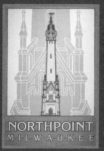

MILWAUKEE
City of Neighborhoods

John Gurda

To Tom Boettcher, with deep gratitude for making
This book a reality. I know Fritz would be proud!

John Gurda

HISTORIC
MILWAUKEE
INCORPORATED

ISBN 978-0-692-45189-2
Library of Congress Control Number: 2015942252

Graphic Design - Market Engineers
mrkteng@att.net

Printed in the United States of America
Burton & Mayer, Inc.
Menomonee Falls, WI 53051

Dedication

To the memories of
Frederick "Fritz" Gerlach (1903-1998),
the Milwaukee artist and historian who could have written *City of Neighborhoods* himself,
and Gregory J. Coenen (1949-2008),
the creative dynamo who is this book's ultimate author

Author's Acknowledgements

Working on books is about as close as I get to being in a band, and the *City of Neighborhoods* ensemble was larger than most. Jan Kotowicz went back to her pencil box after a hiatus of nearly twenty-five years to create new illustrations that blend seamlessly with her original work. Graphic designer Jim Price once again made my words look good, as he's been doing since 1989, this time with able assistance from self-described "second-chair designer" Kate Hawley. A team of talented photographers combed the central city for well over a year in search of compelling images. Christopher Winters and Jessica Lothman covered by far the most ground, but Frank Miller, Jim Hamberg, Anders Gurda (yes, my son), John Ruebartsch, Christopher McIntyre, and I all put on plenty of miles. Cartographer Colter Sikora broke new ground on the neighborhood front with a "Colterrific" set of original maps. Historic photo researcher and copy editor Michael Gauger spared me hours of work and a number of mistakes. Darlene Waterstreet indexed the book with her customary thoroughness. The Milwaukee Department of City Development graciously permitted us to reprint the original poster images.

My relationship with Historic Milwaukee, Inc. goes back nearly thirty years as a speaker and guide trainer. As HMI assumed a new role as my publisher, I had the pleasure of working with executive director Stacy Swadish; her predecessor, Anna-Marie Opgenorth; and the book committee of a very engaged board of directors.

The last and most lavish thank-you goes to the foundations, corporations, and individuals who funded *Milwaukee: City of Neighborhoods*. The entire band offers a deep bow to these supporters for making our appearance possible:

Koeppen-Gerlach Foundation

Coenen Family Foundation
and the Coenen family

David and Julia Uihlein
Charitable Foundation

Greater Milwaukee Foundation, including
the David and Nancy Putz Fund and the
Annette Roberts and Joan Robertson Fund

Northwestern Mutual Foundation

Wisconsin Energy Foundation

Allan "Bud" Selig

Ralph Evinrude Foundation

The family of John Ogden, Sr.

Herzfeld Foundation

Olive and Eunice Toussaint Foundation

Stella H. Jones Foundation

Zilber Family Foundation

Bert and Patricia Steigleder Foundation

Robert W. Baird Foundation

Marcus Corporation Foundation

A.O. Smith Foundation and
the Smith family

Barbara Stein

Table of Contents

USMKE
■ International Port Designation

City of Neighborhoods
■ by Region

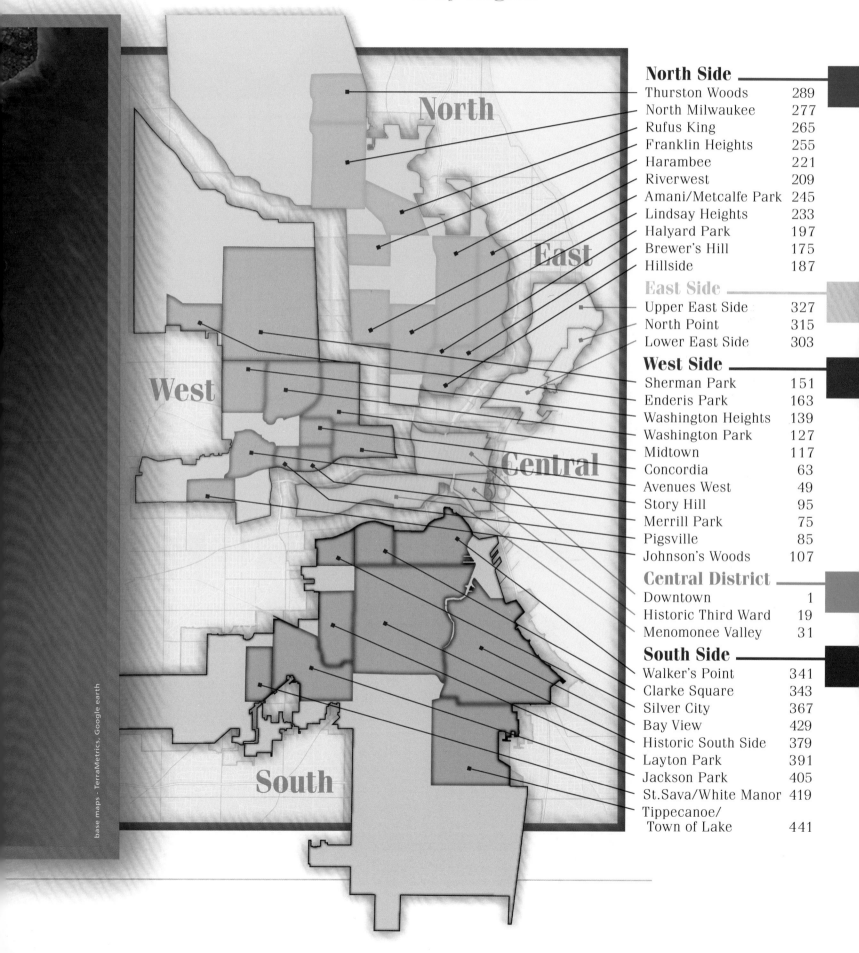

base maps - TerraMetrics, Google earth

Mayor's Foreword

Hardworking, ambitious residents have made Milwaukee strong. They built our industries, promoted our institutions, raised families and made their homes all across this city. Their legacy includes the distinctive neighborhoods that make Milwaukee unique.

These neighborhoods have grown with strong influences from residents' ethnicity, their religious beliefs, their wealth, and their commerce. Neighborhoods often value conformity, yet every neighborhood has its own identity, established by characteristics that, by design, set them apart.

A park, a church, or a school is frequently the centerpiece of a neighborhood. Architecture, a large employer, a body of water, or a major street might further differentiate it. The character of a Milwaukee neighborhood, though, is established by more than its physical aspects; it is defined by the people who live there.

Milwaukee residents identify with their neighborhoods, proudly saying, "I live in the Harambee neighborhood," or "I'm from Jackson Park," or "Enderis Park is my home." They feel a bond with their neighbors, a common connection that adds value.

For almost all my life, Washington Heights has been home. That's the neighborhood just west of Washington Park. I think of Washington Heights as a neighborhood of families and unique homes. It is a place with great features such as nearby parks, prominent churches, a strong neighborhood association, and a local retail area. Many of my neighbors have lived in Washington Heights for decades, and they would never move elsewhere.

Cities are always changing, reinventing and renewing themselves, adapting to new demographics and economic transformation. The same is true of the neighborhoods that constitute a city. And while neighborhoods change, Milwaukee neighborhoods have also stood the test of time. They have remained strong. And they are the foundation of our city's future.

Mayor Tom Barrett

Introduction

Anyone who spends even a day or two in Milwaukee becomes aware of the city's "sidedness." The South Side is a different world from the East Side, the North and West Sides have disparate characters, and the Northwest Side is another territory entirely. Within these and several other composite districts, dozens of smaller communities are embedded — neighborhoods like Bay View, Layton Park, Pigsville, Washington Heights, Rufus King, Riverwest, and North Point, each of them serving as home base for its residents. Viewed from the grassroots perspective, Milwaukee is most definitely a city of neighborhoods, and it is neighborhoods that render the city both intelligible and approachable. They come in many shapes, sizes, colors, and strengths, but together they constitute the fundamental building blocks of the entire community.

Milwaukee: City of Neighborhoods is an attempt to tell the story of grassroots Milwaukee more fully than it's ever been told before. The book is based on my belief that every neighborhood has a story uniquely its own to tell, and that putting a broad range of community chronicles between two covers can encourage a sense of belonging within individual neighborhoods and a sense of mutual respect across neighborhood borders and even beyond the city limits. *City of Neighborhood*s is therefore a sort of intramural ambassador in words and pictures, as well as a fine-grained introduction to Milwaukee for both insiders and outsiders who simply want to know more about what makes the city tick. The book can also be read as the geographic companion to *The Making of Milwaukee,* a general history published in 1999 and updated in 2006.

The subject itself practically guarantees rapid obsolescence. Neighborhoods are quicksilver creations, constantly changing residents, borders, and even names. One generation's Sixth Ward is another's Brewer's Hill. A German enclave in one century becomes an African-American stronghold in the next. All neighborhoods are changing neighborhoods, and always have been. This particular account is forever fixed, as it must be, in the second decade of the twenty-first century, but it will, I hope, have continuing relevance as a benchmark, in precisely the same way that studies prepared by WPA writers in the 1930s retain their value many decades later.

Rapid change is a natural condition of communities that exist not by force of law but by virtue of perception. We codify some lines to identify census tracts or legislative districts or municipalities, but neighborhood borders simply float in our shared awareness, perennially subject to both dispute and revision. Milwaukee doesn't have a Minneapolis-style confederation of neighborhoods with borders set by the city council, and it never attracted anything resembling the corps of sociologists who delineated Chicago's "community areas" in the 1920s. The result, in the context of this book, is an informed and reasonable but patently imperfect interpretation of where one neighborhood ends and another begins.

Not that there haven't been attempts to draw hard lines in the shifting sands of residential Milwaukee. Over the last half-century or so, academics, urban planners, and community activists have made repeated runs at an "official" map of Milwaukee neighborhoods. The most ambitious effort dates to the late 1980s, when the Department of City Development (DCD) launched its Neighborhood Identification Project. The project's goal was "a stable set of neighborhood boundaries" that would become "a recognized and engrained part of the fabric of the City in the future." The map was drafted with social uplift as well as consistent data sets in mind. "This will give every resident of Milwaukee," promised the planners, "an opportunity to develop a sense of place, pride, and belonging in relation to where they live." The problem, if it may be so called, was that the project's leaders were determined to put every square inch of the city in one named neighborhood or another, even when the lack of historical or organizational referents forced them to resort to whole cloth. My favorite fabrication was the area just east of the Allen-Bradley (Rockwell Automation) clock, which, presumably to the surprise of its residents, appeared on the final map as "Clock Tower Acres."

I was part of a similarly well-intentioned stab at the elusive geographic truth, again under city auspices. In 1982 Greg Coenen, manager of communications for DCD, conceived the Discover Milwaukee Program in an earlier attempt to encourage a sense of citizen belonging. The project's signature product was a series of twenty-seven posters painstakingly drawn by Janice Kotowicz, a DCD staff member with deep roots in the city. As the project's writer and researcher, I chose most of the neighborhoods; others were suggested by Greg or dictated by higher-ups in the department. Jan typically used a characteristic architectural feature for her illustration—a bungalow in Sherman Park, a Victorian storefront in Walker's Point, a

Polish flat in Riverwest—while I prepared magazine-length historical essays that appeared on the back of each poster. (My words were consigned to permanent oblivion if the art was ever hung for display.) The posters, which debuted in batches between 1983 and 1990, were hugely popular, showing up in corporate offices, TV interview rooms, public hallways, and thousands of private homes. They made Jan Kotowicz the most famous Milwaukee artist you'd never heard of.

Twenty years later, the posters were still in print and still in demand. In about 2010 I ran into Jan at the South Shore Frolic in Bay View, the neighborhood we've both called home for many years, and she said, almost off-handedly, "We should turn those posters into a book." Her remark led to a much longer conversation. It took a while but, with the sponsorship of Historic Milwaukee, Inc. and the generous support of nearly twenty community-minded funders, the fruit of that conversation is in your hands.

The task seemed relatively simple at first: update the original twenty-seven essays to reflect nearly three decades of change and then write perhaps a dozen new chapters on communities we never got to in the first round. The project evolved, as projects will, into something more complex: hundreds of miles of travel on foot and by bicycle, long days in local archives, and the constant struggle to hit a moving target so that the work seemed neither hopelessly timebound nor overly generic. There were endless decisions to make, the first involving which neighborhoods to include. The roster, you will notice, is not exhaustive. In the interests of time, space, and sanity, I confined myself to the pre-World War II city, an area defined roughly by Silver Spring Drive, Howard Avenue, Sixtieth Street, and the lake. Most of the neighborhoods within those borders were legacies of Greg Coenen's Discover Milwaukee Program, and I added others based on a thoroughly unscientific blend of subdivision borders, major geographic barriers, historic settlement patterns, and current organizational service areas.

I am well aware of the omissions in this account, but it is in prewar Milwaukee that the historical layers are most abundant, the cultural currents most visible, and the stories most resonant, simply because they've been echoing for so long. There are genuine neighborhoods beyond my chosen borders, including nineteenth-century nodes like Granville Station or New Coeln and historic subdivisions like Morgandale or Wedgewood Park, but the postwar city tends to be largely one piece: mile after mile of Cape Cods and then ranches and split-levels, punctuated by apartment corridors and commercial strips. Even in the older part of town, some areas are so diffuse (or so diminutive) that it's difficult to classify them as neighborhoods. Rather than force the issue, I chose to leave a few blank spots on the map.

Choosing a graphic format was significantly easier. Jan's original poster illustrations, augmented by eleven new artworks she created, are the visual anchors of the book. To complement them we've added customized maps and a generous assortment of both historic and contemporary photographs that help bring each neighborhood to life. The result, we hope, is an appealing hybrid between a history book and an art book.

City of Neighborhoods reflects the obvious reality that not every community is created equal. Milwaukee, as much as any large city in America and more than most, is marked by painful inequities in both income and opportunity. But whether a specific neighborhood narrative has led to vibrancy or pathology is not really the issue in these pages. Every story has intrinsic human value, Harambee's no less than North Point's, Metcalfe Park's as much as Bay View's. No understanding of the city—or of America—is truly complete without an understanding of the contrasts that define our society, and no vision of a more hopeful future can emerge without a sure grasp of the past.

For me, it was an undiluted pleasure to make the acquaintance of my hometown at the neighborhood level once again: to bike, to chat, to question, to photograph, and simply to witness Milwaukeeans in the act of being Milwaukeeans. Yes, there's been change and, yes, there are problems, but there is also an undeniable richness to life in grassroots Milwaukee. Chris Winters, our lead photographer, may have said it best: "The deeper you go in the neighborhoods, the deeper they are." It is my hope that *City of Neighborhoods* will help readers discover some of that depth for themselves. There may be no more dynamic human creation than the city, no more compelling expression of energy, aspiration, pain, and potential on the planet. Neighborhoods are the parts that make up the larger organism; it is in seeing our neighborhoods that we see our city whole.

John Gurda

Christopher Winters

Central District

Think of it as a Big Bang. There was nothing particularly explosive about the initial settlement of Milwaukee, and it was a slow-motion boom at best, but the burst of energy that materialized in 1835 provided the spark for everything that followed. Aspiring urbanites from the East Coast joined a savvy fur trader from French Canada to develop a location that promised safe anchorage for their ships and water power for their industries. Together the settlers turned a wilderness outpost into a three-cornered village whose dominant dynamic was the rivalry between its east and west sides.

Separated by the river but united by geographic destiny, the two hamlets eventually coalesced to become Downtown, the commercial core of the entire community. As Downtown assumed its central role, the adjoining Third Ward found its own part to play as a haven for both industries and immigrants. When the choice locations at the heart of the city were all taken, local entrepreneurs transformed the Menomonee Valley wetland into an industrial zone that became an economic engine for all of Wisconsin.

Milwaukee's "sidedness" started in the Central District, and so did its neighborhoods. As the city expanded, new communities came to life on the fringes of the original center, sharing the cultural DNA of the areas they bordered, and the center itself was remade by new development—a cycle that continues to the present. Long after the riverfront trading post and the pioneer cabins around it have all turned to dust, the Big Bang still resounds.

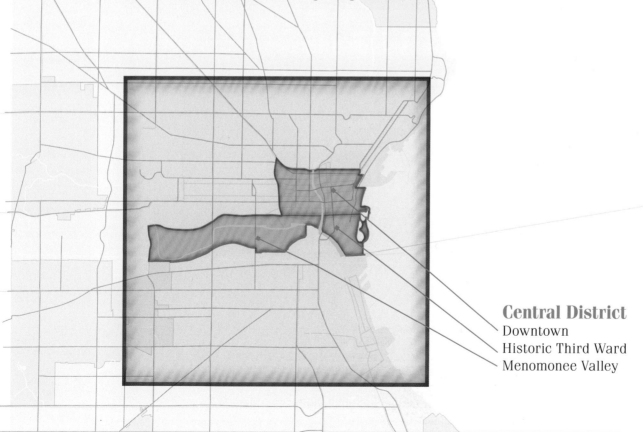

Central District
Downtown
Historic Third Ward
Menomonee Valley

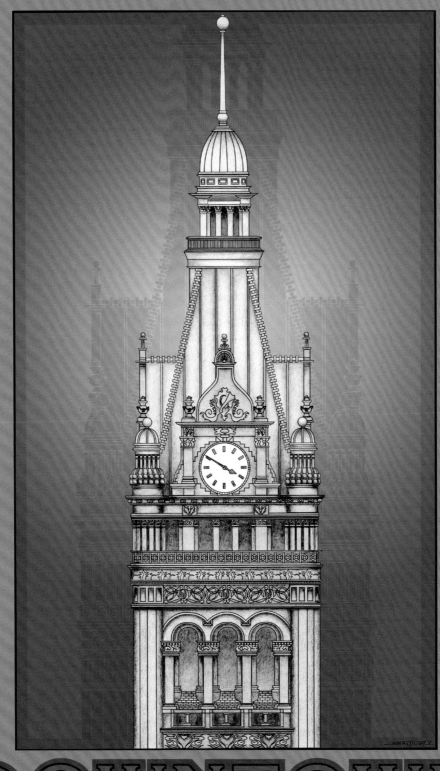

DOWNTOWN
M I L W A U K E E

Downtown

Downtown is the center of the urban universe, the place where all roads converge and every story starts. It is the knot in the pretzel, the hub of the wheel, the nucleus of the primal cell that swelled and split to become the Milwaukee metropolis. Within its borders every stage in the city's evolution is preserved, and within its buildings the essence of the community is expressed in bricks and mortar.

Every American downtown plays the same central role, but the details vary absolutely from place to place. In Milwaukee's case, a river runs through it. From the very beginning of urban time in the region, the city has been bifurcated by the stream for which it is named—an occasion for conflict in pioneer times and still an important line of demarcation in the twenty-first century. The river separates East Town from Westown, and Yankee Hill overlooks them both. The three districts fit snugly inside a belt of encircling freeways, both built and unbuilt, and together they form the common core of a metropolitan region that sprawls across four counties.

Downtown

1. Blatz Brewery Site
2. BMO Harris Bradley Center
3. Boston Store
4. Central Library – Milwaukee Public Library
5. Chase Tower (Marine Plaza)
6. City Hall
7. Cudahy Tower
8. Di Suvero's The Calling sculpture
9. Discovery World
10. Federal Building & U.S. Courthouse
11. Hilton Milwaukee City Center (Schroeder Hotel)
12. Immanuel Presbyterian Church
13. Iron Block Building
14. Marcus Center for the Performing Arts
15. Milwaukee Area Technical College (MATC)
16. Milwaukee Art Museum
17. Milwaukee County Courthouse
18. Milwaukee County Historical Society
19. Milwaukee Gas Light Building
20. Milwaukee Intermodal Station
21. Milwaukee Public Museum
22. Milwaukee Repertory Theater
23. Milwaukee Theatre (Milwaukee Auditorium)
24. Northwestern Mutual Campus
25. Old St. Mary's Catholic Church
26. Pabst Theater
27. Pfister Hotel
28. Plankinton Arcade
29. Riverside Theater
30. Shops of Grand Avenue
31. St. John's Catholic Cathedral
32. The Brewery Redevelopment & Pabst Brewery Site
33. Turner Hall
34. U.S. Bank Center (First Wisconsin Center)
35. UW-Milwaukee Panther Arena (Milwaukee Arena)
36. War Memorial Center
37. Wisconsin Center (Midwest Express Center)

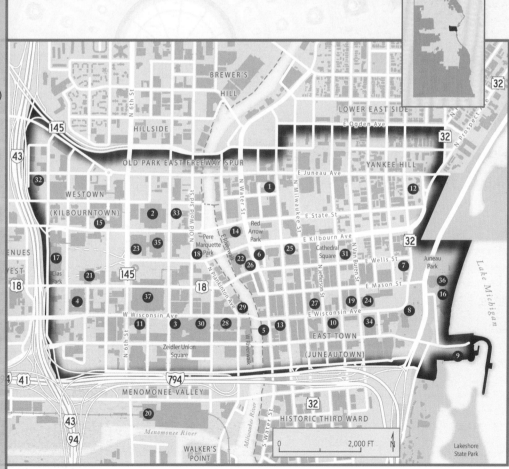

Planted by the Water

It was the river that put Milwaukee on the map. In pioneer days, when everyone and everything in the Great Lakes region traveled by boat, a good harbor was the first requirement for any would-be metropolis. Milwaukee, with

■ *Much of today's Downtown was under water when white settlement began in the 1830s.*

its broad bay and deep river, was one of the most promising ports on all the lakes, but the settlement did not come to life at the river mouth itself. Although it was Milwaukee's front door, the mouth, which opened to the lake at Jones Island, was simply too marshy for permanent development. Walker's Point, not far upstream, was drier, but that modest peninsula was mired in title problems and surrounded by cattails for most of a decade, depriving its founder, George Walker, of his chance for pioneer glory. That left Solomon Juneau, a French-Canadian fur trader who had arrived in 1818, to determine Downtown's location. In 1825 he and his wife Josette, who was part-Menominee by ancestry, opened their trading post on what is now the corner of Water Street and Wisconsin Avenue. Their claim was the first tract of dependably dry ground on the east bank of the river, and the Juneaus' little log cabin became the anchor for all that followed.

When Milwaukee's third founder, Byron Kilbourn, came to town in 1834, he claimed land on the west bank, but not directly opposite Juneau; a tamarack swamp pushed his little settlement nearly a half-mile north, to the solid ground on what is now Third Street and Juneau Avenue. There Kilbourn worked to freeze out his cross-river rival and establish himself as Milwaukee's frontier kingpin. When the Juneau forces managed, over Kilbourn's objections, to build a bridge across the river at today's Juneau

■ *Solomon Juneau's trading post made Water Street and Wisconsin Avenue the commercial crossroads of the infant metropolis— a role the intersection continues to play.*

■ *Solomon Juneau (left)* and Byron Kilbourn maintained a lively intramural rivalry as the principals of Juneautown and Kilbourntown.*

Avenue, the west siders were so annoyed that they eventually severed its footings and dropped the span into the water. Their actions touched off the Bridge War of 1845, a semi-comic conflict that ended with Milwaukee's incorporation as a city in 1846.

Juneautown, Kilbourntown, and Walker's Point were finally one community, at least on paper, but the three sides did not begin on an equal footing. The South Side settlement continued to labor under multiple handicaps, including George Walker's own lack of business acumen and political connections. That left Downtown to develop upstream—one-and-a-half miles above the original river mouth. Even there the east and west banks filled out at different speeds. Juneau's side had the earlier start, as well as the post office, the courthouse, and the land office. In 1850 it claimed a majority of the city's 20,061 residents, nearly 40 percent more people than old Kilbourntown and four times the population of Walker's Point. The east side was clearly the emergent city's business center. The river was Milwaukee's lifeline in the Age of Sail, and Water Street, which paralleled the east bank for more than a mile, became the main street for the entire community. Lots on the lake bluff, however gorgeous their views, were virtually unsalable.

The west bank closed the gap within a decade or two, but only after some aggressive landfill activity. The tamarack swamp south of Juneau Avenue had remained a stubborn obstacle. Amherst Kellogg, who arrived in 1836, described early travel conditions on the west side of Downtown: "We had to be careful to keep on the bogs or roots of trees to prevent from getting into the water and mire." The Kellogg family's cow once foundered in the swamp and had to be helped out with heavy planks. Gravel "borrowed" from the adjoining bluffs eventually provided solid footing for both the cattle and their keepers, and the west bank emerged as a co-equal counterpart to the old Juneau claim on the east side. By mid-century, Downtown's axis was swinging from the north-south ribbon of the river to east-west Wisconsin Avenue. Differences, however, remained. The street systems on the east and west banks were platted independently, and when bridges finally joined the two sides, they crossed the river at an angle—a civic antique that will last for as long as there is a Milwaukee.

Differences notwithstanding, Downtown was one big residential neighborhood in its early years—or, more accurately, several small neighborhoods—simply because

■ (above)
Because the two sides made no attempt to align their street systems, the first bridges crossed the river at an angle—a civic antique that persists to the present.

■ (above right)
Third Street near State had a distinctly rural feel in the 1860s, and a decidedly German accent.

Milwaukee was still too small to support a central business district devoted exclusively to business. German and Irish immigrants lived on both sides of the river in more or less homogeneous groupings. Virtually every merchant on Third Street had to speak German or risk going bankrupt, and the Irish hold on the Third Ward was just as strong. Both groups were highly visible, but it was the Yankees—Anglo-Saxon transplants from New York and New England—who really set themselves apart. Although they were a minority in their own city as early as 1850, the Yankees had come to Milwaukee on the very first wave of white settlement, and they had a virtual lock on wholesale and retail commerce, the grain trade, the professions, and local politics. These Easterners were the frontier elite, and the most successful of them built sumptuous Italianate, Gothic, and Greek Revival homes on the high ground northeast of the business quarter—an area known, appropriately, as Yankee Hill. Lake views began to take on a cachet they have never lost.

The Yankees took their churches with them. Milwaukee's European immigrants had already established religious beachheads of their own—St. John's Cathedral, dedicated in 1853, was an Irish citadel, and German Catholics built what is now "Old" St.

Mary's just down the street in 1847—but the Anglo-American churches of Yankee Hill outshone nearly all their European counterparts. Between roughly 1870 and 1900, Yankee Protestants built elaborate houses of worship in the Presbyterian, Episcopalian, Methodist, Congregational, Baptist, and Unitarian traditions—moving in nearly every case from simpler quarters near the river. There were no Catholic, no Lutheran, and no Jewish congregations on Yankee Hill; those were the immigrant faiths, and their homes belonged elsewhere.

As the residential sections spread outward, so, in time, did the city's commercial center. Milwaukee became less river-bound over the years, in part because railroads had begun to replace schooners and steamships as the economy's prime movers. In 1872 retailer T.A. Chapman moved his department store up the hill from Water to Milwaukee Street. The distance he covered was only two blocks, but journalist Charles Harger praised Chapman for his "broad idea of spreading out rather than confining the retail business of the city to narrow limits." Other businesses followed, and Wisconsin Avenue became a genuine commercial corridor reaching well beyond its original east-west nodes at Water Street and Plankinton Avenue.

■ *The Miller mansion, which still stands on Juneau Avenue, was a typical specimen of Yankee Hill's architectural grandeur.*

It was not only retail establishments that multiplied at the city's center. Before Milwaukee adopted its first zoning ordinance in 1920, anyone could build anything anywhere, and that's precisely what they did. Giants like the Pabst brewery, established on the west side in 1844, and the Blatz brewery, an east side landmark since 1845, expanded in place, and there was an ever-growing number of smaller employers: iron and brass foundries, sausage factories, bookbinders, machine shops, packing plants, tobacco factories, flour mills, pickle factories, and various others. In the later 1800s these industrial enterprises were sprinkled among the shops, churches, homes, and public buildings of earlier eras—frequently in the same blocks. Away from the airy heights of Yankee Hill, the landscape of central Milwaukee was impressively random, a motley assortment of land uses and architectural styles whose patterns could be discerned only with difficulty.

Outward and Upward

Order eventually emerged from the chaos at the heart of town. By 1890, at the very latest, Downtown had developed a robust identity of its own, a life apart from the residential and industrial districts surrounding it. As Milwaukee expanded in every direction but east, Downtown ceased to be primarily a neighborhood and took

■ (left)
The north end of Water Street, near Knapp, was a jumble of mills, stores, and homes—typical of Downtown's pre-zoning landscape

■ (right)
East Wisconsin Avenue was a beehive of activity at the turn of the twentieth century.

on a larger role as the functional heart of the entire city. Its new status required growth in two directions at once: outward and upward. As Milwaukee gained population and area, many of its original elements—ethnic groups, churches, and businesses among them—pushed away from the heart of the city to new layers in the concentric zones surrounding the original core at Water and Wisconsin.

As they moved outward, there was a continual process of scaling up in the space they left behind. Every church and every business headquarters was grander than its predecessor, every new municipal building larger than the last. Immanuel Presbyterian, for instance, built a "little white church" on Mason Street in 1844 and moved to a Victorian marvel on Yankee Hill in 1874. Northwestern Mutual began in a single rented room on Wisconsin Avenue in 1859,

erected an elegant home office on Broadway and Michigan in 1886, and then completely outdid itself with an oversized Greek temple on Wisconsin and Van Buren in 1914. Milwaukee's City Hall grew from a remodeled public market on Wells Street in 1860 to a single wing of the county courthouse in 1873 to the present monumental edifice in 1895—the city's first million-dollar structure and still one of the most beautiful municipal buildings in America. Local residents thought they had crossed a threshold in 1892, when the Pabst Building, Milwaukee's "first skyscraper" at a whopping thirteen stories, went up on Water Street and Wisconsin Avenue— the very site of Solomon and Josette Juneau's old trading post.

The pattern was repeated again and again— fewer, larger buildings replacing many smaller ones—and Downtown's development always kept pace with the growth of the region as a whole. As the district expanded outward and upward, its older residential sections were squeezed out, or at least transformed. Single-family homes of all sizes gave way to free-standing apartment buildings or walk-up rental units above street-level storefronts. One result was a marked increase in density, particularly on Yankee Hill. Although most of the enclave's churches and a dwindling number of its mansions remained, the trend that surfaced in the early 1900s favored apartment blocks and hotels. Homes built for single families and their servants were replaced by residential towers that housed scores of residents.

■ *The Pabst Building, completed in 1892, was celebrated as Milwaukee's "first skyscraper."*

Milwaukee County Historical Society

As Downtown became a genuine central business district, a rough division of responsibilities emerged between its east and west sides—the result of market forces rather than planning protocols. The east side had the major banks, insurance companies, and brokerage houses, as well as the more exclusive retail establishments, led by Chapman's Department Store (1872) and the shops on Milwaukee and Jefferson Streets. It was Milwaukee's version of Wall Street, with a bit of Fifth Avenue added to the mix. The west side's portfolio was somewhat more diverse. Mass-market retail was one specialty, with Gimbel's (1887) and Boston Store (1900) at the head of the pack. Entertainment was another strength, beginning with exhibitions of panorama paintings on Kilbourn Avenue (1885) and accelerating with the advent of vaudeville at the end of the century and motion pictures in the early 1900s; W. Wisconsin Avenue eventually had the highest concentration of first-run movie theaters in the state. The west side of Downtown was also Milwaukee's gathering place, a role it assumed with the opening of the Industrial Exposition Building on Sixth and State in 1881 and cemented with construction of the Milwaukee Auditorium on the same site in 1909.

Although the east and west sides' roles were relatively constant, they were hardly static. Buildings came and went, altering the district's chemistry and adding critical mass to both sides; Downtown's landscape was made, remade, and remade again over the years. There were definite high points in the cycle of construction and destruction. The 1890s introduced such venerable landmarks as the Central Library, the Pfister Hotel, the old Federal Building, and the Pabst Theater as well as City Hall. Development continued at a steady pace after 1900 and reached another peak in the 1920s, when the Schroeder Hotel (today's Hilton Milwaukee), the Cudahy Tower, the Milwaukee Gas Light Building, the Riverside Theater, and the Civic Center all joined the scene.

Then came the lull. Development ground to a halt in the 1930s, when Milwaukeeans had all they could do to keep food on the table, and the standstill continued through the material shortages of World War II. In Milwaukee, at least, the pace didn't pick up with the return of peacetime. For a variety of reasons—the city's innate conservatism, suburban flight, a reluctance to use urban renewal funds, and a simple lack of development pressure—years went by with no major building projects in the pipeline. A *New Yorker* correspondent who visited in 1960 commented on the prevailing state of architectural torpor:

■ (center)
The Milwaukee Auditorium, built in 1909 on the site of an earlier exposition building, cemented the west side's role as the city's gathering place.

■ *Northwestern Mutual's home office was a monumental addition to the east side's skyline in 1914.*

Milwaukee Public Library

Milwaukee County Historical Society

Milwaukee Journal Sentinel

■ *The War Memorial Center (1957) and Marine Plaza (1962) (lower)* were *Downtown's first significant pieces of modern architecture.*

Milwaukee Journal Sentinel

No new large office building has been put up in downtown Milwaukee in more than twenty years, and the skyline, if approached from Lake Michigan, gives the impression of a city that had its picture taken around 1920 and liked the results so much that it decided to leave matters alone.

Downtown's first piece of modern public architecture, Eero Saarinen's War Memorial Center, was completed in 1957—twelve years after World War II. The first modern commercial building of any note was Marine Plaza (now Chase Tower), which was finished in 1962.

The cloud of inactivity had a silver lining. When the historic preservation movement began to hit its stride after 1970, both locally and nationally, Milwaukee had a greater number of historic buildings to preserve than many communities of comparable size and age. It might have been a case of preservation by neglect, but it was preservation nonetheless. The importance of an ample inventory of historic structures was abundantly clear in the 1960s, when Milwaukee, as if to make up for lost time, was as aggressive as any city in clearing land for freeways and replacing older buildings with parking lots. What stands out in every aerial photograph of Downtown

■ *In the 1960s, after years of relative inactivity, Milwaukee joined the rest of America's cities in tearing down large sections of its Downtown for parking lots and freeways.*

■ *The east side financial district reached new heights with completion of the 42-story First Wisconsin Center in 1973.*

in the 1960s is the abundance of blank spots created for the automobile. The inner freeway loop, which was largely completed by decade's end, created borders as real as any river, separating Downtown from the Third Ward on the south, Avenues West on the west, and Hillside on the north. Public opposition killed a planned freeway east of the river, but a block-wide swath of land cleared for the Park East spur separated Downtown, including Yankee Hill, from the Lower East Side. That particular wound was not healed until the development of multi-family housing in the early 1990s. Within the freeway loop, entire blocks were cleared for parking lots.

The period of architectural mayhem was relatively short-lived, due in part to a dawning awareness that Milwaukee's physical heritage was in danger. The pace of land clearance slowed significantly in the 1970s, and Downtown entered an impressive period of redevelopment in the next decade. Patterns of the past were revisited and reinforced. The west side lost its first-run movie theaters, but its historic emphasis on mass-market retail reached a new level with the 1982 opening of the Grand Avenue Mall—for a time the busiest shopping center in Wisconsin. The west bank's role as Milwaukee's gathering place became

even more prominent. The Auditorium (1909) already had the Arena (1950) right next door. They were joined by the MECCA convention center across the street in 1974, which was replaced by the Wisconsin (originally Midwest Express) Center in 1998. The Bradley Center (1988) went up north of the ensemble, rounding out eight square blocks of sports, entertainment, and convention facilities.

The east side's role as Milwaukee's financial center was likewise strengthened. Banking rose to new heights with construction of the First Wisconsin (later U.S. Bank) Center in 1973; at 42 stories and 601 feet, it was Wisconsin's tallest building by a comfortable margin. Literally across the street, Northwestern Mutual spread out from its classical 1914 home office to a four-square-block campus and became the largest individual life-insurer in America. On both banks of the Milwaukee River, businesses and institutions came together to build on the momentum of the Eighties. The East Town Association was formed in 1983 and

■ *The Pabst Brewery, a highly successful mixed-use development with a sudsy heritage, is a potent symbol of Downtown's ongoing resurgence.*

the Westown Association in 1987 to promote their respective sides in the broader context of a healthy Downtown.

At Home in the Heart

Development and redevelopment have been more or less continuous since the 1980s, just as they have been since the 1830s. Not everything has worked—some blocks progressed faster and farther than others, and the Civic Center Plaza adjoining the County Courthouse remained a conspicuous dead zone—but Downtown's resurgence has been impressive indeed. The Pabst brewery, shuttered in 1996, came roaring back to life as a center of nightlife, education, and housing. The lakefront has been in a state of constant creative ferment, sprouting museums, restaurants, and even a state park. The Riverwalk has given Milwaukee a gracious reconnection with the stream that put it on the map. Old buildings have been repurposed and new ones erected to fill the voids left by previous generations. In a striking reversal of the usual trends in urban America, the Park East freeway spur was removed in 2002, a subtraction that opened twenty-six acres of prime land for development.

The results are obvious. In a district always known for its visual variety, the contrasts are more striking than ever. The futuristic Calatrava addition to the Milwaukee Art Museum is linked umbilically to the Saarinen-designed War Memorial Center. Buildings from the mid-1800s— the Iron Block, St. John's Cathedral, Old St. Mary's—share the landscape with structures from the early 2000s. Turner Hall, a mainstay of German life since 1883, is reflected in the gleaming glass panels of the Bradley Center. Some of the trendiest nightspots in town occupy storefronts that once trafficked in hardware and harnesses. An old power plant houses the highly regarded Milwaukee Repertory Theater. The orange asterisk of Mark di Suvero's sculpture, The Calling, punctuates a skyline that has been evolving in place for close to two centuries, and more is on the way.

Perhaps the most notable trend of the recent past has been the proliferation of housing in the heart of the city. Downtown

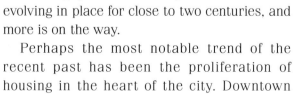

Christopher Winters

John Gurda

■ *The Riverwalk has brought new life—and new investment—to the stream that put Milwaukee on the map.*

Christopher Winters

■ *Since its wings opened in 2001, Santiago Calatrava's soaring addition to the Milwaukee Art Museum has become a civic icon.*

never really stopped being a neighborhood. It provided a home for several ethnic groups in its first century—Greek, Croatian, and African-American as well as German and Irish—but after World War II the typical Downtown resident was a single male with limited prospects living in a residential hotel or a walk-up apartment. (The sole exception was Yankee Hill, where hundreds of older women lived like dowager queens.) The single-male demographic was largely displaced by the land-clearance projects of the 1960s and '70s. Since 1980 the focus has been on upscale development, both apartment towers and condominiums. Yankee Hill has returned to its roots as a prestigious residential district, but developers have been busy on both sides of the river, erecting new buildings and renovating older structures that range from furniture stores to office blocks to an ice cream company's garage.

The residents of Downtown, more than 8,000 strong in 2010, have the educational backgrounds and economic standing to live virtually anywhere in the metropolitan area, but they have chosen to settle in the very heart of the city. The attraction is not hard to fathom. Downtown has the greatest single concentration of employment, culture, entertainment, and historic architecture in the entire state. It is the postcard view, the center of the action, the place where connections are made, but Downtown, like the city it serves, is built at the human scale. Its landscape is more approachable than awe-inspiring. It has plenty of room to accommodate those who crave the spotlight as well as those who prefer the shadows. There are limousines and bicycles, horse-drawn carriages and canoes, private clubs and public landmarks, village greens like Cathedral Square and the sprawling serenity of the lakefront. Downtown is the beating heart of an entire region—a role that has persisted through generations of change and will no doubt endure for generations to come.

Christopher Winters

Jessica Lothman

■ *Downtown is a magnet for events that range from the Komen Race for the Cure (for breast cancer) to the French-themed Bastille Days.*

Jessica Lothman

■ *City Hall's stepped gables are an ode to the city's German heritage.*

Christopher Winters

Christopher Winters

■ *The Wisconsin Avenue bridge still crosses the river at an angle, and a statue of Gertie the Duck memorializes the plucky bird that laid her eggs on a Downtown bridge piling in 1945.*

15

■ *Lakefront fireworks, a fixture of every Milwaukee summer, light up the schooner Denis Sullivan.*

■ (center)
The Manpower Group built its headquarters on the west bank of the river in 2007.

■ (far right)
Milwaukee's theater district is the state's largest center for live music, dance, and drama.

■ (below)
An ore carrier makes her way up the Kinnickinnic Basin into winter layup at Jones Island.

Christopher Winters

Christopher Winters

Jessica Lothman

Christopher Winters

Historic Third Ward

To walk the streets of the Historic Third Ward is to experience urban possibility in its fullest dimensions. The neighborhood began as a marsh, emerged from the muck to become a center of commerce, survived a catastrophic fire, provided a home for two of Milwaukee's largest and poorest ethnic groups, and then, after a period of virtual abandonment, was reborn in the late twentieth century as a destination neighborhood, a capital of chic that bears more than a passing resemblance to SoHo or the South Loop. The Third Ward has had more lives than the luckiest cat. Every stage in its long history has left a visible mark, giving the community a unique sense of place that continues to attract visitors, investors, and homeseekers decades after its latest transformation began.

HISTORIC THIRD WARD

1. Blessed Virgin of Pompeii Catholic Church Site
2. Broadway Theater Center
3. Catalano Square
4. Commission Row
5. Italian Community Center
6. Milwaukee Institute of Art & Design
7. Milwaukee Public Market
8. Marcus Amphitheater

0   500 FT

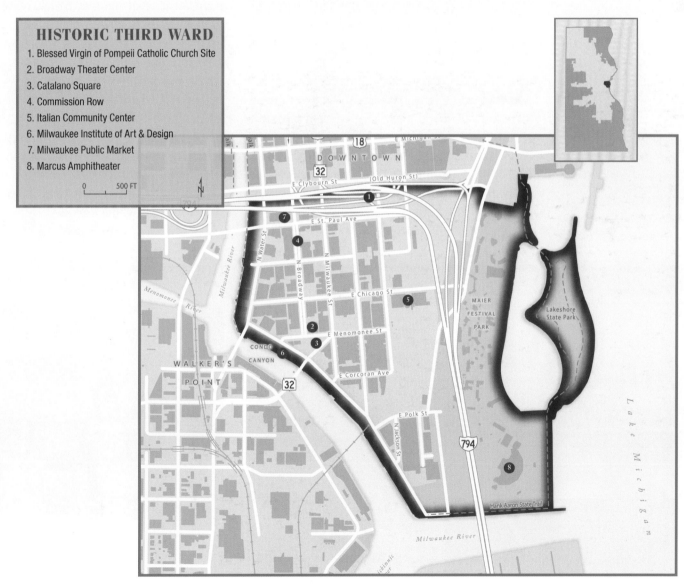

With Muskrats for Neighbors

When the first urban settlers ascended the Milwaukee River—the city's front door in its formative years—dry land was in short supply. Where the Menomonee and Kinnickinnic Rivers met the Milwaukee, newcomers found an expanse of cattails, marsh grass, and wild rice that would become, in time, Walker's Point, Bay View, Downtown, and the Third Ward. Pioneer historian James Buck recalled the Ward in a state of nature. "From Huron [Clybourn] Street south," Buck wrote, "all was marsh and water, except two small islands and the strip along the beach." The two islands underlie today's Milwaukee Institute of Art and Design and the parking structure on Milwaukee and Chicago Streets. The rest of the Third Ward was a paradise for muskrats.

The rodents had less room to maneuver as Milwaukee matured. The river was the community's main artery of commerce, and landfill activities along its shores began almost immediately. Tons of gravel were scraped from the bluffs north of Michigan Street to the waiting wetland below, and the boggy riverbanks were gradually transformed to building sites. Water Street—an aptly named thoroughfare if there ever was one—literally emerged as Milwaukee's main street, years before Wisconsin Avenue would claim that role. By 1855, less than a decade after the city incorporated, Water Street was lined with businesses from Juneau Avenue all the way to the swing bridge to Walker's Point. The river side of the commercial strip was a solid wall of docks where schooners and steamboats called daily during the season of navigation.

The blocks inland from Water Street were largely residential. Milwaukee was divided into five wards when it became a city in 1846, and the Third was universally recognized as the Irish ward. Refugees from famine in their homeland, Irish families were Milwaukee's first major immigrant group, making up 15 percent of the population in 1850. It was largely Irish laborers who filled the marsh, and it was largely they who covered it with modest frame houses as soon as the muck was dry. The neighborhood that resulted, with a population of 4,142 in 1850, was anything but glamorous. Milwaukee's gashouse, which burned copious amounts of coal to produce gas for lighting, was a particularly noxious presence in the heart of the neighborhood, and the surrounding blocks had the highest concentration of saloons in the city. Milwaukeeans who traveled in politer circles knew the Ward as the "Bloody Third," a reputation earned with fisticuffs. When the Milwaukee Police Department compiled its arrest statistics for 1859, 38 percent of the scofflaws were Irish—more than five times their share of the population. Tragedy went hand

■ (below)
After emerging from the primordial muck in the 1850s, the Third Ward became a center of commerce along Water Street (foreground) *and a residential neighborhood closer to the lake. The A.D. Seaman furniture factory towered over Clybourn Street in the 1860s.*

■ (below right)
Irish immigrants made the Ward distinctly their own, and most families were no strangers to poverty.

courtesy Douglas Seaman Family

courtesy Cummings Family

in hand with poverty. The loss of the *Lady Elgin* in 1860 cast a lasting pall over the neighborhood. Nearly 300 people drowned when the excursion steamer sank off Winnetka, Illinois, most of them members or supporters of an Irish militia company on their way home from a fund-raising trip to Chicago.

The Third Ward was, in effect, Milwaukee's first ghetto, but the neighborhood also had its advantages. It was, first of all, close to work—on the docks, on the railroads, and on gangs filling in swamps or grading streets. Employment was never far away, and the dense concentration

of Irish families—and their appetite for civic life—had political implications as well. The Third Ward provided a base of support for several Irish mayors and produced its own crop of legendary politicos. The most notable was Cornelius Corcoran, a local feed merchant who served as the Ward's alderman from 1892 to 1935—a tenure of forty-three years. "Connie da Cork" was Common Council president for thirty of those years, a record in no danger of falling. Corcoran Avenue, near the site of the old gas works, gives the Democratic warhorse a measure of immortality.

■ *The Milwaukee gashouse, shown under construction, cast an acrid pall of coal smoke over the neighborhood.*

Milwaukee Public Library

Milwaukee Public Library

■ *A bird's-eye view of the Third Ward in 1879*

21

By the 1880s the Irish were moving up in the world, and higher incomes meant, for many, a move to higher ground. Although some families migrated to the East Side, the greater movement was westward, first to Tory Hill and then to Merrill Park, where the children and grandchildren of the immigrants established St. Rose Church in 1888. Their exodus from the Third Ward was hastened by the worst fire in Milwaukee's history. The blaze broke out on October 28, 1892, at the Union Oil Company, near the site of today's Public Market. Fanned by gale-force winds, it tore through the heart of the Third Ward in a matter of hours. The modest frame homes erected by the Irish "faded into smoke as fast as tissue paper," according to one eyewitness, and a wall of flame "covered the entire eastern horizon." By the time the fire was extinguished, it had killed 4 people, destroyed 465 houses on 20 square blocks, rendered 2,500 homeless, consumed 25 million gallons of water, and destroyed over $6 million in property.

The 1892 blaze left an impressively blank canvas, and the next generation of Milwaukeeans wasted no time filling it in. Water Street had been the city's commercial center in pioneer days, but Milwaukee's retail axis had rotated ninety degrees, to Wisconsin Avenue, even before the inferno—the natural result of rapid population growth west of the river. The fire accelerated trends that were already under way. Water Street was rebuilt as Milwaukee's wholesale district, and the blocks just inland, between the river and Milwaukee Street, sprouted an assortment of warehouses and light manufacturing plants both larger and more numerous than those they replaced. At the turn of the twentieth century, Third Ward manufacturers made envelopes, cigars, clothing, furniture, gas stoves, lead type, bags, mirrors, biscuits, and a broad assortment of other products. The attractions were obvious: a central location and easy access to both water and rail transportation. A single-track rail line on the Third Ward's lakefront had swelled to a fully equipped freightyard for the Chicago & North Western Railroad, with its own roundhouse at Polk and Jackson Streets.

■ *Ald. Cornelius Corcoran, known to his constituents as "Connie da Cork," served the neighborhood from 1892 to 1935.*

■ *(below left) In 1892 the worst fire in Milwaukee's history nearly leveled large sections of the Third Ward.*

■ *(below right) In true Milwaukee fashion, some of the first structures to rise from the rubble were saloons.*

Milwaukee Public Library

Milwaukee Journal Sentinel

Milwaukee Journal Sentinel

The blocks between the tracks and Milwaukee Street—the eastern portion of the Ward—remained largely residential. Many of the original homes, flimsy as they were, escaped the fire, and a second crop of small frame houses covered the burned-over sections. As the Irish vacated the Third Ward, a new immigrant group moved in behind them: the Italians or, more specifically, the Sicilians. Their Milwaukee population swelled from fewer than 200 in 1890 to 1,740 in 1900 and 4,788 ten years later. The greatest number emigrated from the coastal villages of northern Sicily, including the tiny twin ports of Porticello and Sant'Elia. The Sicilians chose the Third Ward for the same reasons the Irish had: affordable housing and easy access to jobs in the city's tanneries, factories, railroads, and coal yards. The more entrepreneurial newcomers went into the fruit and vegetable trade, beginning with hand-drawn pushcarts and graduating, in a few fortunate cases, to commission houses of their own on Broadway.

The Italian immigrants and their Irish predecessors had something besides poverty in common: Catholicism. The Celtic faithful had worshiped at St. Gall's Church, across the river on Michigan Street, but the Sicilians built their spiritual home, Blessed Virgin of Pompeii, in the heart of the neighborhood, on Jackson Street between Clybourn and St. Paul. Dedicated in 1905, "the little pink church" was a simple brick structure with a decidedly cramped floor area of 5,000 square feet, but its interior was festooned from ceiling to floor with frescoes, ornamental plasterwork, and life-sized statues of Christ and the saints. This Mediterranean wonder quickly became the hub of an urban village—a role most apparent during the summer festa season. The people of Pompeii established thirty-one religious societies, most of them named for the patron saints of their members' home villages. Each saint's feast day became the occasion for an exuberant festa, featuring Italian bands, tug-of-war contests, food stands, and fireworks. At the high point of the celebration, members of the host society paraded through the Third Ward behind a litter bearing a statue of their patron saint. By procession's end, the litter was generally covered with paper money pinned there by the faithful.

■ *Sicilian immigrants poured into the vacuum left by the departing Irish. Some newcomers, including Tony Machi, went into the produce business.*

■ *The most successful peddlers graduated to their own wholesale houses on Broadway, known for decades as Commission Row.*

■ *Blessed Virgin of Pompeii Church, completed in 1905, was the spiritual and social heart of the Third Ward Italian community—and the scene of colorful street festivals that helped relieve the squalor of the neighborhood.*

Renewal, Removal, and Renewal II

The festivals were memorable high points in the life of the Third Ward, but they could not conceal the dinginess of the neighborhood. The "Bloody Third" had not been an especially desirable area during its heyday as an Irish stronghold, and it had not improved with age. As the Sicilians crowded into homes left behind by the Irish or tacked together after the fire, the Third Ward's average household size climbed to 5.89 people per unit—the highest density in the city. In 1910 government investigators pronounced the neighborhood's housing the worst in Milwaukee.

Conditions deteriorated even further as Third Ward businesses shouldered their way into the residential area east of Milwaukee Street. The procession of brick-clad warehouses and light factories made the homes of "Little Italy" increasingly expendable—so expendable that some Sicilians ripped old dwellings apart for firewood. In 1915 historian George La Piana predicted the neighborhood's early demise: "... day after day houses are disappearing to give way to big iron and concrete factories. In ten years this section will be a distinctly business district, and the Italians will be forced to move away."

La Piana underestimated the staying power of some Italians by nearly forty years, but the long-term trend was clear. Although the first generation generally stayed put, their children were much like the Irish families of the 1880s: they left the Third Ward as soon as they could afford to. The Lower East Side was their destination of choice. By 1919 so many families had relocated there that Blessed Virgin of Pompeii opened a small mission to serve them: St. Rita's, on Cass Street near Ogden. Within a decade the mission had 300 children in its Sunday school, compared to 400 at Pompeii's, a clear sign of things to come. As the exodus continued, East Side Italians outnumbered those remaining in the Third Ward, and in 1939 they dedicated St. Rita's Church on Cass and Pleasant. The Blessed Virgin of Pompeii's role became increasingly symbolic. It was still the mother church (and the Third Ward was still the home of hundreds of immigrant mothers), but the life of the second generation lay beyond the borders of the old neighborhood.

The beleaguered community's long downhill slide continued after World War II. Conditions were so wretched that in 1955 the Third Ward became the focus of Milwaukee's first urban renewal project, which took in nearly the entire area between Michigan and Menomonee Streets east of Milwaukee Street. Of the 230 structures in that rectangle, 83.5% were classified as "dilapidated or badly deteriorated." One by one, and despite stubborn resistance from the Third Ward's oldest residents, the City of Milwaukee condemned and cleared hundreds of houses. The area's population plummeted from 2,402 in 1950 to a mere 258 in 1960. Freeway construction dealt the crowning blow; a block-wide swath of the remaining businesses and homes was cleared to make way for Interstate 794 in the mid-1960s. Blessed Virgin of Pompeii was already a lonely sentinel in an urban wasteland by that time, and it lay directly in the freeway's path. In 1967 the little pink church was demolished—shortly after being declared Milwaukee's first official historic landmark.

The wholesale and factory district west of Milwaukee Street seemed destined for the same fate. The area was brimming with what most postwar developers regarded as industrial relics: aging buildings with inefficient multiple floors, impossibly high ceilings, and too many windows. Parking was a perennial challenge, and congestion was a fact of life.

■ *By the 1950s some of the Ward's oldest houses remained standing only by force of habit.*

Milwaukee Public Library

■ *Milwaukee's first urban renewal project, approved in 1955, took in the very heart of the Sicilian residential area. Maitland Field, the city's downtown airport from 1927 to 1956, is in the foreground.*

The smart money was on precisely the kind of structures that had popped up after 1960 in the urban-renewed blocks east of Milwaukee Street: low-slung, geometric boxes that served as both office and industrial space. The old immigrant quarter had been transformed into a suburban-style business park—clean, efficient, modern, and without a shred of historic character. No one seemed to know what to do with the aging (and increasingly empty) buildings on the river side of Milwaukee Street. In the 1970s there were serious proposals to turn the district into a "combat zone"—a headquarters for adult-themed businesses. In the meantime the Third Ward's population plunged to a new low of just seventy-four people in 1980.

Not everyone agreed that the old commercial district was doomed. There was, in fact, a saving remnant of business-owners who believed that the neighborhood's best days were still ahead. In 1976 they formed the Historic Third Ward Association to promote the area's advantages and turn back any and all attempts to denature its landscape. The group's timing was impeccable. It was in the 1970s that Milwaukeeans, and Americans generally, awoke to the enduring value of vintage architecture. Here, on the very threshold of Downtown, was a treasure trove of buildings—no two alike, many designed by prominent architects—with unlimited potential and, not incidentally,

■ (left)
The resulting destruction was reminiscent of the post-fire landscape of 1892.

■ (right)
The crowning casualty was "the little pink church," which fell to the wrecking ball in 1967.

the highest concentration of exposed brick and open beams in the state.

The welcome result was a second renewal more organic, more complete, and far more constructive than the forced dislocations of the 1950s. The resurgence began in the late 1970s and has been more or less continuous ever since. Building by building, block by block, the old Third Ward hummed with new life. A saddlery became a brewpub, a shoe factory became a salon, an old gas works building became a restaurant, a Broadway commission house became a fashion center, and an industrial incubator built on the river in 1920 became the Milwaukee Institute of Art and Design in 1992.

The Third Ward went through an endearingly scruffy period early in its transformation but, today's art students notwithstanding, the bohemian has largely given way to the cosmopolitan. Nowhere else in Wisconsin will you find such a high concentration of bistros, boutiques, and gastropubs. Nowhere else will you find, in a single neighborhood, restaurants showcasing the cuisines of France, Japan, Belgium, Italy, China, Turkey, and Ireland. The Third Ward's specialty shops offer goods that are by turns trendy, kitschy, and edgy. The Milwaukee Public Market, a Water Street landmark since 2005, features some of the city's finest bakery, wine, cheeses, seafood, spices, flowers, salads, coffees, and chocolates. Art galleries abound, and the performing arts have found a welcoming home at the Broadway Theater Center. If you had told any Milwaukeean in 1970 that he or she would one day come to the Third Ward for fine art or a live play, the reaction would almost certainly have been disbelief.

There was new life on the eastern edge of the neighborhood as well. In 1970, after a slow start in other locations, Summerfest moved to Maier Festival Park on the Third Ward lakefront. The event grew so fast that by 1977 organizers could call it the largest outdoor music festival in the world. The area to the west was already in the throes of renewal; now the Summerfest site prompted a return. Hoping to recover, or at least revisit, the sense of community they had known in the old Third Ward, a group of former Blessed Virgin of Pompeii

■ *The Water Street bridge has long been the southern gateway to the Historic Third Ward.*

John Gurda

Christopher Winters

Jessica Lothman

parishioners decided to hold a reunion on the festival grounds and invite the general public. The result was Festa Italiana, which debuted in 1978 and became the model for all the ethnic festivals that followed. Proceeds from Festa Italiana enabled the group to build a permanent home just west of the Summerfest grounds in 1990. Completion of the Italian Community Center marked, in the most literal sense, a homecoming.

There have been hundreds of other homecomings in the Third Ward. One of the most heartening aspects of the post-1970 resurgence is the demonstrated desire of people to live there again. Few communities in the entire metropolitan area have enjoyed such a robust real estate market, both for new construction and for repurposed old buildings. Long-vacant weedlots east of Milwaukee Street have sprouted state-of-the-art condominiums and apartment blocks. Water Street windows that once provided light for garment workers now sport balconies with potted plants and lawn chairs. The Third Ward's

riverfront projects mirror those on the south bank to form what might be called Condo Canyon. The Ward's new residents tend to be younger, better-educated, and more affluent than the metropolitan average—precisely the sort of individuals that every city works to attract and retain.

■ *The Milwaukee Public Market revives a durable Third Ward tradition of fine, fresh edibles available throughout the year.*

Christopher Winters

The Historic Third Ward has shown an endless capacity for reinvention since the 1830s. It began as a watery wilderness and went through a kaleidoscopic existence as a retail center, a manufacturing district, a produce market, and a haven for immigrants before emerging in its modern form. There are still tangible reminders of the past—in street names like Corcoran Avenue, in ghost signs advertising such bygone articles of commerce as "notions and furnishings," and in the ample inventory of historic buildings. Perhaps the deepest connection between past and present lies in the fact that, after years as a demographic desert, residents have returned. From its low point of seventy-four in 1980, the Third Ward's population shot up to nearly 2,400 in 2010. As it was in the beginning, the Third Ward is once again a neighborhood.

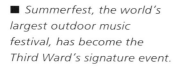

■ *Summerfest, the world's largest outdoor music festival, has become the Third Ward's signature event.*

Jessica Lothman

John Gurda

John Gurda

(left to right)

■ *The Italian Community Center's courtyard provides a gracious outdoor setting for Milwaukeeans of all backgrounds.*

■ *From factories to fine living: A wall of condos rises along the bustling Third Ward Riverwalk.*

■ *The aptly named Renaissance, an elegantly remodeled office building, was built in 1896 as a dry goods warehouse.*

■ *A firefighter and his dog rest outside an old fire station that now houses an upscale clothing store.*

Christopher Winters

MENOMONEE
VALLEY
M◆I◆L◆W◆A◆U◆K◆E◆E

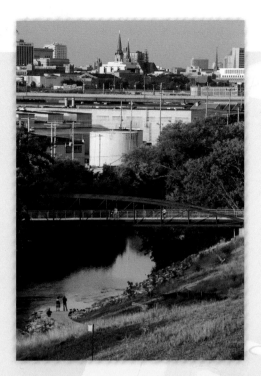

Menomonee Valley

The Menomonee Valley is not a neighborhood in the usual sense of the term. Although it hosts ballplayers in season and gamblers all year, the Valley's only permanent residents are rabbits, rodents, and raccoons. Despite the fact that no one lives there, this distinctive piece of urban real estate has played such an important role for so long that it certainly merits inclusion in any detailed portrait of Milwaukee. As a vital resource for Native Americans, a center of industry for the European newcomers who displaced them, and a continuing source of both employment and recreation in the twenty-first century, the Menomonee Valley occupies a place that is central to Milwaukee's history as well as its geography.

Menomonee Valley

1. Chain Belt Corporation Site
2. Cutler-Hammer Factory Site
3. Falk Brewery Site
4. Falk gear plant (Rexnord Industries)
5. Geuder, Paeschke, & Frey Site
6. Harley-Davidson Museum
7. International Harvester Company, Milwaukee Works Site
8. Joy Global (Harnischfeger Company)
9. Marquette University Valley Fields Athletic Complex
10. Miller Park

11. Milwaukee County Stadium Site
12. Milwaukee Gas Light Structures
13. Milwaukee Road Shops Site
14. Pfister & Vogel Tannery Site
15. Potawatomi Bingo & Casino
16. Red Star Yeast Site
17. Urban Ecology Center – Menomonee Valley Branch
18. Valley Passage
19. Valley Power Plant

0   2,000 FT

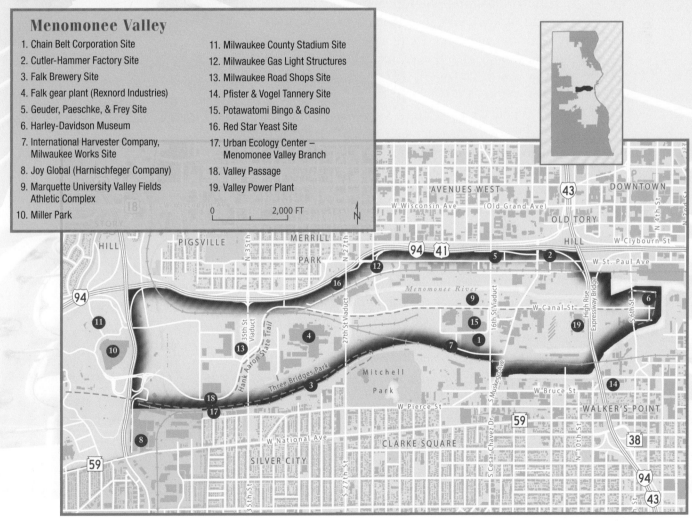

This chapter is an abridged and updated version of a historical essay prepared by the author in 2003 for Menomonee Valley Partners, Inc., and is used by permission.

Beginning with Rice

■ *Native Americans depended on the Valley's abundance of* manomin, *or wild rice, for sustenance centuries before the dawn of urban settlement.*

■ *There were still hundreds of acres of open water when the first whites arrived.*

■ *Pioneer railroads made the Menomonee Valley an important transportation corridor—after some ambitious landfill activity.*

It was Native Americans who named it, naturally. If Milwaukee meant "good land"—the most likely translation of the original word—much of its goodness stemmed from the abundance of wild rice, or *manomin*, at its center. Just upstream from what is now Downtown, the Menomonee River broadened into a sprawling wetland, four miles long and a half-mile wide, that was covered with beds of wild rice and dense stands of cattails, rushes, and reeds. The river was named for the rice, and the Valley provided such a bounty of other resources, including fish and waterfowl, that its bluffs became favored village sites for the Potawatomi, Ojibwe, Odawa, Menominee, and other tribes who settled in Milwaukee over the millennia. There were five villages on the Valley's rim in early historic times, including two in Walker's Point and one in today's Mitchell Park.

When white settlers began to elbow out the Native Americans in the 1830s, it was Milwaukee's superb harbor that attracted them. The central wetland was viewed as a geographic inconvenience, a piece of unproductive real estate that would have to be reclaimed one day, but the Valley served in the meantime as a sort of in-town hunting and fishing preserve. Local sportsmen who braved its meandering channels found it easy to lose their bearings. The *Milwaukee Sentinel* (August 12, 1861) described the adventures of two hunters who spent an unplanned night in the Valley: "A deputation of friends found them in the morning wildly shooting about amid the wild rice opposite Melm's garden, both completely worn out, having rowed some eighteen or twenty miles without getting out of the bayou."

The Valley's days as an urban wilderness were numbered. Milwaukee meant business, and business required first-rate transportation facilities. Ongoing harbor improvements ensured the city's access to eastern markets, but connections with the interior were every

Milwaukee County Historical Society

Milwaukee County Historical Society

1854-55 Milwaukee City Directory

bit as essential. After a failed attempt at canal-building and a number of short-lived plank road ventures, railroads emerged as Milwaukee's most promising path to prosperity. The Menomonee Valley, invitingly flat and open, was an obvious place to put the first tracks. In 1847, one year after the city incorporated, local mogul Byron Kilbourn founded the Milwaukee & Waukesha Railroad and promoted it as a vital artery of commerce, the indispensable link between the lakeshore community and its rich agricultural hinterland. Kilbourn's crews began to build roadbed on the northern edge of the Valley, near Second and Clybourn, in 1849, but they soon ran into problems. Tracks laid on one stretch of landfill disappeared overnight, sinking more than thirty feet into the muck. Pioneer Winfield Smith noted that "months of time and many car loads of earth and timber were consumed in filling this unwelcome cavity."

The marsh's appetite for railroad tracks was eventually satisfied. Solid ground emerged, and Kilbourn's railroad made its maiden run up the Menomonee Valley to Wauwatosa in 1850, traveling at the break-neck speed of thirty miles per hour. By 1857 the pioneer line had reached the Mississippi. As one busy railroad spawned others, Milwaukee realized its destiny as the state's commercial capital and the primary point of exchange between farm products headed east and finished goods coming west.

Enterprising settlers soon realized that there was more money to be made in processing agricultural products than simply shipping them. The city shifted into second economic gear, turning wheat into flour, barley and hops into beer, and hogs and cattle into meat and leather. The early industrialists needed access to both water and rail. Riverfront lots close to Milwaukee's developing rail network were the first to sell, particularly on drier sites near the center of town, but the Menomonee Valley's margins also reflected the economic shift. Before the Civil War began in 1861, Pfister & Vogel were tanning hides, Charles Melms was brewing beer, and the Burnham brothers were making bricks on the south rim of the Valley between Sixth and Sixteenth.

Milwaukee Public Library

■ *The Pfister & Vogel tannery was among the first industries to locate on the south rim. Schooners carried in mountains of tanbark from the Northwoods.*

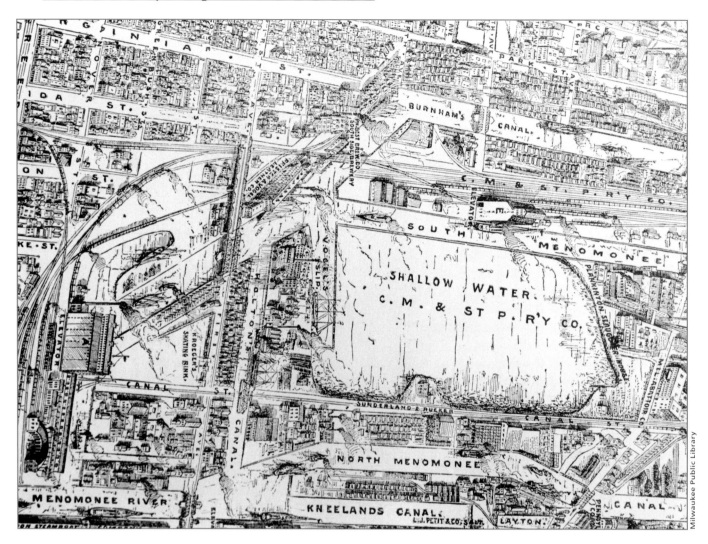

Milwaukee Public Library

■ *Even after twenty years of scraping and filling, "Shallow Water" still filled the heart of the Valley in 1886. The Sixth Street bridge is on the left side of the drawing.*

The marsh proper remained what most Milwaukeeans would have considered a watery wasteland, but not for long. As the banks of the Milwaukee and Kinnickinnic Rivers were filled to capacity, attention turned naturally to the Menomonee Valley, whose open spaces and superb transportation potential seemed ripe for industrial development—after the wetland had been converted to dry land. In 1869 a group of local businessmen launched the Menomonee Improvements and went to work. Concentrating at first on the eastern end of the Valley, they developed a system of canals, boat slips, and rail sidings that may have been Milwaukee's most ambitious infrastructure project of the nineteenth century.

Landfill was the greatest challenge. Using picks, shovels, and horse-drawn scrapers, immigrant laborers pulled down unimaginable quantities of soil and gravel from the adjoining bluffs to the Valley floor. Pioneer historian James Buck estimated the depth of

fill in the central Valley at twenty-two feet on average, and he calculated that the north rim was lowered by as much as sixty feet. Steep bluffs were shaved back to the gentle inclines of the present and, load by load, the marsh began to disappear. Although soil and gravel were the most abundant materials, developers weren't picky about what they used for fill. The *Milwaukee Sentinel* (September 16, 1886) described the scene behind a "Free Dump" sign in the Valley: "Here rotten potatoes and fruit, the contents of paunches and entrails of animals, the refuse of meat shops, and all sorts of filth are deposited in the marsh and a thin covering of ashes and dirt placed over them." Whether the medium was gravel or garbage, landfill activity continued into the twentieth century, but the bulk of the work was done between 1870 and 1900. By the turn of the twentieth century, the days of duck hunts and wild rice harvests were barely memories.

The Bucket Brigade

When the scrapers and shovelers had finished their work, the Menomonee Valley boasted nearly 1,400 acres of "made land," several miles of docks, and some of the best rail connections in the state. Industries moved in almost as soon as the muck was dry, and they represented every phase in the city's economic evolution. Grain elevators continued to receive the bounty of Wisconsin's farms and ship it out again. The processing industries grew by leaps and bounds. Pfister & Vogel continued to tan hides through the 1920s, and meat-packing became a Valley specialty. In 1869 the Milwaukee & St. Paul Railroad opened a large stockyard on reclaimed land just north of today's Mitchell Park. It became a critical source of supply for John Plankinton, Philip Armour, Frederick Layton, and other pioneer packers who built great slaughterhouses on the Valley floor near Muskego Avenue. In 1879 packing was Milwaukee's most important industry, and the Valley was its undisputed center. Because it offered ample room at the intersection of land and water, the Menomonee Valley also became the city's preferred location for the storage of bulk commodities, including lumber, stone, salt, cement, and coal.

Although processing and storage remained important, it was manufacturing that ultimately dominated the Valley's landscape. Milwaukee became the self-proclaimed "Machine Shop of the World" in the late 1800s, with a particular emphasis on all sorts of metal-bending. Utilizing the latest technologies, a small army of local tinkerers graduated from small shops to large factories between 1880 and 1910, and the Menomonee Valley drew them like iron filings to a magnet. On the south side of the Valley, Nordberg (mine hoists and diesel engines) went into business adjacent to the Pfister & Vogel tannery. Chain Belt (chain drives and construction equipment) opened a large factory near S. Sixteenth Street. One block west was the Milwaukee works of the International Harvester Company, whose local plant made farm equipment, gasoline engines, and cream separators. Still farther west, the Harnischfeger Company built a twenty-acre plant (still in operation as Joy Global) that became the world's largest producer of overhead cranes.

Milwaukee County Historical Society

■ (above)
A sprawling stockyard just north of Mitchell Park supplied local meat-packers as the Valley embraced its industrial future.

Milwaukee Public Library

■ *Plankinton was the leading packer in a city famous for its meat.*

Milwaukee County Historical Society

■ *Rockwell & Sanger turned piles of lumber into sashes, doors, blinds, and other millwork for the housing industry.*

Rexnord Industries

■ *Metal-bending became a Valley specialty, and Chain Belt was among the largest manufacturers.*

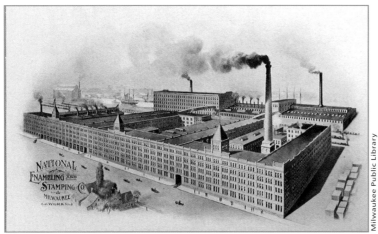

■ *The National Enameling & Stamping Company (known to one and all as NESCO) made roasters on the north rim, and Falk turned out gigantic gears in the Valley proper.*

The filled-in Valley floor west of the gashouse provided a home for two of Milwaukee's largest employers. In 1892 Herman Falk, one of brewer Franz Falk's younger sons, opened a small machine shop in a corner of the old family brewery on the south bluff. By 1910 he had graduated to a large plant in the Valley proper and entered the field that remained Falk's specialty for more than a century: precision industrial gears, including some of the largest in the world. Immediately west of Falk was an even larger enterprise: the main shops of the Milwaukee Road. Virtually filling the Valley floor west of Thirty-fifth Street, the shops made and repaired all the rolling stock for one of America's leading railroads; their cumulative output reached 668 locomotives and nearly 67,000 freight cars by 1937.

Although giants like the Milwaukee Road, Falk, Cutler-Hammer, and Harnischfeger were better-known, the Valley housed scores of smaller enterprises. St. Paul Avenue on the north side and Bruce and Pierce Streets on the south were lined from end to end with modest factory buildings, many of them still in use. In the single square block northwest of Fourth and St. Paul, fledgling industrialists turned out knitwear, decorative marble, furniture, paper boxes, and soap; the melange of sounds and smells must have been almost overpowering. A number of giants put down roots in the Valley, but there were also giants who got away; one soapmaker on St. Paul Avenue was the B.J. Johnson Company, which moved to Chicago in 1923 and found fame as Palmolive.

Businesses of every type and size provided tens of thousands of jobs, and there is little doubt that the Menomonee Valley housed the largest concentration of industrial employment in the entire state. That concentration had a formative impact on Milwaukee's development. The presence of so many jobs so close to the heart of town enabled the community to remain an unusually compact city; in 1902 only Boston and Baltimore had more people per acre. Industrial employers also spawned settlements of industrial employees. Some lived in the

On the Valley's north side, near Tenth and St. Paul, the Kieckhefer brothers opened a tinware plant in 1880 that evolved into the National Enameling & Stamping Company, a firm better known by its initials: NESCO. Two blocks west was the factory complex of Cutler-Hammer, a business that blossomed into one of America's leading manufacturers of electrical controls. Farther west, near Sixteenth Street, Geuder, Paeschke & Frey turned out lunch pails, mailboxes, cuspidors, and other tinware under the Cream City label in a complex that eventually covered seventeen acres. The north side of the Valley also housed an important supplier of industrial energy: a cluster of red brick buildings near Twenty-fifth Street that produced "manufactured gas" from coal. Designed by celebrated local architect Alexander Eschweiler, the Milwaukee Gas Light structures are probably the most distinguished ensemble still standing in the Valley.

■ *The Milwaukee Road shops were a leading local employer for nearly a century.*

Valley proper; blue-collar housing reached all the way to Canal Street at Thirteenth, and a row of houses on Muskego Avenue actually backed up against the hog pens of the Layton packing plant. A far greater number of workers lived in the procession of industrial neighborhoods on the Valley's rim: Walker's Point, Clarke Square, and Silver City on the south bluff; Tory Hill, Merrill Park, and Pigsville on the north. Workers from all those neighborhoods and points more distant formed a "bucket brigade" that streamed into the Valley with their lunch pails every morning and streamed out again at night.

The Menomonee Valley provided jobs for residents of all Milwaukee neighborhoods, but it also created a physical gulf between the North and South Sides. Canal Street, in fact, has long been the baseline—the zero-hundred mark—that determines North and South addresses. As the city grew, it became a practical necessity to bridge the gap, and a series of viaducts, each a half-mile long, became fixtures in the local landscape. The first, completed in 1878, crossed the Valley at Sixth Street; it was replaced by a more durable structure in 1908. Other spans followed at Sixteenth Street in 1895 (replaced in 1929), at Twenty-seventh Street in 1910, and at Thirty-fifth Street in 1933. The first viaducts carried nothing but horse and pedestrian traffic, but all were eventually upgraded for streetcars and then automobiles.

■ *These Harnischfeger factory hands were among the tens of thousands of workers who spent their days (and often their nights) in the Menomonee Valley.*

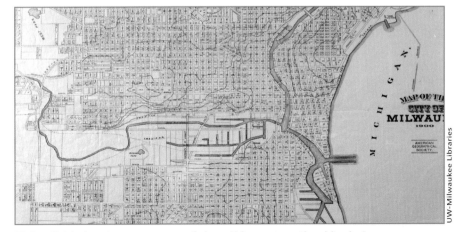

■ *By 1900 the sinuous curves of the wilderness wetland had given way to miles of canals and railroad tracks.*

A Slow Death, a Faster Rebirth

The Menomonee Valley, viaducts and all, was not an aesthetic triumph. As early as 1874, a distillery on the south canal was charged with producing "a nuisance simply stupendous in character." The *Milwaukee Sentinel* (July 17, 1874) described the pollution in graphic terms:

> *Certain it is that from some cause that body of water is a river of death, disgusting in the extreme to the sight and fearfully offensive to the olfactories. From its frightfully filthy depths arise boiling springs and a stench so penetrating and all-pervading as to be utterly unbearable.*

Intercepting sewers were installed in the 1880s, but they simply carried the polluted water out into the lake, where other problems surfaced soon enough.

Liquid waste remained a serious concern, but the Valley was also the site of a novel attempt to solve Milwaukee's solid-waste problems. In 1890 the city installed a "garbage crematory" on the Valley floor east of Sixteenth Street. Summer winds carried the incinerator's odors directly over the mansions of Grand Avenue, and their well-heeled owners howled. U.O.B. Wingate, Milwaukee's health commissioner, expressed surprise at all the fuss. "The whole valley has been a dumping ground for years," Wingate said, and he, for one, did not expect dramatic change any time soon. "We can not very well afford," stated the commissioner, "to lose the $3,000,000 to $4,000,000 invested there."

The city's garbage was eventually diverted to other channels, but the Valley's air pollution problems lasted into modern times. In an era when coal was the universal fuel, locomotives, factories, foundries, and the gas plant belched enormous clouds of acrid smoke into the atmosphere every day. There was a permanent pall over the Valley, and housewives learned not to hang their wash outside when the wind blew from the wrong direction.

For all its economic importance, the Menomonee Valley's persistent pollution problems and the generalized ugliness of much of its development made the district a civic embarrassment to some Milwaukeeans. It was not, ironically, until the Valley's heyday had passed that conditions improved. Local employers expanded in the 1920s, contracted with the rest of the economy in the 1930s, and then climbed to new heights during World War II. Some workers at Falk, Cutler-Hammer, and Chain Belt put in seven-day weeks for the duration of the conflict. It was in the years following World War II that the Valley fell out of favor. As ship and rail traffic lost ground to rubber-tired transport, canal slips and side tracks ceased to be important selling points. Some old-line Valley firms succumbed to technological obsolescence or competitive pressures, but many moved, by truck, to more efficient plants in outlying areas or even other states. A new highway hastened their exit. Interstate 94 opened in stages during the 1960s, following (and obliterating) the route of the Rapid Transit line, a high-speed electric rail corridor that had been in use since 1926.

As the Menomonee Valley began to lose its manufacturing muscle, there were at least a few signs of new life on other fronts. Milwaukee County Stadium opened at the Valley's western end in 1953; four years later, the Braves' triumph in the World Series had Milwaukeeans dancing in the streets. The Valley Power Plant was completed two miles east on Canal Street in 1969; it became America's largest cogeneration facility, providing power for the region's electric customers and steam heat for Downtown buildings. The powerhouse stood in the morning shadow of the High Rise expressway bridge, a high-speed, high-profile version of the viaducts of earlier years. Motorists racing by above the Valley floor might have noticed a number of old standbys that remained in business—Falk, Harnischfeger, and Red Star Yeast among them—but disinvestment was the dominant theme of the post-World War II period. Year by year, the Valley lost economic mass, and quiet reigned where the bluffs had once echoed with the shrill blast of factory whistles and the pounding of heavy machinery.

Milwaukee County Historical Society

■ *By the 1950s the Valley's industrial heyday had passed, and many Milwaukeeans considered it a civic embarrassment.*

■ *There was a scattering of new developments, including Milwaukee County Stadium (1953) and the Valley Power Plant (1969).*

Milwaukee Journal Sentinel

We Energies

Christopher Winters

■ *Potawatomi Bingo and Casino marked the return of the natives in 1991—and the beginning of the Menomonee Valley's rebirth.*

It was probably in the 1970s that the Valley hit rock bottom. Its landscape had degenerated to a forbidding wasteland of junkyards, weed-lots, and some of the most forlorn nightspots in Milwaukee. Local officials were finally moved to take action. Mayor Henry Maier's administration rebuilt roads, cleared blight, and bought land in the Valley for resale to new manufacturers. There was some irony in the creation of an industrial land bank in the middle of a former industrial powerhouse, but Maier was clear about his priorities: "The major goal in the Valley is to provide jobs." The pace quickened after Mayor John Norquist took office in 1988. A series of public and private initiatives, not all of them coordinated, raised expectations for an area that had become one of the most underused in central Milwaukee. Jobs remained the focus, but there was a new emphasis on amenities that would integrate the Valley with the larger community: bicycle trails, open space, and even a proposed golf course. "Ultimately," said Norquist in 1998, "we're going to have a very beautiful valley."

The former marsh was already embracing a post-industrial future, particularly east of Twenty-seventh Street. In 1991 Potawatomi Bingo and Casino opened on Canal Street near Sixteenth. Dispossessed 150 years earlier, the natives had returned, and they brought thousands of gamblers with them. Two years later Marquette University developed its Valley Fields athletic complex across the street, transforming a former coal yard into green space. In 2002 a new Sixth Street viaduct opened, and its bold Calatravaesque design sent a clear message: the Menomonee Valley is no longer an eyesore you cross as quickly as possible; it's a destination. Harley-Davidson heard that message loud and clear. Its museum opened on Canal Street in 2008, drawing visitors from all over the world to soak up the legend of Milwaukee Iron. Another destination emerged at the west end of the Valley: Miller Park, a state-of-the-art replacement for County Stadium that opened in 2001 as the new home of the Milwaukee Brewers.

Christopher Winters

Christopher Winters

■ *The new Sixth Street bridge provided a bold entryway to the Harley-Davidson Museum at the Valley's east margin …*

■ *…while Miller Park opened new possibilities at the western end.*

Christopher Winters

In 1999, as redevelopment efforts gathered momentum, a new organization was formed to focus energy and attention on the Valley: Menomonee Valley Partners, Inc. MVP's

members represent a comprehensive range of interests: Valley business owners, public officials, neighborhood groups, landscape architects, educators, and community advocates. The group's stated goal is nothing less than to "Renew the Valley," with an emphasis on "high-quality, high-yield development." A national competition resulted in a plan that blends parkland, wetland, and recreation with the dominant theme of clean industry.

That plan has fast become an award-winning reality. Twenty-first-century manufacturers have put down roots on the cleared site of the nineteenth-century Milwaukee Road shops. A pedestrian tunnel that connected those shops with workers from the South Side has become the mural-covered Valley Passage, which now connects South Siders with a Valley that's growing greener by the year. In 2013 Three Bridges Park sprouted atop an old freightyard, and the Hank Aaron State Trail carries bicyclists and hikers along a corridor once busy with rail traffic. Just off the trail, at Valley Passage, is the third branch of the Urban Ecology Center, an environmental education pioneer that uses the Valley as an outdoor classroom.

The Menomonee Valley has come a long way from the days when Potawatomi villagers went out in birchbark canoes to harvest wild rice between its bluffs. A natural resource for Native Americans became an industrial resource for European immigrants and then a used-up wasteland that no one seemed to want. The Potawatomi came back to harvest a different kind of bounty in the same location, and a larger transformation is sweeping the entire Menomonee Valley. After 175 years of use and abuse, change and channeling, the Valley is rounding another bend in its long and winding journey, one that holds great promise for the economy, the environment, and the community as a whole.

■ *Bikers navigate the Hank Aaron State Trail through Three Bridges Park, a corridor of greenery that opened in 2013.*

Christopher Winters

Christopher Winters

Christopher Winters

Jessica Lothman

Christopher Winters

■ Bridges spanning the Menomonee Valley at 6th, 16th, 27th, and 35th streets have connected Milwaukee's South Side to the central city since 1878.

■ A pedestrian tunnel that once carried South Side workers to their jobs has become Valley Passage, a mural-covered portal to a much different Menomonee Valley.

Jessica Lothman

■ *The Valley remains a busy rail corridor more than 150 years after the first trains chugged along its northern edge.*

■ *(center right)* The schooner Denis Sullivan *returns to Lake Michigan from her winter berth in the Menomonee Valley.*

■ *(far right)* *The former Milwaukee Gas Light plant at Twenty-fifth Street now houses an architectural firm.*

■ *From its industrial past to its diverse present, the Menomonee Valley has always played a central role in the life of the larger city.*

Christopher Winters

Christopher Winters

Jessica Lothman

West Side

Fanning broadly outward from the edge of Downtown, the West Side spans well over a century of architectural styles and an equally impressive breadth of cultures. Both wealthy and working-class currents were prominent in the district's historical development, intertwined and overlapping to create a formidably complex landscape. Castles and cottages share lot lines in Avenues West. Irish railroad workers, Slavic factory hands, and German aristocrats occupied the same square mile west of Twenty-seventh Street. The phalanx of apartment buildings on Wisconsin Avenue and the classic bungalows of Sherman Park are separated by only a couple of miles, but they might as well be in two different cities.

Culturally, too, the West Side is a study in contrasts. The original residents have long since departed and their descendants with them, but in their place have come other groups who maintain the district's tradition of diversity, from African-American households to Asian refugees to middle-class families of various backgrounds who could easily reside in leafy suburbs but have chosen equally leafy city neighborhoods instead. Together they have developed some of the most energetic grass-roots organizations in the city, and together they have added new layers to the West Side's legacy of human wealth.

West Side
Sherman Park
Enderis Park
Washington Park
Washington Heights
Midtown
Concordia
Avenues West
Merrill Park
Pigsville
Story Hill
Johnson's Woods

AVENUES WEST

M·I·L·W·A·U·K·E·E

Avenues West

How you perceive Avenues West is largely a matter of the direction you're facing. Seen from the east, the neighborhood is the lengthened shadow of Downtown, with an assortment of metropolitan businesses and institutions. Viewed from the west, it's the largely residential extension of two West Side neighborhoods, Merrill Park and Concordia, with the same historic blend of wealthy and working-class homes. Observed from the south, the community reflects the industrial heritage of the adjacent Menomonee Valley.

Although the neighborhood lies at the confluence of several currents, Avenues West is, most visibly, a college campus—the school-year home of more than 11,000 Marquette University students who come from every state and dozens of countries. Beginning with a single building on Wisconsin Avenue in 1907, Marquette has grown to become a major Milwaukee institution, but it exists in the context of its neighborhood. MU proudly declares itself an urban university, and it is Avenues West that provides the urban setting.

Avenues West

1. Ambassador Hotel
2. Aurora-Sinai Medical Center (Mt. Sinai Hospital)
3. Blood Center of Wisconsin
4. Children's Hospital Site
5. Chudnow Museum of Yesteryear
6. Gesu Catholic Church
7. Deaconess Hospital Site (Marquette School of Dentistry)
8. Eagles Club
9. First Marquette College Building Site
10. Gerhard Winner Home Site
11. Irish Cultural & Heritage Center (Grand Avenue Congregational Church Site)
12. Johnston Hall – Marquette University
13. Lutheran Hospital Site (Milwaukee Hospital)
14. Milwaukee Academy of Chinese Language
15. Milwaukee Center for Independence
16. Milwaukee County Courthouse
17. Milwaukee Rescue Mission (Girls Trade & Technical High School)
18. Pabst Mansion
19. St. Emeric Catholic Church Site
20. St. George Melkite Greek Catholic Church
21. Wisconsin Department of Children and Families Regional Office

0   1000 FT

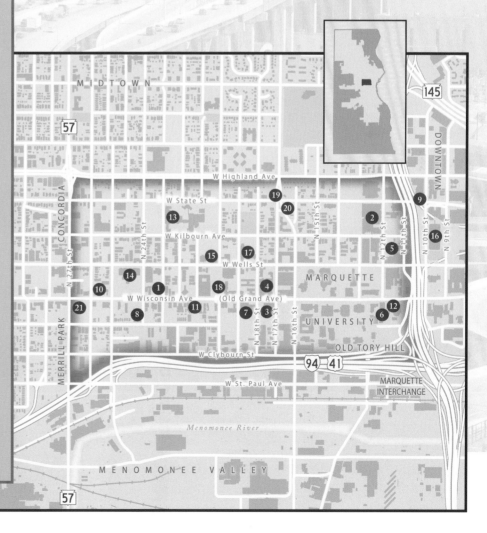

Upstairs, Downstairs

Avenues West began as a community of jarring extremes. It was, in its earliest years, a haven for the wealthy. Beginning in the 1870s, some of Milwaukee's most prominent families lined Wisconsin Avenue (then Spring Street) with homes that were, by Midwestern standards, practically castles. Among the magnates who lived on the avenue were meat-packers Patrick Cudahy and John Plankinton, bankers John Johnston and Rudolph Nunnemacher, and brewers Emil Schandein and Frederick Pabst. In 1876 Spring Street was given a name that more accurately reflected its social standing: Grand Avenue. This early wave of affluence eventually spread north as far as State Street and crossed Twenty-seventh into the Concordia neighborhood.

The blocks south of the avenue were a completely different story. The district bordering the Menomonee Valley east of Sixteenth Street was called Tory Hill, a densely settled and decidedly unaffluent Irish neighborhood. (A short street between Eighth and Eleventh south of Clybourn was named Hibernia—the Latin word for Ireland.) Most Tory Hill residents had moved west from the Third Ward, and practically all worked with their hands. In the decade following the Civil War, the Valley had begun to fill in with stockyards, brickyards, railroads, and industrial shops, all of which needed workers. The residents of Tory Hill took some of the least glamorous jobs in the city, jobs that kept them barely beyond the reach of poverty, while their neighbors to the north lived in conditions that were little short of opulent. It is likely that Tory Hill supplied Grand Avenue with many of its servants and groundskeepers, creating an *Upstairs, Downstairs* social pairing in the very heart of the city.

Most of Grand Avenue's residents worshiped at Protestant churches on the avenue, including Calvary Presbyterian, St. James Episcopal, First Methodist, and Grand Avenue Congregational. The Irish who lived on the slope below them were, by contrast, almost exclusively Catholic. Most Tory Hill residents belonged to St. Gall's, on Second and Michigan. By 1875 that church was filled to bursting, and Holy Name was established on Eleventh and State. Both St. Gall's and Holy Name were administered by the Society of Jesus, an order long known for its commitment to education. The Jesuits had, in fact, come to Milwaukee years earlier with the express intention of opening a college.

■ *Inside and out, meat-packer John Plankinton's mansion defined fine living on Grand Avenue.*

Milwaukee County Historical Society

Milwaukee County Historical Society

The dream finally came true in 1881. Led by Father Stanislaus Lalumiere, the Jesuits erected a four-story brick building on the northwest corner of Tenth and State, next door to Holy Name Church. They named their school Marquette College, after Father Jacques Marquette, the fabled Jesuit missionary and explorer. The building sat at the crest of a gentle hill, giving Marquette an enduring nickname—the Hilltoppers. There were seventy-seven young men in the first class, and their curriculum choices were limited to the liberal arts.

As Marquette College was testing its wings on State Street, the Jesuits opened another landmark institution a few blocks away: Gesu Church. By 1891 Downtown development had begun to encroach on St. Gall's, and Holy Name was chronically overcrowded. The priests decided to merge the two parishes and build a church large enough to accommodate their combined congregations. The result was Gesu, one of Milwaukee's most imposing houses of worship. Designed by Henry Koch, who was also responsible for City Hall, the building was dedicated in 1894. It is a faithful reflection of French Gothic church architecture, a style expressed most grandly in Gesu's model, the Cathedral of Chartres.

■ *The view from Tory Hill was markedly different, featuring long rows of unadorned working-class housing like these dwellings on Clybourn Street.*

Milwaukee Public Library

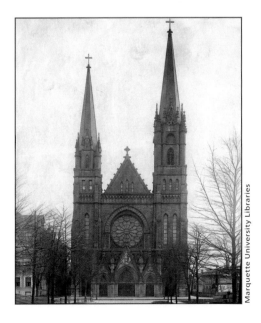

Marquette University Libraries

Marquette University Libraries

■ (left) *Gesu Church was built in 1894 to serve the heavily Irish neighborhood south of Grand Avenue.*

■ (right) *Gesu School, located directly behind the church, educated generations of Tory Hill youngsters.*

Like its predecessors, Gesu began as a parish church, and it anchored a community in the throes of transition. Many of Grand Avenue's more affluent residents stayed through the turn of the twentieth century, but the gold coast's heyday soon passed. Milwaukee was growing, and with its growth came a surge in demand for housing close to the heart of town. As wealthy families moved to greener, quieter pastures, many of their mansions were cut up into multi-family units and ultimately into rooming houses. Other fine homes were torn down to make way for apartment buildings. One notable exception was the grandest of the Grand Avenue mansions, a landmark built for Frederick Pabst in 1892. It became the Catholic archbishop's residence in 1908, four years after the beer baron's death, and housed a succession of prelates until the property was sold in 1975.

Tory Hill remained a densely settled working-class community as Grand Avenue shed its conspicuous wealth. In 1898 there were nearly 300 dwellings squeezed into the area bordered by Tenth and Fifteenth Streets between Wisconsin and St. Paul Avenues. Some Tory Hill homes were literally surrounded by factories. But the neighborhood's ethnic character had changed. Many of the early Irish families had already moved west to Merrill Park, where they founded St. Rose Church in 1888. Tory Hill's inexpensive housing and ready access to jobs attracted

■ *Grand Avenue fell out of fashion at the turn of the twentieth century, but beer baron Frederick Pabst's mansion survived as the residence of the Catholic archbishop.*

UW–Milwaukee Libraries

■ *The neighborhood really began to change when Marquette University moved to Grand Avenue in 1907. Johnston Hall, built in the shadow of Gesu Church, was the entire campus at first. The building is still in use.*

Marquette University Libraries

a new wave of residents, particularly Croatians, Hungarians, and other immigrants from southern and eastern Europe.

Marquette College, meanwhile, was rapidly outgrowing both its building and its curriculum. The original 77 students had multiplied to 200 in 1887 and 300 in 1904. Rising enrollment was accompanied by a demand for new courses, particularly courses that would prepare students for work in the professions. Marquette College took a major step forward in 1907, securing a university charter and adding schools of medicine and law. The institution took a major physical step in the same year, moving from State Street to Grand Avenue. Robert Johnston, a baking magnate and father of a Jesuit priest, funded the construction of Johnston Hall, the school's first and for a few years only building on Grand Avenue. Marquette's new home was literally in the shadow of Gesu Church. As the campus expanded, Gesu developed a dual mission, serving both the neighborhood and the university community.

Change accelerated in the years between 1910 and 1930, a difficult period for Grand Avenue's surviving mansions. As Milwaukee grew, some of the city's leading institutions sought locations near the center of town—on the avenue, if at all possible. Hospitals were prominent in the procession. Deaconess Hospital built a new home on Eighteenth in 1917, Children's Hospital on Seventeenth in 1923, and County Emergency on Twenty-fourth in 1930. All three displaced Grand Avenue mansions. Only blocks away, Mount Sinai Hospital moved into new quarters on Twelfth and Kilbourn in 1914, and Milwaukee (later Lutheran) Hospital—a fixture on Twenty-fourth and Kilbourn since 1863—expanded three times between 1912 and 1932. The presence of five hospitals within walking distance was, of course, a huge advantage for Marquette's medical students.

In 1926, as if to confirm the end of the gold-coast era, Grand Avenue was renamed W. Wisconsin Avenue. Still the institutions came, and they weren't limited to hospitals.

■ *Avenues West developed the largest concentration of hospitals in the state, including Mount Sinai, which moved to Twelfth Street in 1914.*

Jewish Museum Milwaukee

■ *The Eagles Club,*
built in 1926,
featured the state's
largest ballroom.

The local branch of the Eagles, a national fraternal group, built a lavish clubhouse on Twenty-fourth and Wisconsin in 1926; its featured attraction was George Devine's Million-Dollar Ballroom, the largest in the state. Two years later, the Ambassador Hotel opened one block east; the restored building is now one of Milwaukee's major Art Deco landmarks. There were instances of preservation as well as new construction. When the Milwaukee County Courthouse opened on Ninth Street in 1931, a number of rambling old houses in Avenues West were converted to lawyers' offices.

It was in the years after 1910 that Marquette University grew into its role as the neighborhood's largest institution. New schools were added: engineering in 1908, business and journalism in 1910, music in 1911, speech in 1926. As the course offerings multiplied, enrollment soared, climbing from 709 in 1907 to nearly 1,000 in 1910 and 4,357 in 1930. (Although true coeducation developed slowly, the first women were admitted in 1909.) New students and new schools required a larger campus, fueling steady expansion to the south and west. New buildings replaced a number of immigrant dwellings, and old mansions were converted to classroom use.

Although it changed significantly between 1910 and 1930, Avenues West remained a densely settled neighborhood. On some blocks, in fact, the population actually increased, due largely to the construction of apartment buildings where single-family homes and duplexes had stood. Some apartment blocks were nondescript, but others were sufficiently dignified to bear their own names: the Patrician, the Ardmore, Monterey Flats, the Biltmore Grand, and the Stratford Arms among them. The abundance of apartments and the still-plentiful supply of affordable detached homes continued to attract newcomers who had nothing to do with Marquette. Avenues West became a foothold type of neighborhood, a starting place for people from across the ocean and for groups with longer tenure on the continent, including African Americans and Latinos. The greatest number of new arrivals settled in Tory Hill, but they spread out well beyond the old Irish stronghold. One result was an unusual pairing of ethnic congregations on Seventeenth and State. In 1917 a group of Syrian and Lebanese immigrants built St. George Melkite Catholic Church, and in the early 1930s Hungarian newcomers moved into St. Emeric Catholic Church practically across the street. A neighborhood of extremes from the beginning, Avenues West became even more diverse as it evolved.

Milwaukee County Historical Society

Milwaukee Public Library

Rolling down the Avenue

Campus growth and neighborhood change both came to a grinding halt during the Depression, and neither resumed with much vigor until the end of World War II. For Marquette University, the postwar period was a time of full-speed-ahead expansion; for Avenues West, the patterns of change were more ambiguous. The GI Bill got Marquette off to a fast start; returning veterans, taking full advantage of their military benefits, came to the university in droves. Enrollment ballooned from a wartime low of 3,081 in 1943 to 8,603 in 1948 and kept climbing from there, making Marquette the nation's largest Catholic university by the late 1950s. The bulge in the student body put enormous pressure on the prewar campus. Classroom facilities were strained to their limits, and new buildings could not be erected quickly enough. With the addition of new dormitories in the 1950s, the campus enlarged its modest footprint north of Wisconsin Avenue.

The postwar pressures finally receded, but Marquette's leaders continued to look to the future. Despite constant expansion, the campus was anything but cohesive. In the late 1950s the university had two focal points: one cluster of buildings around Gesu Church

and another near Sixteenth and Wisconsin. The clusters were separated by two blocks of apartments, rooming houses, taverns, and aging single-family homes. An integrated campus had been a dream as early as the World War I era, but progress was painfully slow.

What finally made the dream come true was an urban renewal project. In 1964 the City of Milwaukee approved a renewal plan for the area bordered roughly by Eleventh and Seventeenth Streets between Kilbourn Avenue and Clybourn Street. One of the plan's stated goals was "to provide the optimum urban residential environment for the pursuit of higher learning." With the commitment of federal funding in 1965, activity began in earnest. MU had been acquiring mansions since 1907; now it took the apartments that had replaced the mansions. A few were rehabbed, but a greater number were replaced with new classroom buildings or dormitories. Sewer and water lines were relocated, several streets were permanently closed, and Marquette had, for the first time, a self-contained campus.

Tory Hill, in the meantime, was on the verge of extinction. Industrial development had been nibbling away at the working-class enclave for decades, and urban renewal caused additional

■ (left)
Still anchored by Gesu Church, Marquette University's campus expanded dramatically after World War II.

■ (right)
"I think we'll put it there." MU President Edward O'Donnell, S.J., and assorted dignitaries broke ground for a new business school in 1950.

losses. Now freeway development finished the job. Interstates 94 and 43 were completed near the center of town in the late 1960s, and they met precisely at the shrinking heart of Tory Hill. One of the busiest freeway interchanges in the state became an unintended tombstone for a historic community of industrial workers. The Marquette Interchange had a broader impact on Avenues West: it set the neighborhood's southern and eastern borders in concrete. To the west, Merrill Park and Concordia formed an obvious border at Twenty-seventh Street; to the north, State Street marked the line with Midtown. Avenues West, though not yet named as such, occupied an increasingly well-defined space with some imposing borders.

Within those borders, the neighborhood remained a transitional, and in some blocks transient, community of renters in the post-war decades. Drawn by affordable housing and geographic convenience, a shifting cast of characters steadily increased Avenues West's demographic diversity. The local landscape became more diverse as well. The handful of Grand Avenue mansions still standing were put to uses that their builders could hardly have anticipated. In 1952, for instance, an addition was tacked onto whiskey king Gerhard Winner's old home on Twenty-sixth and

Wisconsin as a used-car showroom. Most of the area's hospitals were similarly denatured. One by one, they closed or moved away, until the last health-care facility remaining was Mount Sinai—now Aurora Sinai Medical Center.

There were fears, by the 1970s, that the neighborhood was on a downward slope, but there were signs of hope as well. The turning point might have come in 1975, when a developer bought the Pabst mansion at Twentieth and Wisconsin from the Catholic archdiocese and announced plans to tear it down. Locally and nationally, the historic preservation movement was gaining traction by that time. Rather than see a parking lot replace a beer baron's palace, local activists formed a nonprofit group to purchase the home, restore it to its 1892 splendor, and share the results with the public. The reborn Pabst Mansion quickly became Milwaukee's favorite house museum, and the distinguished survivor established a theme of preservation and renovation that has been part of the neighborhood's character ever since.

Avenues West never stopped being a point of entry for new Milwaukeeans—and new Americans—who were starting on the ground floor, but the note of rebirth sounded by the Pabst Mansion has echoed through other

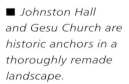

■ *Johnston Hall and Gesu Church are historic anchors in a thoroughly remade landscape.*

all photos on these two pages by Jessica Lothman

neighborhood institutions since the 1970s. The old County Emergency Hospital has housed a succession of public schools. An old nursing home on Wells was replaced by the Milwaukee Center for Independence. The former Girls Trade and Technical High School down the block became the Milwaukee Rescue Mission. The Ambassador Hotel was restored to its Art Deco glory. The Wisconsin Department of Children and Families built a new regional office on Twenty-seventh and Wisconsin. Perhaps the most symbolic transformation took place in 1996, when the former Grand Avenue Congregational Church, once a pillar of polite Yankee society, became the Irish Cultural and Heritage Center. Once confined to a careworn quarter on the edge of the industrial Menomonee Valley, the Irish had moved both uphill and upscale.

The resurgence that began in the 1970s required patient cultivation. Buoyed by positive developments and determined to counter the negative trends, the area's leading institutions and businesses formed the Avenues West Association in 1987. The neighborhood finally had both a name and a voice. Extending its northern border to Highland Avenue,

the association has tackled issues of business development, public safety, landlord relations, housing quality, and aesthetic improvements, all in partnership with the local Business Improvement District (BID). "Together we can" is the Avenues West Association's motto, and the group has done a great deal to make this disparate community a community of interest.

Of all the institutions active in Avenues West—both the association and the neighborhood—none has played a larger role, past or present, than Marquette University. The school's expansion was practically continuous after 1970, but it reached a new level with the launching of the Campus Circle project in 1991. Over a period of five years, the university played the role of real estate developer, investing more than $50

■ (lower left)
The Irish Cultural and Heritage Center occupies the former Grand Avenue Congregational Church.

■ (below)
The aptly named Marquette Interchange sets the neighborhood's eastern border in concrete.

million in the neighborhood around it. Residential properties were purchased and refurbished, new retail centers were built, and Marquette's sphere of influence was dramatically enlarged. With the successful completion of Campus Circle, Marquette took on capital projects closer to its center, including a new school of dentistry, a new library, and new classroom buildings.

In the venerable tradition of Jesuit education, urbanism has been a major theme at Marquette since the beginning. The modern campus has a self-contained, almost insular, atmosphere, with sizable areas of green space and an ensemble of buildings that range from Gothic to post-modern, but Marquette is proudly embedded in the heart of the city. Central Milwaukee serves as both a laboratory and a living environment for students. Urban resources ranging from cultural amenities to internship opportunities are available, in their most concentrated forms, literally at Marquette's doorstep. But it is the daily contact with typical (and not so typical) Milwaukeeans that many graduates remember best. The university is flanked on the north and west by one of the city's most diverse residential districts, an area that provides

homes for African Americans, Latinos, Native Americans, and Indochinese refugees, among many others, few of them with college degrees. Students are an integral part of the community fabric. Generations have learned from their encounters with other neighborhood residents on the street, in local businesses, in off-campus housing, and on the campus itself. "This is real life," said one sophomore. "When I visit friends at other schools, it's like going to a cloister."

Every current in the long history of Avenues West is still swirling in its landscape: the commercial influence of Downtown, the residential character of the West Side, the note of Gilded Age elegance in repurposed mansions, and the dynamism of a major university. Avenues West is like a mixing bowl that blends the homeless with humanities scholars, rooming houses with fine apartments, the bustle of Downtown with the settled air of historic residential streets. The neighborhood is a college campus for some residents and an urban foothold for others. It is that hybrid personality that gives Avenues West its characteristic vitality—and its role as a school of continuing education in the abundant lessons of urban life.

■ *The Kalvelage mansion on Kilbourn Avenue was funded by a fortune made in plumbing fixtures.*

Christopher Winters

Christopher Winters

■ (left)
*Vintage Victorians on
Kilbourn Avenue*

■ (below)
*The Ambassador Hotel is an
Art Deco jewel that has been
restored to its original glory.*

■ (bottom pair)
*The Pabst Mansion has become
Milwaukee's favorite house
museum—where guests can
witness how a beer baron and
his family sat down to dinner.*

Jessica Lothman

Christopher Winters

Christopher Winters

■ (right)
St. George Melkite Church was built in 1917 by Syrian and Lebanese immigrants.

Christopher Winters

MARQUETTE UNIVERSITY

Jessica Lothman

Christopher Winters

Jessica Lothman

Jessica Lothman

Jessica Lothman

■ (top)
The Joan of Arc Chapel is a medieval fixture at the heart of the Marquette University campus.

■ (above)
The Rave nightclub occupies the former Eagles Club, still a Wisconsin Avenue mainstay.

■ (left)
Miss Katie's is a metropolitan dining spot on the edge of campus.

CONCORDIA
MILWAUKEE

Concordia

The college it is named for has left town. The wealthy citizens who built its grandest homes have long since moved on. What began as a suburban haven became an urban community decades ago. The Concordia neighborhood has changed profoundly since its formative years but, in some important respects, the changes have enriched the community. Few Milwaukee neighborhoods encompass so many different worlds. "You name it," said one resident, "and we've got it"—from architects to outlaws and from sprawling Victorian mansions to tiny studio apartments. Some residents are rebuilding the neighborhood's architectural heritage; all are building a new heritage of diversity.

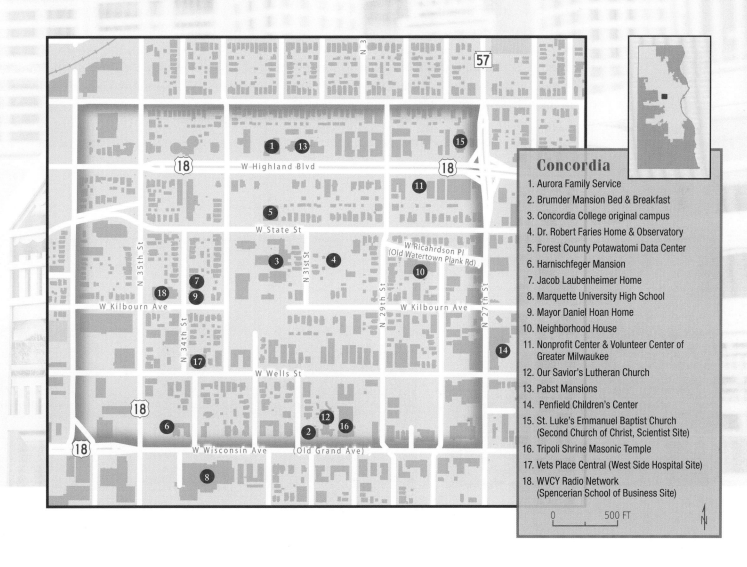

Concordia

1. Aurora Family Service
2. Brumder Mansion Bed & Breakfast
3. Concordia College original campus
4. Dr. Robert Faries Home & Observatory
5. Forest County Potawatomi Data Center
6. Harnischfeger Mansion
7. Jacob Laubenheimer Home
8. Marquette University High School
9. Mayor Daniel Hoan Home
10. Neighborhood House
11. Nonprofit Center & Volunteer Center of Greater Milwaukee
12. Our Savior's Lutheran Church
13. Pabst Mansions
14. Penfield Children's Center
15. St. Luke's Emmanuel Baptist Church (Second Church of Christ, Scientist Site)
16. Tripoli Shrine Masonic Temple
17. Vets Place Central (West Side Hospital Site)
18. WVCY Radio Network (Spencerian School of Business Site)

0   500 FT

Tycoons and College Kids

In Milwaukee's early years, the Concordia area's most important feature was a road that ran through it. The Watertown Plank Road was completed to Wauwatosa in 1849, just three years after Milwaukee received its city charter, and finally reached Watertown in 1853. Farm wagons laden with produce lumbered to market along the toll road every day in season, and it became a crucial link between the city and the surrounding countryside. The meandering highway was straightened in later years, generally following the course of State Street, but one section of its original route remains: Richardson Place, a short diagonal between Twenty-seventh and Twenty-ninth Streets south of State.

The plank road brought farm goods into the city, but it also opened a corridor for Milwaukeeans who wanted to move out to the country. One of them was Dr. Robert Faries, who built an imposing Cream City brick home near what is now Thirtieth and State in the early 1850s. Faries was a dentist by trade, among the first

in Wisconsin, but his passion was astronomy. He used his property as an observatory, gazing at the stars through a telescope he built himself. The Faries home, once again a private residence, is Concordia's oldest building and one of its most prominent landmarks.

Dr. Faries watched the stars in solitude for years, but other members of the gentry settled nearby in the late 1800s. The eastern reaches of Grand (now W. Wisconsin) Avenue had been filling in with grand homes for years, and the wave of wealth finally crossed Twenty-seventh Street in about 1870. One of the first residents of what was called the "west end" of Grand Avenue was Sherburn S. Merrill, general manager of the Chicago, Milwaukee & St. Paul Railroad. The CM&St.P, later known as the Milwaukee Road, was the state's largest line, and its Menomonee Valley shops employed hundreds of Irishmen from Merrill Park, a neighborhood developed by Sherburn Merrill and his family. The Merrills were a power in Milwaukee society, and some of their Grand

■ (left)
Dr. Robert Faries planted the seeds of Concordia's affluence in the 1850s.

■ (right)
Nearby Highland Boulevard blossomed as one of the most prestigious addresses in the city.

Milwaukee Public Library

Milwaukee County Historical Society

Avenue neighbors were just as prominent: the Harnischfegers (overhead cranes), the Wehrs (steel), and the Brumders (publishing).

A second gold coast developed on Highland Boulevard at the turn of the twentieth century. The street was lined with the mansions of brewers, bankers, and other businessmen, among them the Millers, Pabsts, Usingers, Schwaabs, Vilters, Pritzlaffs, and Kieckhefers. A few residents, notably industrialist A.O. Smith and motorcycle manufacturer Walter Davidson, formed an Anglo-Saxon minority, but Highland was so dominated by wealthy Germans that it was dubbed "Sauerkraut Boulevard."

Grand Avenue and Highland Boulevard were two of the most prestigious addresses in Milwaukee, and they served as bookends for the Concordia neighborhood. Between the gold coasts were hundreds of smaller homes (some only slightly smaller) built by professionals and managers in the upper income ranges. There were also prominent public officials on the interior streets. Daniel Hoan, the Socialist who served as Milwaukee's mayor from 1916 to 1940, lived on Kilbourn Avenue near Thirty-fourth for nearly his entire term and stayed until 1954. Just across the alley from Hoan

lived Jacob Laubenheimer, the city's police chief from 1921 to 1936. It's entirely possible that the mayor and the chief stopped to chat when they were taking out the furnace ashes.

The homes that went up during Concordia's early years made the neighborhood a popular stop for out-of-town visitors. Built in the latest Victorian styles (the turreted Queen Anne was easily the most common), they were models of fine craftsmanship. Hardwood floors, lavishly mantled fireplaces, open staircases, and stained-glass windows were standard features. Many of the homes had maid's quarters on the top floor, and a few had coach houses

■ *Although he was a Socialist Daniel in a den of Republicans, Mayor Dan Hoan and his family lived peaceably on Kilbourn Avenue for decades.*

Milwaukee County Historical Society

■ *In 1897 brewer Frederick Pabst, Jr., built a Highland Boulevard mansion that rivaled his father's palatial home on Grand Avenue. Brother Gustav lived next door.*

Milwaukee County Historical Society

Concordia University

Concordia University

■ (top)
The neighborhood's centerpiece and the source of its name was Concordia College, a Lutheran pre-seminary school that moved to the area in 1883.

■ (lower)
Most Concordia students were Midwestern farm boys with German roots. Occasional pillow fights broke the routine of dorm life.

as large as single-family homes in nearby neighborhoods. Beyond a doubt, Concordia was where the gentry lived.

At the center of the community was the institution that gave the neighborhood its name: Concordia College. Operated by and for Missouri Synod Lutherans, Concordia began as a high school for young men who planned to enter the seminary; nearly all its students were German-speaking farm boys from around the Midwest. In 1883 the college moved from Ninth and Highland to a six-acre campus at Thirty-first and State—its home for the next century. In 1890 Concordia added undergraduate courses and became a six-year school, serving about 200 students.

It took nearly twenty years, from 1895 to 1915, for the neighborhood around the college to fill in. By the time the last houses were occupied, the community had already begun to change. As high-density development spread outward from Downtown, apartment buildings began to crop up west of Twenty-seventh Street, particularly on Grand Avenue. The earliest was built in 1907, and the multi-family movement reached its first peak in the 1920s. Metropolitan institutions put down roots during the same period. The Second Church of Christ Scientist (now St. Luke's Emmanuel Baptist) opened on Highland in 1913, and West Side Hospital (now Vets Place Central) was established on Wells in 1924. Marquette University High School was built on Grand Avenue in 1925, and the Tripoli Shrine, a Masonic center inspired by the Taj Mahal, went up a few blocks east in 1928. Twenty-seventh Street itself, a major streetcar route, became a densely developed commercial strip at the same time.

What had begun as a suburban enclave was fast becoming an urban community, and many of its wealthiest residents decided to pull up stakes. Some kept moving west to Wauwatosa, but a greater number resettled in the lakeshore section of the East Side. In 1906, for instance, Gustav Pabst moved from his mansion on Highland to an even larger home on

■ *Twenty-seventh Street became the neighborhood's commercial spine, with establishments like the Tower Theater, a movie palace that opened in 1926, and Traut's upscale grocery store.*

Terrace Avenue, overlooking Lake Michigan. As the exodus gathered steam, the Concordia area experienced a dramatic increase in density. Many of the mansions were converted to rooming houses or fraternity houses, and others were replaced by apartment buildings. Some of Concordia's largest backyards were cut up and covered with smaller homes at the same time. The neighborhood's population increased more than 50 percent between 1920 and 1930.

Concordia College remained a stable presence, and many prominent residents, including Mayor Hoan, were never tempted to leave. The Depression of the 1930s slowed the exodus to a crawl, but the long-term trends resurfaced with new energy after World War II. Once located on the edge, the neighborhood now lay near the heart of the city, and its landscape changed accordingly. More metropolitan institutions moved to the area, among them Doctors (later Family) Hospital and Our Savior's Lutheran Church. Social service agencies, including Family Service, the International Institute, and Lutheran Social Services, built headquarters on Highland Boulevard. Neighborhood House, a magnet for local young people since 1945, opened a new facility on Twenty-eighth south of State in 1967, and the Spencerian School of Business moved into new quarters (now occupied by a

Christian radio network) on Thirty-fifth and Kilbourn. Scores of homes, including some of the finest mansions Milwaukee had ever seen, crumbled before the wrecking ball

Apartment buildings popped up like mushrooms in wet soil as the mansions came down, particularly after a 1961 zoning change. Most of them were large masonry structures filled with efficiencies or one-bedroom units—as many as eighty-five per building. Apartments were most numerous around Twenty-ninth and Wells. Within one block of the intersection, developers ultimately put up 22 structures with a combined total of 685 units. Some buildings housed more people than an entire block of detached houses.

courtesy Florence Rust

John Gurda

■ (left)
As demand for the neighborhood's big homes plummeted, mansion after mansion met the wrecking ball, a wave of destruction that peaked in the 1960s.

■ (right)
Concordia College moved quickly to fill the void, buying over 100 homes to make room for a larger campus. Intense opposition prompted the college to abandon its plans and relocate to Mequon.

Concordia College purchased many of the original single-family homes that remained. In an effort to broaden its appeal to prospective students, Concordia shifted steadily from a narrow pre-seminary program to a Christian, coeducational liberal arts emphasis. The move, college leaders decided, required more room. In 1962 the school announced plans to more than triple its footprint in the neighborhood, and officials targeted 123 properties for acquisition, most within a one-block radius of the existing campus. Concordia eventually purchased more than 100 homes. Roughly half were demolished, and the rest were managed as rental units. By the 1970s the Concordia area was, to put it mildly, an endangered neighborhood.

A countercurrent was soon apparent. Younger families, attracted by the convenience of the neighborhood and the quality of its housing, began to purchase homes around the perimeter of the college's expansion zone. Joining forces with older residents and city officials, they urged Concordia to scale back its plans and take better care of its rental properties.

In an abrupt turn of events, the school abandoned not only its campus expansion plans but its campus. In 1983 Concordia moved to Mequon, taking up quarters in a sprawling convent built by the School Sisters of Notre Dame. (The sisters, ironically, moved back to a Downtown location only a few blocks from their original convent.) The college-owned properties on the West Side were suddenly for sale, and the stage was set for a new and more hopeful chapter in the neighborhood's history.

A Neighborhood Reborn

The resurgence was already under way. As the historic preservation movement gained momentum in the 1970s, Concordia was an obvious choice for people in search of vintage homes. Twenty-ninth Street, between Kilbourn and State, emerged as a particular hotbed of activity. But the "Concordia houses," as the former college properties were known, carried the movement to a new level. Between 1982 and 1984 twenty-five of them were sold to the Westside Conservation Corporation, a nonprofit group established in 1978 to promote owner-occupancy in the district. The homes, all of them late Victorians, were clustered on the east and west sides of the campus. WCC rehabbed the houses inside and out, gave them colorful Victorian paint schemes, and resold them to owner-occupants. Their quality and price ($50,000 to $70,000) attracted eager buyers; the last of the Concordia houses was occupied in 1985.

Twenty-five homes provided room for about as many people as one medium-sized apartment building, but the new residents joined preservationists already on the scene to form a critical mass in the neighborhood. Their combined impact was significantly greater than their actual numbers. Most of the newcomers were first-time home-buyers, and many were first-time parents. A baby boom was apparent by the mid-1980s, bringing new life to what had been an aging neighborhood. Racially integrated, economically secure, and politically active, the new residents represented, in a sense, a rebirth of community. The prevailing spirit soon took organizational form as Historic Concordia Neighbors, Inc., an all-volunteer group that still sponsors, among many other activities, an annual tour of neighborhood homes.

Selling the Concordia houses had been relatively easy, but selling the Concordia campus was not. Rumors swirled for years after the college left in 1983; a prison, senior housing, a Bible college, a conference center, and condominiums were among the possibilities that surfaced. In 1986, finally, the campus was purchased by the Indian Community School, established in 1970 to serve the

■ *Ardent preservationists found plenty of architectural treasures in the homes that remained.*

John Gurda

Native American community's young people. ICS moved its school into one building in 1987 and announced ambitious plans for the rest of the campus. The former Lutheran institution, leaders announced, would become the Wisconsin Indian Cultural Center, providing space for agency offices, a high school, a community college, elderly housing, a museum, and a spiritual center for the Milwaukee area's 8,000 Indians.

■ *The Concordia campus was put to other uses by the Forest County Potawatomi, beginning with a school for young Native Americans.*

Christopher Winters

Large dreams require large amounts of capital, and the Indian Community School proposed high-stakes bingo as a source of the necessary funds. Gambling, however, was an option available only to federally recognized tribes, not to a school that served children from several First Nations. ICS officials invited Wisconsin's tribal communities, which number nearly a dozen, to partner with them, and it was the Forest County Potawatomi who finally agreed. Plans for a bingo hall on the campus itself were shelved after neighbors expressed strong reservations, and in 1991 the Potawatomi casino opened in the Menomonee Valley, on ancestral land where no one lived.

Shared income from the casino, whose dimensions and gaming options kept expanding on the Valley floor, made the Indian Community School the best-endowed elementary school in the state. It was so flush, in fact, that in 2007 the school moved to a stunning new facility in suburban Franklin, where the environmental theme so prominent in Native American culture found physical expression.

Once more the campus was almost entirely empty, and once more the rumors swirled—until 2010, when the Forest County Potawatomi, who owned the property as tribal trust land, unveiled an ambitious redevelopment plan. Historic buildings would be restored and new ones erected to provide space for tribal offices, tribal business operations, community nonprofits (including a charter school), and an "urban Indian center" providing an array of services for Milwaukee's Native Americans. The plan was in many ways an updated version of the Wisconsin Indian Cultural Center proposed in the 1980s, but one of its first elements broke entirely new ground. In 2013 the tribe completed a state-of-the-art data center, a "cloud" that stored and managed information for business clients from throughout the region.

Although the former campus is literally the centerpiece of the neighborhood, it has not been the only center of activity. Concordia is the home of several institutions that serve the entire metropolitan area, including Penfield Children's Center, Aurora Family Service, the Tripoli Shrine, and a Highland Boulevard cluster that includes the Nonprofit Center and the Volunteer Center of Greater Milwaukee. Twenty-seventh Street remains the community's commercial spine, with a pair of new developments bearing the "SoHi" name—for "south of Highland." Concordia is still a restorationist's showcase. Other Milwaukeeans visit the neighborhood to see how it's done, and a number of old mansions have been converted to B&Bs that offer unique lodging experiences.

But the Concordia neighborhood is far more than institutions and buildings. The core of its character is diversity. Although African Americans are in the majority, virtually every major Milwaukee ethnic group is represented. The range of housing choices verges on the extreme. Some families live in cramped one-bedroom apartments overlooking cluttered alleys, while others spread out in homes that are gracious even by North Shore standards. The large number of apartment units gives Concordia a rate of owner-occupancy (8 percent in 2010) that is only one-sixth the city average, but detached houses occupy nearly the same acreage, giving the landscape a diversity that matches its population.

On the human level, the neighborhood is a heady blend of different lives. Some residents never finished grade school, while others have post-graduate degrees. Some blocks pop with energy; others are as sedate as any long-settled suburb. Baby-boomers who bought homes in the 1980s have become empty-nesters, and children born in the 1980s now live in apartment buildings with babies of their own. The neighborhood is, in one sense, a living museum of Victorian houses that provide solid anchors for their owners. It resembles in other respects a bus station, with an abundant supply of low-rent, high-turnover housing that provides its residents with at least a temporary foothold in the city.

Concordia began as a haven for the gentry. The old money has vanished, but the neighborhood has acquired a different kind of wealth: a range of lifestyles, housing types, and cultures that makes it one of the most distinctive, and most dynamic, neighborhoods in the city.

■ *The Schuster mansion, built for a prominent tobacco merchant in 1891, has become a highly regarded B&B, one of several in Concordia.*

■ *Our Savior's Lutheran Church and the Tripoli Shrine Masonic Temple, long-time landmarks on Wisconsin Avenue, form one of the oddest architectural pairings in the region.*

Jessica Lothman

■ The "Lion House" on Highland Boulevard was built for banker George Koch in 1897.

Christopher Winters

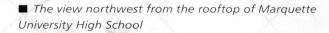

■ Color abounds in the reclaimed Victorians of the Concordia neighborhood.

■ The view northwest from the rooftop of Marquette University High School

Christopher Winters

Jessica Lothman

■ (center left)
Industrialist Henry Harnischfeger's home on Wisconsin Avenue has been converted to apartments.

■ (left)
It's in the details: the ornate gable end of the Schuster mansion.

Christopher Winters

ST. ROSE of LIMA

JAN KOTOWICZ

MERRILL PARK
MILWAUKEE

M·I·L·W·A·U·K·E·E

Merrill Park

It's not hard to tell when you're in Merrill Park. To the south is the constant hum of traffic on Interstate 94. To the west is the quiet of Pigsville, a blue-collar enclave on the banks of the Menomonee River. To the north are Wisconsin Avenue and the once-affluent Concordia neighborhood. To the east is Avenues West, a patchwork quilt of urban life dominated by the Marquette University campus. At the center of that singular frame lies Merrill Park, 40 square blocks housing 3,000 people who share a distinct geography and a strikingly diverse cultural heritage.

Merrill Park

1. Marquette University High School
2. Merrill Park Elderly Housing Community
3. Messmer Catholic Schools West Side Campus
   (St. Rose Catholic School Site)
4. Milwaukee Road Shops Site
5. St. Rose Catholic Church
6. Tripoli Shrine Masonic Temple
7. Zeidler Family Home

Working on the Railroad

Merrill Park is the offspring of a railroad and the namesake of that railroad's guiding light. In 1879 the Chicago, Milwaukee & St. Paul (later known as the Milwaukee Road) began construction of a huge shop complex in the Menomonee Valley, just west of today's Thirty-fifth Street viaduct. The West Milwaukee shops, as they were called, made and repaired all the rolling stock for a line that owned nearly 5,000 miles of track in the Midwest and would eventually reach the Pacific Ocean. By the early 1900s the CM&St.P was one of Milwaukee's largest employers, providing jobs for nearly 3,000 men. They labored inside a cluster of shops, each larger than a football field, that had complete facilities for casting, forging, carpentry, engine work, machining, assembly, and painting.

When the shops opened, the north rim of the valley was covered with the estates of well-to-do Milwaukeeans who were seeking the comfort and open space of the countryside. One of those gentleman farmers was Sherburn S. Merrill, general manager of the Chicago, Milwaukee & St. Paul. In 1868 Merrill purchased roughly fifteen acres at the west end of Grand (now Wisconsin) Avenue and built an elegant brick home on what's now the site of Marquette University High School's cafeteria. Within a decade he owned all the land between Thirtieth and Thirty-fifth Streets south of Grand Avenue—the heart of today's Merrill Park.

Merrill's decision to locate the railroad shops in the Menomonee Valley—almost literally in his own backyard—had an enormous impact on the surrounding area.

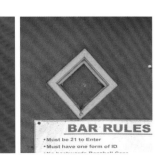

Milwaukee Public Library

■ *Sherburn S. Merrill, general manager of the Milwaukee Road and founder of the neighborhood that bears his name*

■ *Merrill's mansion was one of several grand homes at the west end of old Grand Avenue.*

Milwaukee Public Library

Although the first shop workers commuted from Milwaukee by train, it wasn't long before a resident work force began to put down roots within walking distance of the shops. S. S. Merrill was glad to sell them lots. He began to subdivide his estate in 1883, and "Merrill's Park" (with several "Merrill's Park Additions") provided homesites for hundreds of Milwaukeeans attracted by jobs on the railroad. With characteristic shrewdness, Merrill simultaneously developed an entire neighborhood and employed most of its working adults. The railroad magnate left an estate valued at just under $1 million, a not-so-small fortune in the 1880s.

Most of his new neighbors moved from communities farther east, and Irish families were especially well-represented in the mix. They had been one of Milwaukee's largest ethnic groups since the 1840s, not long after the first public land sale. Most Celtic immigrants had settled in the Third Ward, a densely built neighborhood on the southeast edge of Downtown. When the sons and daughters of "the Ward" started families of their own, many moved west to Tory Hill, on the present site of the Marquette freeway interchange. Merrill Park was the next logical step outward, and settlement there accelerated after a disastrous 1892 fire in the Third Ward.

Even before the fire, Irish newcomers had founded an institution that would become virtually synonymous with Merrill Park: St. Rose Church. The congregation was organized in 1888, and the list of its charter members read like the Dublin phone book. One year later the faithful erected a towering Gothic edifice of Cream City brick at the intersection of Thirtieth and Michigan—on land purchased from the Merrill family. St. Rose became almost literally the heart of the neighborhood: the center of religious, social, athletic, political, and educational life for

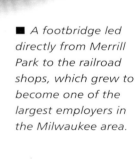

■ *A footbridge led directly from Merrill Park to the railroad shops, which grew to become one of the largest employers in the Milwaukee area.*

■ (right)
A neighborhood developed on the high ground above the Valley, and its focal point was St. Rose Church, a Celtic stronghold dedicated in 1889.

■ (bottom left)
There were still plenty of lots for sale in the heyday of long skirts and horse-drawn buggies.

■ (bottom right)
Carl Zeidler was the older of two Merrill Park brothers who served as Milwaukee's mayor. Carl was in office from 1940 to 1942.

St. Rose Parish

thousands of residents, including the youngest. A large school completed on the church grounds in 1924 soon housed nearly 900 children. Minus its original steeple, St. Rose Church remains the single most important landmark in Merrill Park today.

Catholic churches were fixtures in virtually every Irish neighborhood, but Merrill Park was without another familiar institution. Sherburn Merrill was a teetotaling Yankee who placed deed restrictions on every lot he sold prohibiting "the sale or manufacture of intoxicating beverages." The result was a dearth of saloons in the heart of the neighborhood. One local watering hole, the aptly named Irish Village, became a center of community, but it was on the east side of Thirtieth Street, directly across from the old Merrill estate. Merrill Park developed as a brick-and-mortar oxymoron: a dry Irish neighborhood.

Although they were the largest group, Irish families were by no means the only one. There were numerous German and English residents in Merrill Park, most of whom never

Milwaukee Public Library

Milwaukee Journal Sentinel

set foot inside St. Rose Church. One of them was Michael Zeidler, a barber by trade and a Lutheran by faith, who moved with his wife, Clara, and their children to a corner house at 504 N. Thirty-third Street in 1919. Two Zeidler sons went on to become Milwaukee mayors—Carl from 1940 to 1942 and Frank, a Socialist, from 1948 to 1960. They were not the only sons of the neighborhood who rose to political prominence. Both John Doyne and Bill O'Donnell, proud Irishmen who served multiple terms as Milwaukee County executive, had deep roots in Merrill Park.

Whatever their backgrounds, the first generation of Merrill Parkers shaped the distinctive residential landscape of today. Their typical dwelling was a large two-story frame structure built between 1890 and 1910, and multiple variations on that central theme still fill the neighborhood. Some homes are duplexes, others are single-families, and still others were built for three or four households. Many have fine details—an eyebrow window here, a fish-scale gable end there—that set them apart

from their neighbors, and scores of homes feature spacious front porches with plenty of room for a swing. Hardwood floors are more the rule than the exception, and amenities like oak moldings, built-in china cabinets, and stained-glass window lights grace interiors on virtually every block. Scattered among these more typical houses are both older and newer structures—from nineteenth-century mansions on Wisconsin Avenue to late-twentieth-century apartment buildings in the interior—that make Merrill Park one of the more visually interesting neighborhoods in Milwaukee.

■ (lower left)
Frank Zeidler, Carl's younger brother, held the mayor's seat from 1948 to 1960.

■ (both right)
The Irish Village tavern was a popular Merrill Park hangout from the 1930s (top) through the 1980s, particularly on St. Patrick's Day.

A Neighborhood of Nations

No human community remains static for long, and Merrill Park has demonstrated more dynamism than most. By the 1920s, not many years after settlement was complete, S.S. Merrill would have been surprised at how much his old neighborhood had changed. Wisconsin Avenue, once a genteel address for the city's elite, was transformed into a westerly extension of Milwaukee's main thoroughfare. Some of its mansions were converted to professional offices or studio apartments; others were torn down to make way for metropolitan institutions like Marquette University High School (1925) or the Tripoli Shrine Masonic Temple (1928). An even greater number were replaced by towering apartment buildings.

As Wisconsin Avenue became a more imposing northern border, the population of Merrill Park itself began to change. Just as the original residents had moved west from the Third Ward and Tory Hill, their children kept moving farther west to newer neighborhoods and eventually to suburbs like Wauwatosa and West Allis. Other groups began to make Merrill Park their home: African Americans, Italians, Croats, Slovenes, and Latinos. Most of them followed a well-worn path from the same Downtown neighborhoods that had supplied the first residents.

That pattern of diversity has persisted ever since. Merrill Park became a neighborhood of nations, and its residents have for generations represented a breadth of cultural backgrounds far out of proportion to the community's size. As in the rest of Milwaukee, there was a gradual shift away from the largely European mix of earlier decades. In 2010 the neighborhood's population was 48 percent African-American, 20 percent Latino, 14 percent Asian, and 12 percent white. Hundreds of Hmong refugees, who suffered exile after taking America's side in the Vietnam War, make their homes in Merrill Park, but so do forty-one residents who identify their ancestry as Irish. In the greater Milwaukee area, only Riverwest and sections of the near South Side support comparable cross-sections of the world's cultures.

Although cultural diversity has been the dominant theme for nearly a century, Merrill Park's physical context has clearly changed, particularly since World War II. Interstate 94 cut a broad swath across the southern blocks of the neighborhood in the early 1960s, generating traffic noise but also providing superb access to the rest of the metropolitan area. The Milwaukee Road went bankrupt in 1977 and closed its shops by degrees in the 1980s. Those shops were the neighborhood's original reason for being, and they became part of the general exodus of jobs from central Milwaukee. Small businesses experienced similar stress. Many found it hard to compete against big-box retailers on the edge of town, and there was a gradual thinning of the commercial ranks in Merrill Park. The residential heart of the neighborhood

■ *Whether viewed from on high or from street level, Merrill Park is a richly varied human community.*

Christopher Winters

Christopher Winters

Jessica Lothman

changed by both addition and subtraction. Some homes were lost to freeway clearance and others to neglect, but there were gains as well: new "infill" construction, homes moved from development sites elsewhere, and some of the most impressive restoration efforts in the city.

Merrill Park faces a familiar array of twenty-first-century challenges, but the neighborhood also has a strong tradition of self-help. In earlier decades it was St. Rose Parish that anchored the community. When absentee landlords and residential blight first became issues in the 1950s, the parish organized the Community Beautification and Stabilization Committee to address local concerns. In more recent years St. Rose has adapted to remain relevant to the community. Mass is celebrated in Spanish as well as English—a development that might shock the Murphys and O'Rourkes of the 1880s—and the former parish school continues to educate children as the West Side campus of Messmer Catholic Schools.

In recent years secular organizations have assumed a leading role as community-builders. Neighborhood House, one of the oldest grass-roots groups, has been serving West Siders since 1945 with family-centered programs that currently range from early-childhood services to a school for refugees. One of the newer organizations is the Merrill Park Neighborhood Association, a coalition of neighbors who came together in 1991 with the simple goal of "helping one another." MPNA has since become an important resource as advocate, planner, and organizer for the community.

Merrill Park's organizers and advocates are building on some obvious strengths, beginning with the neighborhood's long-standing tradition of diversity. "There's everybody here," said one African-American homeowner, "and that's what I love about it. We've got Hmong down the block, Spanish across the street, and whites next door." Location is another asset. The cultural and commercial resources of Downtown are barely a mile away, freeway and transit connections are excellent, and yet Merrill Park has both the appearance and the pedigree of a traditional neighborhood—the first west of the central business district.

Few communities in the Milwaukee area demonstrate the effects of geography as clearly as Merrill Park. The neighborhood's strong borders and distinctive landscape have made it, in essence, a geographic shell, a vessel whose contents change but whose identity remains intact. The days of S.S.Merrill and his Irish railroad workers are long gone, but Merrill Park retains an unusually strong sense of urban place. Different from its adjacent neighborhoods and separated from the bustle that practically surrounds it, Merrill Park is a world apart—a heart-of-the-city community with a robust heartbeat of its own.

■ *Soccer in Quad Park and hoops in Merrill Park Playfield*

■ (right)
*Football practice
at Marquette University
High School*

Jessica Lothman

■ (below)
*AFSCME union members pause for
a cookout.*

■ (below right)
*St. Rose School is now the West Side
campus of Messmer Catholic Schools.*

Jessica Lothman

Christopher Winters

Christopher Winters

Christopher Winters

Christopher Winters

■ (above left)
The spirit of renewal on St. Paul Avenue

■ (above)
A Hmong grandmother reaps the harvest of a community garden.

■ (left)
West of Downtown and north of the Menomonee Valley, Merrill Park lies close to the heart of the city.

PIGSVILLE

M·I·L·W·A·U·K·E·E

Pigsville

Pigsville, also known as the Valley, is, to put it mildly, unique. Of all the neighborhoods that make up Milwaukee, it is among the smallest, certainly the most isolated, and without doubt the most unusually named. Sheltered by the bluffs of the Menomonee River, Pigsville is a compact community with a remarkably strong sense of place and a character all its own. Although change has not passed it by, the neighborhood is well into its second century as a distinctive piece of the larger Milwaukee whole.

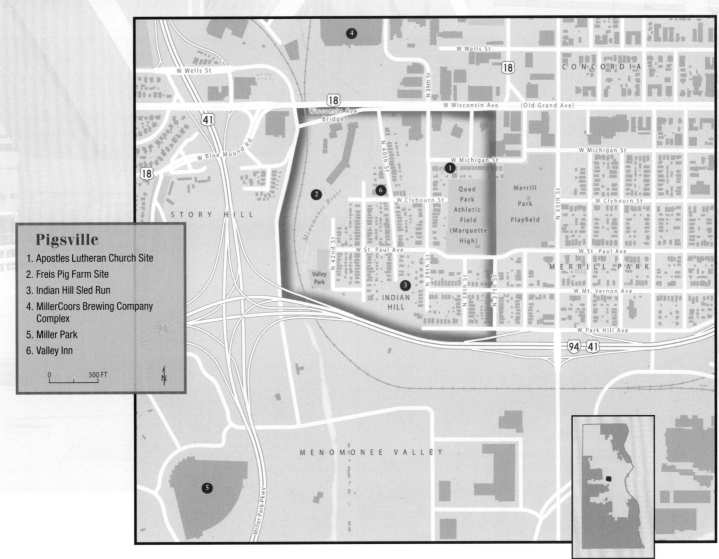

Pigsville

1. Apostles Lutheran Church Site
2. Freis Pig Farm Site
3. Indian Hill Sled Run
4. MillerCoors Brewing Company Complex
5. Miller Park
6. Valley Inn

0   500 FT

Beginning with Pigs

The valley that became the Valley, or Pigsville, was quiet for most of the nineteenth century. The state's first railroad chugged through on its way to Waukesha in 1851. There were occasional blasts from the stone quarry that now underlies Miller Park's north lot. Teamsters entering the valley on Blue Mound Road probably cursed the steep inclines on both sides. A few blocks north, on the Watertown Plank Road, breweries owned by the Miller and Gettelman families kept beer flowing into a city whose thirst was growing as fast as its population. A handful of farmers, most of them German immigrants, tended fields on the valley floor. The most prominent was Adam Freis, whose farm lay on the west bank of the river south of Blue Mound Road. At a time when some of his neighbors were experimenting with dairy cattle, farmer Freis had a different specialty: pigs. At the peak of their operation, Freis and his family kept perhaps 200 pigs on the riverbank.

The valley's pace quickened toward the end of the century. The Milwaukee Road built a massive complex of shops downstream, near Thirty-fifth Street, in the 1880s. Factories upstream manufactured felt, asbestos, and wood products, and the breweries on the

plank road continued to grow. As job opportunities multiplied, urban residents began to arrive. The first houses went up in the 1880s, and by 1910 settlement was nearly complete. The neighborhood's pioneers built a scattering of duplexes and bungalows, but most Pigsville dwellings were modest single-families, including both cottages and Polish flats—those half-basement houses often associated with Slavic immigrants.

As the neighborhood developed, one farm remained in operation—the Freis family's. Their pigs gave Milwaukeeans a handy point of reference for the hamlet taking shape in the valley. The area was called "Pigstown" as early as 1894, and it was widely known as "Pigsville" by the early 1900s. An alternate spelling emerged in later years: "Piggsville." According to a persistent local legend, an innkeeper named George Pigg operated an establishment on Blue Mound Road in pioneer days and bequeathed his name to the settlement. It is more likely, however, that Mr. Pigg was invented by local boosters who had heard a little too much snickering over the years and wanted some distance from their association with ham on the hoof.

Pigsville's early residents were largely Germans, including some who had moved down

■ (left)
Established in 1855, Fred Miller's Plank Road Brewery was one of the first businesses on the valley floor.

■ (right)
Pigsville began to develop a few blocks south in the 1880s.

■ (upper left)
Muddy ruts and all, Blue Mound Road was the main highway through Pigsville for decades. The view is west toward the Menomonee River bridge.

■ (upper right)
The valley's Slovaks maintained a robust cultural life.

■ (left)
Completed in 1911, the Wisconsin Avenue viaduct put a roof over Pigsville and allowed it to develop in peace and quiet.

the hill from nearby Merrill Park. German Lutherans centered their lives around Apostles Church, a Wisconsin Synod congregation established near Thirty-ninth and Michigan in 1897. The church tower was a dominant Valley landmark for seventy years. In the early 1900s the Germans were joined by immigrants from the Slavic nations of eastern Europe: Slovaks, most importantly, but also Serbs, Croats, Czechs, Poles, and Russians. Like the Germans, they transplanted many of their customs and institutions. Pigsville's Slovaks organized their own *sokol*, which combined gymnastics with social activities, as well as an amateur dramatic society.

Both Germans and Slavs depended on nearby industries for employment. A few residents commuted to jobs Downtown, but the vast majority worked in the Milwaukee Road shops, the Miller brewery, and other plants within easy walking distance. Although there were some skilled tradesmen in the neighborhood, most workers began on the lower rungs of the occupational ladder.

As Milwaukee expanded to the west, urban development bypassed Pigsville—or, more accurately, bridged it. Beginning in 1892, a spindly steel trestle carried streetcars across the valley on the Wells Street line. It provided a thrill for paying passengers at no extra

■ (above)
The Steckl bakery was one of more than a dozen Valley businesses.

■ (right)
Rowboats replaced cars whenever the river flooded—a distressingly common occurrence.

charge until the 1950s. The original Wisconsin Avenue viaduct was completed in 1911, after four years of work. It was certainly the most monumental bridge built in Milwaukee before the freeway era, and its concrete arches recalled the graceful symmetry of a Roman aqueduct. In 1925 the Rapid Transit line, a high-speed electric railway, began regular service over yet another bridge just south of Pigsville.

As cars, trains, and trolleys whizzed past on three bridges overhead, the neighborhood on the riverbank was left to develop in peace and quiet. It became an unusually close-knit community, with few intruders and even fewer secrets. The neighborhood was hardly one big family, but many of its residents worked together, drank together, and worshiped together. When the neighborhood's children reached adulthood, intermarriage was not uncommon. The lively sense of community was bolstered by local businesses. In the 1920s Pigsville boasted four grocery stores, three butcher shops, two bakeries, a plumbing business, a dry goods store, and several taverns. Nearly all the necessities of life were a short walk away.

Valley residents paid a price for their privacy. In its early decades the neighborhood was part of the rural Town of Wauwatosa. While city residents on the hilltop to the east enjoyed paved streets, indoor plumbing, and streetlamps, Pigsville made do with gravel roads, backyard wells, and outhouses. Some families added to the rural atmosphere by raising chickens, geese, and even a few pigs on their small lots. The neighborhood's rustic character remained intact until 1925, when, after years of lobbying by local residents, Milwaukee finally annexed the area and began to provide urban services. Another persistent problem was addressed in the 1930s, when federal relief workers lined the banks of the Menomonee River with Lannon-stone walls. Until that project was completed, the river had reached flood stage practically every spring, inundating much of the neighborhood. Although physical conditions gradually improved, Pigsville retained an edge-of-the-city ambience it has never really lost.

Flowing with the River

There was little change in the community until after World War II, and even then the changes were less sweeping than those in nearby neighborhoods. The end of the war itself was an occasion for rejoicing. Pigsville welcomed home its sons with a lavish banquet at Apostles Church, a parade around the neighborhood, and an outdoor party that lasted into the wee hours. In 1948 Valley Park, at Forty-second and St. Paul, opened as a war memorial. A monument to the neighborhood's war dead still stands in the heart of the park, dedicated "By the People of the Valley."

As this surge of civic spirit receded into memory, Pigsville experienced the same juggernaut of forces that transformed cities all across America. Some changes affected the neighborhood's physical landscape. Interstate 94 was built on the community's southern margin in the 1960s, following the old Rapid Transit right-of-way. Apostles Church merged with a Wauwatosa congregation and tore down its building in 1968. (The original school still stands on Michigan Street.) Miller Brewing expanded its physical footprint to Blue Mound Road and beyond. Family-owned local businesses closed, one by one, until the only establishment remaining was the Valley Inn, a long-tenured tavern on Fortieth and Clybourn.

The pace of physical change accelerated toward the end of the twentieth century. In 1993 the old Wisconsin Avenue bridge was replaced by a new span that purposely mirrored the graceful arches of the original. One casualty of the $17 million project was a group of fifteen homes (and two taverns) huddled on the riverbank squarely below the viaduct. Sometimes considered the original Pigsville, the cluster was cleared during construction.

The Menomonee River itself remained an unpredictable neighbor, even with the Depression-era retaining walls in place. A catastrophic flood in June of 1997 prompted the first control measures since the 1930s. The Milwaukee Metropolitan Sewerage District built a levee on the river's east bank and capped it with a decorative floodwall that has so far done its job admirably. Completed in 2001, the project

resulted in the loss of eighteen homes but enlarged the dimensions of Valley Park—and provided relief from the anxiety Pigsville residents felt every time the forecast called for heavy rain.

As the face of the neighborhood changed, so did its demographic profile. Following a script familiar to virtually every immigrant group, the Valley's sons and daughters received better educations than their parents, which enabled them to land better jobs and buy nicer houses—usually outside the neighborhood. As Pigsville's old-line residents aged, more and more of their homes began to change hands. Some were purchased by their children, but not nearly enough to ensure continuity between the generations. The number of Slovak families thinned to a handful, and the community attracted genuine newcomers: African Americans, a variety of working-class whites, Latinos, and a scattering of gay couples. Year by year, the neighborhood looked more and more like the rest of Milwaukee.

At the same time, it continued to look like the only Pigsville in the world. Although change has come to the Valley in recent years, the community has been touched relatively lightly by trends that have remade other sections of the city. Newcomers generally find that they've

■ *A memorial to the neighborhood's war dead was dedicated in 1948 "By the People of the Valley."*

landed in a genuine enclave, one with definite expectations and strong traditions. Pride in property is perhaps the most visible. Many Valley homes are well past the century mark, but their owners have kept them up-to-date over the years. It is not unusual to see repair and remodeling projects underway in the dead of winter. During the warm months many backyards are lush with flower beds, vegetable gardens, and grapevines.

The neighborhood's strong sense of place is reinforced by its geography. Pigsville is not on the way to anywhere. Although it lies at the heart of the city, barely two miles west of Downtown, the neighborhood is cut off from the rest of Milwaukee by some imposing barriers: Interstate 94 to the south, the MillerCoors brewery complex to the north, and fairly steep bluffs to the east and west. Of the eleven

streets that serve the Valley, no fewer than seven terminate in dead ends. Most people who enter the neighborhood are residents, or lost.

Pigsville's location, off every beaten path, has enabled the neighborhood to maintain its traditions with a good deal of integrity. The Valley Park Civic Association, successor to a group organized in 1925, stands ready to resist any threats to the community's stability. The Valley Inn, now in its fourth generation of family ownership, remains a classic neighborhood bar in a classic neighborhood. Fishermen (and some fisherwomen) still angle for salmon in the Menomonee River during the fall spawning run. After subtractions for flood control and bridge construction projects, there are fewer than 150 houses in Pigsville proper—the blocks between the river and Thirty-ninth Street—but residents continue to engage in good-natured

■ *A newer Wisconsin Avenue viaduct carries traffic over Pigsville, but Blue Mound Road* (foreground) *still descends to the valley floor.*

Christopher Winters

debate about the origin, and even the spelling, of their community's name.

In such a small neighborhood, small things are noticed—a sagging porch here, a "For Sale" sign there—and the potential for disruption by physical or demographic changes is high. But many newcomers seem to appreciate Pigsville's island-like atmosphere. They point to its affordable housing, its strong sense of identity, the green space of Valley Park, the little-known sled run on Indian Hill (at the top of Thirty-ninth Street), and the general absence of traffic as appealing assets. One young father put it simply: "It's peaceful down here." Pigsville is not the neighborhood that time forgot, but it remains a special part of the city. The community is unique and, whatever the future brings, it will undoubtedly remain a place unto itself for years to come.

Christopher Winters

Jessica Lothman

Jessica Lothman

■ *Seven of Pigsville's eleven streets terminate in dead ends, enhancing the neighborhood's feeling of separateness.*

Christopher Winters

■ *The Menomonee River is a popular fishing spot during the fall salmon run.*

■ *Miller Park looms just across the freeway, but Valley Park is an island of tranquility.*

Christopher Winters

Christopher Winters

Christopher Winters

Jessica Lothman

■ *The Valley Inn:*
a neighborhood bar
in the best
Milwaukee tradition

STORY HILL

M·I·L·W·A·U·K·E·E

Story Hill

As it tumbles lakeward from Wauwatosa, the Menomonee River creates neighborhoods. The river's broad valley separates the South Side from the rest of Milwaukee, provides an ample bed for Pigsville, and sets borders for several other communities, including Merrill Park, Avenues West, Silver City, Clarke Square, Walker's Point—and Story Hill. Settled largely after 1910, Story Hill is one of the newer neighborhoods in the procession, as well as one of the most distinctive. Perched on a bluff overlooking the Miller Park baseball stadium, the neighborhood lies near the geographic center of Milwaukee County; access in any direction is practically effortless. But the community is much more than a crossroads. Shaped by the valley throughout its history, Story Hill is a neighborhood that stands apart.

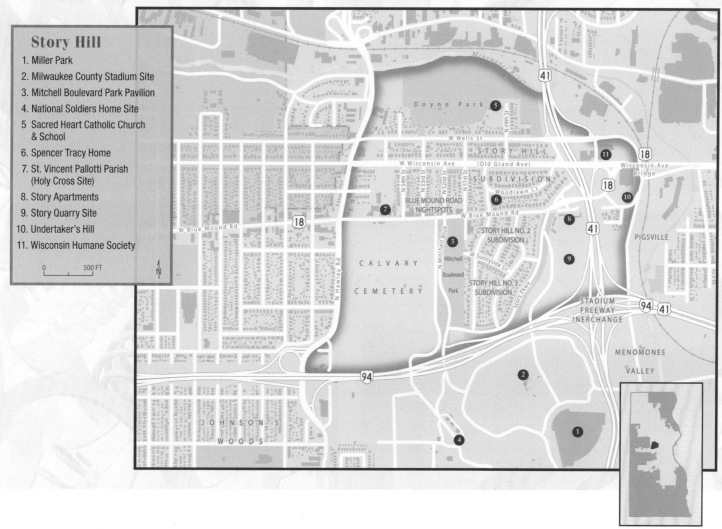

Story Hill

1. Miller Park
2. Milwaukee County Stadium Site
3. Mitchell Boulevard Park Pavilion
4. National Soldiers Home Site
5. Sacred Heart Catholic Church & School
6. Spencer Tracy Home
7. St. Vincent Pallotti Parish (Holy Cross Site)
8. Story Apartments
9. Story Quarry Site
10. Undertaker's Hill
11. Wisconsin Humane Society

0   500 FT

The Storys of Story Hill

Hiram Story was almost a pioneer. He left Vermont at the age of twenty-five and headed west to Milwaukee, arriving in 1843. The first wave of settlement had passed, but there was still plenty of room for an ambitious newcomer. By 1846, the year Milwaukee was chartered, Story owned 160 acres west of the city. The New Englander's land, bordered by Forty-third and Fifty-first Streets between Wisconsin Avenue and Canal Street, included most of the present Story Hill neighborhood.

Story started a farm above the Menomonee River, but an accidental discovery led him to a more lucrative line of work. According to local legend, a storm uprooted a large tree on the farm in the 1850s, revealing a deposit of high-grade dolomite, a form of limestone known regionally as Lannon stone. The farmer became a quarryman, supplying the needs of builders throughout the Milwaukee area. Business was so brisk that Hiram's brother, Horace Story, joined him as a partner in 1857. The Story brothers' quarry eventually covered what is now the north parking lot of Miller Park and the adjacent land beneath Highway 41. The brothers built homes on the high ground above the quarry, and the area was soon known as "Story Hill."

Competing stone quarries opened nearby in the Menomonee Valley, including the Manegold and Monarch operations, which lay just over the hill from the Story quarry. (Filled in years ago, they constitute Doyne Park today.) Between the quarries, at the crest of the hill, was the main road between Milwaukee and all points west. The highway's precursor, little more than two ruts in the wilderness, was blazed in the 1830s to connect the lakeshore city with the little village of Blue Mounds, which lay west and south of what is now Madison. (There was no Madison at the time.) At Blue Mounds the trail joined the military road connecting Green Bay and Prairie du Chien. Most of the route is still in use as Highway 18.

Blue Mound Road, as it came to be called, may have been a quiet country lane in the mid-1800s, but it brought the first non-rural development to the Story Hill area. In 1857 Milwaukee's Catholic diocese opened Calvary Cemetery in a wooded tract on Blue Mound just east of Hawley Road. It had 10,000 burials by 1880, and its "residents" would eventually include such notables as city founder Solomon Juneau, meatpacker Patrick Cudahy, and brewer Frederick Miller.

As Calvary Cemetery began to fill in, a much larger development took shape to the south: the National Soldiers Home. Built in the late 1860s, it was one of the first three homes in the country constructed for disabled Union

■ (left)
Story Hill rests on a solid foundation: 400-million-year-old dolomite that was quarried by the Story brothers and their competitors.

■ (right)
Calvary Cemetery, known for its ornate entrance gate, opened in 1857 as the main cemetery for Milwaukee Catholics.

Milwaukee County Historical Society

St. Vincent Pallotti Parish

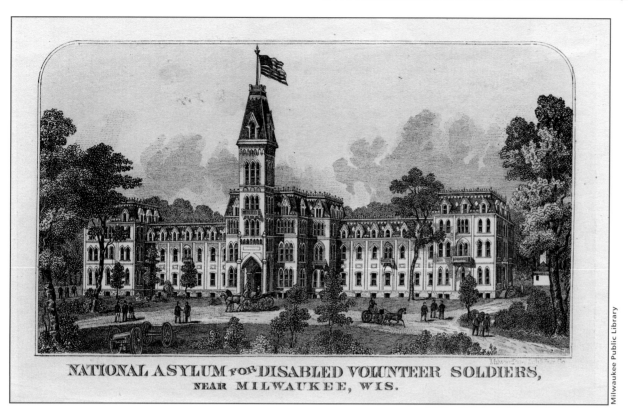

NATIONAL ASYLUM for DISABLED VOLUNTEER SOLDIERS,
NEAR MILWAUKEE, WIS.

■ *The National Soldiers Home was both an asylum for disabled veterans and a major tourist attraction.*

veterans of the Civil War. With its winding carriage paths, picturesque ponds, and gracious Victorian buildings, the National Soldiers Home was a mandatory stop for visitors to Milwaukee. Its main entrances, on Blue Mound Road and "National" Avenue, were soon flanked by saloons that served visitors and veterans alike.

With the Soldiers Home to the south, Calvary Cemetery to the west, and Milwaukee's border only a mile east, Story Hill might have seemed ripe for development. The area lay directly in the path of the city's westward expansion, but a major obstacle retarded its growth for decades: the Menomonee Valley. Blue Mound Road entered and left the valley on grades so steep that they were considered almost treacherous. Although the city was literally in sight, Story Hill remained remote.

The valley's west bluff was called "Undertaker's Hill" because of the challenge it posed to funeral processions bound for Calvary Cemetery. The trip to Calvary was so tedious, in fact, that few city priests could afford the time it took to get there. The Catholic archbishop finally prevailed upon the Capuchin order to open a church across Blue Mound Road from the cemetery. The Capuchins founded Holy Cross Parish in 1879 with a dual

■ *Established in 1879, Holy Cross was a rural German parish whose priests often officiated at Calvary Cemetery across the street.*

■ *Holy Cross School's class of 1894 posed with their slates and lace collars.*

mission: officiating at graveside services and ministering to the German Catholic families in the surrounding farm district. Even after the parish reins passed to the Pallottine order in 1921, cemetery work remained one of the special ministries of Holy Cross.

Milwaukee Public Library

■ *A streetcar trestle linked Story Hill to Milwaukee in 1892, but transit service failed to touch off a housing boom.*

Urban development reached the very edge of Story Hill in the late 1800s. A small settlement named Pigsville (after a neighboring pig farm) spread across the Menomonee Valley floor in the 1880s and '90s. Its residents were drawn by job opportunities in nearby industries, including the Story quarry, but Pigsville was destined to remain an urban village, one of the most isolated communities in the Milwaukee area. Development farther west, on Story Hill, was still blocked by the western bluff.

The area's urban future clearly hinged on easy connections to the city. The first link was forged in 1892, when a local streetcar company built a rickety trestle across the valley at Wells Street. There was soon regular service to Wauwatosa and, after 1901, to West Allis, the manufacturing satellite created by Allis-Chalmers. The West Allis line left Wells Street between Fifty-second and Fifty-third to continue south along the edge of Calvary Cemetery. After negotiating "Cemetery Curve" —a bend still easily visible from Interstate 94 near Miller Park—the streetcars trundled west to Seventieth Street, where they entered the industrial suburb.

Sensing a boom, developers opened subdivisions on the Wells Street section of the west bluff in the 1890s. They found few takers, despite a dependable transit link to Downtown; plenty of

lots were still available on the city side of the valley. Streetcar service, however, continued until 1958, and the trestle was not demolished until 1962. The West Allis roadway, now largely absorbed into neighboring backyards, is still faintly visible between Fifty-second and Fifty-third Streets south of Wells.

A more imposing connection to Milwaukee was completed in 1911, when the Wisconsin (then Grand) Avenue viaduct was opened to traffic. As graceful as a Roman aqueduct, the concrete bridge represented four years of effort by 300 workers. It was apparently the open door that homeseekers had been awaiting. The completion of the viaduct coincided with the beginning of the automobile era, and demand for lots was intense. In 1911 the Story family, by now in its second generation of quarrymen, opened the first Story Hill subdivision, between Blue Mound and Wisconsin east of Fifty-first Street. The tract had never been cleared, and "Story Woods" had provided wildflowers for more than one May crowning at Holy Cross School. Within a few years the "woods" on Woodlawn Court survived only as a scattering of shade trees in an upscale subdivision.

When their first development was filled to capacity, the Story family opened Story Hill 2 (from Blue Mound to Sunnyside) in 1923 and Story Hill 3 (Sunnyside to Story Parkway) in 1927.

■ *The neighborhood eventually developed one of the city's finest collections of Period Revival homes.*

John Gurda

The original subdivisions on Wells Street were settled during the same decade. The Story quarry and its competitors across the ridge continued to operate; dynamite blasts shattered the area's quiet with annoying frequency. But Story Hill became a neighborhood. As if to make the community's status official, the City of Milwaukee annexed the land in 1925.

The homes that went up in Story Hill were above-average specimens of the era's most popular architectural styles. The oldest, dating from the World War I years, reflected the influence of the Prairie School, with gently pitched roofs, broad eaves, and generous porches. Prairie Style homes shared Woodlawn Court and neighboring streets with oversized bungalows inspired by the Craftsman movement, which stressed integrity of form and materials. The focus shifted to Period Revival homes in the 1920s, many of them Tudor and practically all with leaded-glass windows, hardwood floors, and fireplaces. A large number of the Period Revival homes south of Blue Mound are studies in small-scale elegance— almost architectural cameos.

The storybook homes of Story Hill marked a continuation of patterns that had surfaced farther east. Grand Avenue had long been one of the most prestigious addresses in the city,

lined with mansions from Downtown to the lip of the Menomonee Valley. There were few mansions in Story Hill, but the neighborhood's incomes, like its homes, were well above the Milwaukee average. Industrialists like the Harnischfegers and the Nordbergs were joined by lawyers, doctors, and businessmen moving west from the city. One of the new residents was John Edward Tracy, a sales executive whose family lived at 4927 Woodlawn Court after World War I. Tracy's son, Spencer, left Woodlawn in 1921 to begin a career that would lead to durable fame in Hollywood.

Story Hill continued to fill in for several years after the aspiring actor departed. By the early 1930s, however, the Depression had slowed development to a crawl. The Story Apartments near the bluff on Blue Mound Road were built in 1937, but dozens of lots in the southern section of Story Hill remained vacant. Hiram Story's descendants, in the meantime, closed their quarry, after nearly eighty years of operation. Story Hill's very own Story hole was acquired by the city for back taxes and converted to a garbage dump. The Manegold and Monarch quarries to the north met a similar fate.

Soon talk of a new development was in the wind. As early as 1920 Milwaukee's leaders had been discussing plans for a municipal

Milwaukee County Parks Department

■ A cluster of amateur ball diamonds on the valley floor became the site of Milwaukee County Stadium in 1953.

■ Miller Park, County Stadium's successor, looms over the neighborhood's southern border.

Milwaukee County Parks Department

stadium. Intended as a memorial to World War I soldiers, it was envisioned as a venue for the (minor-league) Milwaukee Brewers and local football teams as well as a gathering spot for "civic festivals." The discussion sputtered along until the early 1930s, when the Story quarry, because of its central location, emerged as a leading candidate on the list of possible sites. Endless arguments—about location, cost, and the respective roles of city and county—delayed a decision until 1949. By the time ground was broken in 1950, County Stadium was declared a memorial to World War II soldiers.

The stadium's final site was a corner of the Soldiers Home property that had been covered with amateur baseball diamonds. The old quarry, filled to its brim by that time, became a parking lot. The endless delays were quickly forgotten in 1953, when the stadium opened as the home of the brand-new Milwaukee Braves. The team set a National League attendance record in its very first season and brought Milwaukee a world championship just four years later.

County Stadium dwarfed all previous developments in the Story Hill area, but it was not the only change that took place after World

Christopher Winters

War II. The vacant lots in the southern section of the neighborhood, particularly those on Story Parkway, filled in with new homes, most of them Cape Cods and small ranches. Sacred Heart Catholic Church, a Croatian congregation established on Seventh and Galena in 1917, moved to a new home on Forty-ninth near Wells in 1949; the parish school opened in 1957. And the Stadium Freeway interchange was completed in the late Fifties, bringing rivers of traffic to the neighborhood's southern and eastern borders. Once a quarry site deep in the countryside, Story Hill became a settled neighborhood near the heart of the metropolis.

At Home on the Hill

In some ways, not much has changed. As in its formative years, Story Hill tends to be a community of college-educated Milwaukeeans working in business, the professions, and public service. There are lawyers and teachers, corporate managers and journalists, and—a neighborhood tradition—elected officials. Story Hill's political notables have included Ray Cannon, a congressman in the 1930s; John and Ray Fleming, who served as city attorney and clerk of courts, respectively; John Doyne, Milwaukee's county executive from 1960 to 1976; E. Michael McCann, Milwaukee's district attorney from 1968 to 2006; and Alderman Michael Murphy, who first won election to the Common Council in 1989.

Like the politicians who have settled there over the years, Story Hill is still heavily, but by no means exclusively, Catholic. Many families have long-standing ties to Marquette High School and Marquette University, both a short distance east on Wisconsin Avenue. A significant number are not only Catholic but specifically Irish Catholic. Merrill Park, on the opposite side of the Menomonee Valley, had Milwaukee's highest concentration of Irish families for decades, and Story Hill was a natural destination as their economic fortunes improved. In 2011 a full fifth of the community's residents claimed some Irish ancestry—more than three times the city average.

Ironically, the only churches in Story Hill were founded by members of other ethnic groups: Holy Cross (now the east site of St. Vincent Pallotti Parish) by Germans and Sacred Heart by Croatians. Both of these Catholic congregations welcome worshipers of all ethnic backgrounds today, but Sacred Heart offers the only Croatian Mass in Wisconsin, and its annual picnic draws numerous non-members who appreciate succulent roast lamb and pig prepared in the Old World style.

The bars and restaurants on Blue Mound Road are another neighborhood mainstay. The first watering holes on the old turnpike took advantage of traffic to and from the Soldiers Home, and their successors relied heavily on visitors to County Stadium. Most were filled to capacity, and often beyond, on days when the Braves or the Green Bay Packers played. The roster of establishments has changed with regularity, but the emphasis has traditionally been on sports. The Braves moved to Atlanta in 1966, the Packers now play all their home games in Green Bay, and County Stadium itself was replaced in 2001 by Miller Park, a state-of-the-art home for the Milwaukee Brewers. But baseball continues to bring hordes of visitors to Story Hill, and to the Blue Mound bars, every year. Some neighborhood residents are diehard fans who attend dozens of games each season; others simply accept Miller Park traffic as part of the neighborhood's rhythm. All have found their driveways in demand among friends and would-be friends who want to avoid the cost and congestion of the official parking lots.

From the bars on Blue Mound to baseball in the valley, some powerful local traditions endure, but change is the only enduring constant. By the 1970s the ranks of Story Hill's first residents were thinning rapidly, and a new generation of families was moving in. The newcomers, many with small children, brought with them an appetite for involvement, and they did their best to reinforce the strong sense of community that already existed in Story Hill. Disturbed by sporadic vandalism on Mitchell Boulevard, residents called local officials to a neighborhood meeting in 1976. After brush was cleared and a playground

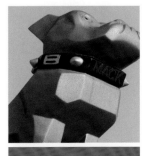

Milwaukee County Parks Department

■ *On Arbor Day in 1970, County Executive John Doyne planted a tree in the park that bears his name.*

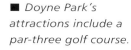

■ *Doyne Park's attractions include a par-three golf course.*

1996 to address a variety of neighborhood concerns, notably a proposed expansion of Interstate 94 that most residents vigorously opposed. The group's first victory, however, was Mitchell Boulevard Park. The boulevard south of Blue Mound was used for overflow parking during Brewers games until residents convinced their elected representatives that there were higher and better uses for the land. Dedicated in 2000, the park includes playfields, prairie plantings, and a pavilion used on a regular basis for community concerts.

Whether gathering in celebration or organizing in protest, the people of Story Hill have displayed a vibrant sense of neighborhood spirit. That spirit reflects the energy of residents both old and new, but it also demonstrates the influence of local geography. Story Hill's location near the center of Milwaukee County has given it a hybrid identity. The community's southern and western borders are Interstate 94 and Highway 41, both high-volume freeways in both senses of the term. A large proportion of the metropolitan area's population whizzes past the neighborhood every day. Story Hill's other borders, by contrast, are parks. To the north is Doyne Park, a reclaimed quarry that features a nine-hole golf course, a soccer field, and a bicycle

installed, the problem disappeared, but the meeting spawned a new tradition. In an effort to strengthen the neighborhood's social networks, residents on both sides of Blue Mound—Story Hill's major internal border— organized events that have since become local institutions. The southern section holds a Fourth of July parade every year, and both sides put on block parties that are among the most spirited in the city. The daylong events feature games for all ages, sidewalk art, potluck suppers, roast corn and, of course, beer.

The community's evolution continues, but its spirit of activism remains. The Story Hill Neighborhood Association was organized in

Christopher Winters

path. Dedicated in 1981, Doyne Park honors the former Story Hill resident who served as Milwaukee's first county executive. The neighborhood's western border is Mitchell Boulevard Park, the generous belt of green space developed by and for the neighborhood. Beyond Mitchell Boulevard is Calvary Cemetery, an oasis of solemn quiet since 1857. Story Hill looks in both directions at once; it is simultaneously engaged and secluded. The neighborhood lies literally at the on-ramp to the rest of the region, but it is also an island of gracious residences and involved residents.

In its larger geographic context, Story Hill is not so much an island as the tip of a semi-suburban peninsula that stretches for miles to the west. That peninsula begins on the site of Hiram Story's old quarry. Just across the Menomonee Valley lie nineteenth-century neighborhoods that are densely settled, extremely diverse, and practically within the shadow of Downtown. The contrasts with Story Hill are obvious. With no pretensions to superiority, the neighborhood is a different world in practically every respect. Set apart by the river as it loops toward the lake, Story Hill has a story of its own to tell, and it's one of the finest in Milwaukee.

Jessica Lothman

■ *A neighborly game of sheepshead*

■ *(below and bottom left) Two storybook homes in Story Hill*

Christopher Winters

■ *The Tree of Life sculpture in Mitchell Boulevard Park*

Jessica Lothman

Jessica Lothman

103

■ (below)
The Wisconsin Humane Society is perched on Story Hill's eastern border.

■ (center right)
Croatian dancers perform at Sacred Heart Church.

■ (bottom)
Calvary Cemetery is an oasis of quiet on Blue Mound Road, but the nightspots to the east are lively indeed.

Christopher Winters

Jessica Lothman

Christopher Winters

104

Christopher Winters

Jessica Lothman

(left pair)
From graveyard to gardens, green space abounds in Story Hill.

(below)
Tailgating at Miller Park is a favorite Milwaukee tradition.

Christopher Winters

Jessica Lothman

JOHNSON'S
WOODS

M*I*L*W*A*U*K*E*E

Johnson's Woods

Johnson's Woods is an in-between sort of neighborhood. Although it's been part of Milwaukee for nearly a century, the community lies squarely between West Allis to the south and Wauwatosa to the north. At closer range, it occupies the space between two very different transportation corridors: Interstate 94 and the Hank Aaron State Trail, a former rail line that now carries bicycles instead of boxcars. In its larger city setting, Johnson's Woods is somewhere between the West Side and the South Side, sharing qualities of both but belonging completely to neither.

The neighborhood's in-between status does not mean that Johnson's Woods is somehow neither here nor there. As with other sharply defined communities, including nearby Story Hill and Pigsville, its unique geographic position has fostered a robust sense of identity. You know exactly where you are when you visit this blue-collar enclave next to the freeway. "It's a nice little pocket," summarized one long-time resident, expressing obvious affection for her district of shady streets, cozy homes, and a central green space that connects the community to its wooded beginnings.

Johnson's Woods

1. Allis-Chalmers Plant Site
2. Burbank Elementary School –
   Milwaukee Public Schools
3. Hunger Task Force
4. Iglesia Jesuchristo Alfa Y Omega
   (Church of the Nazarene Site)
5. Juneau High School Site –
   Milwaukee Public Schools
6. Milwaukee VA Center
   (National Soldiers Home Site)

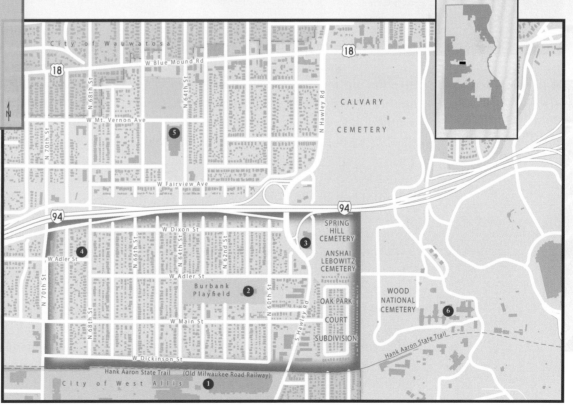

The Johnsons of Johnson's Woods

Nineteenth-century maps identify James Johnson as primary owner of the land that became Johnson's Woods. In 1876 his holdings covered 141 acres bordered by today's Sixtieth and Sixty-eighth Streets between Fairview Avenue and the Milwaukee Road tracks. Johnson was not, as might be assumed, a local farmer who worked the land; he was instead a Milwaukee luminary who held it as an investment. Born in Ireland, the immigrant came to the city in 1844, two years before incorporation, and opened one of its earliest medical practices.

Although he had a busy professional life, Dr. Johnson, like many frontier figures, held more than one public office, serving at various times as alderman, school board member, and Milwaukee's first health commissioner. His duties as commissioner ranged from supervising vaccinations to inspecting slaughterhouses. A devout Catholic, proud Irishman, and loyal Republican, Johnson was also known for his dry sense of humor. That quality was on display when the doctor presented himself as a candidate for alderman in 1849. "I shall get no tickets printed," he wrote. "I ask no man to vote for me or feel under any obligation to any one that does. There is no pay attached to the office that I know of, and I can't thank any man to help put me in a position to work for nothing and board myself."

Practicing medicine was not Dr. Johnson's sole source of income. The *Milwaukee Sentinel* described him as "a careful and methodical businessman [who] at different times was a party to real estate transactions of some magnitude." Johnson owned a fine home in the Yankee Hill neighborhood as well as his extensive acreage in the unincorporated Town of Wauwatosa. In 1877 he sold an undivided half-interest in that land—Johnson's

■ *Dr. James Johnson, the early property-owner who bestowed his name on the neighborhood*

Woods—to his son, Frederick J., who was in his twenties at the time. Trained as a lawyer, Fred Johnson inherited more property when his father died in 1882, and he inherited some of his father's qualities as well, including his staunch Catholicism, Celtic pride, and strong interest in real estate. Johnson's one-time law partner, William W. Wight, recalled him as a skilled attorney who left the field in 1886 "and thereafter subordinated his profession to his large interests in real property." Those interests included corner lots, country farms, and Johnson's Woods.

The woods remained in the family's hands after Fred Johnson's death, at the age of fifty-two, in 1900. His son, James A., took the entrepreneurial tradition even farther. A graduate of the University of Wisconsin Law School, James Johnson worked as an attorney and a banker until 1915, when he became president of the Boggis-Johnson Electric Company, an electrical supply firm he headed until his death in 1935. It was on the third Johnson's watch that today's neighborhood began to emerge, but first came two key incorporations. Wauwatosa, founded as a crossroads trading center in 1837, became a bedroom suburb for Milwaukee workers late in the century. The village secured its charter in 1892, taking in an area that stretched east to Sixtieth Street and south to Wisconsin Avenue. An even more important incorporation, from James A. Johnson's point of view, took place a decade later. The Edward P. Allis Company—soon to become Allis-Chalmers—had run out of room in its Walker's Point shops. In 1900 the firm bought 100 acres of farmland at Seventieth Street and Greenfield Avenue and began to develop a world-class industrial complex. Allis-Chalmers occupied its first buildings in 1902, the same year that the Village of West Allis incorporated. The village limits extended north to the Milwaukee Road corridor (today's Hank Aaron State Trail) and east to Fifty-sixth Street.

Milwaukee County Historical Society

Milwaukee County Historical Society

Johnson's Woods was suddenly in between. Only a mile separated the West Allis border at the railroad tracks from the Wauwatosa line at Wisconsin Avenue. The Johnson property filled most of that gap and, remarkably, it was still "in a state of nature." Most of the adjoining land had been civilized years before. Immediately east was the National Soldiers Home, which became the anchor of today's Veterans Administration complex. The home opened in 1867 as a place of rest for disabled Union veterans of the Civil War, and its cemetery opened as their final resting place. B'nai B'rith, a Jewish fraternal order, added Spring Hill Cemetery in 1876, filling a space between the Soldiers Home and Hawley Road, and Congregation Anshai Lebowitz later opened another graveyard next to Spring Hill. With cemeteries to the east, industry to the south, and cultivated fields to the north and west, Johnson's Woods was a rare fragment of forest primeval. In a 1915 letter to the *Milwaukee Journal*, a woman with the unlikely name of Clara Bell described the property as a bird sanctuary:

> *It is beautifully wooded with trees, shrubs and there is also water. It is one of the most desirable spots for birds in this locality, near the heart of the city. Thousands of people get off the Wells st. car and go to this wood every year, enjoying seeing not only almost every kind of bird that comes to Wisconsin, but also all the different varieties of wild flowers, wild crabapple blossoms, etc.*

Milwaukee Public Library

Another letter-writer, William Orth, painted a similar picture:

> *Soon the crabapples will be in bloom and almost the entire western fringe will be one mass of fragrant pink blossoms. The land is partly marsh and almost every variety of native wildflower and every species of bird find it a natural retreat.*

The retreat's days were numbered. Allis-Chalmers had become the largest corporation

■ (top pair)
First occupied in 1902, the Allis-Chalmers shops formed a mammoth industrial complex at the neighborhood's southern border.

■ (above)
The National Soldiers Home provided a bucolic counterpoint to the east.

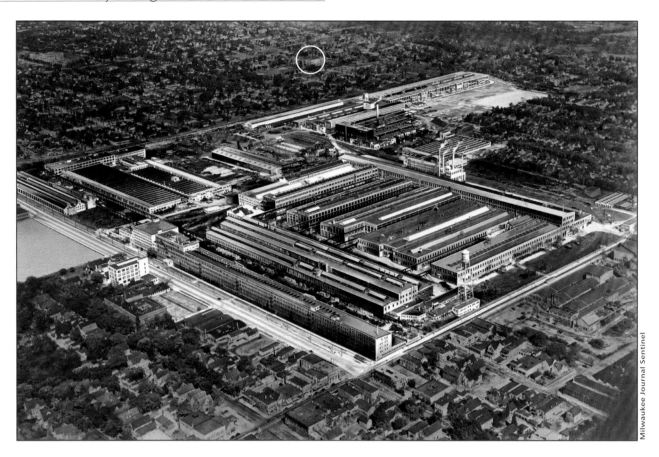

■ *Allis-Chalmers became the largest corporation in Wisconsin, and Johnson's Woods was located just across the railroad tracks. Burbank School is circled.*

■ *A 1915 ad for Milwaukee's newest neighborhood*

in Wisconsin, employing more than 3,200 men in its new works. As other manufacturers followed the giant's lead, West Allis became the state's largest industrial suburb, drawing legions of workers from throughout Milwaukee and well beyond. Many commuted to West Allis on the Wells Street car line, which was extended through the future neighborhood in 1906, but there was growing interest in homesites so close to the factory district. Clara Bell, in fact, had heard rumors of imminent development, and her purpose in writing that 1915 letter was to urge the preservation of her favorite woods. "This city," she declared, "should purchase this land for bird conservation. It will mean as much to our citizens, if not more, than do the parks."

Her pleas went unheeded. James A. Johnson platted "Johnson's Woods No. 1" at the west end of his property in 1915 and finished the job with two more Johnson's Woods subdivisions in 1916 and 1917. Three generations of family ownership came to an end. As the property

was cut up for sale, real estate ads emphasized its proximity ("Only 25 Minutes from Down-Town!"), its pricing ("Any man now supporting a family may have one of these beautiful plots") and, above all, its abundant forest cover:

You know a residence district to be really beautiful and complete must have trees. You can place a high value on every grown tree on your lawn, for don't they add just as much to your comfort and happiness as do certain features of your residence? And every year people pay large sums of money to have grown trees transplanted in their lawns.

Now—just try to take a look into the future and think what it would mean to have your home so near to town and in a regular grove where on hot summer days it will always be cool and shady.

A Blue-Collar Enclave

It was clear from the beginning just what class of buyers the developers expected to seek their shade. Although homeseekers were welcome to buy half-acres if they wished, the proximity of Allis-Chalmers and other industrial employers suggested smaller holdings and a humbler clientele. Most lots were only thirty feet wide, prices started at $99, and the terms were easy indeed: one dollar down and fifty cents a week for any lot costing less than $300.

Johnson's Woods was an attractive proposition for working-class families, but its timing was slightly premature. World War I was under way when the land came on the market in 1915. Although a few lots were sold and a few homes were built, America's entry into the conflict only two years later gave prospective buyers something else to think about, and a sharp postwar recession put a definite damper on sales. As a result, it was not until the 1920s that development began in earnest. Some of the first homes were little more than cottages, and they were joined by scores of Milwaukee bungalows, the decade's signature house type. Bungalows were especially abundant in Oak Park Court, a four-square-block subdivision just east of the original Johnson tract and south of the Jewish cemeteries.

The neighborhood that took shape displayed some distinctive residential patterns. Because it was separated from the city by the National Soldiers Home and the adjoining graveyards, Johnson's Woods did not lie on any main-traveled corridor of settlement. It attracted Germans from the North and West Sides, Poles from the South Side, and other groups from virtually anywhere east of Sixtieth Street. What the new residents had in common was the color of their collars. The neighborhood was part of the unincorporated Town of Wauwatosa in its early years, and a sample page from the Johnson's Woods section of the 1926 town directory offered some occupational clues. The list included five machinists, four laborers, three helpers, three carpenters, two molders, two clerks, two assemblers, a steamfitter, a teacher, a painter, a packer, a draftsman, and a candymaker. The working-class character of the neighborhood was unmistakable, and scores, perhaps hundreds, of local residents walked to work at

Allis-Chalmers, whose factory complex started just across the tracks.

As development intensified, Johnson's Woods shed what remained of its rural character. The City of Milwaukee annexed the area in stages, pushing its limits west to Sixtieth Street in 1925, Sixty-eighth in 1927, and all the way to Eightieth in 1931. City services followed. The dirt roads of the early years were paved and water service was extended, but the most important addition was a school. Local youngsters had attended classes in a crude barracks built by the Town of Wauwatosa at Sixtieth and Adler. Milwaukee replaced the barracks with an attractive brick school in 1931 and named it for Luther Burbank, the celebrated plant breeder. The area's teens went to Juneau High School, which was built in 1932 on Sixty-fourth and Mt. Vernon, just north of Johnson's Woods.

The Depression had dipped to its lowest point by the time the paint on Burbank School's walls was dry. Development virtually stopped in its tracks, and laid-off workers were forced to "pull the coaster" to local relief stations for bulk supplies of cereal, potatoes, flour, oatmeal, beans, and other staples. For residents

■ *After years in cramped barracks (top), the children of Johnson's Woods moved into Burbank School in 1931.*

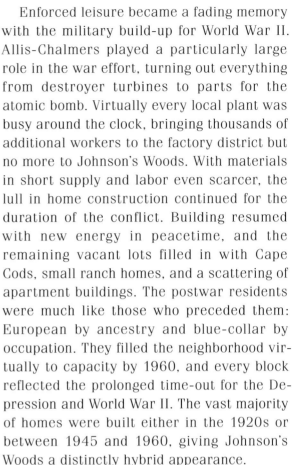

■ (above)
A remnant of Dr. Johnson's original woods is clearly visible in this aerial view of Burbank School and Playfield.

■ (right)
Allis-Chalmers was a major defense supplier during World War II, and women helped keep the plant humming.

Enforced leisure became a fading memory with the military build-up for World War II. Allis-Chalmers played a particularly large role in the war effort, turning out everything from destroyer turbines to parts for the atomic bomb. Virtually every local plant was busy around the clock, bringing thousands of additional workers to the factory district but no more to Johnson's Woods. With materials in short supply and labor even scarcer, the lull in home construction continued for the duration of the conflict. Building resumed with new energy in peacetime, and the remaining vacant lots filled in with Cape Cods, small ranch homes, and a scattering of apartment buildings. The postwar residents were much like those who preceded them: European by ancestry and blue-collar by occupation. They filled the neighborhood virtually to capacity by 1960, and every block reflected the prolonged time-out for the Depression and World War II. The vast majority of homes were built either in the 1920s or between 1945 and 1960, giving Johnson's Woods a distinctly hybrid appearance.

Still in the Middle

Even before its last homes were occupied, the neighborhood underwent a major change. For decades the busiest transportation corridor in Johnson's Woods (and the dirtiest, in the days of coal-fired locomotives) had been the Milwaukee Road branch at its southern edge, which was heavily used by West Allis industries. To the north, along Fairview Avenue, was the electrified Rapid Transit line, a high-speed interurban service inaugurated in 1926. This early version of light rail was popular for years, but Rapid Transit rapidly lost ground to the private automobile. In the 1950s much of its right-of-way was appropriated for Interstate 94. (What remains of the corridor is marked today by high-voltage transmission lines.) The freeway-builders cut a block-wide swath through the northern edge of Johnson's Woods, destroying scores of homes, raising a wall that separated the community from its neighbors to the north, and creating a river of noise. When this first stretch of I-94 opened

of Johnson's Woods, the sole bright spot was a park. In 1928 Milwaukee's Common Council had approved the purchase of the wooded two-block tract just west of Burbank School for public recreation. The Depression made the city's job significantly easier. Some lots were acquired for back taxes, and others were purchased for so little that there was money left over to fund improvements. A softball field and a wading pool were installed in 1933, and a field house and outdoor theater followed one year later, with essential support from New Deal work relief programs. The recreational facilities were popular among residents with time on their hands, but Burbank Playfield's most appealing feature was the remnant of native forest at its western end.

in 1962, it instantly became the busiest highway in Wisconsin.

The railroad tracks were suddenly secondary, and they became even less important as West Allis, with the rest of the Milwaukee area, began to shed industrial muscle. As a global manufacturer of heavy equipment, Allis-Chalmers had always suffered through the vagaries of the business cycle, but the downturn of the early 1980s brought the giant to its knees. Despite massive layoffs and desperate restructuring efforts, Allis-Chalmers was forced into bankruptcy in 1987. A significant number of Johnson's Woods residents lost their livelihoods, and the tracks at the neighborhood's border were so quiet that they were eventually removed. After decades between an electric interurban line and a steam (later diesel) railroad, Johnson's Woods was now bordered by a busy expressway and an empty gravel path.

The neighborhood between those contrasting corridors changed less than the corridors themselves. The first generation of urban settlers was largely gone by the late 1900s, of course, and the second generation was steadily giving way to younger families. Those families were considerably more diverse than their predecessors. African Americans joined the migration, and Latinos were even more numerous, rising from roughly 3 percent of the population in 1990 to 16 percent in 2010. The neighborhood's largest place of worship, a Church of the Nazarene built on Sixty-eighth and Adler in 1940, was purchased by a Spanish-speaking Pentecostal congregation, and the little chapel across the street housed a Honduran faith community.

There have been changes in the recent past, and plenty of them, but just as notable are the things that haven't changed. What Johnson's Woods was, it still is, to a marked degree. Blue-collar and service occupations predominate, with a liberal admixture of public-sector workers. Property maintenance standards remain uniformly high. An old Allis-Chalmers machine shop, now the home of a railcar restoration business, looms over the neighborhood to the south, just as it did in the company's heyday. The rail corridor that

Milwaukee Journal Sentinel

served that shop and many others for nearly a century came back to life in 2011 as the Hank Aaron State Trail. "Johnson's Woods" remains in common use, in part because homeowners—still a majority of households—see the subdivision name on their property tax bills every year.

The neighborhood also retains a thoroughly distinctive sense of place in the twenty-first century. At several points you can see from one end of Johnson's Woods to the other, a span of four blocks between the freeway and the bike path. Oak Park Court, as sheltered a residential pocket as exists in Milwaukee, is the dot on the neighborhood's "i," the cross on its "t," and the enclave's neighbors to the north and east are as quiet as they come. Johnson's

■ *Construction of Interstate 94 transformed the northern border of Johnson's Woods in the 1950s.*

Woods has the only Main Street in Milwaukee, a name of unknown origin that, whether hopeful or humorous, certainly stands out. At the very heart of the neighborhood, on Sixty-fourth and Adler, is its most genuinely iconic space. The western half of Burbank Playfield is covered with a dense growth of oak, maple, hickory, and ash trees, including some that were probably sprouts when Johnsons owned the property. Johnson's Woods it remains—a neighborhood still in between, and glad to be there.

■ (right)
The former Church of the Nazarene now houses a Latino congregation.

■ (far right)
Anshai Lebowitz Cemetery

■ (below)
The Hank Aaron State Trail is a welcome throwback to the neighborhood's rural past.

Jessica Lothman

Jessica Lothman

■ *Burbank School and Playfield*

Christopher Winters

■ (below)
Soldiers' graves in the Veterans Administration Cemetery

Jessica Lothman

Christopher Winters

Jessica Lothman

John Gurda

■ (left)
A former Allis-Chalmers shop looms over this neighborhood of modest homes and quiet streets.

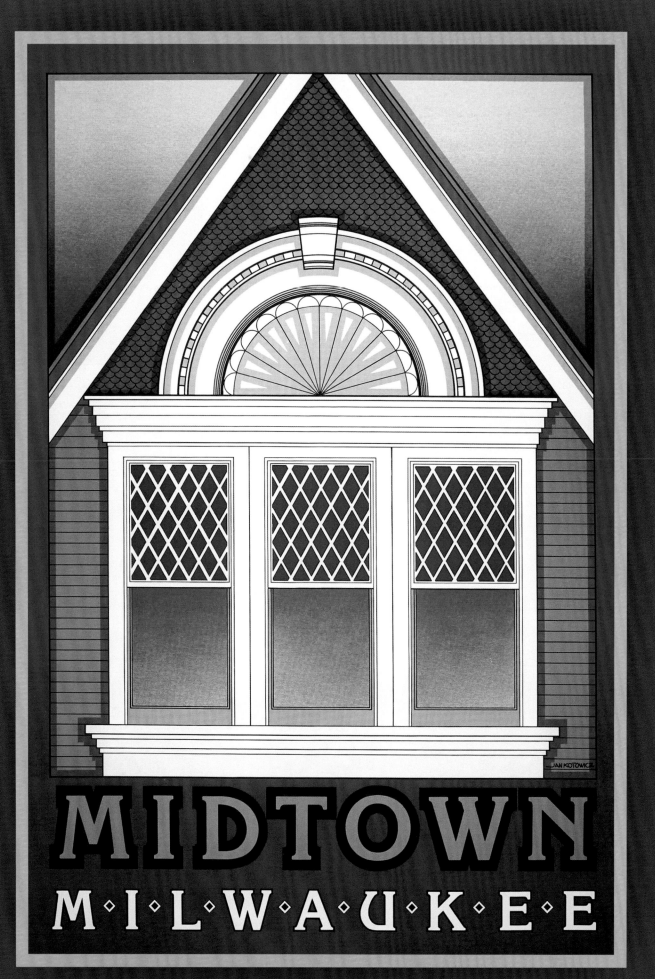

MIDTOWN

M·I·L·W·A·U·K·E·E

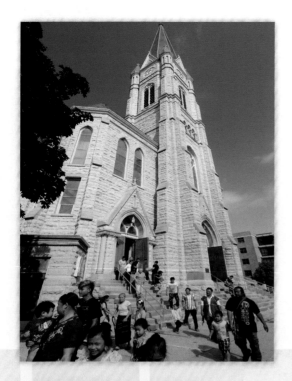

Midtown

Some neighborhoods are new; other neighborhoods are old. Midtown is both. Some Milwaukee neighborhoods participate in the life of the West Side; others identify with the North Side. Midtown splits the difference. Some neighborhoods have always been extremely diverse; others have always been homogeneous, their histories forever linked to one particular ethnic group. Midtown shares aspects of both patterns. Set squarely in the heart of the city, Midtown is a perennial meeting place, a neighborhood where the historical, geographic, and social currents of Milwaukee have always mingled, and the result is a character more complex than you'd find in communities several times Midtown's size.

Midtown

1. Brown Street Academy –
   Milwaukee Public Schools

2. Casa Maria Catholic Worker House

3. CityHomes Development

4. Frank Lloyd Wright Apartments Site

5. Milwaukee High School of the Arts –
   Milwaukee Public Schools
   (West Division High School)

6. Misericordia Hospital Site

7. Salvation Army Community Center

8. St. Michael Catholic Church

9. Starms Discovery Learning Center –
   Milwaukee Public Schools

10. Urban Day School
    (St. Michael Catholic School Site)

11. Voice of Christian Youth
    (Vliet Street State Bank)

Two Streams Converge

In the late 1800s, as industrial growth pushed Milwaukee's population to new heights, the land that became Midtown lay directly between two major corridors of expansion. One followed Wisconsin Avenue west from Downtown and fanned out gently to the north. It carried some of Milwaukee's most affluent families to new neighborhoods generally considered part of the West Side, including Concordia, Story Hill, and Washington Heights. The second corridor followed Fond du Lac Avenue to the northwest. Many of the home-seekers who moved out along Fond du Lac were blue-collar workers from the densely settled area just north of Downtown, and they developed Lindsay Heights, Amani, and other North Side communities.

■ Cold Spring Park began as a popular race track and became an elegant turn-of-the-century subdivision.

from Illustrated Historical Atlas, 1876

The North Side stream was first to reach the Midtown area. By the 1880s working-class families had begun to line the blocks along Lisbon Avenue, an old plank road, with modest frame homes, both single-families and duplexes. Typical lots in the new subdivisions were narrow, creating densities that were intensified by the large number of alley houses—a fixture in many of Milwaukee's older neighborhoods.

The wealthier West Side stream converged from the south near the end of the century and kept flowing well into the 1900s. Wisconsin (then Grand) Avenue was already lined with mansions, and Highland Boulevard, west of Twenty-seventh, was fast becoming another gold coast. Although there were no Harleys or Davidsons, no Pabsts or Millers in the stream that settled southern Midtown, the area attracted middle- to upper-middle-income residents—merchants, professionals, and skilled tradesmen among them—who built massive duplexes and a variety of towered and turreted Victorian single-families.

Some new homes fell little short of the splendor so conspicuously displayed on Grand Avenue and Highland Boulevard. The most prestigious section of Midtown was undoubtedly McKinley Boulevard between Twenty-seventh and Thirty-fifth Streets. From the 1850s to 1890, the long, narrow corridor was the site of a race track called Cold Spring Park, where some of the region's finest trotting horses were put through their paces. The park was enlisted as a military encampment during the Civil War, and it served as the site of the Wisconsin State Fair in the 1870s and 1880s. When urban development reached the area at the end of the century, Cold Spring's owners subdivided the land. Between 1900 and 1910 prosperous Milwaukeeans lined what is now McKinley Boulevard with spacious three-story duplexes and elegant single-family homes. More than a century later, Cold Spring Park remains a distinctive subneighborhood within the larger Midtown area.

Although age and redevelopment have obscured the historical border, the approximate dividing line between the West Side and North Side streams in Midtown was Vliet Street. That border was not hard and fast. Some working-class residents lived south of

Vliet, and there was a scattering of larger homes north of the line. There were ethnic ties across Vliet as well. Although Midtown's residents were economically diverse and, in general terms, geographically split, the vast majority had one thing in common: German ancestry. The area's subdivisions had names like Germania Heights and Von Moltke Park. Small breweries and bowling alleys cropped up even on the side streets. There were churches for German Catholics, German Lutherans, German Methodists, and German Evangelicals. German, not English, was the language of conversation in Midtown's shops, saloons, and living rooms.

The neighborhood's largest church by far was St. Michael's, the Catholic congregation. Established in 1883 with only 125 families, its growth was explosive in the decades that followed. In 1905, the date of the oldest surviving parish census records, St. Michael's numbered 1,101 households: one Bohemian, one Dutch, one Polish, and 1,098 German. In 1893 the congregation built a towering Gothic church of local stone, and it has been Midtown's dominant landmark ever since. A school was opened in 1884, but the neighborhood was growing so fast that the building had to be expanded four times in the next twenty years. St. Michael's became one of the largest parishes in the city, and it was a major hub of social as well as religious life. When a new school was built in 1923, its amenities included four bowling alleys in the basement.

The leader of all Milwaukee Catholics, a German-speaking Austrian, lived only three blocks away. In 1891 Archbishop Frederick Katzer moved into an old mansion on Twenty-third and Juneau. It had been the home of William Pitt Lynde, a prominent lawyer who served Milwaukee as both mayor and congressman. The mansion remained the archbishop's residence until 1908, when it was acquired by the Misericordia Sisters. After remodeling the structure from top to bottom, the nuns opened a general hospital named for their order. They stayed until 1969, when the sisters sold Misericordia Hospital and established Elmbrook Memorial in Brookfield.

(from top)
■ *Midtown's major institutions included St. Michael's Church, a stoutly German parish founded in 1883; West Division High School, built in 1896; and Misericordia Hospital, which took over an old mansion in 1908.*

119

Milwaukee Public Library

Milwaukee Public Library

■ (top pair)
*Retail development
followed residential.
Vliet Street (looking
west at Twenty-
Seventh) and Lisbon
Avenue (west at
Walnut) emerged as
Midtown's major
business districts.*

■ (right)
*An apartment
complex designed by
Frank Lloyd Wright
crowned the corner
of Twenty-seventh
and Highland.*

Milwaukee Public Library

Churches and a hospital were not the only resources close at hand. Vliet Street became Midtown's "downtown," lined with shops from Twentieth to Thirty-fifth. Lisbon Avenue and later State Street were also busy retail districts, and there was no shortage of employers in the area. Beginning in the 1890s, the railroad corridor on the neighborhood's western edge became a bustling industrial district. Plants there produced everything from caskets and cookstoves to cement blocks and worsted cloth.

Hundreds of Midtown breadwinners lived within easy walking distance of work.

Although Midtown was an established neighborhood by 1900, settlement continued into the 1920s, particularly south of Vliet Street. One of the most unusual developments was an eight-family apartment complex built on Twenty-seventh and Highland in 1916. It was designed by Frank Lloyd Wright, a Wisconsin native who became an American legend. Wright had been trying for years to put his architectural designs within reach of moderate-income households. One result was what he called "American System-Built Homes," which featured pre-cut components and simplified construction. The Highland project was the only multi-family complex ever built using Wright's American System.

Preservation or Redevelopment?

Although Midtown remained a stable, German-flavored neighborhood for decades, it changed significantly as the twentieth century progressed. A sizable Hungarian community developed in the 1920s. Like Midtown's first residents, the Hungarians had moved northwest from the Downtown area, and they were by no means the last addition to the neighborhood's demographic mix. More pervasive were the shifts that occurred after World War II. By the 1950s many of Midtown's older homes had begun to show signs of age. Concerned that blight might spread, a group of homeowners and businessmen organized the Mid-Town Neighborhood Association in 1960. MTNA's goal was to shore up the physical condition of the neighborhood from Twentieth to Twenty-seventh Streets between State and Walnut. The group encouraged home repair, painting, and landscaping efforts, and it spread its message through a series of rallies and award dinners. By 1962 the association had 425 members.

Although fresh paint and flowers improved the appearance of scores of homes, MTNA decided that local efforts to upgrade Midtown needed help from outside, and so the group asked the City of Milwaukee for assistance. In

1963 the city designated Midtown an urban renewal area and applied for federal funds to plan and implement a renewal project. Municipal planners extended Midtown's borders north to Lisbon Avenue and west to the railroad corridor that generally paralleled Thirtieth Street. MTNA expanded its own target area accordingly, stretching its borders west to Thirty-fifth Street and north to Brown. The renewal plan was completed in 1966, but red tape and financial problems delayed the start of the project until 1969.

As the neighborhood plan cleared bureaucratic hurdles, the neighborhood itself continued to change. New groups moved into Midtown, most of them following the same corridors that had brought the first urban residents. The presence of African-American families, who had entered Midtown in the 1950s, became more pronounced. The number of Latinos, from both Mexico and Puerto Rico, increased as well. A sizable Native American community developed, particularly in the blocks west of Twenty-seventh Street. There was also an influx of young white residents, many of them Catholic and many of them associated in some way with Marquette University, whose campus began practically on Midtown's eastern border. An active concern for social justice, in both their nation and their neighborhood, united many of the young newcomers. One of their major focal points was

Casa Maria (House of Mary) on Twenty-first Street. Founded in 1966 as a Catholic Worker community, Casa Maria offered hospitality to needy families and individuals from throughout the region.

In 1969, finally, the Midtown Conservation Project began in earnest. Just as two contrasting geographic currents had made Midtown, two contrasting policy currents remade the neighborhood. Earlier renewal projects had stressed land clearance and redevelopment—an approach comparable to clear-cutting a forest and starting over. Later projects emphasized preservation of the existing cultural landscape. Midtown was a watershed project; it combined aspects of both strategies. Local property-owners eventually rehabilitated 650 buildings, their efforts supported by nearly a million dollars in grants and low-interest loans. More visible, however, were redevelopment activities. The final plan, envisioned as a means to eliminate blight, reduce population densities, and facilitate the flow of through traffic, called for the demolition of nearly half the area's buildings, followed by redevelopment of the vacant land.

The proper balance between preservation and redevelopment proved hard to find. There were pitched battles for control of the Mid-Town Neighborhood Association's resident council and sharp disagreements about specific aspects of the plan. The MTNA went on record

■ (above left)
Mike and Nettie Cullen, shown at a community meal with three of their children, founded the Casa Maria Catholic Worker House in 1966.

■ (above)
Midtown residents testified at City Hall regarding a renewal plan many of them opposed.

Milwaukee County Parks Department

Milwaukee County Parks Department

■ *Crowds turned out for the 1978 dedication of Tiefenthaler Park, Midtown's first public green space.*

neighborhood's first, that covered three square blocks north and west of St. Michael's Church. Equipped with ball fields, basketball hoops, and a two-story community building, the park was named for Leo Tiefenthaler, a product of Midtown's German community. Although he never held elective office, Tiefenthaler, as secretary of the City Club, was a widely respected guardian of the public interest in both city and county government. The civic watchdog lived in a Victorian house on McKinley Avenue from his boyhood to his death in 1974 at the age of ninety-four.

The Midtown Conservation Project was the largest renewal effort undertaken by the City of Milwaukee to that point. It lasted nearly six years and cost $25 million, 80 percent of it in federal funds. The project's impact on the neighborhood was enormous. Midtown was an aging community when the activities began. The combination of conservation and redevelopment made it, in effect, a new old neighborhood.

The community has continued down the dual track of preservation and redevelopment since the 1970s. Milwaukee adopted an official preservation policy in 1977, defusing tensions with neighborhood groups and spawning a variety of tools, including low-interest loans and "dollar houses," to upgrade properties and promote owner-occupancy. In Midtown and elsewhere, however, preservation has been largely an individual undertaking. Some of the efforts in the Cold Spring Park section have been particularly impressive, but the spirit of preservation is alive throughout the neighborhood.

Midtown was also affected by a policy that might be described as preservation once removed. In the 1980s, as expansion projects at Miller Brewing, St. Michael Hospital, and other sites put scores of homes in the bulldozer's path, the city bought them, moved them to vacant lots in the central city, and resold them to owner-occupants. The effects of the program are obvious in Midtown, particularly near Twenty-seventh and Lisbon. Dozens of cleared lots were filled with homes ranging from modest post-World War II ranches to imposing duplexes of the World War I era.

against the planned widening of Highland Avenue in 1970, and local preservationists howled when the Frank Lloyd Wright apartments on Twenty-seventh and Highland were demolished for street reconstruction in 1973. In the end the original plan was carried out practically in its entirety. By late 1975, when the initial project was completed, Midtown had new streets and streetlights, upgraded water and sewer lines, new tot lots, and hundreds of new housing units in courtyard apartments, modular multi-family complexes, and scattered-site individual homes. Lisbon, Highland, and Twenty-seventh Street had all been widened, and new institutions had taken root, including a Salvation Army community center. Some residents were grateful for the changes; others wondered where their neighborhood had gone.

Perhaps the least controversial element of the Midtown project was a new park, the

New construction has been even more visible since the 1980s, and acres of vacant land in Midtown have been slowly but steadily reclaimed for residential use—sometimes on individual lots, more often in clusters of homes or entire subdivisions. The CityHomes development northwest of Twentieth and Walnut is especially striking. With spacious yards, detached garages, and plenty of built-ins, the homes are suburban in everything but address. The redevelopment efforts reflect the commitment of city officials, private developers, and nonprofit groups, including Habitat for Humanity. By 2010 their common emphasis on single-family housing had lifted the rate of owner-occupancy in Midtown to 34 percent—a significant jump from the 27 percent who owned their homes in 1960, before redevelopment activity of any kind began.

The Patchwork Neighborhood

The metaphor of the patchwork quilt is sometimes overused in describing urban communities, but it's a perfect match for Midtown. The neighborhood is less whole cloth than a collection of patches, or pockets, one distinct from another and all creating a pattern that takes time to decipher. Former residents revisiting their old haunts tend to become disoriented.

Redevelopment has been so extensive that large sections of Midtown are barely recognizable to them, whether they lived in the community when it was a stable German enclave or during the more challenging period of the 1970s and '80s. One result is a remarkable range of housing choices. Old and new, big and small, restored and relocated, from cottages to nearly castles and from garden apartments to upper flats, Midtown has them all, giving home-seekers perhaps the greatest range of options in the city.

The 7,500 residents of Midtown are nearly as varied as their homes. The neighborhood is a German enclave no longer and hasn't been for more than a generation; Midtown has completed the transition from monolithic to multilingual. African Americans are the largest single group, making up nearly two-thirds of the population in 2010, but the neighborhood also has one of the highest concentrations of Asians in the city: 22 percent in 2010. Most are Indochinese refugees, particularly Hmong, who were persecuted terribly after fighting on America's side in the Vietnam War. There are also nearly 500 Latinos, both Mexicans and Puerto Ricans, and other households representing a variety of European backgrounds, including German. There are no isolated colonies; the groups are spread rather evenly throughout Midtown. "Here," said one resident

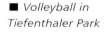

■ *Volleyball in Tiefenthaler Park*

Frank Miller

simply, "there's everybody." The presence of so many cultures gives Midtown a cosmopolitan diversity that feels more like modern Brooklyn than traditional Milwaukee.

It is fitting that St. Michael's Church, once the major cornerstone of the German community, most thoroughly embodies the diversity that is Midtown today. The 2,000 members of the parish include Latinos, African Americans, a variety of whites, Hmong and Laotian families and, since 2010, refugees fleeing persecution in Myanmar. When the groups come together for an all-parish service, the results can be overpowering. Sister Alice Thepouthay, a member of St. Michael's pastoral team who emigrated from Laos in 1981, put it poetically: "We pray to God in many languages, and He understands them all."

The multi-cultural character of Midtown has bred, at the very least, a tolerance for different lifestyles. At their best, local residents display an appreciation of their polyglot culture and an active spirit of cooperation that is most visibly expressed in their organizations. Although there have been losses, chief among them the Mid-Town Neighborhood Association, Midtown retains an impressive concentration of resources. Casa Maria, its mission essentially unchanged, still offers hospitality to the needy in its home on Twenty-first Street. The Salvation Army Center, built during the first stage of renewal, offers a variety of social services, and Voice of Christian Youth (VCY) operates Christian outreach programs from the old Vliet Street State Bank.

Other Midtown organizations are building a base for the future. ACTS Housing, a church-affiliated program that grew out of St. Michael's in 1995, helps low-income families purchase homes of their own. Lake Valley Camp has turned the Tiefenthaler Park pavilion into a center for youth activities. Urban Day School, a community anchor since 1967, has educated thousands of local youngsters in St. Michael's former parish school. West Division High School, a presence on Highland Boulevard since 1896 and in its present building since 1958, came to new life as Milwaukee High School of the Arts, with a much-admired specialty program in the visual, performing, and literary arts. Directly opposite the high school, on Juneau Avenue, the tree-fringed square that once contained the Lynde family's mansion and then Misericordia Hospital has been "renatured" to become Lynden Hill, a green gathering spot for the entire community.

After more than a century, Midtown is still a meeting place—a mid-sized, middle-of-the-city neighborhood where the currents of the larger community continue to mingle. In its organizations, its homes, and its people, the community is a complex blend of old and new, of preservation and renewal. That blend has given Midtown a tangible connection with the past and a foothold on a future whose outline is still emerging.

■ *Sharing the wealth at Alice's Garden*

Frank Miller

Frank Miller

Frank Miller

Frank Miller

Frank Miller

■ (above)
From vintage Victorians to the sparkling new CityHomes, Midtown has an impressive range of housing choices.

■ (left)
Lynden Hill is a square block of green space on the Misericordia Hospital site.

■ (below)
Milwaukee High School of the Arts offers an award-winning program in the visual, performing, and literary arts.

Frank Miller

Christopher Winters

Christopher Winters

WASHINGTON
PARK
M~I~L~W~A~U~K~E~E

Washington Park

The Washington Park area consists of three small-scale residential districts that frame the largest area of green space on Milwaukee's West Side. Those residential pockets—Walnut Hill, Washington Park, and Martin Drive—house no more than 8,000 people among them, but they embody some large-scale contrasts. Their characters, which range from inner-city to almost-suburban, clearly reflect the neighborhood's transitional place near the center of town. There are, at the same time, some powerful unifying influences at work, notably the park itself: an urban oasis that began as a showplace, weathered a lengthy period of decline and, like the residential areas around it, shows encouraging signs of new life.

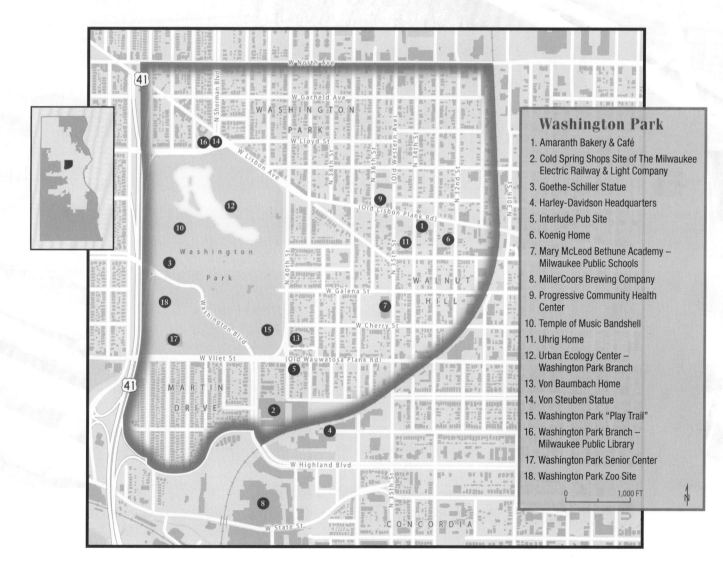

Washington Park

1. Amaranth Bakery & Café
2. Cold Spring Shops Site of The Milwaukee Electric Railway & Light Company
3. Goethe-Schiller Statue
4. Harley-Davidson Headquarters
5. Interlude Pub Site
6. Koenig Home
7. Mary McLeod Bethune Academy – Milwaukee Public Schools
8. MillerCoors Brewing Company
9. Progressive Community Health Center
10. Temple of Music Bandshell
11. Uhrig Home
12. Urban Ecology Center – Washington Park Branch
13. Von Baumbach Home
14. Von Steuben Statue
15. Washington Park "Play Trail"
16. Washington Park Branch – Milwaukee Public Library
17. Washington Park Senior Center
18. Washington Park Zoo Site

0   1,000 FT

Elephants and Immigrants

Long before a neighborhood came to life, the future Washington Park area was fertile farmland served by a pair of busy plank roads. One was a short-haul turnpike called the Wauwatosa Plank Road—today's Vliet Street. The other, and by far the longer, was the Lisbon Plank Road, which cut diagonally through the district on its way to the Town of Lisbon in Waukesha County. (Lisbon, an unincorporated area whose largest settlement is Sussex, lies just west of Menomonee Falls.) In the summer of 1851, the *Milwaukee Sentinel* printed an inviting description of what is now Lisbon Avenue: "Among the pleasantest drives out of town is the Plank Road, leading from this city to Lisbon. It passes through a fertile and well-cultivated region, dotted with neat farm houses and capacious barns, and smiling now with luxuriant crops." Some of those crops were undoubtedly smiling in the Washington Park area. The plank road's first tollgate was at Twenty-seventh Street, the second at North Avenue, and both were surrounded by farmland.

The paired plank roads, which were in business by the early 1850s, made it easier for farmers to bring their crops to market, but they also made it easier for exurbanites to find, even then, relief from the congestion of the city. Gentleman's farms cropped up along the roads soon after they opened. That in itself was not unusual—the same pattern was apparent elsewhere in the county—but the survival of three of the original homes to the present day is remarkable. The Franz Joseph Uhrig mansion, 1727 N. Thirty-fourth Street, was built in 1851 as the summer home of a St. Louis brewer with close ties to the Uihlein family, owners of Schlitz. The residence once crowned a twenty-acre estate that included a fountain, a windmill, orchards, and a separate

■ *Three gentleman farmers, all of them German, built fine homes in the area when it was still completely rural. The dwellings belonged to (clockwise from top) Franz Joseph Uhrig, Frederick Koenig, and Ludwig von Baumbach.*

Milwaukee County Historical Society

Milwaukee Public Library

John Gurda

house just for the gardener. The Ludwig von Baumbach home, 1440 N. Fortieth St., was built in about 1856 for a distinguished German immigrant. The Cream City brick building was moved from ... Vliet Street to its present ... and raised to accommodate ... [th]e Frederick Koenig house, ... ond Street, is a twenty-one- ... vival landmark built in the ... nd purchased from Franz ... hree homes are standouts, ... de a continuing connection ... al beginnings.

... von Baumbachs, and the ... [plen]ty of time to enjoy their ... [surroundings], but it was clear that the ... [directly i]n the path of Milwaukee's ... [onward expansion]. The city limits reached ... Street (then Western Avenue) in 1891, and local developers, including the gentleman farmers, began to subdivide their holdings into urban lots. Before land on the leading edge became prohibitively expensive, the City of Milwaukee purchased 125 acres for a public park—one of six major acquisitions in 1890-91. West (later Washington) joined Lake, Riverside, Kosciuszko, Humboldt, and Mitchell Parks as the anchors of a system that officials projected as "a chain of parks around the city connected by handsome boulevards."

Although the purchases showed great foresight, funds for park development were slow in coming. The city did make some

early progress, drawing on plans for West Park prepared by the firm of Frederick Law Olmsted, America's foremost landscape architect. One of the first tasks was to reforest a landscape that had been largely denuded for agriculture; 4,000 trees were planted in 1894 alone. Other projects showed more immediate results. The high ground in the fledgling park became the site of an observation tower, and the low ground to the north became an island-studded lagoon. (Rowboats were available at ten cents per half-hour in 1895.) Carriageways, a horse-racing track, and a band pavilion attracted more pleasure-seekers, but West Park's major draw was a zoo—or at least the beginnings of one. In 1891 brewer Gustav Pabst and real estate dealer Louis Auer donated five deer to the city for public display. A buck was added one year later, and the herd grew accordingly, swelling to thirty-five animals by 1899. More improvements would come, including Goat Mountain, Monkey Island, and an elephant named Countess Heine, but West Park was an established attraction by century's end. "Situated in the extreme western suburbs," wrote the *Milwaukee Sentinel* in 1897, "it possesses a delightful prospect of picturesque and varied landscape, and while many of its more pleasing features are yet to be developed, what has been done is evidence of the cultivated taste and skillful manipulation of those who have had the work in charge."

■ *Washington Park was designed with broad vistas in mind.*

Milwaukee County Parks Department

■ *Washington Park's attractions included trotting-horse races, rowboats for rent, a zoo starring an elephant named Countess Heine, and events like the Bohemian Sokol's 1918 gymnastics exercises.*

Developments far less picturesque and certainly less cultivated were already under way a few blocks east. Between 1890 and 1910, the railroad corridor that curved north from Miller Brewing along Thirtieth Street became an industrial district of the first magnitude. Trackside factories barely a half-mile east of the park turned out a miscellaneous assortment of caskets, athletic goods, paint and glass, mattresses, paper mill supplies, traveling trunks, windows and doors, lighting fixtures, and sausage. One of the largest employers on the corridor stood just south of Vliet Street, directly across the tracks from the Harley-Davidson plant. Milwaukee's electric utility was also its streetcar utility, and in 1912 the Cold Spring shops of The Milwaukee Electric Railway & Light Company—today's We Energies—opened on the site of an old brickyard. With 300,000 square feet under roof, the Cold Spring shops handled maintenance and repair for the entire fleet, but workers there could also refit old cars and

build new ones from scratch. (The streetcars live on in the Martin Drive area's logo.) From streetcars to suitcases, the trackside industries provided jobs for thousands of people, and many employees walked to work from the surrounding blocks.

With a steadily improving park on one side and a rapidly growing industrial belt on the other, the stage was set for a new neighborhood to emerge. Settlers poured into the open spaces between the park and the rail corridor after 1890, finding enjoyment in one and employment in the other. Not surprisingly, the stream flowed from southeast to northwest, wrapping around the park as it surged outward from the city's center. The park itself preserved the rolling topography that once typified the whole district, but the contours of the surrounding area were softened to facilitate home-building.

Walnut Hill, a large subdivision covering most of the triangle between Thirty-fifth Street, Lisbon Avenue, and the railroad tracks,

was platted in 1889. The neighborhood's settlement started there and accelerated through the next decade, generally following Lisbon Avenue to the north and west. In 1900 Milwaukee's city limits reached the far side of West Park, just ahead of the initial boom in that precinct. The blocks south of the park—the Martin Drive area—were off the main-traveled route from the city, retarding settlement there until the Teens and Twenties. The homes south of Vliet Street are, on average, ten to fifteen years younger than their counterparts north and east of the park. By 1930, however, the entire area was settled to its limits, and the mansions of the gentleman's-farm era were nearly lost in a sea of newer, smaller homes.

Most of those homes were frame single-families and duplexes built on thirty-foot lots by blue-collar workers, both skilled and semi-skilled; the industrial character of the adjoining rail corridor had a major impact on the character of the neighborhood. There was a generous assortment of more imposing houses, including a cluster on Highland Boulevard. Where that street turned north at the railroad bridge to enter Washington Park, it linked affluent Highland Boulevard to the east with equally affluent Washington Boulevard to the northwest. The same upscale pattern was evident on Sherman Boulevard north of the park, and even the side streets had the occasional home built by a doctor or a lawyer.

Although incomes varied, the neighborhood's Germanic flavor was unmistakable, a clear reflection of its origins farther east. There were other ethnic groups in the area, including Irish and Jewish residents, but most newcomers were German-speaking immigrants and their German-speaking children who had moved from neighborhoods closer to Downtown. In 1908, when local German societies were looking for a place to erect a statue honoring two of their homeland's literary heroes, Goethe and Schiller, Washington Park was the obvious choice. In 1921, following the wave of anti-German hysteria that had erupted during World War I, Milwaukee's Teutons put up another statue at the north end of the park. This one honored Frederick Wilhelm von Steuben, a military leader whose service to the Continental Army under George Washington demonstrated the commitment of transplanted Germans to the cause of liberty. Although the more progressive congregations worshiped in English, the area's churches were nearly as Germanic as the statues, and so were the commercial districts. Vliet Street, Lisbon Avenue, and North Avenue became the retail spines of the community, each lined for blocks with bakeries, drugstores, movie theaters, butcher shops, and other small businesses. For the first generation and much of the second, it was possible to satisfy every retail need without speaking a word of English.

■ *The Cold Spring shops of Milwaukee's streetcar company anchored the industrial corridor on the neighborhood's eastern edge.*

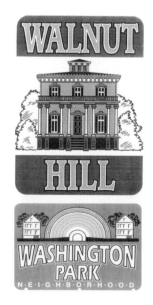

(clockwise)

■ *Hundreds turned out to dedicate the statue of German and American hero Frederick Wilhelm von Steuben in 1921.*

■ *Thousands more attended free concerts at Washington Park's Temple of Music, a 1938 gift from brewer Emil Blatz.*

■ *Everyday people: Thirty-fifth and Vliet in 1950, looking northeast*

■ *North Avenue became the neighborhood's primary shopping center. The view is west from Thirty-fifth Street in the 1930s.*

Milwaukee County Historical Society

Milwaukee Journal Sentinel

Wisconsin Historical Society

Milwaukee Public Library

Rising to the Challenges

The Depression began not long after the last houses went up around Washington Park, and it had the ironic effect of slowing development but hastening assimilation; ethnic differences mattered less when everyone was in the same leaky boat. As the gloom deepened, the Washington Park Zoo began to seem like a civic extravagance. There was talk, not entirely idle, of selling or slaughtering some of the larger animals in the collection. Kinder hearts prevailed, and a grander act of kindness gave the park one of its most durable amenities. In 1938, as the Depression began to lift, brewer Emil Blatz donated $100,000 to build the Temple of Music, an Art Deco bandshell that quickly became one of Milwaukee's major entertainment venues. It was the scene of regular outdoor concerts, including the long-running Music under the Stars series, that drew overflow crowds and set the precedent for today's presentations.

There were also subtractions, particularly after World War II, and once again the park was most directly affected. Clearance for the Stadium Freeway—Highway 41—began in the early 1950s, and it sliced off the entire western edge of Washington Park, including the zoo. By the time the first leg of the freeway opened in 1962, most of the animals had been relocated to a thoroughly modern facility at 100th and Blue Mound. Neighborhood residents were soon joining the elephants and bears in their move westward, drawn by the prospect of new homes, new schools, and new garages for their new cars. Although some area churches built additions to accommodate the postwar baby boom, the new Sunday School rooms weren't in use for long; the wave crested in the 1960s and rolled on to the west.

As traditional residents moved out, new groups moved in, many relocating from the same North Side neighborhoods that had supplied the first Germans. African Americans were most prominent in the migration. In the

■ *The Washington Park Zoo was displaced by the Highway 41 expressway in the 1950s.*

Milwaukee Journal Sentinel

census tracts bordering the park east of Highway 41, their numbers soared from 2 percent of the population in 1970 to 68 percent in 1990 and ticked up to 72 percent in 2010. Churches changed hands, businesses turned over, and schools acquired new students. But the movement was never as monolithic as in other neighborhoods on the North and West Sides. Latinos and Native Americans were a significant presence in the migration, and Asians were even more numerous, most of them Hmong refugees who began to reach Milwaukee from war-torn Southeast Asia in the 1970s.

As the area's population grew both more diverse and younger, its housing stock got older, and the supply of family-supporting jobs grew progressively smaller. Deindustrialization ravaged the Thirtieth Street rail corridor in the 1970s and '80s; dozens of employers closed their doors, and the minority who remained open slashed their payrolls. As income levels dropped, local retailers suffered as well, and

slow bleeding was apparent up and down the Vliet, North, and Lisbon shopping corridors. The only sector that seemed to be thriving was the illegal drug trade. As blight claimed an increasing number of houses, rising crime rates fueled a perception that the neighborhood's centerpiece, Washington Park itself, was unsafe. In a central-city scenario all too common across the United States, the neighborhood began to lose mass, buying power, and confidence at the same time.

There were countervailing attempts to stem the tide and restore the sense of civic balance that had traditionally characterized the neighborhood. Milwaukee's West Side was a hotbed of grassroots activity in the 1970s and '80s, much of it involving the Washington Park area. The roster of community groups included the Cooperation West Side Association (COWSA), the Westside Community Development Corporation, the Westside Home Buyer's Clinic, Lisbon Area Neighborhood Development, and a number

Milwaukee Journal Sentinel

■ *The Interlude Pub was a liquid experiment in community-building.*

years, a tongue-in-cheek sign still adorns its entrance: "No Jacket Required.") In the years since that burst of 1970s energy, the Washington Park neighborhood has acquired new residents, new challenges, and new resources. The Asian community's growth accelerated through the turn of the twenty-first century. In the single census tract covering most of Walnut Hill, the proportion of Asian residents, principally Hmong families, rose from 11 percent in 1990 to 41 percent in 2010—one of the highest concentrations in the Milwaukee area. The Hmong have been joined since 2000 by refugees from Myanmar (Burma), Somalia, and other troubled regions of the world.

of church-affiliated organizations supporting everything from housing rehabilitation to block clubs. The area had its own newspaper—the *Westside News,* which debuted in 1979—and even a community-owned tavern: the Interlude Pub on Fortieth and Vliet, directly across the street from Washington Park. Established by the Community Development Corporation in 1980, the Interlude enjoyed some years of popularity as what its founders called "a place for dining and socializing in an atmosphere supportive of the community and its culture."

All of these grassroots ventures played their parts and departed the scene. (Although the Interlude has been closed for

■ *The mansions built by the Koenigs, von Baumbachs, and Uhrigs continue to grace the landscape of Washington Park ...*

Efforts to increase homeownership among the refugees and their neighbors hit a major stumbling block with the foreclosure crisis that followed the real estate collapse of 2008. As residents lost their homes, there was a disturbing increase in the number of board-ups and an even more distressing rise in the number of tear-downs. The singular exception was the Martin Drive area. Just as its position outside the mainstream had delayed initial development until the Teens and Twenties, the area's relative isolation helped to preserve a higher rate of homeownership and a stronger sense of identity in the twenty-first century. The Martin Drive pocket bears a strong resemblance to sections of nearby Story Hill and Washington Heights.

Christopher Winters

Elsewhere in the neighborhood, keeping up with blight has been a full-time job for community activists. Some census tracts have lost more than half their housing stock since 1970, but there has been tangible progress in reversing the trend. Habitat for Humanity has made Washington Park an area of special concern, and developers have used tax-credit financing to build a number of sleek new apartment complexes. Throughout the area, there has been a greater emphasis on brick-and-mortar projects since 2000, a shift in focus from the grassroots efforts of the 1970s and '80s. In addition to the residential projects, major landmarks of the recent past include the Washington Park branch of the Milwaukee Public Library, built on the site of the old Boulevard Inn in 2003; Mary Mc-Leod Bethune Academy on Thirty-fifth Street (2005); and Progressive Community Health Center's new clinic on Lisbon Avenue (2015). Art installations and community gardens have also brought vacant lots back to life, and grassroots organizing has by no means been forgotten. Washington Park Partners, a cooperative effort of residents, businesses, and nonprofit agencies, was convened in 2010 to help secure a sound and sustainable future for everyone in the neighborhood.

Of all the developments of the recent past, perhaps the most significant have taken place in Washington Park itself. Never abandoned but definitely neglected, the park received some overdue attention after 2000. A "Play Trail" of imaginative early-childhood equipment weaves through its southeast corner, balancing the well-used senior center on the southwest. On the Lisbon Avenue side of the park, soccer fields have replaced the baseball diamonds, which replaced the original horse track decades earlier. In 2005, with help from neighbor Harley-Davidson, the Temple of Music was renovated to welcome a new generation of concert-goers, and in 2007 the Urban Ecology Center, established in Riverside Park sixteen years before, made Washington Park its second home. An underused pavilion became the Ecology Center's education building, and the park itself became an outdoor classroom for young people attending school within a two-mile radius. The cumulative result of all the changes has been a genuine blossoming of new life in the neighborhood's defining green space.

The Uhrigs, the von Baumbachs, and the Koenigs would probably find that news heartening—if they could begin to comprehend the scale of the changes that have occurred since their tenure in the neighborhood. Washington Park has indeed traveled an enormous distance from the days of plank roads and pachyderms. Its path has included valleys as well as peaks, with more of both ahead, but the trio of distinguished homes remains in a most dynamic present—silent witnesses to all that has passed, and all that is to come.

■ ... *while General von Steuben still keeps watch at the foot of Sherman Boulevard.*

■ (right and below)
From ice-skating on the frozen lagoon to working on crafts at the senior center, Washington Park is a magnet for area residents.

Urban Ecology Center

Jessica Lothman

■ (center right)
Fancy cakes on Vliet Street

Christopher Winters

■ (below)
Oversized duplexes are plentiful in Washington Park.

Christopher Winters

Christopher Winters

■ *Historic amenities updated for a new generation: the Washington Park lagoon and the Temple of Music*

Jessica Lothman

WASHINGTON
HEIGHTS

M·I·L·W·A·U·K·E·E

Washington Heights

Washington Heights, straddling Washington Boulevard on the high ground between Washington Park and Washington Highlands, could hardly have a more appropriate name. The neighborhood fits snugly into the geography of today's West Side, but its roots reach back much farther—all the way to the heart of the city. It was there, in the mid-1800s, that Milwaukeeans of ample means—some of extravagant means—developed one of the city's first mansion districts. The pluto-crats built their way west for generations, finally reaching Washington Heights in the early decades of the twentieth century. The result was a new link in the long chain of middle- to upper-income settlements that would eventually reach the western limits of Brookfield.

More than a century later, Washington Heights is what it has al-ways been: one of the most solidly residential communities in the city, with some of the most substantial housing stock as well. Updated by a new generation of residents, the character of the neighborhood blends the privacy and comfort of the suburbs with the diversity and convenience of city life. The people of Washington Heights wouldn't have it any other way.

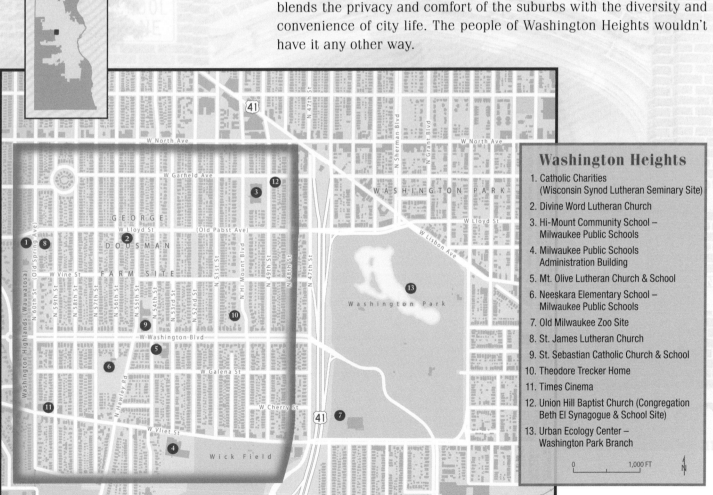

Washington Heights

1. Catholic Charities
   (Wisconsin Synod Lutheran Seminary Site)
2. Divine Word Lutheran Church
3. Hi-Mount Community School –
   Milwaukee Public Schools
4. Milwaukee Public Schools
   Administration Building
5. Mt. Olive Lutheran Church & School
6. Neeskara Elementary School –
   Milwaukee Public Schools
7. Old Milwaukee Zoo Site
8. St. James Lutheran Church
9. St. Sebastian Catholic Church & School
10. Theodore Trecker Home
11. Times Cinema
12. Union Hill Baptist Church (Congregation
    Beth El Synagogue & School Site)
13. Urban Ecology Center –
    Washington Park Branch

0   1,000 FT

A Rolling Wave of Affluence

Most of the land that became Washington Heights belonged to one family for half of Milwaukee's history. The family's head was George Dousman, a Michigan fur trader's son who came to Milwaukee on the very first wave of European settlement in 1835. Dousman claimed a 250-acre parcel whose present borders are Vliet Street and North Avenue between Fifty-first and Sixtieth Streets. As the rest of Milwaukee County was carved up

■ *George Dousman, the pioneer who once owned most of Washington Heights*

■ *One of his family's liquid assets was spring water bottled under the Nee-Ska-Ra label.*

Milwaukee County Historical Society

Nee-Ska-Ra Mineral Spring.

THIS spring is located about two miles from the City of Milwaukee, on high ground, remote from habitation and secure from contamination.

Analysis and microscopic examination by noted chemists and physicians shows the water to be of unprecedented purity, there being no trace of organic matter.

Analysis and experience also show that the medicinal properties of the water are equal to those of the most celebrated waters of Wisconsin.

As a table water it has no equal. Its clearness and purity, its delightful flavor, and freedom from any objectionable taste or odor, recommend it beyond all others. At least 5,000 people in Milwaukee drink Nee-Ska-Ra daily. Send for analysis, price list, etc.

NEE-SKA-RA MINERAL SPRING CO.,
110 Mason Street,
MILWAUKEE, WIS.

from *Milwaukee's Great Industries*, 1892

into small farmsteads (averaging 65 acres in 1860), Dousman's claim became one of the largest holdings in the region.

The pioneer could afford to keep his property intact. He actually lived downtown, where he presided over the largest commission house in Milwaukee. In the mid-1800s three-fourths of all incoming freight passed through Dousman's warehouse. He eventually retired to his gentleman's farm on the city's western outskirts, where he resided until his death in 1879. Dousman's son, George P., continued to farm the land, but he also bottled mineral water from a large spring on the estate. His company, Nee-Ska-Ra Mineral Spring, remained in operation for nearly forty years. In 1924 the present Neeskara School was built on or near the site of the spring.

The Dousman family's nearest neighbor to the west was another Milwaukee luminary, brewer Frederick Pabst. His 225-acre parcel on the far side of Spring Avenue (Sixtieth Street) was Captain Pabst's summer home, and its centerpiece was a house described in 1892 as "an airy abode with all the charms of a castle on his beloved Rhine without the architectural inconveniences." The property doubled as a working farm. The beer baron raised hops for his brewery on the land, and he developed one of the nation's premier herds of Percheron draft horses, which were used to pull his finished product to market. The Pabst and Dousman farms covered a huge tract of open land between the emerging suburb of Wauwatosa and the maturing metropolis of Milwaukee.

The beginnings of modern development can be traced to four events that took place in the single momentous year of 1892. Preliminary designs for Washington (then West) Park were completed. The Village of Wauwatosa was incorporated, taking in three square miles that included the entire Pabst farm. An electric streetcar line backed by the Pabsts went into service on Lloyd Street (then Pabst Avenue) between Milwaukee and Wauwatosa. And a

Milwaukee County Historical Society

Milwaukee Public Library

Milwaukee Public Library

Wisconsin Synod Lutheran seminary—the area's first non-agricultural development—opened on the streetcar line at Sixtieth and Lloyd. The neighborhood's urban future was assured. George P. Dousman remained on the homestead at Hawley and Vliet until his death in 1927, but the bottler and his neighbors began to sell their farms, piece by piece, to developers. The first subdivisions were recorded in the early 1890s.

Washington Park played an especially pivotal role in the district's transformation. One of the first major purchases in the Milwaukee system, the park was designed by Frederick Law Olmsted's firm, which was also responsible for Lake Park on the East Side and Central Park in Manhattan. The park featured carriage drives, a horse-racing track, an observation platform, a bandshell, a scenic lagoon, and the Milwaukee zoo. There had been a small herd of deer on display as early as 1891. As the menagerie expanded to include birds, bears, a pair of sea lions, and an elephant named Countess Heine, the zoo emerged as a popular tourist attraction.

Washington Park became a recreational resource for the entire region, but its impact on the surrounding area was particularly profound. The park increased the value of residential real estate, promoting middle- and upper-income settlement. It influenced the development of park-like boulevards (Washington, Hi Mount, Sherman, Grant) to the west and north. Most

important, it acted as both a border and a green link between the old Dousman farm and the heart of Milwaukee, contributing to a sense of seclusion and, at the same time, connection. In the twenty-first century, the park's dual role remains vitally important.

Although the first signs of urban development surfaced in the 1890s, it took a few years for urbanites to reach the blocks west of the park. Residents of the Grand Avenue gold coast, a corridor of affluence anchored by the Alexander Mitchell mansion (now the Wisconsin Club) at Tenth and Wisconsin, had been migrating west and north for decades. They crossed Twenty-seventh Street in the

■ *Washington Park was a metropolitan attraction on the neighborhood's doorstep, with a popular zoo, a scenic lagoon, and wooded walking paths.*

■ *A neighborhood takes shape:* (left) *Washington Boulevard under construction (looking west toward Hawley Road) and* (right) *open for traffic in the 1920s (looking east from Hawley). Mt. Olive Lutheran Church was built in 1923.*

late 1800s and created the Concordia neighborhood, lining Highland Boulevard with some of the city's most opulent homes. In the next generation they crossed Washington Park and made Washington Boulevard a zone of comparable affluence. Other West Siders with smaller bank accounts filled in the side streets. The building boom began in about 1910 and continued without interruption for twenty years. By 1930 Washington Heights had been transformed from farmland to a settled residential neighborhood. Nearly 95 percent of the community's present homes were built between 1910 and 1930, and the vast majority went up between 1915 and 1925.

Milwaukee's city limits pushed west with the newcomers. The municipal border moved from Forty-seventh Street in 1900 to Forty-ninth in 1906 and finally reached the Wauwatosa line at Sixtieth Street in 1924. Wauwatosa experienced the same building boom. The Pabst family had moved its farming operation to Oconomowoc years before, and in 1919 their old hops-and-horses farm became Washington Highlands, which remains one of the most genteel residential enclaves in the Milwaukee area. Nestled between the Highlands and Washington Park, Washington Heights developed a semi-suburban character that owed something to both.

Washington Heights was not as uniformly affluent as Washington Highlands, but the neighborhood signified, for every newcomer, at least a measure of success. The majority of its residents held middle-income positions in both white- and blue-collar occupations. The breadwinners on a typical street in the 1920s

might have included a bank clerk, a die-maker, a teacher, a foreman, a salesman, a building contractor, a mail carrier, a cigarmaker, and a bookkeeper. It was the most successful residents who attracted the most attention. Washington and Hi Mount Boulevards became two of the toniest addresses in the city—the West Side counterparts of Newberry Boulevard on the East Side. These oversized streets were lined with the imposing homes of families whose names were household words: Trecker (milling machines), Gallun (tanning), Steinman (lumber), Gettelman (brewing), Brumder (publishing), and both Harley and Davidson. Deed restrictions insured that Hi Mount, in particular, would remain "a first-class residence district"; anyone who bought a lot on the boulevard was required to build a home worth at least $3,500.

Whatever their economic status, residents of Washington Heights tended to favor one of two house types. The first was the Milwaukee bungalow. Enormously popular between 1910 and 1930, the typical bungalow is one-and-a-half stories in height, with a gently pitched roof and a porch framing the front entrance. What distinguishes the bungalows of Washington Heights is their variety and quality. The homes come in a range of sizes (including a large number of "bungalow duplexes"), and many show the influence of the Craftsman movement, which sought to express the American spirit through the artful use of natural materials. Hardwood floors and moldings, built-in cabinets, working fireplaces, ornamental plasterwork, and stained-glass window lights are typical features of the Craftsman bungalow.

The neighborhood's other houses include tall Milwaukee duplexes near the park and a scattering of Prairie-style dwellings, but the most abundant type, after the bungalow, is the Period Revival. Architects and builders of the pre-Depression years revived the styles of continental Europe and colonial America and adapted them to city lots. In some blocks, bungalows and Period Revival houses are present in almost equal proportions.

The homes of Washington and Hi Mount Boulevards are, simply put, larger and more lavish versions of the bungalows and Period Revivals on the side streets. More than 80 percent are built of brick or stone, and dozens are as large as the mansions bordering Lake Park. In a neighborhood filled with success stories, the boulevards attracted people who were more successful than most.

Whether they lived in the simplest bungalow or the most elegant Tudor mansion, the original residents of Washington Heights tended to be German Milwaukeeans who had moved from older neighborhoods farther east. Three of the area's largest churches reflected the prevailing cultural patterns. The oldest and still the largest is St. Sebastian's. The parish's first Mass was said in a rented storefront on Vliet Street (now a tavern) in 1911, and many of its charter members had roots in St. Michael's Parish, an intensely German community around Twenty-fourth and Cherry. "St. Seb's," as the congregation is familiarly known, moved into its present landmark building in 1929. Mt. Olive Lutheran, just across Washington Boulevard from St. Sebastian's, moved in 1923 from Fourth

■ (above)
The community's major house types include Craftsman bungalows on the side streets (left) *and imposing Period Revivals on the boulevards.*

■ *St. Sebastian's Church, the neighborhood's largest, was built to serve local Catholics in 1929.*

and Walnut, another old German neighborhood. Reflecting the growing comfort of its members in the American mainstream, Mt. Olive was the first major Lutheran church in Milwaukee to use English rather than German in its services. In sharp contrast, the third original church, St. James Lutheran (Wisconsin Synod) on Sixtieth and Lloyd, did not discontinue German-language liturgies until 1967. St. James was organized in 1921 by a professor from the Lutheran seminary across the street. (The seminary moved to Thiensville in 1929; its site is now occupied by Catholic Charities.)

Not every Washington Heights resident was a German Catholic or German Lutheran. There were numerous Irish families at St. Sebastian's, and a sizable Jewish community developed in the neighborhood's northeastern corner. Members

Jewish Museum Milwaukee

■ *Built in 1921,
Congregation Beth El
was the first
synagogue west of
Twentieth Street.*

of Congregation Beth El erected an attractive Mediterranean-style synagogue on Forty-ninth and Garfield in 1921. It was Milwaukee's first Jewish house of worship west of Twentieth Street and the first Conservative congregation in the entire region. As the children of immigrants adapted to life in America, many sought a middle way between the strictures of Orthodoxy and the liberalism of the Reform tradition. They found a welcoming home at Beth El—and in Washington Heights.

Changing in Place

Washington Heights was an established community by 1930; construction of its homes, schools, and places of worship was virtually complete. What followed was fifteen years of anxious quiet. The neighborhood, like practically all American neighborhoods, was frozen in place during the Depression and World War II. When peacetime returned in 1945, Washington Heights entered a period of gradual change. Quonset huts went up at Fifty-first and Vliet to relieve the severe postwar housing shortage, covering land now occupied by the Milwaukee Public Schools

administration building. Congregation Beth El followed its members north to Sherman Boulevard in 1951, and St. Thomas Lutheran Church moved into the former temple. (The round of musical churches continued in 1984, when St. Thomas merged with Washington Park Lutheran to form the present Divine Word congregation at Fifty-fifth and Lloyd. The old synagogue became Union Hill Baptist Church and the adjoining Hebrew school its education building.) In the late 1950s the western edge of Washington Park was sheared off for what is now the Highway 41 freeway. The new road displaced the Milwaukee County Zoo, but not everyone missed the animals. "With an east wind," said one long-time homeowner, "you could smell the goats and the bears all the way to St. Sebastian's." The freeway enabled local residents to reach the rest of Milwaukee with relative ease, but it was also a concrete border that heightened the area's long-standing sense of relative seclusion.

By the time the zoo moved to the city's edge on Blue Mound Road, the original residents of Washington Heights had reached retirement age. Their children had matured and married during

Milwaukee Public Schools Recreation Division

the Depression and World War II. Although hundreds of second-generation couples stayed to raise families of their own, a greater number joined the postwar move to the suburbs. As the first generation stayed put, the median age in Washington Heights climbed to 38.3 in 1960— eight years above the city median. Property values began a slow decline relative to the city average, and there was growing concern about the neighborhood's future.

The next stage of the cycle was apparent in the 1970s. Younger couples, with or without children, moved to Washington Heights in droves, attracted by its obvious amenities, particularly what one resident called "a lot of house for a reasonable amount of money." By 1980 the median age had plummeted to 30.1 years, only a few months above the city median, and housing values had once again climbed above the city average.

The cycle has been repeating itself ever since. New residents continue to move in as older residents move on, but there has also been significant change. The original home-builders had typically moved to the area from neighborhoods east of Washington Park. The newcomers of recent years are from

exactly the same neighborhoods, but they are more likely to be African-American than German, Jewish, or Irish. Between 1985 and 2010, black residents grew from about 5 percent of the community's population to roughly 25 percent. From the beginning of settlement, Washington Heights has represented the very best housing its residents could afford. Whether they buy or rent, the pattern is as true of African Americans in the twenty-first century as it was of Germans in the early twentieth. The changing demographic patterns have created some interesting cultural shifts. German carols are no longer sung at the round-robin Christmas party on Hi Mount Boulevard, but gospel music can be heard every Sunday at Union Hill Baptist Church.

What unites the residents of this increasingly cosmopolitan community is a shared awareness of its unique assets. Vliet Street and North Avenue—the bookends of Washington Heights—are lined with neighborhood-oriented businesses. Downtown Milwaukee is minutes away. The neighborhood is surrounded by parkland: Washington Park to the east, the athletic facilities of Wick Field to the south, the park-like streets

■ *Wick Field and the Milwaukee Public Schools central office have defined the southern border of Washington Heights for decades.*

of Washington Highlands to the west, and a residential "park"—Sherman—to the north. Washington Park itself has been revitalized since 2000, with new playgrounds and soccer fields, an updated bandshell, and the second branch of the Urban Ecology Center, which introduces local schoolchildren to the wonders of nature in their own backyards. St. Sebastian's bells still toll the hour for everyone, and the schools of St. Sebastian's and Mt. Olive have provided parochial educations for generations of local youngsters. Washington Heights remains a solidly middle-income neighborhood with a definite appeal to families. "When you're in college," said one young father, "you live in places like the East Side. When you have kids, you come here."

Most of the community's assets have been decades in the making, but the current residents of Washington Heights may be less inclined to take them for granted than previous generations. As the neighborhood has become more diverse, it has also become more attractive to people who value diversity and see it as a distinct advantage. In 1990

residents of all backgrounds came together to form the Washington Heights Neighborhood Association. The group sponsors crime watches, assists block clubs, and sponsors a year-round schedule of special events, all in an effort to build on common strengths and work on solutions to common problems.

There is a great deal to build on. When residents are asked to describe their feelings for Washington Heights, they use the word "love" with a frequency that any community activist would find heartening: "I love my home," "I love this neighborhood," "I love living here." These statements of affection are not difficult to understand. More than a century after the first urban residents arrived, "solid" is still the word for Washington Heights. Solid homes. A solid citizenry. Solid institutions. Solidly residential land use. Solid rows of trees shading impressively well-kept homes and yards. These have been the major attractions since the first years of settlement in Washington Heights, and they represent a solid foundation for the future of this urban-suburban neighborhood.

■ *St. Sebastian's Church remains the neighborhood's dominant landmark.*

Christopher Winters

Christopher Winters

Jessica Lothman

■ *There's plenty of activity in Washington Heights, including softball at Wick Field, block parties, and weddings at "St. Seb's."*

Christopher Winters

147

■ (right and below)
Showing off outside the Sho-N-Out barber shop on North Avenue and singing out on the Washington Park stage

■ (bottom)
This Washington Boulevard gem was built in 1928 for Frank Hochmuth, a dealer in musical instruments.

Christopher Winters

Jessica Lothman

Jessica Lothman

Christopher Winters

Jessica Lothman

■ (left)
Bandshell concerts are a summertime staple at Washington Park.

■ (below)
Union Hill Baptist Church was originally a Conservative Jewish house of worship.

■ (bottom)
Washington Heights, where the living is easy

Christopher Winters

Jessica Lothman

149

SHERMAN PARK
MILWAUKEE

Sherman Park

Sherman Park is one of Milwaukee's largest neighborhoods. With 32,000 residents and nearly four square miles of land, the community is so large that it is best understood as a confederation of smaller neighborhoods—Grasslyn Manor, Sunset Heights, Uptown Crossing, and several others. Each has its own visual character and its own cultural patterns, but all pledge allegiance to the same Sherman Park flag. Together they lend a small-scale atmosphere to an area that dwarfs its adjoining communities.

The entire neighborhood is defined neatly by some imposing borders: the Thirtieth Street industrial corridor on the east, the Wauwatosa city limits and a large cemetery on the west, post-World War II development to the north, and Washington Park and its neighborhoods to the south. Those borders frame a community with a distinguished heritage of diversity and some of the most distinctive—and most desirable—housing in the entire metropolitan area.

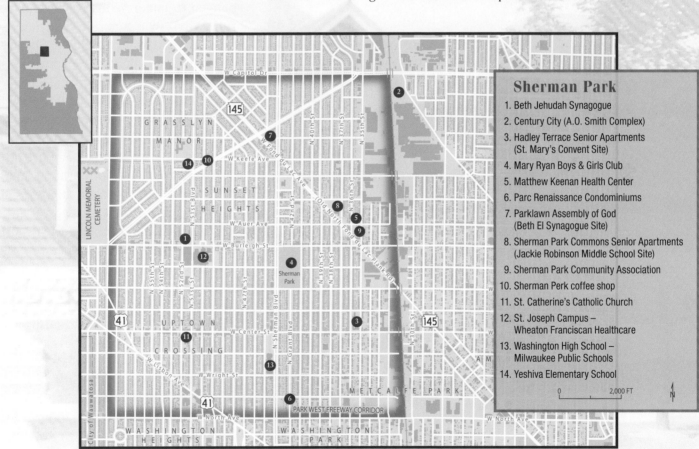

Sherman Park

1. Beth Jehudah Synagogue
2. Century City (A.O. Smith Complex)
3. Hadley Terrace Senior Apartments (St. Mary's Convent Site)
4. Mary Ryan Boys & Girls Club
5. Matthew Keenan Health Center
6. Parc Renaissance Condominiums
7. Parklawn Assembly of God (Beth El Synagogue Site)
8. Sherman Park Commons Senior Apartments (Jackie Robinson Middle School Site)
9. Sherman Park Community Association
10. Sherman Perk coffee shop
11. St. Catherine's Catholic Church
12. St. Joseph Campus – Wheaton Franciscan Healthcare
13. Washington High School – Milwaukee Public Schools
14. Yeshiva Elementary School

0   2,000 FT

The North Side Once Removed

■ *Pastoral scenes mingled with industrial at Sherman Park's beginning. The park itself was the scene of church picnics in the early 1900s, and major employers like the Fuller-Warren Stove Company lined the nearby railroad tracks.*

Sherman Park was still farmland in the late 1800s, but it was farmland on the verge of urban development. A few rural landmarks persisted—a tollgate on the Fond du Lac plank road at Burleigh, a country schoolhouse up the road near today's Thirty-ninth Street—but they would soon vanish under a wave of settlement from the city. Immigration and industrialization fueled a 77-percent increase in Milwaukee's population during the 1880s, one of the greatest ten-year gains in the city's history. The heavily German neighborhoods on the North Side were growing rapidly to the north and northwest, and the land that became Sherman Park lay squarely in their expansion path. The name of an early subdivision revealed the ethnic make-up of the approaching wave: Prussian Heights, platted in 1887.

A park was waiting for the new residents. In 1891 the city's Park Commission purchased a tract of land at the present intersection of Sherman Boulevard and Burleigh Street. Its most prominent feature was one of the last native woodlots in the area, and by 1895 there was a small pavilion on the property. It was called Perrigo Park at first, after the previous owners, but the name was soon changed to honor William Sherman, the celebrated Civil War general. The commissioners showed remarkable foresight. Sherman Park was not even inside the city limits when it was acquired, and it took another thirty years for the surrounding blocks to develop. But the park filled a conspicuous corner of the commission's map: it lay due north of Washington Park and due west of Lake Park. Sherman Park would provide both a name and a focal point for the neighborhood as it took shape.

Development of a less pastoral nature was occurring along the railroad tracks that paralleled Thirtieth Street. Between 1890 and 1910 the corridor was lined with factories that produced everything from bridges and barrels to cement mixers and shoes. The largest employer was A.O. Smith, whose car frame factory eventually covered more than 100 acres south of Capitol Drive. The industrial belt fixed the border between Sherman Park and the North Side, and it provided jobs for many of the new residents. At least one employer, the Fuller-Warren Stove Company, developed a subdivision near Wright Street that practically bordered its factory.

Sherman Park's first urban residents crossed the railroad corridor in the early 1890s. St. Anne's Catholic Church (Thirty-sixth

Milwaukee County Parks Department

Milwaukee Public Library

and Wright) was established in 1894 as an offshoot of St. Michael's in the Midtown area; sermons were preached in German. By 1900 there were roughly 200 houses in the neighborhood, nearly all of them clustered in the southeastern corner, within walking distance of St. Anne's and the trackside factories.

The community's growth in the next thirty years was nothing short of explosive. By 1920 the settled area extended as far west as Sherman Boulevard and as far north as Burleigh Street; the neighborhood park at the intersection finally served a neighborhood. By 1930 the entire southern half of the district (below Burleigh) had filled in, and development of the northern half (especially east of Sherman) had started in earnest. New institutions followed the new residents. Construction of Washington High School began in 1913, St. Joseph Hospital erected its first buildings in 1929, and dozens of churches were established. Nearly all had roots on Milwaukee's near North Side.

Sherman Park was a new kind of urban community. Older neighborhoods to the south and east were largely blue-collar settlements characterized by narrow lots, high densities, and a patchwork of land uses. Their residential sections were dotted with corner stores, corner saloons, backyard cottages and, in some areas, small factories. There were islands of affluence on the North Side, but they were nearly submerged in a sea of working-class homes. Sherman Park was noticeably different. It was settled by members of Milwaukee's emerging middle class, and it symbolized, in a sense, the maturing of the city's economy. After 1900 the growth of a social layer between industrialists and industrial workers was increasingly obvious. Merchants, middle managers, and skilled tradesmen wanted homes that reflected their growing prosperity, and Sherman Park became one of their most representative neighborhoods.

The patterns were obvious in the southeast quadrant. The blocks near Thirty-fifth Street, where settlement began before 1900, were much like those on the near North Side. As settlement moved west, lot widths

■ *Washington High School earned a reputation as the city's finest.*

■ *St. Joseph Hospital met the area's health care needs, growing from an empty shell ...*

■ *... to a finished facility in 1929.*

■ *There were still open lots along Thirty-ninth Street near Burleigh in the 1920s.*

increased steadily, from 30 feet on Thirty-eighth Street to 40 feet on Fortieth to 50 feet on Grant Boulevard (Forty-second). Grant and Sherman Boulevards, both named for Civil War heroes, became Sherman Park's most prestigious addresses. They were lined with the homes of professionals, business leaders, and industrial managers, including some whose plants were located on the nearby railroad corridor. Fifty-first Boulevard (north of Burleigh) played a comparable role three decades later. Although some blocks were more affluent than others, the homes in all sections of Sherman Park were substantial, and the neighborhood's median household income was well above the city average.

Two more factors shaped Sherman Park's character: public land use controls and the automobile. Setbacks from the curb line and distances between homes were regulated more strictly after 1900, and single- and multi-family dwellings were separated more carefully. New zoning laws restricted

commercial development to major arterials, giving rise to neighborhood-oriented retail corridors along North, Center, Burleigh, Fond du Lac, and Lisbon. Sherman Park had a much tidier appearance than areas developed earlier, and its residents had more mobility as well. With the rise of the automobile after 1900, there was less need for homeowners to cluster near major employers or streetcar lines. As a result, Sherman Park became a uniformly settled community of middle-class homes with something new in their backyards: detached garages. Most breadwinners commuted to jobs outside the area by car. Sherman Park was part of the city (annexed in stages between 1891 and 1928), but its atmosphere was, in a word, suburban.

Although it was a new kind of community, Sherman Park reflected the cultural patterns of the North Side neighborhoods it evolved from. The community was, in fact, the North Side once removed. The vast majority of the first arrivals were German by birth or ancestry, and their descendants made up more than 40 percent of the neighborhood's population as late as 1980. The early Germans were soon joined by other ethnic groups—Irish, English, and Polish among them—and a sizable Czech community developed around St. John de Nepomuc Catholic Church, established at Thirty-seventh and Keefe in 1927. Like their German neighbors, the newcomers looked back to roots on the North Side.

Only one group rivaled the Germans in size: Jewish Milwaukeeans, particularly Jews from eastern Europe. They had found their way to Milwaukee in the 1880s and settled just north of Downtown, most of them renting hand-me-down housing near a haymarket at Fifth and Vliet. By the early 1900s the Haymarket neighborhood had 5,000 residents and nearly a dozen synagogues. Like the Germans they had replaced, the Jews moved north and west as their fortunes improved, reaching Sherman Park in the 1920s. Although they settled throughout the neighborhood, the heart of the Jewish community was Fifty-first and Center Streets. Before the Twenties were over, local

■ *Completed in 1926, the Uptown Theater served Sherman Park moviegoers for more than fifty years.*

Milwaukee Public Library

residents could patronize Guten & Son's grocery store, the Sanitary Kosher Market, the New Method Hebrew School, Abraham Morris's tailor shop, the Yiddish Folk School, Leon Cohen's bakery, and delicatessens run by the Lipkin and Tischer families—all within two or three blocks of Fifty-first and Center. The synagogues would not follow their members northwest until after World War II, but Sherman Park's Jewish presence was well-established before the stock market crash of 1929.

A Neighborhood of Homes

The architectural legacy of the neighborhood's formative decades is still a major influence on life in the community. In an important sense, Sherman Park is its homes. Other sections of Milwaukee are intensely residential, but none have both the number and the variety of well-built houses that are present everywhere in Sherman Park. Development proceeded in an orderly fashion, from southeast to northwest, moving at a rapid pace between 1900 and 1930, slowing down during the Depression, and concluding with a quick burst of activity just after World War II. There are a few surprises—an opulent brick-and-fieldstone bungalow on Fifty-fourth Street, an International Style house on Fifty-fifth—but the neighborhood consists of broad bands of settlement, each containing the types and styles representative of its age.

The southeastern corner was developed first. Modest frame single-family homes built before 1900 are numerous, but duplexes constructed between 1900 and 1910 are even more prevalent. This section has, in fact, the highest proportion of duplexes in the city. They increase in size and ornamentation west of Thirty-fifth Street. Some are absolutely massive, with as much as 2,000 square feet of living space per unit.

Grant and Sherman Boulevards border the duplex zone, and the homes that line both streets are certainly among the most attractive in Sherman Park—and in the city. Most houses south of Burleigh were built between 1910 and 1920, when architects

were reviving the styles of earlier periods: Tudor, Georgian, English cottage, Mediterranean, and others. There are also a few custom-built bungalows and even one or two homes influenced by Frank Lloyd Wright and his Prairie School colleagues. Nearly all the houses are built of brick or stone. The substantial homes and the generous setbacks give Grant Boulevard, in particular, an air of settled gentility.

The blocks west of Sherman Boulevard (Forty-third Street) and south of Burleigh Street have been aptly described as "bungalow heaven." No other neighborhood in the city has a comparable assortment of bungalows. They range in size from modestly scaled "bungalowettes" in the southwest corner to towering "bungalow flats" (duplexes) west of

■ *Uniform setbacks and stricter zoning laws gave the neighborhood a distinctly tidy appearance.*

■ (bottom) *Bungalows were Milwaukee's signature house type in the 1920s, and Sherman Park was their particular stronghold.*

Milwaukee County Historical Society

Milwaukee Public Library

Washington High School. Some are relatively simple tract-built homes; others are richly detailed both inside and out. (The 2500 block of Forty-seventh Street is so exceptional that it's been designated a historic district.) Sherman Park's bungalows differ widely in building materials, roof treatments, and stylistic details, but all have gently pitched roofs, prominent front porches, efficient floor plans and, above all, a feeling of impressive bulk. Nearly all date from the 1920s.

Sherman Park's northeastern blocks are decidedly mixed, but Period Revival homes dominate the neighborhood's northwest quadrant, north of Burleigh and west of Sherman. Builders of the Thirties and Forties revived the same styles that were popular earlier on Grant and Sherman Boulevards, but they worked at a somewhat reduced scale. (The almost-mansions on Fifty-first Boulevard are a distinguished exception.) The vast majority of homes in the quadrant are built of brick or Lannon stone; entire quarries must have been emptied to keep pace with the demand for stone. Both materials were relatively cheap and readily available during the Depression and war years, and the presence of so much masonry lends the area a tangible sense of permanence.

A last spasm of development filled Sherman Park to its northwest corner immediately after World War II, a time when Period Revival homes were giving way to simpler styles and smaller footprints. Cape Cods are dominant, but the neighborhood's outer fringe has an assortment of other housing types that were popular in the postwar years, including a group of Lannon-stone ranch homes. By 1950 settlement was practically complete.

Sherman Park is probably the best place in the city to study the types and styles of homes built in the first half of the twentieth century, particularly the years between 1900 and 1930. It is, however, much more than a sampler. Three distinct phases—the duplex, the bungalow, and the Period Revival home—reach a peak of development in Sherman Park, and both earlier and later homes are present in quantity. What unites them is their feeling of substance. The community's homes reflect the solidity and pride of their original owners, and they remain the neighborhood's outstanding feature more than a century after development began.

■ Fifty-first Boulevard emerged as one of Sherman Park's most prestigious streets. This Period Revival standout was built for grocer Max Kohl in 1939.

John Gurda

■ With development stalled for the duration of World War II, victory gardens sprouted along Roosevelt Drive instead of houses.

Milwaukee Public Library

An Urban Experiment

Sherman Park's long building boom came to an end after World War II, but change, of course, did not. Change, in fact, has been a dominant theme in the neighborhood's modern history, as new groups and new institutions have added their influence to the prevailing mix.

The Jewish community grew most rapidly in the immediate postwar years. The exodus from the Haymarket neighborhood had been under way since the 1920s, and it was practically complete in the 1950s. As Jewish families settled in the residential sections, Jewish institutions—businesses, schools, and synagogues—sprang up on the commercial corridors, particularly Center and Burleigh Streets. In the 1960s six of the Milwaukee area's eleven synagogues were located in Sherman Park. The community's young people swelled the enrollments of local public schools, and some used the lessons they learned there to launch high-profile careers. Washington High School's post-World War II graduates included baseball commissioner Bud Selig, former U.S. Senator Herb Kohl, and actor Gene Wilder.

African-American families were not far behind in the procession of ethnic groups. They came from the same North Side neighborhoods as the Germans and Jews before them, and they settled in Sherman Park for the same reason: to improve their quality of life. The first families crossed the Thirtieth Street industrial corridor in the 1960s, but their real growth began in the 1970s. By decade's end African Americans made up 26 percent of Sherman Park's population. Older church buildings were repurposed for new congregations, and local business districts evolved to serve new customers.

The 1970s also witnessed a new level of community involvement. A block-wide swath of homes just above North Avenue was cleared for construction of the Park West freeway in the late 1960s, and local residents rallied to stop the project in its tracks. Legislative support for the project weakened as opposition grew, and in 1978 freeway authorities released the land for redevelopment. The long

■ *A postwar traffic jam on Thirty-fifth and Fond du Lac. The view is southeast.*

■ *Beth El Ner Tamid was one of several synagogues that followed their members to Sherman Park after World War II.*

■ *Beth El's move was complete with the relocation of its Torah scrolls in 1951.*

■ *Center Street, pictured at Forty-seventh in 1950, became one of Sherman Park's major retail corridors.*

scar in the local landscape began to heal in 1983, when the first phase of the Parc Renaissance condominium project was completed.

The freeway controversy was a key factor in the establishment of a powerful grassroots organization. In 1971 the Sherman Park Community Association (SPCA) was founded to present a united front against outside threats and to build on the community's inherent strengths. The group united behind a simple affirmative slogan—"Sherman Park: A Nice Place to Live"—and made cultural diversity a top priority. As the vehicle for what local activists called an "urban experiment," SPCA quickly became one of the strongest and most sophisticated neighborhood groups in Milwaukee, involved in everything from fair housing efforts and home repair programs to soccer leagues and a sprawling network of block clubs. One by-product of all the activity was the creation of a strong community "brand." In previous decades, local residents had considered themselves part of the undifferentiated West Side. Since the 1970s "Sherman Park" has become one of the most recognizable neighborhood names in Milwaukee.

The Sherman Park Community Association has had no shortage of issues to address since its inception. Deindustrialization ravaged the Thirtieth Street industrial corridor

in the 1980s, leading to a sharp rise in unemployment, particularly in the areas nearest the tracks. The foreclosure crisis of the early 2000s left Sherman Park with hundreds of vacant homes, often on streets that were otherwise strongholds of pride. Like bad apples in the larger barrel, the abundance of board-ups has posed a serious threat to the neighborhood's stability. Diversity remained an important community goal but, as African-American households grew to 83 percent of the population in 2010, it took on different dimensions.

The richest expression of diversity surfaced in the northwest quadrant. As other Jewish congregations moved to suburban locations, only one—Beth Jehudah—remained in the old neighborhood, and it became a nucleus for new life. Under the leadership of Rabbi Michel Twerski, Beth Jehudah transformed itself into a "full-service Orthodox community," complete with an elementary school and an adult education center. Membership climbed to nearly 500 people, from newborns to ninety-year-olds, all within walking distance of the synagogue on Fifty-second and Burleigh. Full beards, black hats, and long skirts are standard dress for many residents of the northwest quadrant, creating cultural contrasts that carried over to the commercial districts. Sherman Park became the only place in Milwaukee, and perhaps in the United States, where you could find a kosher meat market next door to an African hair-braiding salon.

Other institutions joined Beth Jehudah in making distinctive contributions to the neighborhood's vitality. St. Joseph Hospital, a community mainstay since 1929, has grown to become a medical complex of regional importance. The Matthew Keenan Health Center, housed in an Art Deco landmark on Thirty-sixth and Auer, has been providing public health services since 1932. Community nonprofits, from the Sherman Park Community Association to Common Ground, have worked diligently to reverse the impacts of the foreclosure crisis. Sherman Park itself remains the neighborhood's green focal point more than a century after it was acquired, and its centerpiece is the Mary Ryan Boys & Girls Club, a major resource for the community's young people.

There is new development as well. North Avenue east of Thirty-fifth Street, an area shared with Metcalfe Park, has sprouted a number of mixed retail and residential projects that would gladden the heart of any New Urbanist. The former Jackie Robinson Middle School has been restored to life as a residence for senior citizens, and Hadley Terrace, in what was once the shadow of St. Mary's Convent on Center Street, is a new apartment complex with the same older clientele. Much larger things are planned for Century City, a "modern business park" on the former site of the A.O. Smith car-frame factory at Sherman Park's eastern border.

The matrix for all these activities is four square miles of tree-lined residential streets that stretch, block after comfortable block, for miles, Sherman Park is still a haven of fine older homes and a confederation of small communities sharing a large section of the city. Its settings vary from inner-city to almost-suburban, and its status as an urban experiment continues in the twenty-first century. The progress of that experiment holds some important lessons for Milwaukee, and for America.

■ *Sherman Park marches to the beat of many drums.*

Jessica Lothman

Christopher Winters

Jessica Lothman

Jessica Lothman

■ (below)

The Keenan Health Center has been serving Sherman Park since 1932, and St. Joseph Hospital has been a neighborhood institution since 1929.

Christopher Winters

Christopher Winters

Christopher Winters

Christopher Winters

Jessica Lothman

Jessica Lothman

■ *Artisanal shops and artful benches grace the walkways of Sherman Park.*

AT WORK, WE
MAKE A LIVING;
AT LEISURE,
WE MAKE A LIFE.
DOROTHY
ENDERIS

Jan Kotowicz

ENDERIS
PARK
M·I·L·W·A·U·K·E·E

Enderis Park

The Enderis Park neighborhood is all angles. In a city developed on the rigid rectangular street grid, there is nothing remotely predictable about this leafy West Side enclave. It has straight streets, curved streets, dead ends, cul-de-sacs, and two major arterials, both diagonals, that slice through the community like pipelines, creating triangles at every intersection. Just off these main-traveled roads, all is quiet. The street layout calms traffic by its very nature, and the design—or lack of it—creates well-defined pockets that feature some of Milwaukee's best examples of residential architecture from the 1920s through the 1940s. You can look at Enderis Park from any number of angles, but they all reveal a neighborhood of distinctive homes, engaged residents, peaceful integration, and an enviable quality of life.

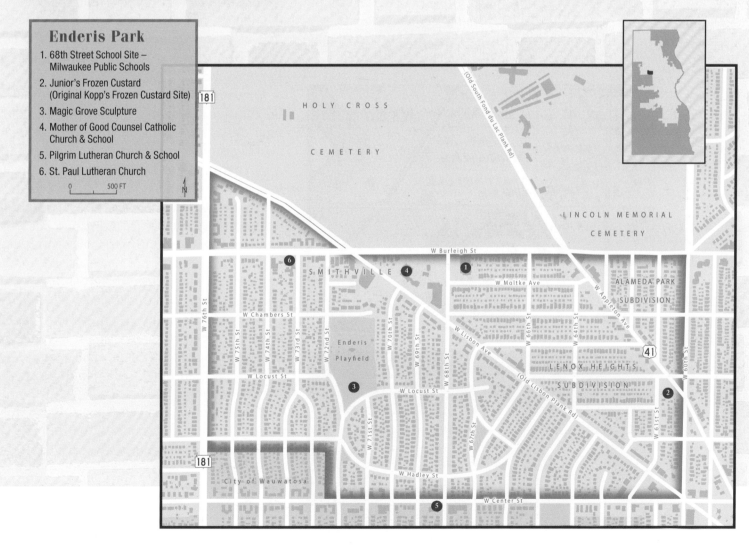

Enderis Park

1. 68th Street School Site – Milwaukee Public Schools
2. Junior's Frozen Custard (Original Kopp's Frozen Custard Site)
3. Magic Grove Sculpture
4. Mother of Good Counsel Catholic Church & School
5. Pilgrim Lutheran Church & School
6. St. Paul Lutheran Church

0   500 FT

N

The Dead before the Living

■ *The crossroads hamlet of Smithville developed at the present intersection of Lisbon Avenue and Burleigh Street.*

■ *The neighborhood's first permanent "residents" were the deceased Germans in Wanderers' Rest Cemetery.*

Both of Enderis Park's major arterials— Lisbon Avenue and Appleton Avenue—began as plank roads in the 1850s, and both were named for their destinations. Lisbon led to the Town of Lisbon in northeastern Waukesha County, and Appleton (originally South Fond du Lac) connected Milwaukee to the cities on and around Lake Winnebago. Small settlements were strung like beads along the turnpikes, each containing a tavern, perhaps, and a post office or general store that served local farmers as well as travelers. One such hamlet developed at what is now the intersection of Lisbon Avenue and Burleigh Street. Named Smithville after Erastus Smith, a local farmer, its major landmark was a wayside inn called the Five Mile House simply because it was five miles from Milwaukee.

from *Illustrated Historical Atlas*, 1876

John Gurda

It was clear to anyone with even minimal foresight that Milwaukee would one day come much closer. The city was expanding rapidly in the nineteenth century and, limited by Lake Michigan, had nowhere to grow but west. Ironically, deceased Milwaukeeans were the first urbanites to settle permanently in the area. In 1894 a group of nine Lutheran parishes—all on the North Side, all German-speaking—joined forces to purchase eighty-five acres north of Burleigh and west of Sixtieth Street for a cemetery. They called their project Wanderers' Rest, and a thousand German Lutherans gathered to dedicate the burial ground with hymns and speeches in September 1894. The location was so remote that attendees had to be ferried out by carriage from the end of the streetcar line at Twenty-seventh Street.

Milwaukee's Catholics were next to choose the future Enderis Park neighborhood as their final destination. Since 1857 their primary burial ground had been Calvary Cemetery, a sylvan abode at Hawley and Blue Mound Roads. It took a half-century, but that site was eventually filled to capacity, forcing the archdiocese to look outward for a new location. The result was Holy Cross Cemetery, which opened in 1909 north of Burleigh and west of Appleton Avenue, directly across from Wanderers' Rest. Spread over nearly 200 acres, Holy Cross was still well beyond the leading edge of urban settlement, and it became the obvious choice for German, Irish, Italian, Polish, Czech, and other traditionally Catholic families who had lost loved ones.

Established fifteen years apart, Wanderers' Rest (now Lincoln Memorial) and Holy Cross were large cemeteries that served Milwaukee's two largest religious denominations. They brought a steady stream of Lutherans and Catholics out to the peace and quiet of the countryside, first in funeral processions and then to visit family graves. The cemeteries also attracted a cluster of florists and monument dealers. The Schwebke family, for one, erected a large greenhouse at Sixty-ninth and Burleigh, on the present site of Mother of Good Counsel Church. H. Schwebke & Son advertised their location as "Opp. Holy Cross Cemetery" and assured prospective customers that "We Do Cemetery Planting." More than a century after the burial grounds opened, grave decorations and tombstones are still sold in the Enderis Park neighborhood.

It took a few decades for the living to join the departed. Milwaukeeans had been pushing north and west since pioneer days, creating neighborhoods as they went. Washington Park and Sherman Park began to take shape in the 1890s and continued to grow through the early years of the twentieth century. As homeseekers kept surging northwest, developers looked beyond Sixtieth Street for opportunities. Milwaukee's city limits reached Sixty-fourth Street in 1925 and jumped all the way to Ninety-second just two years later. Real estate promoters began to advertise lots for sale in Alameda Park, the northeastern corner of today's neighborhood; Lenox Heights, the wedge of land between Appleton and Lisbon Avenues; and more than a dozen subdivisions south of Lisbon. Center Street became the border between suburban Wauwatosa and a brand-new neighborhood.

Although development commenced in the 1920s, it did not proceed in the orderly east-to-west sequence that might have been predicted. One of the striking features of Enderis Park's landscape is the internal diversity of its housing stock. Typical bungalows from the 1920s can be found on practically any street between Sixtieth and Seventy-sixth. Even more numerous, and somewhat more concentrated, are Period Revival homes from the late Twenties and Thirties, a time when architects were adapting Tudor, Colonial, Gothic, and English cottage styles to American tastes and middle-class budgets. Period Revivals are especially plentiful in the blocks around the Enderis Park playfield, but again, they can be found practically anywhere. Most are constructed of brick or stone—relatively inexpensive building materials during the Depression. Rounding out the catalog of styles

are Cape Cods and small ranch homes built in the immediate post-World War II years. They are most numerous close to Seventy-sixth Street, but postwar homes appear as infill all the way back to Sixtieth.

Enderis Park, in short, represents a narrow but richly varied slice of American architectural history. Development began in earnest during the 1920s and, in a sharp break from the usual pattern, continued through the Depression; some blocks date largely from the 1930s. The parade of new homes ground to a halt during World War II and resumed with a final burst of energy in the five years after the war. Very few homes were built before 1925 and just as few after 1950. The neighborhood that Enderis Park most closely resembles is Jackson Park on the South Side, particularly its Harder's Oak Park section, but the housing stock there is somewhat more uniform. It is not unusual to find homes from the 1920s, the 1930s, and the late 1940s on any given block in any section of Enderis Park.

■ *Schwebke Florists advertised prominently in the 1940 city directory.*

■ *A typical Enderis Park mix of pre- and post-World War II housing*

Jim Hamberg

The people who built those homes had a great deal in common. Most were moving from neighborhoods closer to the heart of town, and most were German by ancestry, with a scattering of Irish, Slavic, and other ethnic backgrounds. Nearly all were in the middle income ranges, with a generous assortment of public-sector workers. In the long 2700-2800 block of N. Sixty-seventh Street, which was developed between 1929 and 1949, the original residents included two police officers, a mail carrier, a parks employee, three salesmen, a lawyer, an engineer, a factory foreman, an office supervisor, and the owners of a clothing store and a gas station. For all of them, moving to Enderis Park was a step up in both status and comfort.

A Park for the People

One element the neighborhood lacked in its formative years was a centerpiece, a focal point powerful enough to command the attention of every resident and promote a common sense of identity. City officials were at work on just such a feature. The Recreation Division of the Milwaukee Public Schools, led since 1920 by a legendary figure named Dorothy Enderis, completed a study of the city's "playground and playfield needs" in 1928. Enderis and her colleague, playground engineer Gilbert Clegg, submitted a full menu of proposed recreation sites to the Common Council, and it included the square block bordered by Seventy-first and Seventy-second Streets between Chambers and Locust. Even though practically no one lived there yet, Enderis recommended that the city establish a "supervised playground" on the site by 1936. Recreation, she believed, was something essential to every neighborhood, even the newest ones, and her conception of it went well beyond fun and games. Enderis saw recreation as a vital part of the larger effort to built solid citizens and solid human beings. "During working hours, we make a living," she said. "During leisure hours, we make a life."

The Recreation Division was authorized to purchase the land in 1928, but the initial asking price was too steep for Enderis and her colleagues. Then came the Depression. In 1931, with the real estate market in free fall, the parcel's owner was only too glad to settle for much less, and Milwaukee acquired

■ *Dorothy Enderis became a nationally recognized advocate for leisure activities through her work for the Milwaukee Public Schools.*

■ *(center)*
The playfield that would be named for her was taking definite shape in 1941.

Milwaukee Public Schools Recreation Division

some adjoining lots for back taxes. Facing financial shortfalls of its own, the city was in no hurry to develop the property. "This site was acquired well in advance of the need of a playground in this neighborhood," reported the Department of Public Works in 1932, "and the complete improvement thereof is not recommended at this time."

The advent of work relief programs prompted a change in plans. First under city sponsorship and then with more ample federal funding, unemployed workers planted trees, installed lights, laid water pipes, and erected buildings. The park was modestly expanded and steadily improved in later years, but it was the functioning heart of the neighborhood by the time World War II began. Originally known as the Chambers Street Playfield, it was named after Enderis's retirement to honor the visionary leader who had made it possible.

As Dorothy Enderis was busy planning the neighborhood's future, other institutions were becoming part of its present. Mother of Good Counsel Parish, a ministry of the Salvatorian order, was established in 1925. After worshiping in a cramped bungalow for a few years, parishioners built a combination church and school on

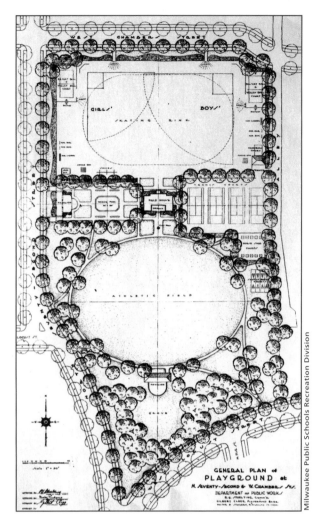

GENERAL PLAN of
PLAYGROUND at
DEPARTMENT OF PUBLIC WORKS

Milwaukee Public Schools Recreation Division

■ *The 1937 master plan for Enderis Playfield*

■ *The community building under construction in 1949*

Milwaukee Public Schools Recreation Division

Milwaukee Public Schools Recreation Division

■ *In 1928 Mother of Good Counsel Parish, the neighborhood's largest institution, built a combined church and school where angels rubbed wings with priests.*

the corner of Sixty-eighth and Lisbon in 1928. Catholic families, many with young children, were particularly prominent in the outward migration from Milwaukee's North Side; they swelled the parish rolls and made three additions to the school necessary before 1950.

Mother of Good Counsel, known to virtually everyone as "MGC," played a central role in Enderis Park, but there were other institutions in the neighborhood. MGC's playground was literally across the street from District School No. 7, built by the unincorporated Town of Wauwatosa in 1925. When the City of Milwaukee annexed the area two years later, the red brick building on Moltke Avenue became Sixty-eighth Street School, part of the MPS system and the neighborhood's only public school.

It was not until after World War II that the neighborhood and its institutions reached maturity. After the slowdown of the 1930s and a virtual freeze during the war, development accelerated in peacetime. The major streets— Lisbon, Appleton, Center, Burleigh—became important commercial corridors. Perhaps the best-known local business was Kopp's Frozen Custard, which began as a drive-in on Sixtieth and Appleton in 1950 and grew to become a kingdom of custard in the Milwaukee area.

Protestant congregations broadened the neighborhood's religious choices; Pilgrim Lutheran built a church on Sixty-eighth and Center in 1949, and St. Paul's Lutheran followed on Seventy-third and Burleigh a decade later. The green acres at the community's center matured as well. Trees planted during the Depression began to provide shade, the Lannon stone pergola aged gracefully, and local residents used Enderis Playfield for softball, ice skating, wading, chess and checkers tournaments, Fourth of July celebrations, and a full range of other leisure-time pursuits.

Many of the park's patrons were children. A baby boom was in full swing following the war, and Mother of Good Counsel experienced it most directly. Enrollment in the parish grade school soared to more than 2,000 in the 1950s, making MGC one of the largest Catholic educational institutions in the country. The parish even spun off a fondly remembered boys' high school— Francis Jordan, named for the founder of the Salvatorian order—that operated next door from 1959 to 1969. After forty years in the lower level of the church-school building, MGC dedicated its strikingly modern present church in 1968, directly over the footprint of the Schwebke family's greenhouse.

Jim Hamberg

Reclaiming a Heritage

From its peak of postwar stability in about 1970, the neighborhood entered a period of slow but inevitable change. As the original residents departed the scene, their children, in many cases, took over the family homes or bought nearby, but there was also substantial turnover, particularly in the closing years of the twentieth century. With its tree-lined streets, picture-book Period Revival homes, and an attractive swath of well-used green space at its center, Enderis Park attracted a new generation of homeowners significantly more diverse than those they replaced: Protestant and unchurched as well as Catholic, both gay and straight, black alongside white. The proportion of African Americans in the census tract covering most of the neighborhood rose from just over 1 percent in 1990 to 30 percent in 2010. What did not change was the neighborhood's economic profile; Enderis Park remained a solidly middle-income community whose homes reflected a definite measure of success.

Whether old or new, local residents began to feel growing concern about their central playfield in the mid-1990s. As municipal budgets tightened, there were fewer activities in Enderis Park, fewer workers to maintain the property, and a troubling increase in crime. Instead of passively accepting what some might have considered inevitable, local residents resolved to halt the erosion of their signature open space and reclaim the vision of Dorothy Enderis. The result was the Enderis Park Neighborhood Association (EPNA). Led by the late Bruce Cameron, a lawyer who was himself a 1988 transplant, the group raised funds and lobbied for city support to restore the playfield to its former green glory. The results include a splash pad, a soccer field, new playground equipment, a volleyball court, an improved softball diamond and tennis courts, and a welcome infusion of energy. There was even a new centerpiece for the community's centerpiece: the Magic Grove, a colorful metal sculpture dedicated at the south end of the park in 2007. "Bringing back the park was like starting the neighborhood's heart," said Scott McGroarty, EPNA's president in 2014. "It really took on a life of its own."

The energy was by no means confined to the park itself. The association sponsors activities designed to build a broader sense of

■ *Forty years later the parish moved into a thoroughly modern house of worship next door.*

participation: Easter egg hunts, the traditional Fourth of July parade, a community-wide yard sale, nighttime trick-or-treating, a newsletter and website, and concerts "on the green" that draw hundreds of people during the summer months. EPNA concentrates its efforts south of Lisbon Avenue, but Lenox Heights and Alameda Park, the subdivisions north of Lisbon, travel in the same orbit and participate in many of the activities.

Enderis Park is definitely an urban neighborhood, but it retains a settled, semi-suburban air in the twenty-first century. The only way to distinguish the community from Wauwatosa, its neighbor to the south, is by the color of their street signs—blue on Wauwatosa's side of Center Street, green on Milwaukee's. The abundance of curves and corners continues to encourage a sense of small-scale belonging. This is a community whose residents—a few, at any rate—still wave to strangers, a place where block parties and Independence Day parades have been going on for decades but have taken on a new sense of purpose. There is a shared awareness that the best way to ensure an engaging neighborhood is to be engaged neighbors. The people of Enderis Park know what they have, and they are determined to preserve it, angles and all.

■ *Installing the Magic Grove sculpture in 2007*

■ *(center right) A backyard barn recalls the neighborhood's rural past.*

Jim Hamberg

■ *Holy Cross Cemetery lends an air of otherworldly quiet to a community of unique businesses and distinctive homes.*

Jim Hamberg

Jim Hamberg

John Gurda

Jim Hamberg

North Side

There was no North Side in Milwaukee's earliest days. The central rivers that put the young city on the map divided it into three distinct zones: east, west, and south. It was not until the later 1800s, when the West Side had grown too large to be contained by a single compass point, that the North Side began to elbow its way into the intervening space on the edge of Downtown. Lacking major geographic barriers—no rivers, no railroads, no major parks—the district's settlement pattern was impressively uniform. Newcomers followed diagonal plank roads into the countryside, and major arterials became the borders between their neighborhoods.

The cultural patterns were nearly as uniform. Milwaukeeans usually think of the North Side's development in a sort of cultural shorthand: Germans came first, and African Americans followed. That perception is accurate, broadly speaking, but many more groups have found homes in the district, including a United Nations of immigrants, college-educated young whites in Riverwest, and a variety of urban professionals in Brewer's Hill. The North Side is likewise viewed as the most troubled section of Milwaukee. That, too, has a basis in reality—in a city with disturbingly high poverty rates, North Side neighborhoods are the poorest—but the district also has a core of deeply invested residents who not only resist the stereotype but are working to relegate it to history.

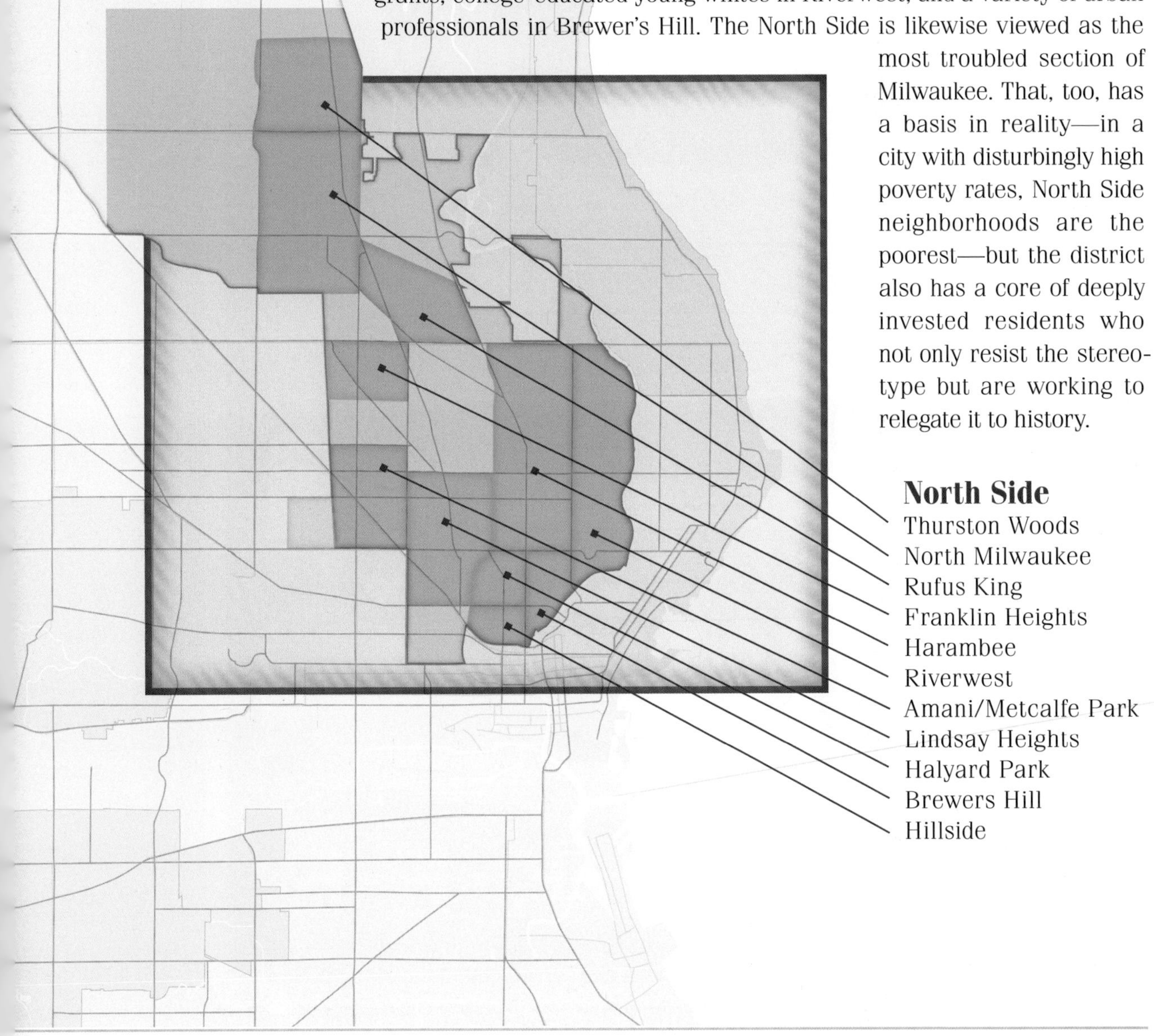

North Side

Thurston Woods
North Milwaukee
Rufus King
Franklin Heights
Harambee
Riverwest
Amani/Metcalfe Park
Lindsay Heights
Halyard Park
Brewers Hill
Hillside

BREWER'S HILL

M·I·L·W·A·U·K·E·E

Brewer's Hill

To visit Brewer's Hill is to see firsthand the American city's capacity for reinvention. One of Milwaukee's most historic—and most desirable—neighborhoods was, not many years ago, one of its most blighted, a place where few callers came on legitimate business after dark. As recently as the 1980s, the community was pockmarked with vacant lots where homes had once stood, and those that remained seemed destined for the wrecking ball. Slowly at first, preservationists began to buy up the distressed properties that had survived, creating a ripple that became, before long, a wave. House by house, then block by block, the spirit of renewal spread inward, generating a market so robust that some of the city's most prominent developers chose Brewer's Hill for some of their most ambitious projects. The result is a uniquely urban hybrid of old and new that has drawn a remarkable variety of home-seekers.

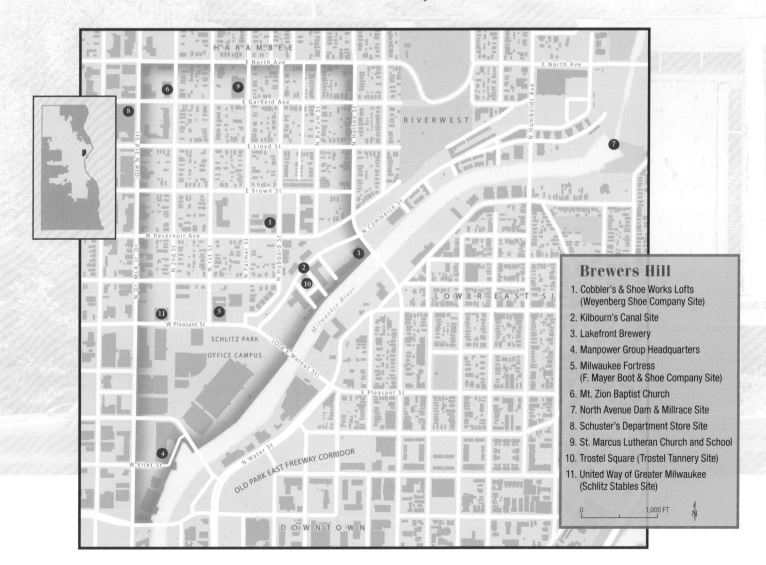

Brewers Hill

1. Cobbler's & Shoe Works Lofts
   (Weyenberg Shoe Company Site)
2. Kilbourn's Canal Site
3. Lakefront Brewery
4. Manpower Group Headquarters
5. Milwaukee Fortress
   (F. Mayer Boot & Shoe Company Site)
6. Mt. Zion Baptist Church
7. North Avenue Dam & Millrace Site
8. Schuster's Department Store Site
9. St. Marcus Lutheran Church and School
10. Trostel Square (Trostel Tannery Site)
11. United Way of Greater Milwaukee
    (Schlitz Stables Site)

0   1,000 FT

The Old Sixth Ward

Brewer's Hill was created, in more ways than one, by the Milwaukee River. It has always been a bi-level community, rising from the stream's low west bank to a broad plateau with a commanding view of the city's center. The hill itself is actually a gentle bluff that emerged as the river, century by century, cut into its valley. By the 1800s the top of today's Brewer's Hill stood nearly eighty feet above the water line. Early Indian tribes found the high ground especially attractive, gracing the area with a number of effigy mounds. A small ravine carried water down the face of the bluff; it is still visible as a gentle depression that now carries Hubbard Street.

Byron Kilbourn, one of Milwaukee's three founders, claimed much of the west bank wilderness in 1835. He was soon engaged in an intense rivalry with the east bank's promoter, Solomon Juneau, and he enlisted the river to help his cause. In 1838 Kilbourn broke ground for a canal that would connect his settlement with the Rock River and thereby the Mississippi and ultimately New Orleans. His dream was a commercial waterway that would place his settlement at the junction of the eastern and southern trade routes of the central United States. As soon as the necessary surveys were completed, Kilbourn's crews dammed the Milwaukee River near what is now North Avenue and proceeded to dig a canal along the west bank below.

Work came to a halt just south of Vliet Street in 1842, a casualty of political intrigue and the realization that railroads were the transportation mode of the future. Although dreams of transcontinental glory faded quickly, enterprising Milwaukeeans soon realized that the mile-long section of completed canal offered a dependable source of water power. By 1848 there were twenty-five mills and factories on Kilbourn's ditch. When railroad tracks were laid alongside it in 1852, development intensified, and "the Water Power" became Milwaukee's first large-scale industrial district. Riverfront flour mills helped make the city one of America's largest milling centers by the mid-1860s. Nearly a dozen tanneries were built below the North Avenue dam in the same period, their yards piled high with hemlock bark (an early source of tannin) from the Northwoods. By 1890 Milwaukee was the largest leather-tanning center in the world. The Schlitz brewery, which had opened in 1849 at Fourth and Juneau, moved to a Walnut Street location near the canal in 1870. Within four decades the company was brewing 3 million barrels a year of what it called, with justification, "the beer that made Milwaukee famous."

As the major riverfront industries—milling, tanning, and brewing—grew in sales and size, satellite businesses appeared. Cooperage shops made barrels for flour and beer. Ice dealers, who harvested their product from the river itself, provided a convenient means of refrigeration. Shoe companies turned locally tanned leather into footwear. The F. Mayer Boot and Shoe Company, which opened a massive red brick factory at First and Walnut in 1880, was soon producing 3,000 pairs a day. Thirty years later the Weyenberg Shoe Company built a large plant on Brown Street that outdistanced F. Mayer, turning out 10,000 pairs daily at its peak.

■ *A riverside canal intended for transportation in the 1840s became a water-powered industrial corridor instead.*

Milwaukee County Historical Society

■ *The industries that developed along the canal included (clockwise from top) the Schlitz brewery, almost a dozen tanneries, and several flour mills that served a national clientele.*

Milwaukee County Historical Society

Milwaukee Public Library

Milwaukee Public Library

In the late 1800s nearly all of the area's industries turned to steam power, rendering Kilbourn's canal obsolete. The long stretch between Humboldt Avenue and Walnut Street was filled in completely by 1886, and the old waterway became a road named, fittingly, Commerce Street. A channel created for canal boats now carried horse-drawn vehicles.

Although the commercial importance of the Milwaukee River diminished, the stream had sparked an important sequence of events. The river made construction of the canal possible, and the canal attracted industries. The industries, in turn, led directly to the formation of a neighborhood. There had been one false start before settlement began in earnest. In 1837,

■ *Steam power replaced water power in the late 1800s, and Byron Kilbourn's canal (left side of photo) was filled in to become Commerce Street.*

Milwaukee County Historical Society

John Gurda

■ *One of the neighborhood's largest homes is an Italianate mansion that belonged for many years to Joseph Phillips, Milwaukee's mayor in 1870-71.*

only two years after Milwaukee's first public land sale, a pioneer speculator platted a subdivision called Sherman's Addition. Covering all of today's Brewer's Hill, it was the northernmost subdivision in the city. Sherman's Addition drew scant attention at first. Urban settlers had been edging outward from the center of Kilbourntown (Third and Juneau), but their progress was slow. In the 1850s, when the industrial district along the canal began to boom, they finally crossed Walnut Street and colonized the high ground to the north. Hundreds of newcomers built homes overlooking the river, and by 1880 the area was filled practically to North Avenue.

Brewer's Hill was an attractive residential choice for the same reasons it is today, including grand views and easy access to Downtown. In the nineteenth century, however, there was an even greater attraction: proximity to employment on the riverfront. Brewer's Hill became a neighborhood of industrial workers who walked to jobs on the river's edge, and they were not exclusively blue-collar workers by any means. Between 1850 and 1880, the peak years of development for Brewer's Hill, Milwaukee, like most of its urban counterparts, was a walking city—not by design

but by necessity. Public transit, of the horse-drawn variety, was limited and slow, and most Milwaukeeans had no choice but to live within easy walking distance of work, worship, shopping, and social life. One obvious result was economic diversity, and Brewer's Hill was a striking example of the pattern. Successful industrialists lived among their employees. Wealthy merchants lived among their customers. All walked to work on the same streets. A tannery owner and a tannery sweeper might have been next-door neighbors, one living in a castle, the other in a cottage.

Many of Brewer's Hill's original homes still stand, despite the drastic attrition of the post-World War II years, and they constitute a guidebook of nineteenth-century architectural styles. The earliest are in the Greek Revival mode: classically simple, austere but graceful. They were followed by Italianate homes, still symmetrical but built with more flowing lines and a greater emphasis on ornament. Finally came the Queen Annes, harmonious ensembles of surfaces and textures. Palmer Street has two mansions, an Italianate at 1823 and a Queen Anne at 1843, that are outstanding examples of their types, but even the most modest houses show the influence of particular design periods. The contrast between large and small is extreme on some blocks, and the neighborhood's visual variety is one of its most important qualities.

The people who settled the Sixth Ward, as the area was known after 1857, were less diverse than the houses they built. The vast majority were German immigrants, a pattern that persisted for decades. Milwaukee was the nation's most German city in the later 1800s, and nearly two-thirds of Milwaukee's Germans lived on the west side of the river, an area that included Brewer's Hill. North Third Street, now Martin Luther King Drive, became their leading commercial district. As settlement on the hill grew denser, Third Street was lined with dry goods stores, saloons, butcher shops, bakeries, and other retail businesses. Schuster's Department Store opened in 1884 and soon became the district's anchor. The Vorwaerts (Forward) Turner Hall provided both a social and an athletic outlet for local Germans. At

■ *St. Marcus Church, shown during and after construction, served the area's German Lutherans.*

■ *Schuster's Department Store anchored the commercial district on nearby Third Street.*

least two businesses on the street divided their time between undertaking and the operation of livery stables. Third Street became, in an important sense, the North Side's downtown, and for years it was second only to Wisconsin Avenue in retail sales volume. There were German-flavored businesses on the side streets as well. Miller Brewing opened at least one saloon within view of Schlitz, and Meyer's Park, a small beer garden on Garfield near Buffum Street, attracted thirsty patrons during the summer months.

The prosperity of Brewer's Hill was based on the thriving industrial district along the river, the busy shops on Third Street, and a stable residential area in between. This three-sided partnership endured for decades, but the area also witnessed change, particularly after 1900. As the original settlers died and many of their children relocated to newer neighborhoods, other groups moved into the area. Although Germans were still numerous, the Sixth Ward became extraordinarily diverse during the World War I era. Hungarians, eastern European Jews, and African Americans moved up Third Street from Downtown, just as the original Germans had, and Italian and Polish families moved across the river

from the East Side. As the wealthier families moved away, many of the largest homes were converted to rooming houses, and a number were replaced by apartment buildings. Although there were still Hafemanns, Heidemanns, and Hoecherls on the same block in the 1920s, Brewer's Hill became both denser and more diverse.

Change continued in the years after World War II. The riverfront industries, some nearly a century old, slowly slid into obsolescence. Tanneries began to close when foreign competitors and synthetic leather upended their traditional markets, and local shoe factories

■ *African Americans became a major influence on the neighborhood after World War II. Mt. Zion Baptist (top) built a new church on Garfield Avenue in 1950, and St. Marcus Lutheran (above) became an integrated congregation.*

pressing economic problems, they developed a strong neighborhood culture; churches, businesses, and other institutions were established to meet community needs, often in buildings erected in the 1800s. Many African Americans came to refer to Brewer's Hill as the "East Side"—of the North Side.

Although the newer cultures had inherent strengths, high rates of absentee ownership and the advanced age of the neighborhood's buildings led to an epidemic of blight. Riverfront industries, Third Street storefronts, and scores of homes were torn down and replaced by nothing at all. The blocks south of Brown Street lost more than half their population between 1950 and 1970, as nearly 700 housing units were demolished. A neighborhood with an uncommonly rich past faced a most uncertain future.

An Urban Lazarus

Brewer's Hill sank to its low point in the 1970s. Third Street was a commercial ghost town. Commerce Street was reduced to little more than a weedy shortcut between the East Side and Downtown. The neighborhood's housing stock thinned each year, and low rents and high crime discouraged reinvestment of any kind.

There were, at the same time, seeds of renewal. A number of Third Street merchants refused to leave their traditional places of business. Brewer's Hill's churches refused to believe that their neighborhood had reached the end of the line. Mt. Zion Baptist, a largely African-American congregation, built an apartment complex for the elderly that covered an entire block of Second Street between Garfield and Lloyd. St. Marcus Lutheran, a pillar of the German establishment since 1875, opened its doors to the community and dramatically expanded its school on Palmer Street.

And then there were the houses. Despite the losses of earlier years, Brewer's Hill had a critical mass of Victorian homes that made the community a magnet for restorationists. As the historic preservation movement gained traction, younger Milwaukeeans with a newfound taste for vintage architecture began to buy up properties in the southern

felt a similar chill. The struggling Schlitz brewery was sold to Stroh's of Detroit and closed permanently in 1982. The Third Street corridor began to decline as well, particularly after suburban shopping centers sprang up and the riot of 1967 frightened away longtime customers. In the residential heart of the neighborhood, newer groups rose to dominance. Puerto Ricans moved across the Holton Street bridge from the Lower East Side and developed a distinctive community on the eastern edge of the neighborhood. African-American residents exercised the greatest influence, rising from 9% of the population in 1950 to 42 percent in 1960 and 78 percent in 1970. Despite

blocks of the neighborhood. The first was Ron Radke, a bricklayer by trade, who purchased an Italianate mansion on Palmer Street in 1975. It had been the home of Joseph Phillips, Milwaukee's mayor in 1870-71, and had been used as a rooming house since 1911. Radke became, at the age of twenty-two, an urban pioneer. Word spread informally as he began the arduous task of restoration, and within a few years the hillside was home to two or three dozen preservationists, including some who had grown up in the neighborhood. Many paid only a few thousand dollars for their homes, and they typically arrived one step ahead of the wrecking ball.

The preservationists formed what was surely one of the most unusual groups of neighbors in the city. Most were Milwaukee-area natives in their twenties and thirties, but the similarities in background ended there. They were gay and straight, single and married with small children. They earned their livings as accountants, machinists, secretaries, psychologists, waitresses, and steel workers. Some restored their homes with scrupulous attention to period detail; others simply remodeled. What united the pioneers was an almost-religious devotion to preservation of some of the city's most historic homes. All of the new residents literally shoveled out their dwellings at the beginning, and horror stories abounded, from piles of discarded syringes in bedrooms to rats floating in toilet bowls. Most newcomers lived in construction zones for years. They completed projects as time and resources permitted, and spent thousands of dollars on houses that more conventional home-seekers would have considered marginal at best. Some learned the histories of their houses better than most Americans know their family trees. The past was alive to them, and their firm intention was to create a shared future.

The preservationists' influence extended to the naming of the neighborhood. If other Milwaukeeans were aware of the community at all, they considered it part of the North Side or, if they had attained a certain age, the Sixth Ward. In 1981 an informal block club started by the newcomers became Historic Brewer's Hill of Sherman's Addition, Inc. As

the name for a historic district perched on a hillside overlooking a famous brewery, it fit perfectly, and the neighborhood has been known as Brewer's Hill ever since.

The brewery itself played a major role in the neighborhood's rebirth. In 1983 a team of home-grown Milwaukee developers led by Gary Grunau bought the vacant Schlitz complex and proceeded to make ambitious plans for the shuttered hulk. The result was Schlitz Park, a mixed-use development that blended preservation with new construction. It was a singular success, drawing a mix of businesses and nonprofit groups that collectively employed more people than the brewery at its peak.

Robert Wiegert

Not only did Schlitz Park provide a solid anchor at the foot of Brewer's Hill, but its success sparked reinvestment on North Third Street, which was renamed in 1984 to honor Dr. Martin Luther King, Jr. With ample help from the City of Milwaukee, King Drive recovered much of its historic vitality, attracting merchants who sold everything from fine chocolate to athletic shoes. Vintage storefronts were restored, and new buildings went up on lots that had been empty since the 1960s.

Commerce Street, in the meantime, was languishing. Its fortunes had ebbed so low that in 1983 the State of Wisconsin purchased the vacant Trostel tannery and announced plans to convert it to a prison. That proposal sparked an uproar in the neighborhood, as

■ *Schlitz was gone by 1982, but its brewery came to new life as an office park whose energy spread to the surrounding neighborhood.*

older residents and newer preservationists closed ranks against it. Mayor Henry Maier took up their cause, and the prison plans were ultimately scrapped. The controversy taught local residents a valuable lesson in the power of community, and it brought welcome attention to a movement that had been practically unknown beyond the neighborhood's borders.

As restoration activities on the high ground gathered momentum, Commerce Street finally stirred to life. The Lakefront Brewery, which had been producing fine craft beers since 1987, moved from an old Riverwest bakery to an equally antique power plant on Commerce in 1998. With a major boost from Mayor John Norquist's administration, other projects followed, particularly condominium developments. A forlorn mile of riverfront was transformed in the early 2000s, as vacant lots sprouted sleek compositions of brick, chrome,

and glass that would have been right at home in much larger cities. The Commerce Street condos attracted everyone from corporate transplants to recovering suburbanites.

Similar construction projects were going on up the hill. As the beachhead of the 1970s became a united preservation front in the 1990s, the way was paved for new development. Lots that had been vacant for decades became homesites again, and most of Brewer's Hill's new homes were reasonable facsimiles of the old styles—reasonable enough to blend in almost seamlessly. New multi-family developments went up as well, and older industrial buildings were creatively repurposed. The former Weyenberg shoe factory was converted to condominiums, and the F. Mayer Boot and Shoe plant became the Milwaukee Fortress, a complex of offices, workshops, and studios that was eventually converted to apartments.

■ *Old and new coexist happily in Brewer's Hill. The neighborhood has an appealing assortment of nineteenth-century buildings ...*

As its vitality returned, Brewer's Hill benefited greatly from a transportation decision—or the reversal of one. In 1971 the Park East freeway spur had opened just south of the neighborhood. It was designed as part of a loop encircling Downtown but, as opposition to freeways mounted, construction was halted at Milwaukee Street. For more than thirty years, the Park East functioned as a long and lightly traveled exit ramp from Interstate 43 to the east side of Downtown. In 2002, largely as the result of pressure from John Norquist's administration, the freeway spur was removed. The decision opened twenty-six acres of prime real estate to redevelopment, but its most important impact, from Brewer's Hill's perspective, was the elimination of an imposing physical and psychological barrier. With the concrete bulwark gone, the energy of Milwaukee's Downtown flowed more freely into the residential areas immediately north.

Like any dynamic neighborhood, Brewer's Hill is a work in progress, and its transformation has not been entirely without controversy. Soaring property values have led to soaring property taxes, putting pressure on long-time residents who have no interest in moving. But the benefits of reinvestment vastly outweigh the hazards of gentrification. Since the 1980s Brewer's Hill has experienced a welcome infusion of new residents, new capital, and new energy. Bright strands of contemporary development are woven into its historic fabric, giving the neighborhood an uncommon vibrancy. Like Lazarus, Brewer's Hill has come back from the dead. Its resurrection stands as an object lesson for similarly challenged neighborhoods in Milwaukee and throughout urban America.

■ ... *and an equally impressive number of twenty-first-century landmarks. The result is a visual variety uncommon for such a compact community.*

■ *Overlooking Downtown and the Lower East Side, Brewer's Hill has views that are unmatched in the city.*

■ *Milwaukee's Riverwalk runs to the eastern edge of Brewer's Hill, where the Lakefront Brewery (right) stands ready to share some of the region's finest craft beers.*

Jessica Lothman

Jessica Lothman

Christopher Winters

Jessica Lothman

■ *Lakefront Brewery and the neighborhood's sudsy heritage go hand in hand.*

Jessica Lothman

HILLSIDE
M·I·L·W·A·U·K·E·E

Hillside

Some neighborhoods are born, and others are made. Hillside belongs in the second category. The surrounding landscape took more than a century to evolve, but Hillside came to life in a single burst of activity after World War II. The Milwaukee Housing Authority "made" the neighborhood in an effort to alleviate blight and to relieve a critical shortage of housing, but Hillside evolved to become the city's pioneer foray into the field of public housing for low-income residents. Today its 470 homes constitute a residential island bordered by a historic industrial district, both of them carved into a gentle slope overlooking the west side of Downtown. True, there are other public housing developments in Milwaukee, each a neighborhood in its own right, but, as the city's first venture and the one with the most historic setting, Hillside merits special attention.

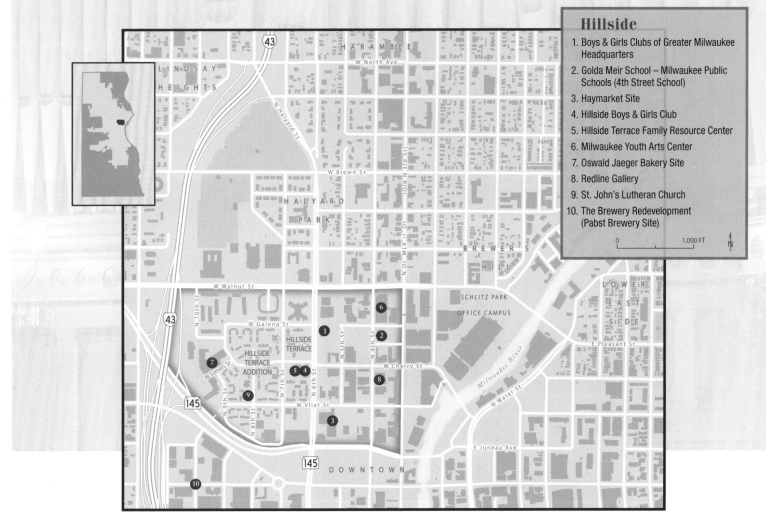

Hillside

1. Boys & Girls Clubs of Greater Milwaukee Headquarters
2. Golda Meir School – Milwaukee Public Schools (4th Street School)
3. Haymarket Site
4. Hillside Boys & Girls Club
5. Hillside Terrace Family Resource Center
6. Milwaukee Youth Arts Center
7. Oswald Jaeger Bakery Site
8. Redline Gallery
9. St. John's Lutheran Church
10. The Brewery Redevelopment (Pabst Brewery Site)

A North Side Mosaic

Hillside rests on the site of a much older neighborhood. In the 1850s, when Milwaukee was barely a decade old, European immigrants began to build homes on the high ground above the town's center. Although they included a generous sprinkling of Dutch and Czech families, the vast majority of newcomers were from Germany, and their economic circumstances differed widely. The greatest number of immigrants were blue-collar workers who put up modest wooden homes on the typically narrow lots of the time. There were wealthier residents as well, some perched on the highest rungs of Milwaukee's economic ladder. So many Uihleins (owners of the Schlitz Brewery) lived on or near Galena Street that the area was known as "Uihlein Hill," conveniently overlooking the family's Third Street brewing complex. One of their mansions, which stayed in the family until the 1940s, stood just north of what is now the Hillside Terrace Family Resource Center. Whether working-class or upper-class, settlement continued into the 1870s, when the area was filled to its limits.

At the foot of the hill, around Fifth and Vliet Streets, was a haymarket that served as a magnet for the entire district. Farmers from the adjoining countryside brought in loads of hay—fuel for hungry horses—as well as a seasonal round of fresh vegetables and fruits that nourished the whole neighborhood. The haymarket area's residents shared the German ancestry of their neighbors on the hillside, and they shared the landscape with a wide range of businesses. The area was filled with cigar factories, butcher shops, shoe factories, a weiss beer brewery, blacksmith shops, and a number of bakeries. One of the bakeries was operated by Oswald Jaeger, an Austrian immigrant who lived above his shop on Somers Street. Jaeger's Butter-Nut brand was advertised as "the finest bread you ever tasted," and the mouth-watering smell of fresh-baked bread wafted over the neighborhood for more than a century. The Jaeger complex shipped its last loaf in 2005; the buildings are now used as warehouses.

The area's Germans started churches as well as businesses. In 1890 St. John's Lutheran, a Wisconsin Synod congregation organized in 1848, moved into a new church on Eighth and Vliet Streets. The graceful Gothic building was among the largest Lutheran churches in the city, and the parish school next door served thousands of children before closing in 1960. St. John's

Milwaukee Public Library

Milwaukee County Historical Society

Lutheran is Hillside's major landmark today, its Gothic steeple providing a dramatic link with the neighborhood's early years.

By 1900 a new group was making the neighborhood its own: eastern European Jews. The original Germans and their descendants were migrating steadily to the north and west, clearing the way for immigrants who had fled poverty and persecution in the Russian Empire. The haymarket area's Jewish enclave grew to nearly 5,000 people in an area of just twenty-five square blocks, and the Orthodox faithful established roughly a dozen synagogues. One of the younger arrivals was Goldie Mabowehz, an eight-year-old who settled with her family in a two-room apartment on Sixth and Walnut in 1906. Goldie was valedictorian of her graduating class at Fourth Street School. Years later, as Golda Meir, she became prime minister of Israel and perhaps the most famous ex-Milwaukeean in history. Her former school is now named in Golda's honor.

Like their German predecessors, the eastern European Jews moved north and west as their fortunes improved, and their old neighborhood gradually became one of the most diverse in Milwaukee. Greeks, Slovaks, Croatians, and African Americans joined the earlier Germans and Jews, each group establishing its own businesses and places of worship. In the 1920s Jews and African Americans worshiped side by side on Sixth Street, the first group in Anshe Sfard synagogue and the second in the Church of God. The Home for the Jewish Aged stood down the block from Sacred Heart (Croatian) Catholic Church on Galena Street. Although it eventually became an integral part of the African-American community, the neighborhood maintained its rich ethnic diversity for a full generation.

As the area's cultural mix changed, its houses aged in place. By the 1940s some were nearly a century old, and the years had not been kind. Too many absentee landlords let their buildings fall into disrepair, and city officials finally declared the area blighted. Milwaukee faced an apparently unrelated

■ *The membership of St. John's Lutheran Church reflected the German heritage of the neighborhood's first residents.*

Milwaukee Public Library

■ *Jewish immigrants from eastern Europe gradually replaced the Germans. One of the newcomers, circled at far right, was Goldie Mabowehz, the future prime minister of Israel.*

Milwaukee Public Library

■ *As its houses aged and Milwaukee industrialized, living conditions deteriorated, and the haymarket area became a hodge-podge of conflicting land uses.*

Milwaukee Public Library

Milwaukee County Historical Society

(above)
The social center at Fourth Street School served a rapidly integrating neighborhood in the 1920s. The Schlitz brewery is visible in the background.

African-American churches arose to serve the newest residents. Some were of the storefront variety, like the Church of God in Christ on Eighth Street. Others stressed more formal worship, including St. Mark African Methodist (both center right), a sacred presence on Fourth Street from 1914 to 1953.

problem at the same time. During World War II nearly all the city's industries became defense plants, and they were uniformly swamped with military orders. "War workers" swarmed into Milwaukee from across the region, creating an acute housing shortage.

The Housing Authority of the City of Milwaukee (HACM) was established in January 1944 to address the twin problems of blight and overcrowding. Sharing costs with the federal government, the Housing Authority focused first on the haymarket area. Officials made plans to clear two square blocks (from Sixth to Seventh Streets between Galena and Vliet) and replace the battered homes there with "permanent housing." It was felt that the initial project should be small to "avoid displacement of families now living in the blighted area." The Housing Authority's intent was to build homes for war workers that would be "converted to low-rent housing after the war."

The "Sixth Ward project," which soon became the more descriptive "Hillside Terrace," was delayed by political conflict and government red tape. By the time the land was cleared, the war workers had all gone home, and Hillside was redefined as "a slum clearance housing project for persons of low income." Ground was finally broken on January 8, 1948. The Lincoln High School band serenaded a crowd of 150, and Mayor John Bohn said, "Today we are finally digging . . . after a long, tiresome task of following down miles and miles of red tape." The building crews moved quickly, enabling Hillside's first residents to move in during the Christmas season of 1948.

The first phase of the Hillside development provided homes for 232 families. In early 1950, as the last of them were getting settled, planning for a 388-unit addition began. The Housing Authority used federal funds to

Milwaukee Journal Sentinel

Milwaukee Public Library

Milwaukee Journal Sentinel

Milwaukee Public Library

purchase land bordered by Seventh, Ninth, Galena and Vliet Streets—just west of the original Hillside. Once again, progress was slow. Groundbreaking for the Hillside Terrace Addition did not take place until July 7, 1954, and the development was not fully occupied until 1956.

Hillside was built in two phases but featured only one architectural style. The basic unit is a simplified English cottage, with brick siding, a steep roof, and (on the original homes) a brick chimney. The homes vary in size from one-bedroom apartments to five-bedroom rowhouses, and there is an eight-story high-rise on the summit of the hill as well. They clearly met a need: there were at least four applicants for every available unit. The project was also racially integrated from the very beginning. Mayor Frank Zeidler, the Socialist who held office from 1948 to 1960, was a tireless advocate for public housing. When

the Hillside Terrace Addition was dedicated, Zeidler presented keys to a black and a white family and said, "Let's give these people who are to live here a chance to really mean it when they sing *God Bless America*."

The landscape around Hillside changed steadily after the project's completion. In the early 1960s new freeways set Hillside's southern and western borders in concrete. In the same years, the city's Redevelopment Authority cleared the northern border, a narrow strip of land on Walnut Street between Sixth and Tenth Streets. Multi-family developments there, including Mayflower Court, Plymouth Manor, and Walnut Park, brought hundreds of new residents to the neighborhood. In the early 1970s the old haymarket area just east of Hillside was redeveloped as a center for commerce and light industry. All of the new developments helped to strengthen Hillside's island-like character.

(clockwise from upper left)
■ *As the neighborhood became a genuine slum, land was cleared to the bare ground, and the city built a housing project called Hillside Terrace. The first residents took occupancy in 1948.*

New Look, New Life

Hillside evolved with the city around it. From the very beginning, Housing Authority officials wanted to provide more than housing. In the 1950s they encouraged residents to use an on-site day care center, a supervised playground program, and Scouting activities sponsored by the Kiwanis Club. Those programs and similar efforts expanded steadily. In 1970 three buildings were emptied to provide space for social service programs. In 1978, with help from a federal grant, Hillside Community Center was built on the site of a former playground. It quickly became the gathering place for hundreds of local residents. The Boys & Girls Club, Hillside's largest social services agency, offered a full range of programs for local young people, and the Community Center served all ages.

The most extensive changes took place in the 1990s. The federal government, through its Hope VI program, set out to transform public housing in America, and Milwaukee was among the nation's earliest and most creative users of Hope VI funds. Some Housing Authority developments were rebuilt to serve a broader spectrum of incomes, but Hillside's economic criteria remained the same. What did change was the appearance of the community. In an effort that lasted from 1992 to 1998 and represented an investment of $46 million, Hillside was given a substantially new look. Interiors were modestly upgraded, porches were enlarged, green space was expanded, and the original cul-de-sacs were converted to through streets, all of which enhanced a feeling of neighborhood. Another enhancement was the Hillside Terrace Family Resource Center. The Hillside Boys & Girls Club and an adjacent day care center remained community magnets, while the Resource Center provided an array of educational, employment, and health care services as well as community meeting spaces.

Ann Wilson, a long-time Hillside resident who manages the Family Resource Center, spoke of the development's human qualities. "We have a closeness as much as any community in Milwaukee," Wilson said, "and more than most. Most of us know each other and watch out for each other. I'm not saying everyone who lives here is good, but we've got some fabulous people." Hillside, in fact, is much like many other Milwaukee neighborhoods. Its residents are largely African Americans, but not exclusively. Some families have been there for two generations, and others moved in yesterday. Some plant their front yards as carefully as any suburban plot; others let the litter pile up until they're ordered to remove it. There is no shortage of Christmas decorations and Packers banners in season—and sometimes out. Numerous residents get along with everybody, while others barely get along with themselves. Hillside is a community of nearly 1,200 people, and their outstanding quality is variety.

When the people of Hillside talk about the neighborhood's high points, they often mention their homes first. The units are comfortable, the rents are affordable (limited to 30 percent of household income), and the Housing Authority keeps the buildings in good repair. "The city's a good landlord," said one long-time Hillsider. Attractive landscaping—trees, shrubs, and flowers—sets an example that most residents do their best to follow.

Location is another attraction. Hillside is perched barely a stone's throw from Downtown, and the views are every bit as grand as they are from the pricier heights of nearby Brewer's Hill; residents enjoy million-dollar vistas at public-housing rents. They also live within easy walking distance of shopping, entertainment, and education. The resources of the redeveloped Pabst Brewery complex are just across the freeway by way of a pedestrian bridge. The blocks east of Sixth Street have attracted an eclectic mix of businesses and nonprofit groups. A number of them are oriented to

the arts, notably the Redline Gallery and the perennially busy Milwaukee Youth Arts Center. St. John's Lutheran Church, whose members held weekly German services until 1986, still provides a nineteenth-century focal point for a development very much at home in the twenty-first.

With decent housing, an enviable location, and a wide range of resources, it's no wonder that many Hillside residents are satisfied with their community. "It gets so you can't move," said a twenty-year resident. "You just get comfortable." But the homes of Hillside are not castles, and life in the development is not heaven on earth. Hillside is a low-income community, where life for many is a continuing struggle. "If I can get through the month with my bills paid and my kids out of trouble, I'm doing fine," said one resident.

The struggle need not go on forever. Dozens of residents have used the relatively safe haven of Hillside as a springboard to something better. Hillside's "alumni" include "Downtown" Freddie Brown, one of the finest shooting guards in NBA history, and Howard Fuller, former Milwaukee Public Schools superintendent and a nationally known advocate for educational reform. Fuller, whose family was among the first to move into Hillside, looks back on his growing-up years there with pride. "It was a positive place to live," he said. "Hillside gave me a solid foundation to build from in later years." Other former residents are playing an active part in Milwaukee's business and professional life. All serve as role models; they are examples of what's possible.

Since its founding, the Milwaukee Housing Authority has worked to provide "decent, safe and sanitary housing" for those city residents least able to afford it. Hillside has been meeting that need since the middle of the last century. For those with the vision to use it, the development offers something more: a foothold on the future.

■ *The neighborhood's business residents include the Bartolotta Restaurant Group.*

■ *St. John's Lutheran Church remains a distinctive Hillside landmark, inside and out.*

All photos this page by Christopher Winters

Christopher Winters

■ (above) *Named for its most famous graduate, Golda Meir School serves gifted and talented youngsters.*

■ *The nearby Youth Arts Center offers programs in dance, theater, and a wide range of other pursuits.*

Milwaukee Youth Arts Center

Milwaukee Youth Arts Center

Christopher Winters

■ *The Hillside Boys & Girls Club has long been a magnet for the neighborhood's young people.*

Hillside Boys & Girls Club

Jessica Lothman

■ *National Ace Hardware serves a metropolitan clientele.*

Hillside Boys & Girls Club

■ *Perched on the edge of Downtown, Hillside features million-dollar views at public-housing rents.*

Christopher Winters

HALYARD
PARK

M·I·L·W·A·U·K·E·E

Halyard Park

If a typical Milwaukeean were blindfolded and dropped off in the middle of Halyard Park, he or she might be confused when the blindfold came off. Ranch homes on large lots? Late-model cars in the driveways? This must be Brown Deer or Brookfield. But Halyard Park is no suburb. It lies near the heart of Milwaukee's North Side, and the neighborhood's amenities do not conform to the usual image of the inner city.

Halyard Park has been a widely admired addition to the urban landscape since the 1980s, and it has become such a strong presence that its borders now encompass several blocks of older buildings to the north and south. Whether they live in newer homes or vintage Victorians, residents consider their neighborhood both an act of faith and an expression of pride. As much as any development in Milwaukee's modern history, Halyard Park symbolizes new life in the central city.

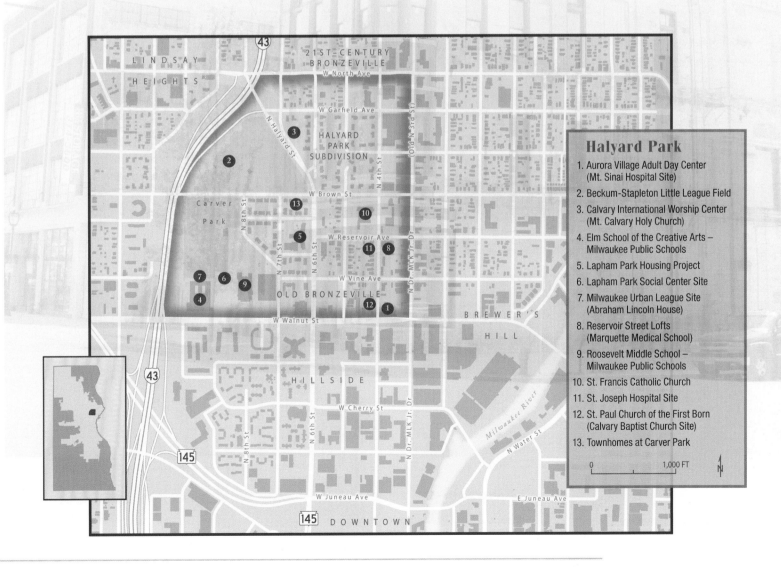

Halyard Park

1. Aurora Village Adult Day Center (Mt. Sinai Hospital Site)
2. Beckum-Stapleton Little League Field
3. Calvary International Worship Center (Mt. Calvary Holy Church)
4. Elm School of the Creative Arts – Milwaukee Public Schools
5. Lapham Park Housing Project
6. Lapham Park Social Center Site
7. Milwaukee Urban League Site (Abraham Lincoln House)
8. Reservoir Street Lofts (Marquette Medical School)
9. Roosevelt Middle School – Milwaukee Public Schools
10. St. Francis Catholic Church
11. St. Joseph Hospital Site
12. St. Paul Church of the First Born (Calvary Baptist Church Site)
13. Townhomes at Carver Park

0   1,000 FT

Homes and Hospitals

The area that became Halyard Park was settled when Milwaukee was still emerging from its pioneer period. The first houses went up in the 1850s, just a few years after the city was incorporated. Development thereafter was rapid, and the community was filled to capacity by 1890. Like most neighborhoods west of the Milwaukee River, the area was dominated by German immigrants who lived within walking distance of every necessity. During the week many walked to work in the industries that lined the nearby riverbanks—tanneries, mills, shoe factories, and the mammoth Schlitz brewery. They lightened their pay envelopes in the shops on Third Street, the North Side's downtown for generations. On Sunday mornings the area's German Catholics walked to Mass at St. Francis Church, a congregation established by the Capuchin order in 1870. (The present Gothic landmark on Fourth and Brown was built in 1877.) When Sunday services were over, Germans of all faiths, or no faith, walked to the Schlitz beer garden near Eighth and Walnut. It featured an amphitheater with seating for 5,000, a rustic lookout tower, entertainment ranging from light opera to diving horses and, of course, plenty of Milwaukee's finest beverage.

Schlitz Park was a metropolitan attraction, and there were other prominent institutions in the area. In 1883 a group of Franciscan nuns opened St. Joseph Hospital on Fourth and Reservoir, a four-story structure with room for fifty patients. It was so highly regarded that in 1898 a medical school opened across the street: the Wisconsin College of Physicians and Surgeons. That college became Marquette University's medical school, which became, in

■ *St. Francis Church, built in 1877, was filled with German Catholics on Sunday morning, while the Schlitz beer garden* (below) *attracted German families of all kinds in the afternoon.* (below right) *St. Joseph Hospital was a pillar of health care in the community for nearly fifty years.*

St. Francis Parish

Milwaukee Public Library

Wheaton Franciscan Healthcare

turn, the Medical College of Wisconsin. The original building has been converted to condominiums, but the school's name is still faintly visible high atop its east elevation.

By 1900 the area's German families were moving on to newer homes north and west of their original settlement, and the neighborhood they left behind was becoming one of the most diverse in Milwaukee's history. In addition to the remaining Germans, there were African Americans, Hungarians, Italians, Czechs, Slovaks, Poles, and a large concentration of Jews from eastern Europe. One of the new residents was a young girl named Goldie Mabowehz, whose family emigrated from what is now Belarus to an apartment on Sixth and Walnut in 1906. More than sixty years later, as Golda Meir, the ex-Milwaukeean rose to world fame as Israel's prime minister.

Local institutions evolved to meet the needs of the newcomers. In 1909 the city bought Schlitz Park and renamed it for Increase Lapham, a legendary pioneer scientist; the purchase gave this densely settled neighborhood some much-needed breathing space. In 1911 Milwaukee's Jewish leaders established Abraham Lincoln House on Ninth and Vine as a full-service Jewish community center. Three years later and practically next door, the legendary Lapham Park Social Center, a unit of the Milwaukee Public Schools, began to offer classes in the English language, civics, and other subjects with particular appeal to immigrants; generations of newcomers learned how to become Americans at Lapham Park. Many of their children attended Roosevelt Junior High School at Eighth and Walnut. Completed in 1926, Roosevelt was the first junior high in the city.

Health care received a boost as well. In 1903 the Jewish community opened Mount Sinai Hospital in a former German YMCA on Fourth and Walnut. Perennially pressed for space, Mount Sinai moved to larger quarters on nearby Twelfth Street in 1914, but its original building is still in use as the Aurora Village Adult Day Center. Two blocks north, St. Joseph Hospital was also running out of room. In 1930 the Franciscans moved their institution to Fifty-first and Chambers, in the Sherman Park neighborhood, but they maintained a clinic in the old location. That clinic, St. Joseph Annex, eventually became St. Michael Hospital on Villard Avenue.

By the time St. Joseph relocated to Sherman Park, its old neighborhood was well on its way to becoming the core of Milwaukee's African-American community. Like the early Germans, black families had started on the edge of Downtown and moved steadily north. Like the first European settlers, they established their own churches, businesses, and other institutions. Calvary Baptist Church, a

Jewish Museum Milwaukee

UW-Milwaukee Libraries

■ (center left)
Mount Sinai Hospital, founded in 1903, was established by the Jewish community to serve patients of all faiths.

■ *Halyard Park's Jewish immigrants included young Goldie Mabowehz, the future Golda Meir.*

■ *Halyard Park is the historic heart of Milwaukee's African-American community. Its major institutions included the Milwaukee Urban League, founded in 1919 and headquartered for many years in the former Abraham Lincoln House on Ninth and Vine. The League's programs ranged from violin lessons to amateur baseball teams.*

■ *The faithful of Calvary Baptist Church gathered outside their Fourth Street home in the 1920s.*

pillar of African-American Christianity since 1895, moved to Fourth Street near Walnut in 1923 and stayed for nearly fifty years. Although Third Street remained a popular shopping district, Walnut Street emerged as the commercial heart of Bronzeville, the name commonly used for the North Side's African-American community. Walnut Street was lined with grocery stores, offices, restaurants, and nightspots, including some that attracted national touring acts. Abraham Lincoln House, built to serve Jewish immigrants, became the home of the Milwaukee Urban League. Lapham Park remained Bronzeville's major recreational area, but the park was renamed in the 1960s for George Washington Carver, the celebrated African-American scientist and educator.

all photos on these two pages from the Wisconsin Black Historical Society

The neighborhood's appearance did not change dramatically until the mid-1960s, when the Interstate 43 expressway ripped through the North Side. A block-wide swath of houses west of Seventh Street was taken, disrupting the community's social networks. Walnut Street was widened at about the same time—a catastrophe for downtown Bronzeville's remaining businesses. In 1964

several blocks of dilapidated structures were torn down to make way for the Lapham Park housing project, which included 170 units of multi-family housing and an eight-story high-rise for senior citizens. As surface roads were rearranged on both sides of the freeway corridor, a new diagonal emerged between Brown and Garfield. It was named Halyard Street in 1965 to honor a distinguished

■ *The Community Drug Store was one of many businesses that made Walnut Street the center of Milwaukee's Bronzeville.*

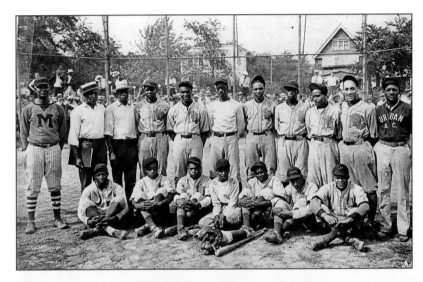

CALVARY BAPTIST CHURCH MILWAUKEE WIS. PHOTO BY WARREN

African-American couple: Wilbur and Ardie Halyard, who had come to Milwaukee from Beloit, Wisconsin, in 1923. Concerned about housing and social conditions in their new community, the Halyards organized Columbia Building and Loan in 1925—Milwaukee's first black-owned financial institution—and became leaders in the local chapter of the NAACP. Wilbur died in 1963, but Ardie remained a vital community force until her own death in 1989.

Some of the homes near Halyard Street, especially those occupied by their owners, remained in fine condition. As the years passed, however, many fell victim to neglect, fire, and age. Vacant lots multiplied, and the community's long-term prospects seemed doubtful indeed. In 1968 Mt. Calvary Holy Church, a congregation with deep Milwaukee roots, moved from Eleventh and Brown to Halyard Street. Mt. Calvary's was the first new building to grace the area in decades, but there was scant evidence that anyone would follow suit.

■ *Wilbur and Ardie Halyard, the community leaders for whom the neighborhood is named*

Wisconsin Black Historical Society

■ *By the 1970s blight posed a serious and growing threat to the community's future.*

Milwaukee Public Library

Milwaukee Public Library

A Spirit of Renewal

The pace of change quickened in 1972, when the blocks east of Mt. Calvary Church were slated for urban renewal. Delineated by the city and supported by federal funds, the Halyard Renewal Area consisted of five square blocks bordered by Halyard, Fourth, Brown, and Garfield. The plan was to demolish most houses, rehabilitate those that were still sound, relocate residents to better housing, and redevelop the cleared land. Work proceeded steadily for almost two years, but in 1974 the Nixon administration imposed a freeze on federal housing funds. The Halyard project was shut down with its activities only half-completed. One longtime resident compared the area in 1974 to "a mouth with half the teeth knocked out."

City officials didn't lose faith in the area's potential, and they worked to stir interest in redevelopment, but there were no solid plans until 1976, when the United Realty Group entered the picture. Organized only two years earlier, United Realty was the product of a merger of several black-owned real estate firms. The company's leaders sensed a market for high-quality new houses in the central city, and they proposed a subdivision of privately financed single-family homes in the old renewal area. The Redevelopment Authority accepted their proposal and agreed to complete acquisition and clearance of the houses that remained. Halyard Park was born.

There were doubters when the plans were announced. Some Milwaukeeans were sure that buyers, lenders, and the media would give Halyard Park a cool reception. There was also controversy. Some residents expressed a strong desire to remain in their homes, and some community activists questioned the wisdom of replacing high-density development with a low-density subdivision. But United Realty, under the leadership of Beechie Brooks, remained both confident and determined. In 1977 Brooks built the first new home in Halyard Park for his own family, and he acted as general contractor on several that followed. When a reporter asked if the project would work, he replied, "I wouldn't be spending $50,000 if I didn't think it really would."

Brooks was right. With the backing of public officials, local lenders, and the market, progress was steady. Year by year, Halyard Park was transformed from an area of rundown houses and weedy lots to a brand-new community. Redevelopment activity was constant through the 1980s, and by the decade's end Halyard Park was an accomplished fact.

The forty-three homes that emerged are as spacious and comfortable as any you'd find in a middle- to upper-income suburban subdivision. All are single-families, all have attached garages and at least three bedrooms, and nearly all have brick or stone trim. Most residents

HALYARD
URBAN RENEWAL AREA

ACQUISITION MAP

☐ PARCEL TO BE ACQUIRED

▦ PARCEL CURRENTLY EXCLUDED FROM ACQUISITION

2 BLOCK NUMBER

∞ PARCEL NUMBER

■■■ PROJECT BOUNDARY

| Neighborhood Development Program Milwaukee, Wisconsin | Map No. ND 401-3a |

Milwaukee Public Library

Milwaukee Journal Sentinel

chose to build ranch houses, but there are also colonials, split-levels, and homes influenced by Tudor and Spanish styles. "Luxury built-ins," as contractors call them, are common in Halyard Park. Nearly every home has a fireplace in the family room, and some residents added whirlpool baths, saunas, and even, in one residence, a heated indoor pool.

■ *Launched as an urban renewal project by the City of Milwaukee and completed as a private subdivision by United Realty, the Halyard Park development was an upscale addition to the central city.*

There were no celebrities among the first homeowners: no professional athletes, no well-known ministers, no prominent politicians. The residents, all of them African Americans, were instead a combination of teachers, small-business owners, skilled industrial workers, secretaries, supervisors, and health-care workers, most living in two-income households. Although there were no millionaires in the group, they could certainly have afforded homes on the edge of the city rather than in its heart. What attracted the first residents, and what has kept many of them there, is a rare combination of amenities. "Quiet" is the one that the people of Halyard Park invoke most often: quiet homes, quiet streets, and quiet neighbors. Carver Park offers ample green space within easy walking distance, and the community's location is enviable: barely a mile from Downtown, two blocks from the freeway, and close to major bus lines. In the view of many residents, Halyard Park combines the comfort of the suburbs with the convenience of the city. Not surprisingly, turnover has been extremely low. Many of the original builders have stayed through retirement, and the small number removed by death or relocation have been replaced by homeowners with the same backgrounds and expectations.

Halyard Park residents are understandably proud of their accomplishment. "I think it's wonderful progress," said one. "It gives us something to build up and make beautiful," said another. But Halyard Park is very much a part of Milwaukee's North Side. Many residents lived in the area before redevelopment occurred. They are active in local churches and community organizations. They patronize local businesses. And they see themselves as part of a growing trend in the inner city:

■ (below left)
A Halyard Park homeowner still cuts her own grass at the age of ninety-one.

■ (below right)
Martin Luther King Drive, formerly N. Third Street, remains the neighborhood's retail backbone.

■ (bottom right)
Halyard Park's ranch homes are suburban in everything but address.

all photos on these two pages by John Gurda

revitalization. Halyard Park is one building block, and an important one, in the ongoing transformation of the near North Side. To the east, the vintage homes of Brewer's Hill have made that neighborhood a hotbed of restoration activity and one of the city's most vibrant real estate markets. To the south, the energy of Brewer's Hill has spread across King Drive to remake the area that was once the home of both St. Joseph and Mount Sinai Hospitals—an area now considered part of Halyard Park. The older homes that survived the wrecking ball have been extensively restored, and there have been some high-end new developments: townhouse condominiums, gracious single-family homes, and even an art-filled hotel on Sixth Street. To the west, Carver Park is home field for the nationally known Beckum-Stapleton Little League, and in 2002 the public housing project on the other side of Brown Street was completely remade as a mixed-income community, with a blend of subsidized and market-rate units. To the north, city officials are planning a development called 21st-Century Bronzeville in the section of North Avenue between King Drive and Seventh Street. The intent is to create a cultural and entertainment district reminiscent of Walnut Street in its prime.

Halyard Park has clearly been the catalyst for some impressive activities in one of the oldest sections of Milwaukee. Beechie Brooks, the man most closely identified with the neighborhood, firmly believes that it contributes to the city as a whole. "The city's like a wagon wheel," he said, "and Downtown is the hub. If you let the spokes get too loose, the wheel falls apart and the wagon breaks down." Halyard Park is an important spoke, and it will help keep Milwaukee rolling into the far-distant future.

■ (below)
The lower level of the Lapham Park senior housing complex preserves memories of nearby Bronzeville.

■ (left)
A handful of Victorian "painted ladies" remain from the neighborhood's earliest days.

■ (bottom)
The Townhomes at Carver Park

■ (right)
St. Francis Church remains a community anchor, particularly for Milwaukee's Puerto Rican Catholics.

John Gurda

Christopher McIntyre

Christopher McIntyre

■ *Just as it was during its days as historic Third Street, King Drive is a commercial hub for Milwaukee's North Side, offering everything from haircuts to stemware.*

John Gurda

John Gurda

John Gurda

Christopher McIntyre

Christopher McIntyre

RIVERWEST

M·I·L·W·A·U·K·E·E

Riverwest

From its headwaters in Fond du Lac County, the Milwaukee River meanders slowly, past farms and through villages, to the city that was named for it. The river turns abruptly east as soon as it enters Milwaukee, at Lincoln Park, and inscribes a graceful arc on the landscape until North Avenue, where it bends west again and descends to the lake. Within this easternmost bend, defined neatly by Holton Street, lies the neighborhood called Riverwest. Like the river, it is a venerable part of Milwaukee and, like the river, it is a scene of both constant change and impressive continuity.

Riverwest

1. Charles Whitnall Home
2. COA Youth and Family Center
3. Friends Meeting House
4. Fuel Café
5. Holton Youth & Family Center
6. Jerusalem Lutheran Church
7. Kadish Park Amphitheater
8. Kellner's Greenhouses
9. Lakefront Brewery
10. North Avenue Dam & Millrace Site
11. Octagon House
12. Outpost Natural Foods
13. Peace Action Center
14. Polish Falcons Bowling Alley
15. Riverwest Co-Op
16. Snail's Crossing Park
17. St. Casimir Catholic Church –
    Our Lady of Divine Providence Parish
18. St. Mary of Częstochowa Catholic Church –
    Our Lady of Divine Providence Parish
19. T'ai Chi Ch'uan Center
20. Woodland Pattern Book Center

0   2,000 FT

Beginning on the River

It was the river that brought the first non-native settlers to the neighborhood. In about 1851 John J. Orton, an enterprising lawyer from New York State, built a dam just south of today's Capitol Drive. The channel below was soon lined with mills that produced paper, flour, and linseed oil. To house the workers, Orton established the small village of Humboldt on the high ground west of the dam.

Humboldt's prosperity was short-lived, as repeated flooding eventually forced the mills out of business. By the 1870s the river was attracting Milwaukeeans who came to the area for recreation rather than work. Another dam, this one at North Avenue, created a long, narrow flowage that was lined with swimming schools, rowing clubs, beer gardens, amusement parks, and resorts. Thousands of urbanites took a steam launch from the dam to the pleasure spots every summer weekend, paying fifteen cents for a round trip.

Some visitors stayed longer. As the resorts grew in popularity, a number of affluent Germans bought land on the west bank and built imposing summer homes. The Uihleins, Meineckes, Puelichers, Kerns, and other families transformed old Humboldt from an industrial village to a warm-weather gold coast. Kern Park, once the estate of the flour-milling Kern family, is a lasting reminder of Riverwest's days as a summer colony.

There was also a scattering of year-round residents. Frank Whitnall built ten

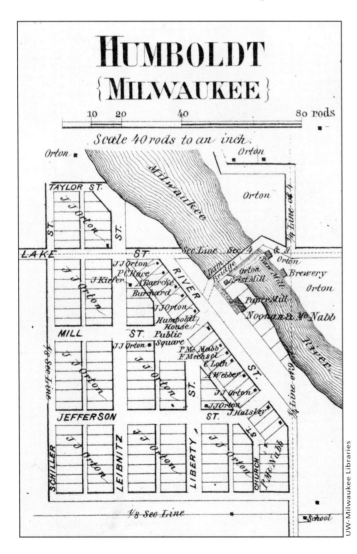

UW-Milwaukee Libraries

Milwaukee Public Library

Milwaukee County Historical Society

greenhouses behind his home near Humboldt and Locust and earned a reputation as one of Milwaukee's finest florists. Frank's son Charles, a Socialist and life-long area resident, followed him into the plant business and went on to a distinguished career as Milwaukee's foremost urban planner and chief architect of its celebrated park system. The benevolent spirit of Charlie Whitnall still hovers over the green river corridor he knew so well as a child.

Large-scale urban development began in the 1880s, and its character was strongly influenced by the neighborhood's geographic position. Settlement north of Downtown had always followed two fairly distinct corridors. One stream of settlers, heavily German, flowed along Third Street into what would become the North Side. The other stream, multi-ethnic in character, curved up the East Side between the lake and the river. Today's Riverwest lies squarely between the two channels, and in the 1880s they converged. For well over a century since that time, the neighborhood's character has been determined by the mingling of currents from the North and East Sides. It might be said, in fact, that Riverwest is the east side of the North Side and the north side of the East Side.

The North Side stream—the Third Street German channel—was first to spill over into Riverwest. Dozens of substantial Victorian homes went up near the North Avenue water reservoir after 1880. Many of the urban pioneers were relatively affluent (several Booth Street residents were listed on the social register), but Germans of more modest means were in the majority. One such group established Jerusalem Lutheran Church on the corner of Holton and Chambers in 1888. It was the neighborhood's first church and the nucleus of a small Teutonic settlement.

Germans of all classes were quickly outnumbered by Poles moving up from the East Side. Although Milwaukee's South Side is the home of the city's best-known *Polonia* (Polish-American community), there have been Poles on the north side of the Menomonee Valley for nearly as long. In the 1860s immigrants from the Kaszuby region on Poland's

Baltic seacoast began to settle the riverbank north of Brady Street. Attracted by riverfront industries, the "Kaszubs" created one of the most densely populated neighborhoods in Milwaukee. In 1871 they established St. Hedwig's Church—the city's second Polish congregation, after St. Stanislaus—and the East Side *Polonia* developed literally in the shadow of its steeple.

In the 1880s, as the Brady Street settlement outgrew its original borders, hundreds of Polish families crossed the

Milwaukee County Historical Society

■ *Charles B. Whitnall, Milwaukee's godfather of green and a lifelong Riverwest resident*

■ *Whitnall's wagons distributed nursery stock throughout the Milwaukee area.*

Pieter Godfrey

Milwaukee Public Library

Archdiocese of Milwaukee

Milwaukee Public Library

■ (upper left)
The establishment of St. Casimir's Church in 1893 represented "the birth of a neighborhood," as Polish families made Riverwest their own.

■ (upper right)
St. Mary of Czestochowa grade school's class of 1930

■ (above)
Bremen Street north of Center was a typical Riverwest block: dense, unpretentious, and definitely cozy.

Humboldt Avenue bridge and established a new community west of the river. With a characteristic passion for home ownership, they covered block after block with modest frame houses, and in 1893 they established a church of their own: St. Casimir's. Tom Tolan, Riverwest's historian, characterized that event as nothing less than "the birth of a neighborhood." St. Casimir's provided a focal point, a touchstone of identity for a majority of the community's residents. Within two years the congregation had more members than St. Hedwig's, its mother church. The western edge of the neighborhood remained heavily German, but Riverwest's *Polonia* continued to grow. By 1907 a second church was required, and St. Mary of Czestochowa was established on Burleigh Street.

Whatever their origins, residents had little reason to leave the neighborhood. Nearby tanneries and factories provided jobs. Church and school, family and friends were within easy walking distance. (In 1923 St. Casimir's School had over 1,300 students.) The river provided abundant recreational opportunities, including a swimming beach in Gordon Park and ice-skating during the winter months. The neighborhood was dotted with bakeries and butcher shops, corner stores and corner taverns. Life revolved in a close, comfortable circle for generations, a circle reinforced by the density of the neighborhood. The typical Riverwest dwelling, particularly south of Locust Street, was a small frame home on a small lot, but many homeowners practiced what scholars have labeled "additive architecture." They often began with a single-story cottage and then, as finances permitted, raised the house with heavy jacks and built a basement apartment beneath it—the origin of the "Polish flat." Other residents moved their original homes to the rear of their lots and built larger ones in front. Still others tacked on storefronts to accommodate businesses they had begun in their living quarters. The cumulative result was more people in less space than was typical in adjacent sections of the East and North Sides.

Milwaukee County Parks Department

■ *Gordon Park had its own beach and bathhouse on the river near the Locust Street bridge*

■ *Winter activities at Gordon included "icycle" races on the frozen river and ski-jumping from the bluff above.*

Milwaukee Public Schools Recreation Division

Milwaukee Public Schools Recreation Division

New Streams

This compact neighborhood was a cultural crossroads from the beginning, and it became even more so as the years passed. As in the earliest years, new residents arrived from both the south and the west. Italian families, most of them Sicilian, had settled in the Third Ward in the 1890s. Pushing steadily northward, they reached the old Brady Street Polonia in the Teens and then crossed the river in the late 1920s, just as the Poles had done forty years earlier. They were joined after World War II by Puerto Rican families who had originally settled north of St. John's Cathedral, on the edge of Downtown.

When urban renewal claimed that area in the 1950s and '60s, the Puerto Ricans crossed the Holton Street viaduct into Riverwest. A broader movement reprised the original German settlement. African Americans had been a presence in Milwaukee since pioneer days, eventually clustering on the western side of Downtown. As their population swelled in the post-World War II years, African-American families moved up the Third Street corridor, just as the original Germans had, and then, still following in the Germans' footsteps, crossed Holton Street into Riverwest in the 1950s and '60s.

A less predictable influx came from the east in the 1970s. It consisted largely of

courtesy Marian Aviles

■ *The south end of Holton Street became an important center of Puerto Rican settlement.*

■ *A phalanx of duplexes lines Holton Street on the neighborhood's western border.*

young people, most of them single, most of them white, many of them associated in some way with the University of Wisconsin-Milwaukee. The East Side was already the established center of Milwaukee's counterculture, especially the area around Brady Street. High rents, congested streets, and natural expansion eventually pushed the young people across the river, where they found a neighborhood more cohesive, more affordable, and more laid-back than the one they had left. They tended to use Riverwest as a sort of dormitory community at first, commuting back to the East Side for school, work, and social life. In time, however, they

established institutions of their own on the west side of the river.

Some transplants saw the community as an outpost of a new social and political order, a place to put their principles into practice. Perhaps the most significant fruit of their efforts was ESHAC, which began as the East Side Housing Action Committee in 1972 and soon moved across the river to become an engine of activism. It was ESHAC and its allies who gave the neighborhood its name, and it was they who saved Locust Street. In the 1970s transportation engineers wanted to transform Locust from a two-lane urban corridor lined with homes and businesses into a four-lane straightaway lined with not much at all. They prevailed west of Holton, but the engineers met fierce resistance to the east. The activists fought a successful holding action, and the result is the neighborhood-oriented, neighborhood-serving street that provides a home for some of the community's most important institutions, including arts-related enterprises. Many of the neighborhood's traditional small businesses had closed in the postwar decades, and artists moving from the East Side found that Riverwest's vacant storefronts made ideal gallery and studio spaces.

Whether they were artists, activists, or simply bystanders, the newcomers added a distinctive layer to the already rich tapestry of neighborhood life. They also contributed a

John Gurda

great deal to the larger Milwaukee community. Riverwest was the birthplace or is still the home of such metropolitan mainstays as Woodland Pattern Book Center, Outpost Natural Foods Cooperative, the Peace Action Center, the Milwaukee River Greenway, and Lakefront Brewery, whose signature beer is Riverwest Stein, one of the best craft brews in town.

T'ai Chi and Chai Tea

What is remarkable about Riverwest is that every group who ever settled in the neighborhood is still there—not the original residents, of course, but their physical or spiritual descendants. You will find a generous scattering of Polish and German families whose ancestors came on the first wave. You will find Italians whose families arrived a generation later. You will find Puerto Ricans in significant numbers. In fact, St. Casimir and St. Mary of Czestochowa Churches have merged to form a new parish named Our Lady of Divine Providence, the patroness of San Juan, Puerto Rico. You will find African Americans, who have created their own distinctive blend of institutions, and you will also find children, and now grandchildren, of the counterculture. Riverwest resembles the United Nations; not everyone eats together, but everyone has a place at the table.

There is not much question that Riverwest is the most diverse neighborhood in Milwaukee,

and has been for decades. It is a classic crossroads community, where a multitude of paths converge and numerous currents mingle. Its diversity is something you can see and touch and hear and taste. In some blocks, you feel as if you're in the heart of the inner city. Others have a prim, almost-suburban quality. In still others, especially the unique river's-edge enclave east of Humboldt, the atmosphere is practically rural. In the neighborhood's newest green space, Kadish Park, you can watch live music and theater on a hillside with commanding views of Downtown and the East Side.

An edgy sort of energy pervades the neighborhood. It's hard for Riverwest to sit still. The cast of characters, like the roster of businesses, is constantly changing, but the greater constant is a proud urbanism, an openness to currents outside the mainstream. Where else would you find a hookah lounge next to a yoga studio next to the most eclectic video store in town and down the street from a brew pub and a storefront church? Where else would you encounter so many walking canvases of body art? With the possible exception of the Milwaukee Bucks locker room, Riverwest probably has more tattoos per square inch of skin than anywhere else in town—and more wild gardens per square foot of yard. Cuisines range from Vietnamese to Italian to African to Caribbean to the peanut-butter-apple-and-bacon sandwiches at Fuel Café. If you compiled a list of every tune on

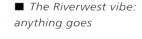
The Riverwest vibe: anything goes

John Ruebartsch

every jukebox and turntable in Riverwest's taverns, it would likely be the most cosmopolitan in the city, perhaps in the entire state.

Some Riverwest residents have PhDs and others have GEDs. Some are cashing pension checks and others are nursing newborns. The neighborhood has Buddhists and Baptists, activists and pacifists, T'ai Chi and chai tea, hipsters and the homeless, echoes of the Old World and stirrings of the New Age. The only thing it might have a shortage of is Republicans—and you could probably find a few of those if you looked hard enough.

Riverwest, in short, is a continuing urban experiment and an eloquent urban statement. And it is the river. Within the eastward-bending bow defined by Holton Street lies a unique human community, one the river serves as both border and metaphor. Like the river, the neighborhood has changed over the decades but, like the river, it keeps on rolling, constantly fed by currents from the world around it and creating from those currents something ever ancient and always new.

■ (right)
The Beerline Trail links Riverwest with the Milwaukee River.

■ (below)
Music on Center Street

■ (below right)
The octagon house on Gordon Place is a rare survivor from the 1850s.

Jessica Lothman

John Ruebartsch

John Ruebartsch

■ Co-ops, bookstores, and restaurants add to Riverwest's cultural vibrancy.

■ The Rowing Club dock provides access to the urban river.

John Ruebartsch

John Ruebartsch

Christopher Winters

Christopher Winters

■ Filled to the brim with cutting-edge condos, Riverwest's south end presents a new face to the morning sun.

Christopher Winters

217

■ (top row)
From the Milwaukee River Greenway to green ballfields to well-stocked greenhouses, Riverwest keeps close ties with the natural world.

■ (right)
The Riverwest Artist Association organizes the Art Cart Race as part of "Center Street Daze" every year.

Jessica Lothman

■ *The "marsupial bridge" is suspended from the Holton Street viaduct.*

John Ruebartsch

Denny Rauen

Jessica Lothman

■ (top)
Riverwest has its own community-produced radio station.

■ (above)
Creating street art on Burleigh was a bonus checkpoint during the annual Riverwest 24 bike race.

■ *Audiences take in live theater—and a gorgeous view of Downtown—on a midsummer evening in Kadish Park.*

HARAMBEE

MILWAUKEE

Harambee

"Harambee" is the Swahili word for "pulling together." It is also the name of a historic neighborhood that lies near the heart of Milwaukee's North Side. Draped across a steep ridge left by the last glacier, Harambee enjoys panoramic views of Downtown and preserves within its borders an impressive panorama of the city's past. The neighborhood stretches from North Avenue to Capitol Drive, a distance of two miles, and its homes, churches, and businesses span nearly six decades of development, from the 1870s through the 1920s. But the past is most important as a highly distinctive vessel for the present. Harambee is the home of nearly 15,000 Milwaukeeans, and its name signifies two things: the African heritage of most residents, and a spirit of "pulling together" that local leaders have been nurturing since the 1970s.

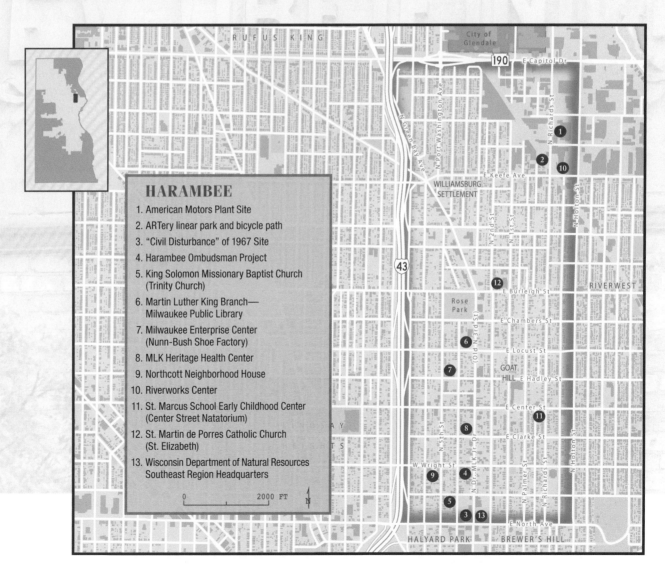

HARAMBEE

1. American Motors Plant Site
2. ARTery linear park and bicycle path
3. "Civil Disturbance" of 1967 Site
4. Harambee Ombudsman Project
5. King Solomon Missionary Baptist Church (Trinity Church)
6. Martin Luther King Branch—Milwaukee Public Library
7. Milwaukee Enterprise Center (Nunn-Bush Shoe Factory)
8. MLK Heritage Health Center
9. Northcott Neighborhood House
10. Riverworks Center
11. St. Marcus School Early Childhood Center (Center Street Natatorium)
12. St. Martin de Porres Catholic Church (St. Elizabeth)
13. Wisconsin Department of Natural Resources Southeast Region Headquarters

Beginning with Germans

The Williamsburg settlement's early landmarks included a genuine Dutch windmill. Frank Seemann's grocery store (lower) was a more traditional Green Bay Avenue business.

In the mid-1800s, when memories of the frontier were still fresh in Milwaukee, the area that became Harambee was a farming district dominated by immigrants from Germany. Most of them lived so far beyond the city limits—North Avenue at the time—that they developed their own crossroads trading center at the triangle formed by Green Bay Avenue, Port Washington Road, and Keefe Avenue. The little settlement was called Williamsburg, or Wilhelmsburg, and at its peak boasted a flour mill, greenhouses, feed stores, harness shops, blacksmiths, bakeries, and its own post office. Williamsburg even had a working windmill built by the Grootemaats, a family that was not *Deutsch* but Dutch.

As Milwaukee grew, the city limits moved steadily north, reaching Center Street in 1855 and Burleigh Street a year later, but the future Harambee neighborhood remained essentially rural. In 1866 a German shooting society bought several acres of land at Third and Burleigh for use as a rifle range. Schuetzen (Shooter's) Park doubled as a beer garden, complete with dance hall, bowling alley, and saloon. It became a popular weekend retreat for city residents who craved the quiet of the countryside—and a good glass of beer.

In the 1870s that quiet countryside began to disappear. Milwaukee was adding residents at the rate of nearly 400 each month, and city-dwellers were covering the old farming district above North Avenue with new homes. Urban settlement continued through the end of the century, edging up the glacial ridge like a rising tide. In 1891 Williamsburg, by then a suburban community of blue-collar workers, became part of Milwaukee. In the same decade Pabst Brewing purchased Schuetzen Park and turned it into an amusement park. The beer garden remained, but the rifle range was replaced by a roller coaster, a miniature railroad, a carousel, and a funhouse called Katzenjammer Castle. Pabst Park soon had plenty of customers from the surrounding area. By 1900 the wave of settlement had reached the crest of the ridge, near Burleigh, and was beginning to spill down the other side east of old Williamsburg.

Like the farmers they replaced, the newcomers were overwhelmingly German. Third Street became their primary "downtown," and the Williamsburg section of Green Bay Avenue blossomed as its northerly extension. The adjoining residential areas were dotted

with German saloons, German stores, and dozens of German churches: Catholic, Methodist, Episcopal, Adventist, Evangelical, and several varieties of Lutheran. Most of the congregations served blue-collar families whose breadwinners walked or took the streetcar to skilled jobs in Milwaukee's booming factory districts. Some of them didn't have far to walk. In 1915 the Nunn-Bush Shoe Company built a large factory in the heart of the neighborhood at Fifth and Hadley, a facility that would later house the Milwaukee Enterprise Center.

There was one notable exception to the prevailing blue-collar pattern. First, Second, and Palmer Streets became the North Side German community's gold coast, particularly between North Avenue and Center Street. The thoroughfares were lined with the imposing homes of merchants, manufacturers, and professionals, all of whom built monuments to their own success. Perhaps the best-known resident of First Street was Edward Schuster, who founded what was for decades Milwaukee's largest department store chain. Between 1890 and 1910, Schuster and his neighbors built exuberant Queen Annes, symmetrical Colonial Revivals, and elegant variations on medieval and Renaissance themes. Elaborate woodwork, stained-glass windows, and ornate fireplaces were common features, and a few homes had

Milwaukee County Parks Department

■ *With roots in a Civil War-era shooting park, the Pabst Park beer garden drew patrons from throughout Milwaukee. Its attractions included a full-sized wooden roller coaster.*

Milwaukee County Historical Society

223

■ *First Street developed as the North Side's gold coast. Wealthy residents lined the blocks from North to Center with fine homes, and the Millioki Club on Wright Street (right) became their social center.*

carriage houses larger than the single-family residences on nearby streets. While other Germans socialized at neighborhood saloons, the wealthy residents organized the Millioki Club and built a lavish clubhouse at First and Wright. The club is long gone, but the surviving homes are so exceptional that in 1984 the First Street corridor was added to the National Register of Historic Places.

While members of the Millioki Club sipped their champagne, the tide of home-seekers continued to surge north, washing down the north side of the ridge to Keefe Avenue before 1910 and finally reaching Capitol Drive in the 1920s. The sheer size of the neighborhood, and the six decades it took to develop completely, make Harambee a case study of architectural change. The southern blocks are covered with homes from the late 1800s—Victorian houses with ornamental "gingerbread," single-family cottages, and a scattering of Cream City brick structures. The northern section, above Keefe Avenue, is dominated by bungalows, Milwaukee's signature house type in the 1920s. In between are towering duplexes and tidy single-families from the 1900-1920 period. All varieties are present, in varying states of

■ *Green Bay Avenue remained a busy retail corridor as old Williamsburg was absorbed by the city.*

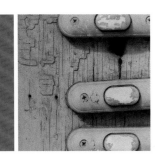

repair. The neat chronological order is broken by Williamsburg, which remains an island of older homes and storefronts in the northwest corner of the neighborhood.

A very different kind of development transformed the northeast corner of what is now Harambee. Drawn by the district's open land, access to workers, and superb rail service, manufacturers turned the blocks north of Keefe Avenue into a large-scale industrial district. They produced everything from shoes to pianos and from elevators to wooden toys, but the largest factory by far was the Seaman auto body plant. Built in stages between 1920 and 1928, the Richards Street plant contained more than 1,000,000 square feet of floor space and employed 6,500 workers at its peak in 1926. Seaman workers supplied all the auto bodies for Nash Motors of Kenosha (which later became American Motors), and many of them lived in the immediate neighborhood.

There was a new recreational amenity near the center of the community, but its setting was familiar. The advent of Prohibition brought Pabst Park's days as a beer garden to an end. In 1921, two years after Milwaukee's favorite beverage was declared illegal, Pabst Brewing sold its park to Milwaukee County, and county officials renamed it for James Garfield, twentieth president of the United States. One of the most popular attractions in Garfield (now Rose) Park was a pavilion that offered open-air dancing during the summer months.

The surrounding neighborhood remained heavily German through the 1920s, but there were clear signs of ethnic change. Many of the new residents in the northern sections were Polish and Italian families who had moved across Holton Street from the Riverwest neighborhood. Both groups looked back to roots on the Lower East Side. In the southern sections, scores of German families moved out to newer neighborhoods, and they were succeeded by a wide variety of ethnic groups. Puerto Rican families moved from the Lower East Side to the vicinity of Holton Street and North Avenue, particularly after World War II, but the African-American influence has been even more profound. The first

black families arrived in the 1930s, buying or renting homes in the blocks above North Avenue, and their numbers swelled in the decades that followed.

The African-American migration was, in many respects, a twentieth-century reprise of the original German settlement. Moving from the same blocks north of Downtown and motivated by the same desire for better housing, African Americans followed the same path up the Third Street corridor as the Schmidts and Schneiders of the previous century. They established new spiritual homes in the old churches, opened new businesses in the old storefronts, and instilled

■ *The Seaman body plant (later American Motors) on Richards Street was the neighborhood's largest industry, employing 6,500 workers at its peak.*

■ *(lower) There were opportunities for play as well, including the open-air dancing pavilion at Garfield (now Rose) Park.*

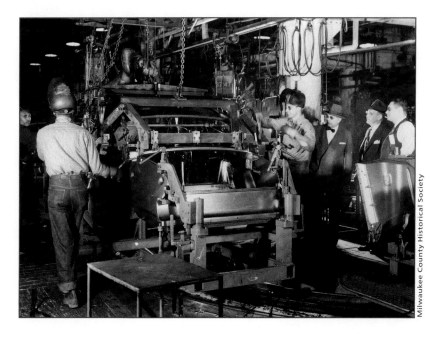

■ *The Harambee neighborhood emerged as a stronghold of African-American culture even before World War II.*
(counterclockwise from right)
The group's presence was apparent in the YMCA on North Avenue, in local schools, in athletic programs at Garfield (Rose) Park, and in the widespread popularity of Juneteenth Day, a celebration of freedom that the neighborhood first hosted in 1972.

Milwaukee Public Library

Milwaukee Public Library

Milwaukee County Parks Department

a new culture in the old neighborhood. They also continued to make history, taking an active part in the civil rights struggles of the 1960s and weathering the riot of 1967, a tragic spasm of violence that began on the corner of Third and North. There was reason for celebration as well. Juneteenth Day, which commemorates the abolition of slavery, was observed in the neighborhood, on Third Street, for the first time in 1972. It became the black community's largest continuing celebration, and Harambee is Juneteenth Day's permanent home. Third Street itself, the neighborhood's dominant artery since pioneer days, received a new name that better reflected its new culture. In 1985, at the request of local residents, the street was rechristened to honor the memory of an American hero, Dr. Martin Luther King, Jr.

Building Community

Even the most casual visitor could not help but notice the blend of old and new that marks the Harambee neighborhood today. The words "Dreieinigkeits Kirche"—German for "Trinity Church"—are carved in stone above the entrance to a Fourth Street landmark that is now King Solomon Missionary Baptist Church. The old public natatorium crowning the glacial ridge at Center Street has become St. Marcus School's Early Childhood Center. The regional office of the Wisconsin Department of Natural Resources rises behind the façade of an old neighborhood bank. Barbecue barrels sit on Victorian front porches in Harambee, and long-tenured taverns play music that an earlier generation of residents wouldn't recognize. It is this layering of past and present, this blending of stories, that gives American cities such visual and cultural vitality.

Not every landmark from Harambee's earlier years has survived to serve a new purpose. Grass-covered vacant lots mark the ghosts of old homes, and a scattering of derelict buildings underlines the challenges facing a historic neighborhood with above-average maintenance needs and below-average incomes. Harambee's economic struggles are due in part to the loss of manufacturing jobs in the neighboring industrial district. The mammoth Seaman body plant on Richards Street was purchased in 1936 by Nash Motors, which became part of American Motors in 1954. Workers continued to stamp out bodies for Ramblers and other AMC vehicles until the plant was shut down for good in 1988. The loss of American Motors was the largest in a round of closings that affected the entire area.

The twenty-first century has so far been more positive for Harambee than the late twentieth. The Riverworks Center initiative has brought new employers into the industrial district north of Keefe Avenue. A number of fine old homes in the First Street historic district have been restored to their original glory, leading some residents to describe Harambee's southern blocks as "the new Brewer's Hill." As older homes are rescued, dozens of new houses have gone up in the strip between King Drive and Interstate 43. Elsewhere in the neighborhood, it is not unusual to see a blighted house on one end of a block and smell new drywall and fresh paint on the other. King Drive has experienced a renaissance, both residential and retail, and community gardens have literally sprouted at several locations in the neighborhood.

■ *Repurposed landmarks abound in Harambee, including an old bank that now houses the regional headquarters of the Wisconsin Department of Natural Resources.*

Kate Hawley

Milwaukee Journal Sentinel

■ *Aurora Weier turned the vacant Center Street natatorium into a well-used educational center for local youngsters.*

A number of home-grown organizations have worked to build on that momentum, including one that gave the community its name. In 1969, when the neighborhood was rapidly integrating, the pastors of St. Elizabeth's Church, an old German Catholic congregation on Second and Burleigh, decided to close their parish school. St. Elizabeth's was soon renamed for St. Martin de Porres, the son of a slave, and its old elementary classrooms were reopened as a nonsectarian community school whose name, Harambee, was borrowed from the Swahili language of eastern Africa. The name was in turn adopted for a project launched by the University of Wisconsin Extension in 1974. The Extension staff had offered a course on political awareness co-taught by Ben Johnson, the area's alderman, at the Martin Luther King Library on Locust Street. On one memorable evening, a group of neighbors showed up to seek their alderman's help. The tall grass on Goat Hill, a steep bluff at First and Hadley, had become a breeding ground for juvenile crime. Johnson, after cutting through several layers of red tape, had the grass cut, and the complaints stopped.

The episode proved that local residents were willing to work together on local problems, and the UW-Extension staff built a grassroots program around that willingness, using the ombudsman approach pioneered in Sweden. Outreach workers identified block leaders who became the voices of their neighbors, monitoring complaints and referring problems to the ombudsmen in the UW-Extension office. The ombudsmen then worked with the appropriate agencies until a problem was solved. And so

the Harambee Ombudsman Project was born, probably the only organization in America whose name combined Swedish and Swahili words. Before long the block-work approach had carried the Harambee name to every corner of the neighborhood.

The Ombudsman Project eventually shifted its focus to other social services, and newer organizations continued the effort to promote pride and stability. In 1977 Panamanian-born activist Aurora Weier opened an educational center for Latino children and soon moved it to the Center Street natatorium. When Weier was murdered by a rival in 1985, the center was named for her. It evolved into a well-regarded Head Start program and then the early-childhood campus of St. Marcus School. In 1982 Garfield Park was renamed in honor of Clinton Rose, the area's long-time county supervisor, and the park's old pavilion was replaced by a state-of-the-art senior center. Other bulwarks of community include Northcott Neighborhood House (broad-based social services), the MLK Heritage Health Center, and the Martin Luther King branch of the Milwaukee Public Library.

Harambee's oldest grassroots organization is the Central North Community Council, an all-volunteer group formed in 1960. Until his death in 2006, the Council's perennial president was Frank Zeidler, mayor of Milwaukee from 1948 to 1960 and a neighborhood resident since 1946. The area's churches have been building community for an even longer time. There are dozens of them in Harambee, representing a broad cross-section of the Christian denominations. A few congregations still gather in their original homes, others have recycled older buildings, and still others have built new houses of worship. Every church is a bulwark of faith for its members and an anchor of stability for the surrounding community.

Whether sacred or secular, Harambee has an abundance of institutions that are striving to meet the area's human needs and build on its human strengths. Local leaders point to a number of built-in neighborhood advantages: a distinctive blend of fine old homes, a prime location on the edge of Downtown, a rolling landscape like few others in the city, an eclectic mix of businesses, and positive momentum. "It's building up," said one long-time homeowner. "There's been a lot of change, and lately for the better." For many residents, "Harambee" is both a name and a spirit. No one expects the area's long-term problems to disappear quickly, but hope keeps company with realism in this uniquely historic neighborhood.

■ (center left)
Frank Zeidler, Milwaukee's mayor from 1948 to 1960, lived with his family on Second Street near Locust from 1946 to his death in 2006.

■ (left)
St. Martin de Porres Church, formerly St. Elizabeth's, remains a community anchor.

■ (below left)
King Drive looking south from Burleigh Street

Milwaukee Journal Sentinel

John Gurda

John Gurda

Kate Hawley

■ (right)
Growing Power is a newer presence on King Drive.

■ (opposite page top)
The ARTery bike and walking path makes use of a reclaimed rail corridor.

■ (opposite page middle)
The Roselette Dancers have been representing the Clinton Rose Senior Center for years. Their average age is seventy-five.

■ (below)
Martin Luther King School's paint scheme incorporates African motifs.

■ (lower panorama)
Harambee is close to Downtown and yet a world of its own. The view is from atop the Holton Terrace senior apartments

John Gurda

Kate Hawley

John Gurda

Kate Hawley

John Gurda

LINDSAY HEIGHTS
WALNUT WAY
M·I·L·W·A·U·K·E·E

Lindsay Heights

Lindsay Heights has always been a central square in the patchwork quilt of Milwaukee neighborhoods. As one of the oldest squares, it has been woven of several threads—first German, then Jewish, finally African-American—and it has carried several names, including the Seventh Ward and North Division before Lindsay Heights prevailed. The neighborhood has also suffered more wear than most squares in the urban quilt, the result of highway construction and poverty as well as age. Since the 1950s Lindsay Heights has lost both people and buildings, but it never lost hope. In recent years the neighborhood has spawned some of the most impressive redevelopment efforts in the city, as residents old and new work to restore the community's fabric.

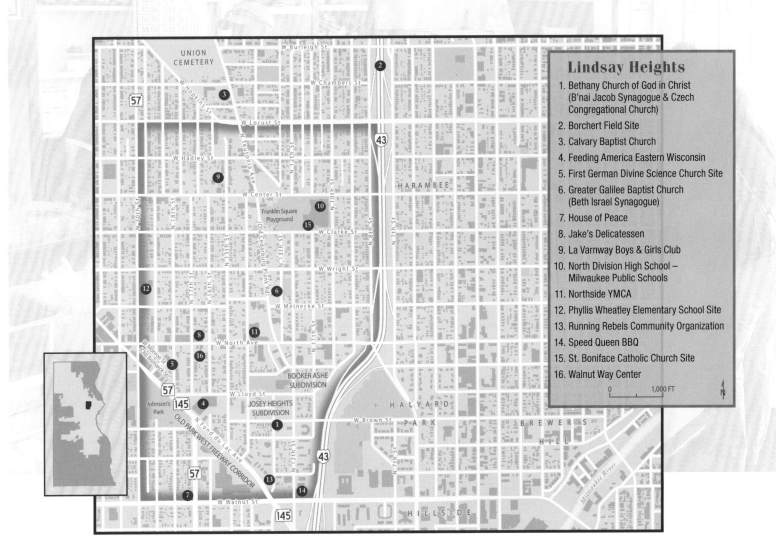

Lindsay Heights

1. Bethany Church of God in Christ (B'nai Jacob Synagogue & Czech Congregational Church)
2. Borchert Field Site
3. Calvary Baptist Church
4. Feeding America Eastern Wisconsin
5. First German Divine Science Church Site
6. Greater Galilee Baptist Church (Beth Israel Synagogue)
7. House of Peace
8. Jake's Delicatessen
9. La Varnway Boys & Girls Club
10. North Division High School – Milwaukee Public Schools
11. Northside YMCA
12. Phyllis Wheatley Elementary School Site
13. Running Rebels Community Organization
14. Speed Queen BBQ
15. St. Boniface Catholic Church Site
16. Walnut Way Center

0   1,000 FT

The Teutons of Teutonia Avenue

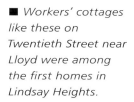

■ *Workers' cottages like these on Twentieth Street near Lloyd were among the first homes in Lindsay Heights.*

■ *(bottom) Built in 1907, North Division High School quickly filled to capacity, enrolling more than 1,600 students in 1927.*

It was German immigrants and their children who built the first houses in Lindsay Heights. Germans had been a presence in Milwaukee since the late 1830s, several years before the hopeful little village became a city in 1846, and they typically settled on the west side of the Milwaukee River. The group migrated north and west from that foothold, reaching the Lindsay Heights area in the 1870s. Their primary path outward was an old plank road to Cedarburg that was soon renamed Teutonia Avenue—an apt choice for an area so saturated with Teutonic families. They lined block after block with frame houses—first single-story cottages and then the towering two-story duplexes that are still the neighborhood's signature house type. By 1910 settlement was nearly complete. The area's teenagers attended North Division High School, the city's fourth secondary school, which was completed in 1907. The red brick building on Center Street was the community's dominant landmark for nearly seventy years.

The North Side was the most German section of America's most German city at the turn of the twentieth century, and the landscape of Lindsay Heights reflected the prevailing culture. Teutonia Avenue, the neighborhood's main street, was lined with German shops. Monroe Street was named Bismarck, for the "Iron Chancellor" who had united Germany. The Bahn Frei (Independent Way) Turner Hall at 1122 North Avenue provided a place for neighborhood residents to socialize and practice gymnastics. More than a dozen churches offered services in German, including a little building on Eighteenth and Monroe whose cornerstone still reads *Erste Deutsche Gotliche Wissenschafts Kirche* (First German Divine Science Church). Milwaukee's favorite beverage was always in ample supply, and brewery-run saloons provided most of the suds. At least three pre-Prohibition "tied houses" survive in the area, including one on Twelfth and Chambers whose antique Pabst logo is still intact.

The German community's most permanent legacy turned out to be a burial ground. Union Cemetery, between Teutonia and Twentieth near the neighborhood's northern border, was established in the Civil War years by a "union" of three German Lutheran churches. It contains some of Milwaukee's finest examples of the stonecarver's art—angels, wreaths, and effigies of the deceased—as well as dozens of monuments that bear the inscription *Ruhe Sanft,* or "Rest in Peace." Among those resting in Union Cemetery are scores of veterans of the Civil War.

The majority of Lindsay Heights' living residents worked with their hands, turning

Milwaukee Public Library

Milwaukee Public Schools

out machinery and other durable goods in the city's abundant factories. That generally meant walking or taking the streetcar to the industrial districts on the Milwaukee River or along the Thirtieth Street railroad corridor. In the days before zoning, however, there were numerous industries in the neighborhood itself: a twine manufacturer on Meinecke, a "stair works" on Seventeenth, a muslin underwear factory on Fond du Lac, and a Briggs & Stratton automotive parts plant on Center, plus a sausage works, an ice cream maker, and even a macaroni factory.

The neighborhood also had a surprising association with America's pastime. No fewer than three minor-league ballparks were built in or near Lindsay Heights, all of them drawing fans from throughout the city. The first was the "baseball grounds" on Eleventh and Wright, which was followed by a more elaborate park on what became Seventeenth Street between North and Lloyd—the exact site of the Walnut Way Conservation Corporation's most visible activities. The third park, Borchert Field, was shoehorned into the single city block bordered by Seventh and Eighth Streets between Burleigh and Chambers, and it proved to be the most durable of the neighborhood diamonds. Built in 1888 as Athletic Park, Borchert Field was the home of the minor-league Milwaukee Brewers from 1902 to 1952. The team won three American Association pennants during its years at Borchert, earning the enthusiastic support of local residents, even those who had to put up

with the occasional home-run ball through their living room windows.

Although the greatest number of fans in the neighborhood were German by ancestry, Germans were not the only group in Lindsay Heights. Bohemian Hall on Twelfth near Brown provided a community center for local Czechs, and a little Czech Congregational

■ (top pair)
Commerce flourished in such a densely built neighborhood. The busier establishments included Bitker's Department Store (left) on Fond du Lac Avenue and the Trupke & Goetter carriage works on Teutonia.

■ *There were also plenty of places to play. Lindsay Heights had some of the city's earliest ballparks, including one on Seventeenth Street near Lloyd (above) and another on Eighth and Chambers—the fabled Borchert Field.*

■ *Center Street was another busy retail corridor. The view is west from Sixteenth Street.*

■ *(bottom) Beth Israel Synagogue, built in 1925 for $250,000, was a social and spiritual anchor for Jewish families in the neighborhood.*

church was erected one block west. A few blocks away, on Tenth and Brown, immigrants from Holland built a Dutch Reformed church. There were also scattered individuals from other ethnic groups, including Carl Sandburg, a young Swede from Illinois who lived at 2469 N. Eighteenth Street for a time. He commuted to City Hall, where he worked as secretary for Mayor Emil Seidel, Milwaukee's first Socialist chief executive. Sandburg left the city in 1912, on his way to becoming one of the nation's most celebrated poets and a renowned Lincoln biographer.

A second wave of settlement began in the early 1900s and accelerated after 1920. As the German community pushed north and west into newer neighborhoods, there was a steady influx of Jewish families in their wake.

Milwaukee Public Library

Jewish Museum Milwaukee

Like the Germans, they were moving up from neighborhoods closer to Downtown, and they added a distinctive flavor to Lindsay Heights. Most of the newcomers traced their roots to eastern Europe. Yiddish was heard almost as often as German in some sections of the neighborhood, and nearly a third of the students at North Division High School were absent on the Jewish High Holy Days. The former Czech church on Thirteenth and Brown became B'nai Jacob Synagogue, and Beth Israel, completed in 1925, was the largest of several new places of worship. Built for $250,000—an imposing sum in 1925—Beth Israel's tan brick synagogue on Teutonia Avenue featured matching towers, fine stained-glass windows, a gymnasium, an auditorium, a full kitchen, and a ten-room Jewish school. There was also an abundance of Jewish businesses. Miller's Bakery, Cohen's Kosher Meats, and Guten's Deli drew customers from a wide area, while several ma-and-pa grocery stores met the daily needs of the neighborhood. One of those little stores, on Tenth and Meinecke, was the boyhood home of Joseph Zilber, the future Milwaukee real estate mogul.

No neighborhood stands still for long. Jewish families made Lindsay Heights their home for a full generation, but a third wave gathered force in the 1940s. African Americans, following the same Teutonia Avenue corridor that had brought Germans and Jews into the area, moved up from the neighborhoods adjoining Downtown. Black families had been part of Milwaukee since the city's infancy, and the community was large enough to support a church (St. Mark African Methodist Episcopal) as early as 1869. It was in the 1920s, however, when restrictive immigration laws created a demand for industrial workers from the South, that African Americans became a significant Milwaukee ethnic group. By the end of World War II, they had reached Lindsay Heights, and their influence on the neighborhood expanded steadily in the next two decades.

The process of racial change was neither easy nor automatic. In 1950 Twelfth Street was the neighborhood's vividly drawn "color line"; the census tracts east of Twelfth were 47-percent African-American, and those to

Milwaukee Public Library

Milwaukee Journal Sentinel

PHOTO BY BOTZ

the west were less than 2 percent. Before long, however, the line was breached and the community became thoroughly mixed. By the late 1950s the Milwaukee Hebrew Home and the NAACP had their headquarters on the same block of North Avenue, and the graduation pictures from North Division High School showed increasing integration. In the 1960s the outdoor courts at Franklin Square, just west of the high school, attracted some of the city's best basketball players, many of them African-American, and North Division teams began to make regular appearances at the state tournament in the same decade.

Peaches and Planning

In the closing decades of the 1900s, as the process of change accelerated, Lindsay Heights became, like the neighborhoods surrounding it, an African-American stronghold. The community's black population surged from 22 percent of the total in 1950 to 95 percent in 2010. The Twelfth Street dividing line was entirely forgotten, and the cultural landscape was transformed. Tavern jukeboxes traded rock and polka music for rhythm and blues. Stores that had once sold matzo and corned beef began to stock collard greens and okra. The little house of worship on Thirteenth and Brown, after serving Czech and then Jewish believers, became Bethany Church of God in Christ, an African-American congregation. On the other end of the scale, the splendid Beth Israel

Synagogue on Teutonia Avenue was repurposed as the home of Greater Galilee Baptist Church, a transfer that took place in 1960.

The transformation was accompanied by demolition. In the early 1960s, crews building Interstate 43 cut a broad swath through the eastern flank of the neighborhood. Hundreds of homes, churches, and businesses were destroyed, and the grandstands at old Borchert Field were reduced to splinters and then only memories. To the south, along Fond du Lac and North Avenues, a second corridor was cleared for the Park West Freeway—a road that was never built. Opposition in Sherman Park and elsewhere killed the project, but not before significant damage had been done to Lindsay Heights. Between the freeway corridors, virtually every block shed housing stock—the consequence of rising absentee-ownership rates, falling income levels, and sheer age. The net result of all the clearance was a staggering loss of population. Within substantially the same census-tract boundaries (Seventh to Twentieth, Locust to Galena), the area's population plummeted from 39,440 in 1950 to 8,685 in 2010. Lack of open space is not a problem in this particular section of Milwaukee's North Side.

The past has not been totally erased. You can still enjoy hot pastrami sandwiches and matzo ball soup at Jake's Deli on Seventeenth and North, a culinary holdover from the days when Jewish families made the area their home. Union Cemetery, its fences gone, is

■ *A winning tradition: North Division High School's 1916 championship track team and a tournament-bound North basketball team in the 1970s*

Milwaukee Journal Sentinel

Milwaukee Journal Sentinel

■ *As African Americans became the neighborhood's largest group, old landmarks changed hands and new institutions emerged. Greater Galilee Baptist Church (above) purchased Beth Israel Synagogue in 1960, and black merchants banded together to promote business on the near North Side.*

■ *(lower) Brother Booker Ashe accepted donations for the House of Peace, a community resource center he founded in 1968.*

Milwaukee Public Library

still a popular neighborhood shortcut—and still a place where local youngsters indulge in ghostly games of hide-and-seek, just as they have for generations. The remaining older homes of Lindsay Heights, some dating to the 1880s, provide an even more tangible connection with the past.

Nor have the neighborhood's central institutions crumbled. Churches have been local mainstays since the first days of settlement, and their number actually increased as Lindsay Heights became an African-American community. More than thirty congregations were active in the early 2000s, some worshiping in landmarks erected by European groups in the nineteenth century, others in remodeled storefronts, and still others in custom-built quarters. One of the largest "new" African-American churches is actually one of Milwaukee's oldest: Calvary Baptist. Established in 1895, Calvary moved in 1970 to a striking home on Teutonia Avenue designed to

resemble two African huts. A number of area churches sponsor schools, day care centers, youth activities, food pantries, and other programs for residents of the larger community.

Social service organizations add another dimension to life in Lindsay Heights. The La Varnway unit of the Boys & Girls Club, a local fixture since 1957, and the Running Rebels on Walnut Street both serve hundreds of young people every week. The House of Peace, a Catholic ministry on Walnut, has been reaching out to the area's neediest families since 1968. On the south end of Teutonia Avenue, the Northside YMCA offers a full range of athletic, wellness, and community-building programs in a sprawling facility completed in 2002. The area has an assortment of charter schools and medical clinics, and Feeding America supplies dozens of food pantries and meal programs from its warehouse on Fond du Lac Avenue.

Some of the physical damage done since the Fifties has been repaired in recent years. Nearly every block has homes with new roofs, fresh paint, and carefully tended flower gardens, and these grassroots efforts are complemented by a variety of larger developments. Spacious suburban-style homes have sprouted at several points in the neighborhood, most visibly in the Booker Ashe subdivision, an enclave overlooking I-43 that was named for the Capuchin brother who founded the House of Peace. Habitat for Humanity crews have been active in Lindsay

■ *Once a center of German Catholicism, St. Boniface Church became a stronghold of civil rights activism in the 1960s under Father James Groppi.*

Heights, and there is a generous scattering of apartment and townhouse complexes, some built by churches and nonprofits for the elderly and disabled, others put up by developers for anyone interested in quality housing near the heart of the city. The result is a physical landscape of extreme contrasts. The homes of Lindsay Heights are new and old, large and small, decaying and restored, detached and multi-family—sometimes in the same block. There is also a welcome patch of green space: Johnson's Park, thirteen acres of reclaimed freeway land on Fond du Lac Avenue. The park's name honors Clarence and Cleopatra Johnson, husband-and-wife tailors who settled in Milwaukee in 1920 and became pillars of the African-American community.

The physical renewal of Lindsay Heights, slow and selective though it may seem, reflects one of the neighborhood's most important assets: a tradition of community activism that dates to the earliest years of the African-American presence. St. Boniface Church, on Eleventh near Center, had been serving German Catholics since it was built in 1888, but the congregation found new purpose as its traditional members died or moved away. St. Boniface became a center of Milwaukee's civil rights movement in the 1960s, a place perpetually busy with rallies, mass meetings, and marches as well as worship. The church was especially active between 1963 and 1970, when Father James Groppi served as a pastor there.

The activist tradition surfaced again during discussions for a new North Division High School. Built in 1907, the original structure was nearly obsolete by the mid-1960s, and students and parents mounted a vigorous campaign for a new facility. The School Board decided to build a larger school on the site of the old, a decision that required the demolition of St. Boniface Church. The congregation ultimately merged into St. Martin De Porres Parish in the Harambee neighborhood, and the new North Division opened in 1978 as one of the largest, best-equipped, and most attractive schools in the system. The story took a sharp turn in the next year, when the School Board decided to make North Division a city-wide magnet school for the health sciences—part of an overall plan to encourage voluntary desegregation. Area residents and

their allies (many of them North graduates) argued that the plan would exclude hundreds of neighborhood teenagers, and they organized the Coalition to Save North Division in an effort to preserve local access to the school they had labored so long to see built. In 1980, following court-guided negotiations between coalition leaders and school authorities, North was reclassified as a neighborhood school, and so it has remained ever since.

A third wave of energy began to coalesce in the late 1990s under a new name. Known for a time as North Division, the area was increasingly identified as Lindsay Heights, honoring Bernice Lindsay, an African-American dynamo who came to Milwaukee in 1928 and spent the next two decades as executive secretary of the North Side YWCA. The name was chosen by a public-private consortium working to spur the development of new housing in Lindsay Heights, and one of the most energetic participants was the Walnut Way Conservation Corporation. The group's guiding light was Sharon Adams, who grew up on Seventeenth and North. After a notably successful career on the East Coast, Adams came back to her family home in 1997 and found the neighborhood in a troubling state of decline. She and her husband, Larry, rallied neighbors to turn the community around, founding Walnut Way in 2000.

Their efforts received a welcome boost in 2008, when Joe Zilber, the Meinecke Avenue grocer's son who grew up to make a fortune in real estate, decided to invest some of that fortune in his old neighborhood. The Zilber Neighborhood Initiative made Walnut Way its lead agency in Lindsay Heights. Working from a plan developed with local residents, the group

■ *Lindsay Heights has a variety of public, private, and charter schools. The Running Rebels (lower right) have focused on after-school activities since 1980.*

all photos on these two pages by James Schnepf for the Zilber Family Foundation

has launched some highly successful projects in community-building, wellness promotion, and urban agriculture, including its signature peach orchards. Although Walnut Way took the lead, it has never worked alone. The organization collaborates with other neighborhood groups—including the Walnut Area Improvement Council and associations representing the Josey Heights, Johnson's Park, Phyllis Wheatley, and Clarke Street areas—all in an effort to build a better future for everyone.

Lindsay Heights has traveled a long distance since the 1870s, and in recent decades its journey has seemed marked by too many wrong turns. With Walnut Way and its resident partners at the steering wheel, the neighborhood is changing its course to become, year by year, resident by resident, a community that Sharon Adams calls "a loving place of destination."

■ *Founded in 2000, the Walnut Way Conservation Corporation brought new energy to the heart of Lindsay Heights. A vacant lot next to the group's headquarters has been reborn as a peach orchard.*

(clockwise from upper left)

■ *Walnut Way's activities include beekeeping, community planning, daily walks in Johnson's Park, and ongoing efforts to beautify and empower the neighborhood.*

■ *Sitting tight in Lindsay Heights*

all photos on these two pages by James Schnepf for the Zilber Family Foundation

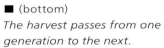

■ *Jake's Deli is a delicious holdover from the neighborhood's days as a center of Jewish life.*

■ (bottom)
The harvest passes from one generation to the next.

AMANI

METCALFE PARK

M · I · L · W · A · U · K · E · E

Amani/Metcalfe Park

The neighborhood's map resembles a geometry exercise. A diagonal road and a rail corridor cut across two overlapping rectangles, turning Amani/Metcalfe Park into triangles, squares, and a variety of other shapes. Whether the result seems symmetrical or splintered depends on your point of view, but splintering is more apparent at ground level. Vacant lots abound within the district's borders, and its housing stock includes too many board-ups on the verge of becoming teardowns. Age, poverty, and their attendant problems have given Amani/Metcalfe Park a reputation as one of the most careworn sections of the central city in recent decades. Many residents consider that reputation an undeserved affront, and they point to energetic efforts to improve conditions for every household. The names themselves were adopted in the 1990s to provide focus and context for community development initiatives—initiatives that have borne tangible fruit and continue in the present.

Amani/Metcalfe Park

1. Bethel Baptist Church (Zion Lutheran Church)
2. Capitol Stampings (Steeltech Plant)
3. Center Street Branch- Milwaukee Public Library
4. Dominican Center for Women
   (St. Leo Catholic Church)
5. Fondy Farmers Market
6. Jefferson Hall
7. Master Lock Factory
8. Metcalfe Park Community Center
9. Next Door
10. Project Respect
11. Sears Store Site
12. Wisconsin Black Historical Society & Museum

Rails and Retail

In the mid-1800s, when Milwaukee was growing into its role as Wisconsin's commercial capital, plank roads were the primary links between the city and its surrounding farm region. One of the busiest was the North Fond du Lac Road, which connected Milwaukee with a long string of settlements to its northwest. (There was also a South Fond du Lac Road, known today as Appleton Avenue.) The turnpike ran straight as an arrow through the heart of the present Amani/Metcalfe Park area, with a toll gate stopping travelers just north of Burleigh Street. The highway became a lifeline for local farmers, including those who were still clearing their land of its abundant forest cover. In 1843 one Fond du Lac Road resident advertised "500 cords of good wood … sold cheap for cash … 3 miles from town"—a location south of today's Capitol Drive.

The highway remained a vital link between city and country through the nineteenth century. In 1897 the *Milwaukee Sentinel* reported that "wheelmen" (bicyclists) considered it "one of the most interesting tours out of Milwaukee," a route known for its "pleasant farming country" and "uniformly good" road conditions. But the southern end of the Fond du Lac Road was fast becoming an urban thoroughfare. Milwaukee's population swelled from 19,963 in 1850 to 204,468 in 1890, and the city limits expanded accordingly. Beginning in the 1870s, Fond du Lac Avenue—no longer just a road—became a primary migration route for urbanites moving to the northwest. The vast majority were first- and second-generation Germans who earned their livings as tradesmen or industrial workers. By 1910 the newcomers had covered the interior blocks with sturdy frame duplexes and single-families, turned Fond du Lac Avenue into a commercial corridor, and built perhaps a dozen churches whose services were conducted in German. The intersection of Fond du Lac and North Avenue—the gateway to the neighborhood—was flanked by a bowling alley on one corner and Zion Lutheran Church on another. The bowling alley was eventually replaced by a Sears store, and Zion "Kirche" is now Bethel Baptist Church, an African-American congregation.

■ (below)
A neighborhood in the making: Twenty-first Street north of Center in 1904

■ (right)
"Zions-Kirche"— The original German inscription still crowns the entrance of what is now Bethel Baptist Church.

Milwaukee Public Library

John Gurda

Although Fond du Lac Avenue was the neighborhood's spine, an equally important corridor developed immediately west. Between 1890 and 1910, the Milwaukee Road tracks running next to Thirtieth Street spawned one of the greatest concentrations of industry in the entire state—surpassed in Milwaukee only by the Menomonee Valley. The corridor stretched for nearly four miles, from Miller Brewing on the south to the Cutler-Hammer industrial controls plant on the north, and the Amani/Metcalfe Park section included such giants as Briggs & Stratton (small engines), Master Lock (padlocks), Fuller-Warren (stoves), and Koehring (construction equipment). Dozens of factories employed thousands of workers, making the neighborhood a destination and shaping its industrial character.

As the area filled in with factory hands, North Avenue developed a commercial base comparable to Fond du Lac Avenue's. By the 1920s merchants on North sold everything from violins to fishing poles, and there were even two movie theaters—the Tivoli and the Comet—on opposite corners of the 3300 block. Fond du Lac Avenue, in the meantime, continued to reflect the German flavor of the surrounding blocks. In 1921 local residents could shop at Schachtschneider Hardware, Engelhardt Bakery, and Liesenfelder Schwister

Clothing. Jefferson Hall, at 2617 Fond du Lac, was the home of a *Freie Gemeinde* (freethinker congregation) and a popular gathering spot for the city's Germans, complete with bowling alleys in the basement. It was probably inevitable that the neighborhood's biggest store would rise at the intersection of its two busiest retail strips. In 1927 Sears opened a three-story department store at the corner of Fond du Lac and North. Designed as a sister store of the Sears on Mitchell Street, it was soon drawing patrons from across Milwaukee's North Side.

Milwaukee County Historical Society

■ *Factory workers like this Koehring Company machinist were prominent in the first wave of urban settlers.*

■ *Built in 1927, the Sears department store anchored the shopping district at North and Fond du Lac Avenues.*

Milwaukee Public Library

LEGACY

Changes and Challenges

With plenty of industrial jobs a short walk away, an abundance of opportunities for shopping and recreation, and a large supply of homes within relatively easy reach of working-class budgets, the neighborhood prospered for decades, even through the tumultuous years of the Depression and World War II. It was not until the 1950s that change began on the large scale, and it reflected developments taking place both north and south of the neighborhood. Milwaukee had continued to expand ever since the Amani/Metcalfe Park area was first settled, of course. The pace accelerated significantly after World War

■ *Two views of Amani/Metcalfe Park in the 1920s: a solid row of duplexes on Twenty-fifth Street, and the triangle formed by Twenty-seventh and Center Streets at Fond du Lac Avenue*

II, when returning soldiers and their spouses wanted new houses for their new families. There was a general movement away from the city's older neighborhoods, and new forms of commerce appeared on the urban fringe to match the new ranch homes and split-levels. In 1956 Capitol Court Shopping Center opened on Fond du Lac Avenue and Capitol Drive, two miles northwest of Amani/Metcalfe Park. Merchants closer to town noticed a disturbing dip in their sales.

As older residents were moving out, new residents were moving in, and they were coming from the same heart-of-the-city neighborhoods that had supplied the area's very first urban residents. The near North Side had become the primary address for Milwaukee's African Americans in the pre-war years. Just like the Germans of a previous generation, they moved north and west in search of better housing at mid-century, crossing North Avenue in the 1950s and '60s. The number of African Americans in today's Amani/Metcalfe Park area surged from virtually none in 1950 to 53 percent of the population in 1970. One by one, and not without conflict, houses turned over, churches changed hands, and businesses learned to serve a different clientele.

The newcomers found a neighborhood that appeared to be under attack by transportation authorities. In the late 1960s a block-wide swath of land along North Avenue was cleared for the Park West freeway. Hundreds of homes and stores were leveled, displacing families, disrupting social networks, and weakening local institutions, including some venerable churches. When plans for the freeway were dropped—the result of intense opposition farther west—the damage seemed both unnecessary and unnecessarily severe.

The next blow was a wave of plant closings that eventually turned the Thirtieth Street rail corridor into an industrial ghost town. Multi-story factories next to railroad tracks began to seem obsolete in the new era of single-floor facilities and rubber-tired transport. Some employers, including Briggs & Stratton,

Milwaukee Public Library

Milwaukee County Parks Department

248

moved to more efficient plants in the suburbs, but a greater number simply closed their doors, particularly after the savage recession of the early 1980s added "deindustrialization" to the American vocabulary.

The net result of the post-1960 changes was something resembling a perfect storm. Simply put, the area was shedding resources—homes, retail businesses, and industrial employers—at precisely the same time it was becoming more African-American (on the way to 94 percent in 2010) and significantly poorer as well. The stresses were greatest in the 1980s, when chronic joblessness, educational deficits, and an active drug trade fueled a spike in crime and what appeared to be an epidemic of homicides. The North Avenue corridor—precisely the area that bore the brunt of the Park West demolitions—was widely considered the most dangerous neighborhood in Milwaukee.

In 1990 Mayor John Norquist's administration launched a coordinated attack on the prevailing problems. City officials identified a specific geographic area, bordered by Twenty-seventh and Thirty-eighth Streets between North and Center, and called it Metcalfe Park—"in the hope," wrote one reporter, "that it will give the area a sense of community." There was an actual Metcalfe Park in the area, a grassy swath of abandoned freeway corridor just west of Twenty-seventh Street. (It was claimed in 1992 for the Steeltech manufacturing plant.) The name honored Ralph Metcalfe, an African-American legend who had won a gold medal for track at the 1932 Olympics, graduated from Marquette University in 1936, and gone on to a notable career in Chicago politics.

The new and enlarged Metcalfe Park district, which included a carved-out corner of Sherman Park, was more a target area than an organic neighborhood, but it sent a clear message. Here, Milwaukee's leaders were saying, is a community that matters, and they followed up with a multi-department push to reclaim the area for its residents. Streets were repaired. A police substation was opened. A neighborhood association was organized and with it a network of block clubs. A number of blighted houses were razed and others

were rehabilitated. Hundreds of abandoned cars were towed away, along with dumpsters piled high with trash. New development was actively encouraged. The intersection of Thirty-fifth and North—long a neighborhood hub—was virtually remade, as public and private partners built townhouse apartments, a full-service grocery store, athletic fields, and the Metcalfe Park Community Center, which opened in 2000 as a combination school, family resource center, and Boys & Girls Club.

As the Metcalfe Park initiative gathered steam, a related effort was under way directly to the east. In 1976 a nonprofit group called Project Respect was organized to combat crime and build community on Milwaukee's North Side. Its signature activity

Milwaukee Public Library

■ *St. Leo's Church, a pillar of German Catholicism since 1923, became a largely African-American congregation in the 1960s and '70s.*

AUTHORIZED PERSONS
ONLY
BRIGGS & STRATTON CORP.
OWNER

John Gurda

■ *As deindustrialization gathered speed, all that remained of most local employers was their signs.*

was a high-flying basketball league that kept young people occupied and helped develop some future collegiate and professional talent. Project Respect eventually left the athletics to other groups and developed a broader range of services for an area bordered by Twentieth and Thirty-first Streets between North and Burleigh. In 1997 organizers christened the area "Amani"—the Swahili word for "peace"—and put up signs proclaiming the new identity all over the district. Just as big men are sometimes nicknamed "Tiny," the new name signified what was all too often the opposite of the neighborhood's reality, but it expressed a powerful aspiration for the community.

In the Balance

Their names are relatively new additions to the landscape, but the neighborhoods are not. The overlapping Amani/Metcalfe Park area has been a distinctive part of Milwaukee's geography since the 1870s, and evidence of its deepest roots is still apparent. *Freie Gemeinde* and *Zions-Kirche* are still inscribed on a pair of local landmarks: Jefferson Hall and Bethel Baptist Church. You can, if you look hard enough, still find signs identifying Briggs & Stratton, Koehring, Perlick, and other former factories along the Thirtieth Street industrial corridor, and one valued employer, Master Lock, is still doing business in its long-time location on the tracks. Although Sears left

the building years ago, clothing and jewelry are still sold in its former department store on Fond du Lac and North.

Some old landmarks have been converted to new and highly constructive uses. The Wisconsin Black Historical Society and Museum tells the state's African-American story in a former public library at Twenty-seventh and Center—right across the intersection from the "new" Center Street Library, which opened in 1989. A one-time carbon products plant on Twenty-ninth has become the home of Next Door, a well-respected specialist in early childhood education, and the former rectory of St. Leo's Catholic Church on Locust houses the Dominican Center for Women, whose staff works with Amani residents to tackle the broad array of problems facing the neighborhood.

There are also newer landmarks that continue some old traditions. The Fondy Farmers Market, a purveyor of fresh food on Fond du Lac and Twenty-second since 1981, is a popular throwback to the days when local producers sold directly to consumers all over the city. One new industry has taken root near the old industrial corridor: Capitol Stampings, a metal fabricator that moved into the former Steeltech plant at Twenty-seventh and North in 2001. The COA Goldin Center opened on Burleigh in 2005 and quickly became one of the state's largest youth and family centers. The Metcalfe Park Community Center remains a vital anchor even after other programs of the Nineties have gone dormant or

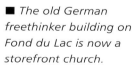

■ *The old German freethinker building on Fond du Lac is now a storefront church.*

2617

FREIE GEMEINDE

John Gurda

disappeared, and new energy has coalesced around the Amani United initiative.

The fate of the earlier programs amounted to a hard lesson in the realities of inner-city life. The most obvious was that all the municipal services in the world won't turn a neighborhood around if people don't have gainful employment, or the education and skills to make employment possible. Home-ownership rates have proven particularly difficult to budge—a problem aggravated by the foreclosure crisis that emerged in 2008. In the meantime, age and blight have continued the wave of demolition that began with clearance for the Park West freeway in the 1960s. As a direct result, the population of Amani/Metcalfe Park dropped from approximately 21,000 in 1950 to 8,600 in 2010.

The problems are apparent, but the other side of the coin is just as visible. Lower densities mean more open space, and there is a generous assortment of new "infill" homes that are in every case sounder than those they replaced. Grassroots organizations are working diligently to build a sense of engagement and commitment among local residents that will counter the isolation and apathy so toxic to any neighborhood's well-being. Some blocks are models of decorum, and it's not unusual to see a house being torn down on one side of the street and a new roof being installed on the other. Challenges remain, but some impressive forces are creating a new, more hopeful geometry in this neighborhood of angles, giving shape to a solid future for all who call it home.

■ (below left)
Master Lock has been turning out padlocks in the same Center Street factory since 1939.

■ (above)
The Metcalfe Park Community Center offers a full range of programs and services for local residents.

all photos this page by Frank Miller

251

■ *The neighborhood's key institutions include (counterclockwise from pair below) the Fondy Farmers Market, the Gospel Lighthouse Chapel, the Wisconsin Black Historical Society and Museum, and the Center Street Library.*

James Schnepf for Zilber Family Foundation

all photos on these two pages by Frank Miller except as noted

FRANKLIN
HEIGHTS

M·I·L·W·A·U·K·E·E

Franklin Heights

Franklin Heights is a neighborhood in the middle. It occupies a gentle summit near the heart of Milwaukee's North Side, and it lies squarely between nineteenth-century housing to the south and post-World War II development to the north. Economically, too, Franklin Heights occupied a central position for most of its history. It came to life as a middle-income community settled by blue-collar Milwaukeeans who walked to work in the industrial corridor along Thirtieth Street.

No company in that corridor employed more people than A.O. Smith, the largest manufacturer of automobile frames in the world. Wages from the Smith plant helped the heavily German work force of the 1920s fill the neighborhood with bungalows, and wages from Smith helped a later generation of African-Americans maintain the local tradition of homeownership.

The A.O. Smith complex was sold in 1997 and closed entirely a decade later—the greatest loss in a long line of casualties along the Thirtieth Street corridor. The closing placed Franklin Heights in a different sort of middle: between the stability of its past and the challenges of its post-industrial present. In 2009 the City of Milwaukee unveiled plans for a bold development called Century City on the former Smith site. As the business park took shape, Century City became the focus of hopes that new jobs would help restore Franklin Heights and its neighboring communities to the prosperous middle of their formative years.

Franklin Heights

1. A.O. Smith Research & Engineering Building
2. Benjamin Franklin School – Milwaukee Public Schools
3. Koehring Factory Site
4. New King of Kings Baptist Church (Grace Evangelical & Reformed Church)
5. Rays of Sunshine Community Garden
6. Siloah Lutheran Church & School
7. All Saints Catholic Church (St. Agnes)

0   1,000 FT

Plank Roads and Car Frames

The in-between community of Franklin Heights began between two historic highways. In the mid-1800s, when Milwaukee was in its infancy, the rectangle that became Franklin Heights was part of a fast-developing agricultural region. As fields replaced forests, local farmers, many of them German-born, desperately needed roads to bring their crops to market in Milwaukee. Local promoters saw an opportunity. In the early 1850s a group of Milwaukee businessmen hired crews to lay planks for a toll road to Fond du Lac. By 1854 the highway had reached Cedarburg—"where it stopped," according to one terse contemporary account. What began as the New Fond du Lac Plank Road became instead the more accurately named Cedarburg Plank Road. Near the city, the highway was called Teutonia Avenue, reflecting the Teutonic, or German, character of the communities it served. The Hopkins Road, named for an early settler who plotted its course, was built a half-mile west at about the same time. Franklin Heights developed squarely between Teutonia and Hopkins.

The two diagonal roads brought farm produce into the city for decades. By the late 1800s they were bringing something else out into the countryside: Milwaukeeans in search of homes. Keefe Avenue was the northern edge of the city in the 1890s, but new streetcar service opened the area beyond Keefe to development. The Hopkins Street line was extended from Seventeenth Street (near Locust) all the way to North Milwaukee (Thirty-fifth and Villard) in 1899, creating a link between the center of the city and its expanding outskirts. To the east, the Teutonia Avenue streetcar line did not cross Keefe until more than a decade later, and so Franklin Heights' first homes went up at the neighborhood's western margin, close to Hopkins Street.

Milwaukee's North Side was expanding naturally, but the newcomers were also responding to a powerful attraction: jobs. The railroad corridor that ran parallel to Thirtieth Street had been filling in with industries for years; Fuller-Warren (stoves) and Koehring (concrete mixers) were among the companies that built factories near Franklin Heights. In 1910 the largest of them all arrived: A.O. Smith. Founded as a machine shop in 1874, the company had become a national leader in the metal trades. By 1895 Smith was the largest manufacturer of bicycle parts in America, shipping hundreds of frames, forks, and sprockets every month from its plant in the Walker's Point neighborhood.

In the early 1900s the company graduated to automobile frames, and it was soon growing in lockstep with an industry that would leave the bicycle business in the dust. Henry Ford himself placed an order for 10,000 frames in

■ The A.O. Smith car frame plant was one of the largest industrial complexes in Wisconsin. As the sparks flew, employment grew, and many Smith workers built homes in Franklin Heights.

■ *Building crews on Twenty-second and Concordia paused for a photo in 1912. Before there were dump trucks, horse-drawn wagons did the job.*

1906. Since there was no room to expand in Walker's Point, A.O. Smith looked north, purchasing 125 acres—a parcel nearly as large as the Franklin Heights residential area—west of Twenty-seventh and Hopkins. The company put up a brick office building and a huge factory in 1910, and A.O. Smith moved from the South Side to its new home "out in the country."

The Smith plant was soon turning out 100,000 car frames every year, and demand kept growing. In 1921 A.O. Smith opened an automated plant just south of its first factory that could produce 10,000 frames every *day*. More buildings were added to the complex in the mid-1920s, and the Research and Engineering Building was finished in 1930. The seven-story landmark, a much-admired specimen of Art Deco design, still dominates the western skyline of Franklin Heights. The products developed there ushered in a new era of growth, but A.O. Smith was already a huge enterprise. By 1930 the company employed nearly 6,000 workers.

With a major employer at its western border, Franklin Heights grew rapidly. The trickle of newcomers in the early 1900s became a flood after 1915, and the neighborhood was settled to Capitol Drive, its northern border, by

■ *Bungalows were the housing type of choice for most Franklin Heights residents.*

1930. The vast majority of new residents were blue-collar Milwaukeeans, German by ancestry, who worked at A.O. Smith and other industrial plants along the railroad corridor. Most had moved up from older sections of the North Side, and they viewed Franklin Heights as a welcome change from the congestion of their old neighborhoods.

The newcomers showed a definite taste for the latest word in residential design: the Milwaukee bungalow, a widely popular house type in the 1920s. Generally one-and-a-half stories tall and nearly as wide, the typical bungalow has considerably more space than seems apparent from outside—the result of an extremely efficient floor plan. Although other styles are present in

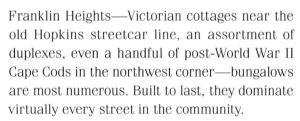

■ *Dedicated in 1924, Franklin School embodied what officials called "some of our most up-to-date ideas in school architecture." Those ideas included fireplaces in the kindergarten room.*

Franklin Heights—Victorian cottages near the old Hopkins streetcar line, an assortment of duplexes, even a handful of post-World War II Cape Cods in the northwest corner—bungalows are most numerous. Built to last, they dominate virtually every street in the community.

Urban services followed the new residents. Milwaukee annexed the area in stages between 1910 and 1924, and city crews installed miles of water mains and sewer pipes. They also built a school to serve the soaring population of youngsters. In 1924 Benjamin Franklin School opened on Twenty-third and Nash, the neighborhood's high point. "Franklin" was already a prominent name in the community. Vienna Avenue had been Franklin Street in earlier years, and a subdivision near Twenty-seventh Street was called Franklin Heights—a name later adopted for the entire neighborhood.

Local churches reflected the heavily German character of the new community, and Siloah Lutheran (Wisconsin Synod) was the

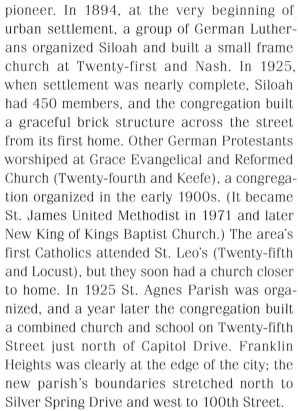

pioneer. In 1894, at the very beginning of urban settlement, a group of German Lutherans organized Siloah and built a small frame church at Twenty-first and Nash. In 1925, when settlement was nearly complete, Siloah had 450 members, and the congregation built a graceful brick structure across the street from its first home. Other German Protestants worshiped at Grace Evangelical and Reformed Church (Twenty-fourth and Keefe), a congregation organized in the early 1900s. (It became St. James United Methodist in 1971 and later New King of Kings Baptist Church.) The area's first Catholics attended St. Leo's (Twenty-fifth and Locust), but they soon had a church closer to home. In 1925 St. Agnes Parish was organized, and a year later the congregation built a combined church and school on Twenty-fifth Street just north of Capitol Drive. Franklin Heights was clearly at the edge of the city; the new parish's boundaries stretched north to Silver Spring Drive and west to 100th Street.

Although Franklin Heights became an urban neighborhood, traces of its rural past lingered. Frank Stelzl, a cement contractor who lived at 2426 W. Nash, operated a hobby farm that covered most of the block behind him; the sounds of his sheep, pigs, and chickens mingled with factory noises from farther west. Just down the block from Stelzl, at 2401 W. Nash, was a large greenhouse built in about 1911 by a pair of German florists. Nash Floral stayed in business until the late 1950s, when it was replaced by an apartment building that has since been converted to a church.

Franklin Heights matured as "an honest, German, common-person sort of neighborhood," in the words of one early resident, but it didn't stand still for long. The Depression struck almost as soon as the last houses were finished. A.O. Smith's work force was cut in half, and hundreds of residents struggled to make ends meet. World War II marked a return to full employment as Smith and other factories worked overtime to aid the military effort. When the war ended in 1945, the neighborhood entered a period of relative prosperity and more rapid change. Membership in local churches swelled. Siloah Lutheran peaked at 2,700 members in 1956, making it one of the largest Wisconsin

Siloah Lutheran Church

Siloah Lutheran Church

Synod churches anywhere. St. Agnes Catholic Church had more than 2,000 families at the same time, and the congregation built an imposing modern church on Twenty-fifth Street in 1961. A.O. Smith remained the dominant local employer. As late as 1960 more than 11 percent of the neighborhood's workers walked to their jobs—well above the city average—and the greatest number walked to Smith.

As the years passed, young people who had been raised in Franklin Heights moved north and west to newer neighborhoods. Their parents stayed behind for a time, but the area was poised for a new wave of settlers. Like the early Germans, African Americans had been moving up from the near North Side for years and, like the early Germans, they were responding to both push and pull forces. In the 1950s and '60s, urban renewal and freeway construction displaced thousands of families, and their natural migration path led north. The pull was provided by jobs. Employment at A.O. Smith increased to 9,000 on all three shifts in the postwar years, and a significant number of those jobs were held by African Americans. After years on the lower rungs of the occupational ladder, they were finally earning union wages in a union town.

Pushed from the south and pulled to the north, African Americans soared from less than 1 percent of Franklin Heights' population in 1960 to 68 percent in 1970 and 94 percent in 1980. A new culture took root in the neighborhood, as churches were repurposed and businesses changed hands. The transition was not painless but, in some important ways, very little changed. Whether its residents were German or black,

Wisconsin Black Historical Society

A.O. Smith Corp.

■ (top pair)
Siloah Lutheran Church, a German congregation, built a simple house of worship in 1894 and moved to a more imposing brick structure across Nash Street in 1925.

■ (above)
A.O. Smith's labor force integrated steadily after World War II, earning the company a reputation as one of Milwaukee's best places for African Americans to work.

■ *As employment climbed, so did the stacks of car frames awaiting shipment to Detroit and other automotive centers.*

Lutheran or Baptist, Franklin Heights offered the same amenities to all: substantial homes, larger lots, and quieter streets. For the African-American residents of more recent years no less than for their German-speaking predecessors, the neighborhood has meant, quite simply, the attainment of a better life.

Hope along the Railroad Tracks

A better life is still one of Franklin Heights' major attractions. Roughly half the community's residents own their homes, and you'll hear regular expressions of pride during a walk through its settled streets. "It's a pretty nice neighborhood," said one long-time resident. "This is a good place to live," added a more recent arrival. But expressions of satisfaction are tempered by feelings of concern. Franklin Heights was never a company town built around a single employer or group of employers, and its ties with A.O. Smith, in particular, slackened as Milwaukeeans became more mobile and the company's workforce became more metropolitan. But the connection between the neighborhood and the manufacturers on its western border remained important. When a wave of deindustrialization began to cascade down the Thirtieth Street industrial corridor in the early 1980s, it was felt sharply in Franklin Heights.

The A.O. Smith plant was the most visible casualty. The company suffered major losses when the automotive industry abandoned steel frames for less costly unibody construction. Concluding that there was more opportunity in its non-automotive lines, Smith sold the frame business to Tower Automotive in 1997. Tower bumped along for a decade but finally gave up the ghost in 2006. A complex that once contained more than 100 buildings sprawling across 140 acres of land was absolutely idle.

As manufacturing's decline became general, the blue-collar households of Franklin Heights struggled to adjust. Unemployment rose, home maintenance suffered, and young people faced uncertain futures. Franklin Heights did not, however, succumb to the despair that has claimed other formerly industrial neighborhoods throughout America. Announced in 2009, the city's plans to transform the A.O. Smith site into Century City generated real enthusiasm. Mayor Tom Barrett described the development as "a modern business park with roads and rail connections, with modern storm water management, and with new buildings, new companies, and employment opportunities." Local residents have followed Century City's progress with cautious optimism.

The same optimism applies to local institutions. In 1962, when it was obvious that the area's racial makeup was changing, Siloah Lutheran Church opened a school on Twenty-first Street, and it has since grown, both physically and academically, to provide a tuition-free Christian education for nearly 200 neighborhood children. Siloah is distinguished as the community's oldest congregation, but virtually every church in the neighborhood— and they are numerous—offers some form of outreach ministry.

On the public side, Franklin School, the neighborhood's dominant landmark since 1923, offers a variety of traditional and specialized programs for local youngsters from kindergarten through

■ *Siloah Lutheran Church remains a neighborhood linchpin, operating a tuition-free school for local children.*

John Ruebartsch

John Ruebartsch

eighth grade. Long-time residents still refer to the school's commanding location as Franklin Hill. A variety of nonprofits serve the people of Franklin Heights as well. Some, like the COA Goldin Center, lie just beyond the neighborhood's borders. Others, like the YWCA and Northwest Side Community Development Corporation, include the community in much larger target areas. And there are home-grown initiatives, like the Rays of Sunshine community garden on Twenty-fifth and Keefe, that have planted hope in the landscape.

More than a century after its first urban houses were built, Franklin Heights is still a neighborhood in the middle. It lies squarely between the densely settled blocks of the central city and the open spaces of suburban-era developments, and its residents express both satisfaction with the present and concern for the future. What will tomorrow bring? Much depends on developments taking shape on their western border, but the people of Franklin Heights can look back on a tradition of stability and pride as old as the neighborhood.

■ *The buildings are largely empty, but the plans are fully developed, and the former A.O. Smith complex is taking on a new identity as Century City.*

John Ruebartsch

Milwaukee Department of City Development

Mike Ford

■ *Young residents take part in a neighborhood clean-up.*

■ *(bottom) Area churches large and small serve as anchors of community in Franklin Heights.*

John Gurda

all photos on these two pages by John Ruebartsch except as noted

■ (above)
*The Rays of
Sunshine
community garden*

John Gurda

■ *The A.O. Smith
Research and
Engineering
Building is Franklin
Heights' dominant
landmark and a
touchstone of
hope for the future.*

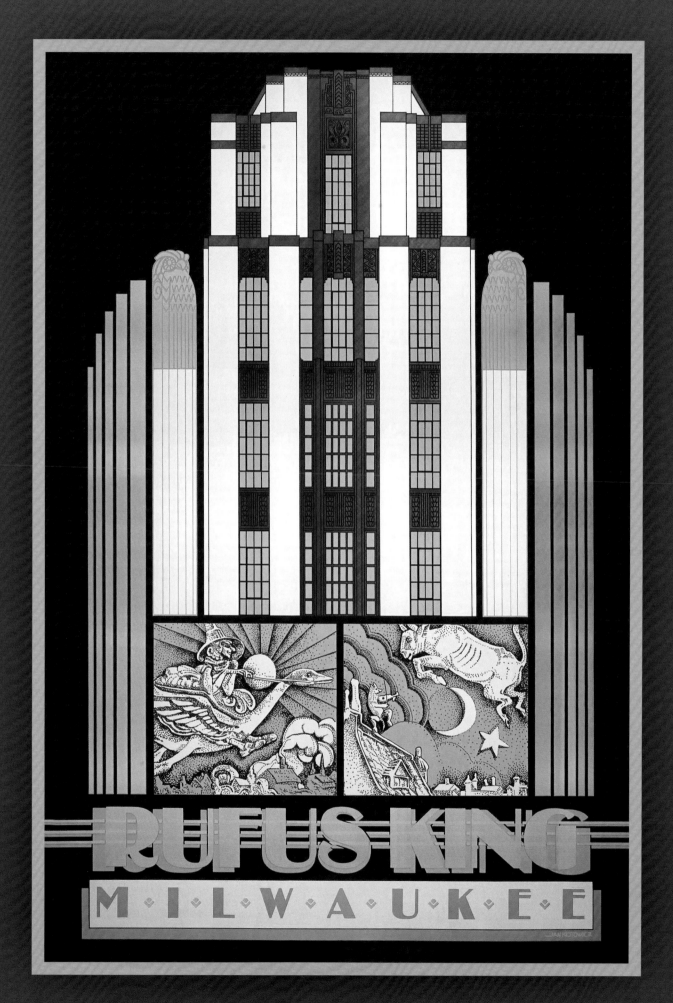

Rufus King

It has the look and feel of an older suburb. Quiet streets, substantial homes, an obvious feeling of pride—these have been the hallmarks of the Rufus King neighborhood since settlement began in the first decades of the twentieth century. The neighborhood takes its name from a public high school at its center. Like the school, the neighborhood has undergone sweeping changes in recent decades, but one quality has remained constant. For every resident—from the Germans of the 1920s to the African Americans of the twenty-first century—the neighborhood has been a symbol of solid achievement.

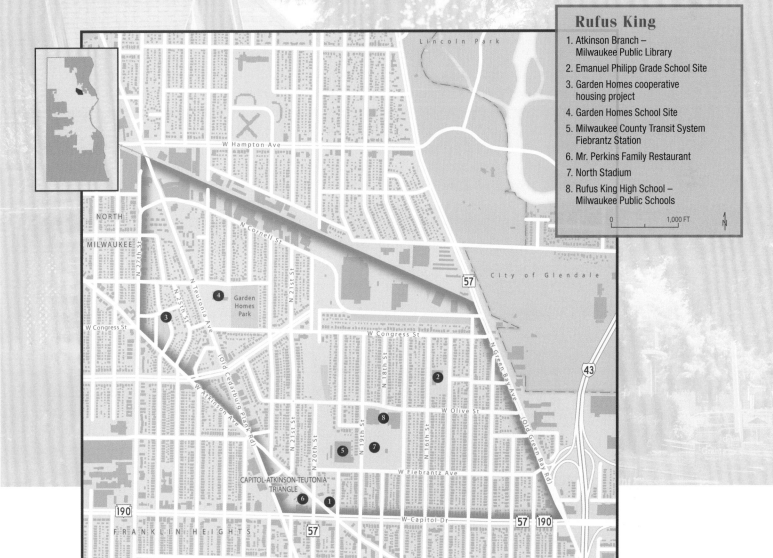

Rufus King

1. Atkinson Branch – Milwaukee Public Library
2. Emanuel Philipp Grade School Site
3. Garden Homes cooperative housing project
4. Garden Homes School Site
5. Milwaukee County Transit System Fiebrantz Station
6. Mr. Perkins Family Restaurant
7. North Stadium
8. Rufus King High School – Milwaukee Public Schools

A Place for the Middle Class

It began with a road. In 1839, when most of Milwaukee was still covered with towering maple and oak trees, the federal government built a road connecting the little settlement with Green Bay—Wisconsin's metropolis at the time. The new road, now Green Bay Avenue, wasn't much more than a wagon track at first, but it was among the earliest highways in the region, and it quickly became one of the busiest. Immigrants, most of them Germans, trekked north from the lakeshore village, buying land along the Green Bay road and carving farms out of the forest.

By 1876 the area that became the Rufus King neighborhood supported perhaps thirty small farms, nearly all of them owned by Germans and most of them fronting on the Green Bay road. With such excellent access to the city, local farmers raised crops they could sell directly to urban residents: vegetables, fruits and, by the late 1800s, flowers. A floral greenhouse covered several acres just north of the present Atkinson Public Library.

Access to the heart of the city got even better in 1908. The Milwaukee Northern Railway, an electric line, was completed between Milwaukee and Sheboygan in that year. The Northern's tracks followed Sixth Street north of Downtown, veered west on Atkinson Avenue, and then entered a dedicated right-of-way just north of Capitol Drive at Twentieth Street. Milwaukee Northern trains clattered through the farming district every two hours, carrying passengers and freight to and from Sheboygan and all points in between. It wasn't necessary to wait at a particular stop. In those days of pitch darkness after sunset, anyone who wanted to stop a train had only to "Stand Clear of Track and show a light or strike a match."

The darkness became less absolute as the district began to urbanize. To the northwest, near Thirty-fifth and Villard, was the industrial suburb of North Milwaukee. Built around the intersection of two rail lines that attracted several manufacturing firms, the village incorporated in 1897 and boasted more than 2,000 residents by 1918. The suburb's borders touched the northwest corner of the present Rufus King neighborhood at Twenty-seventh and Congress.

To the south, the City of Milwaukee was edging closer and closer each year. The farming district along the Green Bay road became a belt of open land sandwiched between two urban communities, and its days were clearly numbered. Urban residents finally crossed Capitol Drive in the 1920s. The city annexed the entire district, piece by piece, between 1924 and 1930, and the greenhouses and truck farms were replaced by block after block of new homes. Most were built by former North Siders. The Rufus King neighborhood lay directly in the path of the Near North Side's natural expansion, and the new residents reflected the ethnic patterns of the old communities. Although there were Czech, Jewish, Polish, and Scandinavian families in the mix, the vast majority of newcomers were German.

The ethnic patterns persisted, but the new neighborhood was by no means simply an extension of the old. The Rufus King community came to life as a haven for the middle class.

■ *Milwaukee Northern streetcars were a lifeline for the first generation of Rufus King residents.*

Milwaukee Public Library

John Gurda

John Gurda

It attracted small business-owners, professionals, skilled industrial workers, foremen, salesmen, civil servants, and other residents with above-average incomes. The homes they erected were above-average as well: noticeably larger and more substantial than those they had left behind. The vast majority were single-families, and most were built of brick or Lannon stone. Leaded-glass windows, hardwood floors, and built-in cabinets were common, and more than 10 percent had fireplaces.

Two housing types were especially popular among the neighborhood's charter residents. The first was the Milwaukee bungalow, a sturdy one-and-a-half-story home nearly as wide as it is tall. Bungalows are still most numerous in the blocks that were settled first, between Capitol and Fiebrantz. The second major type was actually a family of designs that historians lump together as "Period Revival." In the 1920s and '30s, architects were reviving historic European styles—Tudor, English Cottage, and Mediterranean—as well as American colonial designs, and the Rufus King area has all of them in quantity. Like Period Revival homes elsewhere, most are built of brick or stone.

A less-traditional housing development took shape at the northwest corner of the new neighborhood, and this one was unique in all the nation. In 1923, under the leadership of Mayor Daniel Hoan, a Socialist, the City of Milwaukee completed a cooperative development called Garden Homes. Designed to provide affordable housing for working-class citizens, Garden Homes was the very first municipally

Milwaukee County Historical Society

Milwaukee County Historical Society

sponsored public housing project in America. Located on former farmland near the crossing of Teutonia and Atkinson Avenues, the development was a highly compact cluster of ninety-three stucco-clad houses (twelve of them duplexes) situated on curving streets around a central park. The homes were cozy variations on the English Cottage theme, and gardens were definitely encouraged. The project began

■ (top pair)
Scores of spacious Period Revival homes went up north of Capitol Drive in the 1920s and '30s.

■ (above)
To the west was a nationally important experiment in affordable housing: the Garden Homes cooperative development. Most of its residences were modeled after English cottages.

as a cooperative whose bylaws were drafted by Dan Hoan himself, an attorney in his pre-mayoral career. Residents made monthly payments to a corporation instead of paying rent, but in 1925, as the project's property values soared, they voted to terminate the cooperative and take individual title to their homes. A public experiment became a private development, but Garden Homes remains a landmark success in the history of affordable housing.

Maturity and Change

As Garden Homes was filling out and the nearby blocks were filling in, the United States was inching toward an economic catastrophe. By the time the stock market crashed in 1929, just over half of the Rufus King area's homes were in place. The blocks closest to Capitol Drive looked much as they do today, but there were plenty of lots for sale in the northern reaches of the neighborhood. The Depression virtually killed the real estate market. Residential growth slowed to a crawl as the newcomers struggled to make their house payments, but building of a different sort continued. The neighborhood

was filled with families in their child-raising years, and there was an obvious need for new schools. Emanuel Philipp Grade School, on Sixteenth near Olive, was completed in 1931. It was named for a prominent Milwaukee industrialist who served as Wisconsin's governor from 1914 to 1920. Although the school's architects, Eschweiler and Eschweiler, described it as "one of the first to express the trend toward simplicity," Philipp School was covered with fanciful decorations: stone carvings of animals and fairy-tale figures, tiles depicting characters from Mother Goose, and a kindergarten room with a working fireplace and a fish pond. Garden Homes School, more traditional but much larger than Philipp, was built on the northwestern edge of the neighborhood in 1931. Its Saturday-afternoon movies and bake sales drew families from throughout the area.

Local teenagers attended a school that quickly became the pride of the entire neighborhood. Rufus King High School, towering over the blocks around Eighteenth and Olive, was finished in 1934. It was named for a Civil War general and newspaper editor who was also a passionate supporter of public education. Rufus

■ *Two striking examples of Art Deco design graced the landscape in 1931: Emanuel Philipp Grade School* (left) *and Rufus King High School.*

John Gurda

King, in fact, was Milwaukee's first superintendent of schools. As the city's only high school north of Center Street, his namesake served more than 1,400 students by the end of its first year. Like Philipp School, King showcased the Art Deco style popular in the Thirties, with elaborate woodwork, tiles, and stone carvings, many done in bold geometric patterns. North Stadium was finished just south of the school in 1934; with 15,000 seats, it became the home field for several North Side high schools.

Churches were built to serve the area's religious needs during the same period. Garden Homes Lutheran Church, a heavily German congregation, completed its building on Twenty-fifth and Atkinson in 1928, a few years after the housing cooperative around the corner was occupied. Gospel Lutheran, whose members moved into an imposing Lannon stone church on Sixteenth and Capitol in 1939, was even larger and just as German. Augustana Lutheran, originally a congregation of South Side Swedes, moved to a new building on Twenty-first and Congress in 1936. Area Catholics worshiped at Holy Angels or St. Agnes, both a few blocks outside the neighborhood's borders.

A number of Rufus King residents continued to rely on the Milwaukee Northern streetcar line for transportation to their Downtown jobs. In 1922 the Northern was purchased by a forerunner of We Energies, which built the imposing red-brick car barn on Nineteenth and Fiebrantz in 1931. Streetcar service ended in 1948, but the car barn eventually found a new and continuing use as a facility for Milwaukee County buses. The original Northern Railway right-of-way persists as a belt of green space—a sort of unintended (and untended) park—parallel to Twentieth Street.

■ *North Stadium, which filled the square block behind Rufus King, was the home field for a number of North Side high schools. The school and the stadium were surrounded by row after row of well-built, well-kept homes.*

269

■ (top pair)
■ (top pair)
The Fiebrantz transit station was built by the Milwaukee Northern Railway in 1931. Its features included a car wash—for streetcars.

■ *The Atkinson branch of the Milwaukee Public Library replaced a facility demolished for freeway construction.*

Schools, churches, and car barns were the major landmarks that emerged during the Depression, and residential development resumed with the gradual return of better times. Nearly 220 houses were built in the Thirties, another 230 during the war-torn Forties, and 160 more in the boom period of the Fifties. It was not until roughly 1960 that the last vacant lots filled in with houses. The postwar additions tended to be simpler than the homes closer to Capitol Drive—Cape Cods, scaled-down colonials, and modest ranch homes predominated—but all were in keeping with the comfortable single-family character of the entire neighborhood.

Other kinds of development occurred along Rufus King's borders in the postwar years. To the north, between Cornell Street and the Milwaukee Road tracks, new factories and warehouses formed a sizable industrial belt dominated by a large box factory at Nineteenth Street. To the east, Green Bay Avenue, the original lifeline to the city, became an important commercial district, particularly well-known for its car dealerships. To the west, the Capitol-Atkinson-Teutonia triangle strengthened its position as a local shopping center. One of the neighborhood's last major landmarks appeared on the triangle in 1961: the Atkinson branch of the Milwaukee Public Library. Sometimes called the "ski lodge" because of its open floor plan and soaring ceiling, Atkinson replaced a Green Bay Avenue library taken for freeway construction in 1959.

By the time settlement was complete in 1960, the neighborhood's earliest residents had been in their homes for almost forty years. Their children had graduated from Philipp or Garden Homes, gone on to King, and then pursued homes and careers of their own. Rufus King became a neighborhood of older residents; their median age—thirty-nine years in 1960—was fully nine years above the city median. The stage was set for the next chapter in the neighborhood's evolution.

Just as the original German families had moved naturally from Milwaukee's North Side as the city expanded, a new wave of settlers began to arrive from the same area. The first African-American families crossed Capitol Drive in the late 1950s; they included doctors, businessmen, and celebrated slugger Hank Aaron. As their movement gained momentum, entire blocks changed in a matter of months. Black residents made up 0.4 percent of Rufus King's population in 1960, 58 percent in 1970, and 89 percent in 1980.

Ricco's Swingin' Door

Milwaukee County Historical Society

Although the transition generally occurred without trauma, one troubling statistic demonstrated the influence of race on the real estate market. Between 1960 and 1980—the years of greatest change—the median value of Rufus King's homes dropped from 9 percent above the city's median value to 23 percent below—for exactly the same properties. On the other hand, the newcomers got a great deal of house for their money, and they made the most of it. The neighborhood was jokingly referred to as "Blackfish Bay," the African-American equivalent of the largely affluent (and largely Caucasian) suburb of Whitefish Bay.

Continuity was every bit as important as change. It was clear from the beginning that the new residents were, in all respects but race, nearly identical to the original settlers: similar income levels, similar educational status, similar occupations. Although its racial profile shifted dramatically, Rufus King remained a comfortably middle-income neighborhood.

Pride and Property

A clear majority of Rufus King's current residents own their own homes. The ratio is above the city average and, as always, ownership goes hand in hand with pride. Most lawns are tended carefully, most sidewalks are shoveled promptly, and hundreds of backyards are filled with summer flowers. The weeping mulberries and juniper trees planted by an earlier generation have long since matured into striking specimens. At least one mail carrier has been gently reminded not to walk across the lawns on his rounds through the neighborhood. "This is the best place I've ever lived in Milwaukee," said one woman. "People are proud of it, and people stay."

The people who share this obvious pride are among the city's busiest. As it has been since the 1920s, Rufus King is the home of white-collar workers and the upper echelon of blue-collar workers. There are supermarket-owners and independent barbers, federal administrators and private accountants, welding shop foremen and plant supervisors, public officials and salesmen, teachers and nurses, and a sizable congregation of ministers. Rufus King houses a large proportion of the African-American community's leadership—political, economic, cultural, and religious.

Whatever their backgrounds, local residents share some important amenities, beginning with their houses. Whether they were built in the 1920s or the 1950s, the homes of Rufus King were generally designed to impress and built to last. Location is another advantage. The neighborhood lies only

■ *Milwaukee Braves slugger Henry Aaron was one of Rufus King's first African-American residents.*

■ *St. Mark African Methodist Church moved into a new home just south of Capitol Drive in 1969. Rufus King residents have long been prominent in its membership.*

three miles from Downtown, but it's at the edge of the city and practically adjacent to the inviting green spaces of Lincoln Park. Convenience is still another asset. The shops of Bayshore Town Center are only minutes away in Glendale, and a variety of local businesses serve local needs. The Capitol-Atkinson-Teutonia triangle remains the most important neighborhood shopping center, anchored by food, drug, and discount stores. One of the triangle's best-known businesses is Mr. Perkins Family Restaurant, a community institution since 1969 and a favorite meeting place for black Milwaukeeans. The restaurant's owners happen to be Rufus King residents.

The neighborhood shares a variety of other resources. Atkinson Library offers traditional library services, but it also has a full complement of computers and a variety of job-search information. The area's churches continue to serve as community anchors. Some of the original congregations, including Garden Homes Lutheran and Gospel Lutheran, chose to minister to the neighborhood as it changed, and both operate full-service schools. Other congregations, including Antioch Missionary

Baptist and New Covenant Temple, worship in buildings purchased from their predecessors. Still others, among them Jerusalem Missionary Baptist and Mt. Zion Assembly, gather in new sanctuaries.

Like the neighborhood's churches, local schools are both landmarks and resources. Rufus King High School is still the neighborhood's focal point, but the school's reputation has spread far beyond the community's borders. With the advent of Milwaukee's desegregation initiative in 1978, King became a city-wide specialty school for the college-bound. It offers the most rigorous academic program in the public school system. By any number of measures—college acceptances, test scores, academic decathlons—King compares favorably with the best private schools in the metropolitan area. The school's prestige has heightened the sense of pride already present in the surrounding neighborhood. It also provides a more tangible amenity: Local walkers and joggers use the running track behind Rufus King High School from morning to night throughout the year.

■ *Rufus King High School, widely regarded as the city's best, is still the neighborhood's focal point, and the old North Stadium running track (far right) remains a well-used local amenity.*

The neighborhood is not without its challenges. Some of the area's smallest houses, including those in the Garden Homes district, have begun to show signs of age and neglect, but even that urban experiment continues to draw attention. Although the gardens are fewer and most of the original stucco has been replaced by vinyl or aluminum siding, Garden Homes remains every bit as distinctive in its way as the New Deal suburb of Greendale, a better-known planned community in southwestern Milwaukee County.

Rufus King has some impressive physical resources, but the core of its character is something less tangible. When asked to describe their community, residents typically use the word "quiet." King is a neighborhood of quiet streets, quiet homes, and quiet pride. For many, it marks a kind of arrival. After struggling in earlier years and older communities, many residents view their current addresses as the American dream come true. "It's a family neighborhood," said one sixteen-year homeowner. "You get to know everyone, and everyone knows what we have here. We're going to work to keep it that way."

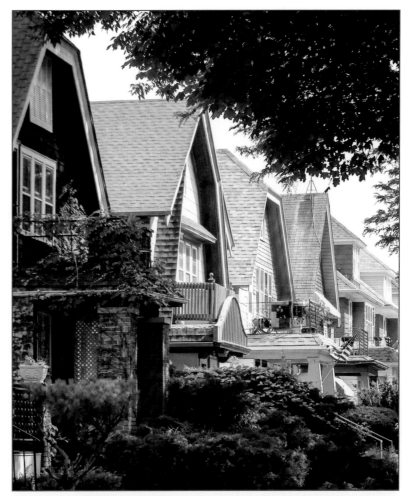

■ *Numerous blocks present a united front of bungalows.*

■ *Manicured lots, mature trees, and plenty of brick and stone are all Rufus King signatures.*

■ (bottom)
Mr. Perkins Family Restaurant is the neighborhood's leading culinary institution.

all photos on these two pages by Jim Hamberg except as noted

■ *Bungalows and Period Revival homes are still the dominant housing types.*

John Gurda

■ *Several historic churches, including Gospel Lutheran on Capitol Drive, have kept faith with the neighborhood for decades.*

NORTH
MILWAUKEE

North Milwaukee

North Milwaukee is a city that joined a city. For more than thirty years, from 1897 to 1929, it was an independent suburb, operating its own schools, publishing its own newspapers, and developing its own personality. The old suburb is an urban neighborhood today, as it has been for generations, but the past, as always, casts a long shadow. The landscape that began to take shape in the nineteenth century is still largely intact in the twenty-first. It provides a unique setting for the community's current residents, most of them African Americans, who are writing their own chapter in the long history of one of Milwaukee's most interesting neighborhoods.

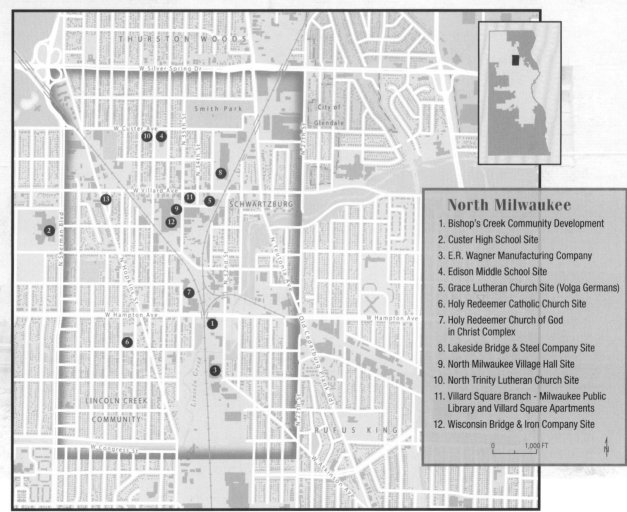

North Milwaukee

1. Bishop's Creek Community Development
2. Custer High School Site
3. E.R. Wagner Manufacturing Company
4. Edison Middle School Site
5. Grace Lutheran Church Site (Volga Germans)
6. Holy Redeemer Catholic Church Site
7. Holy Redeemer Church of God in Christ Complex
8. Lakeside Bridge & Steel Company Site
9. North Milwaukee Village Hall Site
10. North Trinity Lutheran Church Site
11. Villard Square Branch - Milwaukee Public Library and Villard Square Apartments
12. Wisconsin Bridge & Iron Company Site

0   1,000 FT

Industry at the Junction

■ "X" marks the spot: The crossing of two major railroad lines spawned a busy industrial suburb.

■ Wisconsin Bridge & Iron was among the first employers to build on the tracks.

North Milwaukee began its career as Schwartzburg, an undersized trading center at what is now the intersection of Teutonia and Villard Avenues. Named for a pioneer farmer, Schwartzburg was little more than a post office, a saloon, and a handful of houses. There were dozens of tiny hamlets just like it in the Milwaukee area, but the settlement had one resource that others lacked: railroads. By the 1870s Schwartzburg lay just east of the junction of two major rail lines, one connecting Milwaukee with Minneapolis, the other reaching north to Green Bay and ultimately Upper Michigan. Both were part of the sprawling Milwaukee Road system, and they were among the busiest lines in the state. Their crossing carved a huge "X" on the neatly tilled farmland north of Milwaukee. Schwartzburg soon developed an alternate name: Northern Junction.

The Junction presented some intriguing possibilities. Milwaukee became a major industrial center between 1870 and 1910, and nearly all of its major industries were located on railroad corridors. In that vanished era before Mack trucks and double-bottom trailers, it was trains that brought raw materials into the city and carried finished goods away to market. As Milwaukee industrialized, trackside sites near the heart of the city became increasingly scarce and prohibitively expensive. By the 1890s manufacturers were looking farther afield for industrial land.

Although Northern Junction was well beyond the city limits, its rail connections were irresistible. In 1893 the Wisconsin Bridge & Iron Company moved from the West Side to a sprawling new plant on Thirty-fifth Street, just south of today's Villard Avenue. In 1896 the Meiselbach (later American) Bicycle Company built its factory across the street. Bridges and bicycles thus formed the foundation of a new community: North Milwaukee.

Other industries followed, and the settlement grew with astonishing speed. Before 1893 North Milwaukee barely existed. Only four years later, the editor of the city directory described it as "a manufacturing suburb of Milwaukee ... not yet incorporated as a village, although its boundaries are thoroughly defined." In 1897 North Milwaukee received its official charter from the state, and the new village took in nearly all the land within the rectangle bordered by today's Congress Street, Silver Spring Drive, Twenty-seventh Street, and Sherman Boulevard.

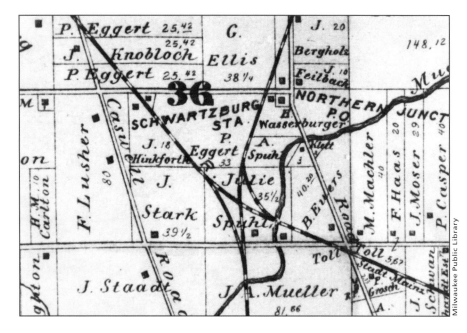

Milwaukee Public Library

Milwaukee Public Library

North Milwaukee's appeal was obvious, and the village attracted a small army of developers who worked tirelessly to enlarge its place on the map. (Similar efforts were under way at precisely the same time on the opposite side of the county, in a suburb named, fittingly, South Milwaukee.) Nearly a dozen development companies were launched, the most prominent of them headed by Henry Clay Payne, an East Side Yankee who wielded enormous political and economic power in Wisconsin. Payne served as Milwaukee's postmaster, chaired the state Republican Party, and managed the local streetcar monopoly for Henry Villard, a New York capitalist whose other holdings included the Northern Pacific Railroad. Payne enlarged his own fortune through land sales in North Milwaukee, and he used his position to ensure the community's future prosperity. In 1899 he extended a streetcar line from Keefe Avenue to Thirty-fifth and Villard—a distance of more than two miles through largely open land. North Milwaukee's main street was named Villard Avenue in honor of Payne's boss in New York.

Connected to Milwaukee by streetcar and to the rest of the country by train, North Milwaukee seemed to have unlimited potential for growth. More factories sprouted along the tracks after 1900, among them E.R. Wagner (metal stampings), Greenbaum Tannery, and Lakeside Bridge and Steel. By 1915 the "X" of the railroad crossing marked one of the densest industrial districts in the Milwaukee area. Although it was clearly a manufacturing suburb, North Milwaukee was not as dependent on a single company as West Allis (Allis-Chalmers), South Milwaukee (Bucyrus-Erie), or Cudahy (Patrick Cudahy).

■ *Henry Clay Payne was North Milwaukee's well-connected godfather. He extended streetcar service to the suburb and named its main street for his boss, Henry Villard.*

Milwaukee County Historical Society

■ *The Meiselbach bicycle factory was another prominent local industry. One of its early employees was William Harley, co-founder of Harley-Davidson.*

Milwaukee County Historical Society

It had a large number of medium-sized employers, and factory hands routinely moved from one to another in search of better wages and working conditions.

North Milwaukee's prosperity was reflected in the growth of Villard Avenue. In 1897, the year of incorporation, there was only a handful of businesses on the village's main artery, including a lumberyard, a grocery store, and a butcher shop. By 1909 there were nearly thirty establishments, among them two workingman's hotels, a hardware store, a bakery, medical offices, a pharmacy, a notions store, and a variety of well-patronized saloons. All were clustered within a block or two of Thirty-fifth Street. North Milwaukee's village hall was located on Thirty-fifth just south of Villard, practically in the shadow of the Wisconsin Bridge shops. Built in 1901, the hall housed the fire and police departments, the jail, meeting rooms, the library, and living quarters for the janitor. It remains the neighborhood's most distinctive landmark today.

Although industry brought it to life, North Milwaukee was, first and foremost, a residential community. Drawn by the promise of employment, industrial workers and their families poured into the young village. North Milwaukee's population was roughly 600 at the turn of the century, up from practically nothing

a decade earlier. By 1910 there were 1,860 residents, with more coming every year.

The vast majority of them looked back to roots in Germany. Most North Milwaukeeans moved to the village from the heavily German North Side of Milwaukee or the heavily German farming communities north of town. They relaxed in saloons like Wasserburger's Grove and Eggert's Opera House, and they organized churches like Holy Redeemer Catholic, North Trinity Lutheran, and the German Full Gospel Church, all of whose pastors preached in the tongue of their ancestors. Until at least World War I, German was more commonly heard on Villard Avenue than English.

North Milwaukee's German community included a subgroup that was one of the most unusual, and least-studied, immigrant populations in Wisconsin—the Russian Germans, or Volga Germans. In the 1760s Tsarina Catherine the Great, a former German princess, persuaded thousands of German farmers and craftsmen to colonize the sparsely settled lands along the lower Volga River. They lived and prospered in almost complete isolation from the cultures around them, retaining the German language, German customs, and German religions for more than 150 years. In the early 1900s many of the Volga Germans departed

■ (below)
Villard Avenue was the commercial heart of North Milwaukee.

■ (center)
Thirty-fifth Street was the suburb's other major thoroughfare. North Milwaukee's village hall is at far left.

Milwaukee Journal Sentinel

for America, some to avoid military service, others to find larger opportunities, still others to escape the aftermath of the 1917 Communist revolution. Between 1910 and 1920, hundreds of them found their way to North Milwaukee.

Although they shared the German heritage of their neighbors, the newcomers maintained, as they had in Russia, a distinct identity. In 1913 they established Grace Lutheran Church on Thirty-fourth just south of Villard. They also remained true to their agricultural roots. Many women and children spent their summers tending sugar beet fields on southern Wisconsin farms, and they were joined by the men of their families during periods of unemployment. Although they settled throughout North Milwaukee, the Volga Germans were concentrated south of Villard and east of the tracks. Other residents began to call the area "Red Town," much to the irritation of the people who lived there. After suffering persecution in the wake of the 1917 revolution, none of the immigrants had a shred of affection for the Communists. The Volga Germans had been glad to leave the Old World behind, and they put down deep roots in their chosen corner of the New World. As late as 1950, 1,186 North Milwaukeeans—nearly 10 percent of the population—gave Russia as their place of birth.

Annexationists vs. Hometowners

As immigrants and older Americans continued to flock to the village, North Milwaukee filled out nearly to its limits. In 1918, when its population reached 2,200, the community secured its charter as a fourth-class city and continued to grow. North Milwaukee stood out boldly on the region's map. At its core was a busy downtown centered around Thirty-fifth and Villard. Radiating out from that core were four rail corridors lined with factories and, filling the spaces between them, a range of residential districts. The oldest homes, built in the 1890s, ranged from spacious Victorians near Smith Park to simple cottages on the neighboring streets. The next layers of development were dominated by two-story duplexes and then by bungalows. Built during the 1920s, bungalows are still the most abundant house type in the community. Scattered among them are Period Revival homes from the same decade, most showing the influence of traditional English styles.

At the time of cityhood in 1918, North Milwaukee was a compact cluster of urban development surrounded by small farms and semi-rural homesteads. It was a remarkably self-contained community.

■ *"Volga Germans," uprooted from tsarist Russia, established Grace Lutheran Church in 1913.*

Milwaukee County Historical Society

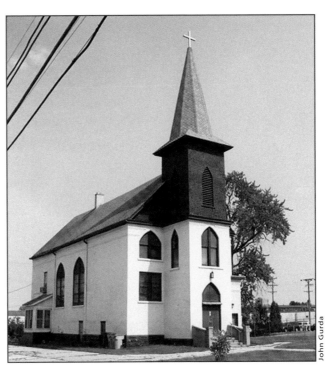

John Gurda

281

First Administration City of North Milwaukee

Milwaukee County Historical Society

■ *North Milwaukee graduated from village to city status in 1918 with a full roster of local officials.*

■ *The suburb was still flanked by farmland in this pre-World War II aerial photograph. The view is north up Thirty-fifth Street.*

Milwaukee County Historical Society

In addition to its industries and businesses, North Milwaukee had its own sewer and water systems, two elementary schools, a six-member common council, an independent street numbering system, a newspaper, a locally owned bank, and (the mayor boasted) eight miles of cement sidewalk.

As North Milwaukee was growing to maturity, however, so was its larger neighbor to the south. At the time of incorporation in 1897, the village was separated from Milwaukee by nearly two miles of farmland. (Holy Redeemer's first priest commuted from Ninth and Center every other Sunday—by bicycle.) Year after year, fueled by the same blend of industries and immigrants that drove North Milwaukee's growth, the larger city edged closer and closer to its northerly suburb. In 1924 Milwaukee's city limits touched the southeastern corner of North Milwaukee. It was increasingly clear that Milwaukee would either surround or absorb its neighbor.

North Milwaukee Will Die With the Old Year

aj. Gen. Wahl Dies Suddenly

Baths Are No Easier to Get in Chicago, So Runaway, Is Back

Art Teaching Brightened Up
City School Pupils Enjoy Work Now, Once Drudgery

Pocket Flasks Will Be Safe
Dry Agents to Confine Efforts to Clubs and Cabarets

Will the House of Tomorrow Look Like This?

Theodore Tomanek, Deputy Sheriff, Dies

Suburb to Be a Part of City
Annexation to Benefit by Gas Rate Cut and Fire Protection

Pastors Refute Barnes Theory
Smith College Professor's Statement Is Denounced

■ *After more than thirty years of independence, North Milwaukee joined the City of Milwaukee in 1929.*

Not everyone was alarmed by the prospect. Most North Milwaukeeans were transplanted Milwaukeeans, and continued movement from city to suburb nearly doubled North Milwaukee's population during the 1920s. The newcomers chafed under what they considered an inferior form of government. They found their property taxes more burdensome, their utility rates much higher, and the level of municipal services significantly lower than Milwaukee's. Cost-conscious residents began a movement to consolidate the two cities in 1921, and it rapidly gathered momentum. In a 1922 referendum, a slim majority of North Milwaukee voters expressed their desire to join Milwaukee.

Other residents, particularly those who had been part of the community since its village days, were determined to keep North Milwaukee independent. Among them was Mayor Emil Klamp, who dismissed the consolidation campaign as "the work of a few radicals." Most voters may have favored annexation, but they also returned Klamp and like-minded aldermen to office repeatedly. The result was a stalemate.

The battle between "annexationists" and "hometowners" simmered for years and finally reached its climax in 1927. With their patience exhausted, local activists organized the North Milwaukee Civic Club, which quickly claimed 1,800 members. Its sole issue was consolidation. The Civic Club started a newspaper (the *North Milwaukee Annexationist*), launched a voter-registration drive, and in 1928 sponsored a slate of candidates for local office. The entire ticket won, and the battle was over.

North Milwaukee's new leaders immediately opened discussions with Milwaukee officials and scheduled a referendum on consolidation. The outcome: 1,186 in favor and 548 opposed, a margin of more than two to one. Civic Club members celebrated with an impromptu parade down Villard Avenue. Mayor Daniel Hoan sent his congratulations, stating that the annexation would "place Milwaukee ahead of Buffalo in point of population and assist us in becoming a great metropolitan center."

On January 1, 1929, North Milwaukee officially became part of Milwaukee. The new high school on Custer Avenue (later Edison Middle School) was absorbed by the city's public school system. Smith Park, a scenic hardwood grove on Thirty-fifth Street, became a city and later a county park. The old village hall was used as a ward yard for Milwaukee sanitation workers. North Milwaukee, once a village and then a city, had become a neighborhood.

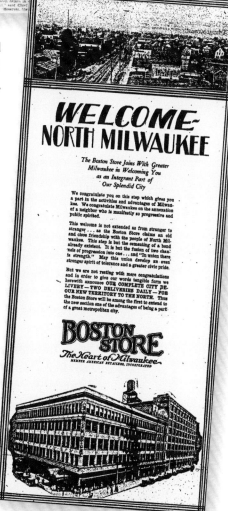

WELCOME NORTH MILWAUKEE
The Boston Store Joins With Greater Milwaukee in Welcoming You as an Integral Part of Our Splendid City

BOSTON STORE
The Heart of Milwaukee

In the City, Body and Soul

It took another thirty years for the city to completely surround its former suburb. After a long pause for the Depression and then World War II, development resumed in the 1940s. Empty lots inside North Milwaukee's original borders were covered with Cape Cods and modest ranch houses, and the same wave of construction swept around both sides of the community and kept surging to the northwest. By 1960 the process was complete. North Milwaukee became a residential island, a prewar neighborhood surrounded by postwar development. Generations later, the community still has Milwaukee's greatest concentration of pre-1930 houses outside the central city.

For two or three decades, the neighborhood retained a measure of its original independence. With its traditional industries, the familiar mix of stores in its commercial district, a wide variety of historic churches, and a full range of housing choices, North Milwaukee was, in many respects, practically self-sufficient. In this it resembled another strong community—Bay View, which happens to be the only other Milwaukee neighborhood that was once an independent suburb. Bay View, however, was isolated from the rest of the city. It began as a company town built around an iron mill in a sequestered corner of the south lakefront, and it was not until 1977, when the Daniel Hoan Bridge opened, that local residents had convenient access to central Milwaukee. North Milwaukee, by contrast, was part of an unbroken expanse of land that stretched from Downtown to the northwest for miles; it was connected to the heart of town by rail, by road, and by tradition.

■ *Exotic pets are one of Villard Avenue's specialties.*

Both early and late, it was the city's North Side that exercised the greatest influence on North Milwaukee. The North Side supplied most of the suburb's original residents, and the same district supplied most of the neighborhood's newcomers after 1970. What did change was the cultural background of the new arrivals. In the early 1900s the village was dominated by Germans who had moved north in search of new homes. In later years the neighborhood attracted African-American families following the identical path for identical reasons. The process of integration was calm, for the most part, and it was rapid as well. From less than 1 percent in 1970, North Milwaukee's black population surged to 40 percent in 1985 (roughly equal to the community's German stock) and kept climbing to 60 percent in 1990 and almost 90 percent in 2010.

These most recent North Milwaukeeans repurposed old institutions and created new ones. Churches that had once known only German hymns resounded to the joyful strains of gospel music. On Villard Avenue, fried chicken and collard greens ruled where pizza had once been sold and, across the street, country ham and crowder peas took the place of bratwurst and mettwurst. The suburb had joined the city bodily in 1929, and now it was bound in soul as well. The crisp borders of the original village blurred to the vanishing point and, in the view of many residents, North Milwaukee simply became part of the greater North Side. It was probably inevitable that the community's given name would lose its early potency. The surest sign of transformation may have come in 1994, when the name of the local public library branch was changed from "North Milwaukee" to "Villard Avenue."

What did not change to any appreciable extent was the neighborhood's landscape. North Milwaukee's present geography is as distinctive as its past history. The major rail corridors still inscribe a gigantic "X" over the heart of the community. Reinforced by diagonal highways and the meandering channel of Lincoln Creek, those corridors have sliced North Milwaukee into a sort of urban pie—a collection of wedge-shaped subneighborhoods, each with its own sense of

John Gurda

place. Some "slices" have fared better than others in the twenty-first century. The well-tended calm of the Lincoln Creek community near Sherman Boulevard and the village atmosphere of the Smith Park quadrant are counterbalanced by sections showing definite signs of struggle. Along the rail corridors themselves, deindustrialization has taken its toll. Wisconsin Bridge and Iron, the neighborhood's first major employer, closed its doors in 1983, and other old standbys have followed.

Although the challenges are obvious, so are North Milwaukee's advantages. There are still industries along the tracks, and Villard Avenue remains a viable business district, but one of the community's most important assets is its tradition of civic activism. In the 1920s local residents came together around the issue of consolidation. In the 1970s, during the peak years of integration, two organizations emerged to ensure a smooth transition: North Milwaukee CONCERN and North Milwaukee ACTION. The second group's slogan could have applied almost anywhere: "You don't have to move to live in a better neighborhood."

The activist spirit has taken different form in more recent years. The Northwest Side Community Development Corporation, established in a former firehouse on Hopkins Street in 1983, has expanded its target area and broadened its mission to include business loans, workforce development, and planning services. One of the CDC's major achievements grew out of a partnership with the Milwaukee Public Library. In 2011 the partners teamed with a private developer to build Villard Square, a pioneering mixed-use project on Thirty-fifth and Villard. A state-of-the-art branch library on the ground floor replaced an antiquated facility down the street, and the three upper floors contained forty-seven units of "grandfamily" housing—apartments designed for grandparents raising their school-age grandchildren. Villard Square provides vital services to local residents and has added new life to North Milwaukee's oldest business district.

An even more ambitious project came to life in the neighborhood's southeast quadrant—the section closest to the City of Milwaukee in suburban days. When North Milwaukee was young, churches were the leading centers of community. Holy Redeemer Church of God in Christ has revived that tradition and carried it to an entirely new dimension. Established in 1986, Holy Redeemer is a largely African-American congregation that has grown, under the leadership of Bishop Sedgwick Daniels, into a Milwaukee powerhouse. Although the church proclaims itself "unashamedly Pentecostal and unapologetically sanctified," it ministers to the whole person. Holy Redeemer's sprawling complex on Thirty-fifth and Hampton houses schools, a Boys & Girls Club, a credit union, a health clinic, and a conference center as well as worship space. Just across the tracks, at Thirty-second and Hampton, is Bishop's Creek, a mixed-use development that includes an apartment complex, a youth dormitory, a prayer tower, and plenty of space for future projects. Year by year, Holy Redeemer has reclaimed the long-idle industrial plants of an earlier age to meet the needs of North Milwaukee's current residents.

That spirit of reuse, even of redemption, has become a significant theme in the North Milwaukee of the twenty-first century. The annexation battles of the 1920s are long-forgotten, but the neighborhood remains a place apart. Shaped by its history and defined by its geography, North Milwaukee is an island in the urban stream. The residents of the island have changed over time, and the banks show signs of erosion in places, but the neighborhood remains a thoroughly distinctive part of Milwaukee, one that can look back to the strengths of a common past to build a stronger future.

■ *Sunday morning at Holy Redeemer Church of God in Christ*

John Gurda

The shadow of North Milwaukee's industrial past still lingers as life goes on in the twenty-first century.

all photos on these two pages by John Gurda

■ *A range of housing choices, a fondness for greenery, and a fighting spirit are all key assets as North Milwaukee faces the future.*

THURSTON
WOODS

M · I · L · W · A · U · K · E · E

Thurston Woods

Thurston is gone, but his woods remain. Trees, in fact, are the first thing you notice when you enter this far North Side neighborhood: a stately conclave of oaks and ashes, maples and hickories, some of them much older than the homes they shelter. The trees recall the area's rural past, as do place names like Berryland and Florist Avenue, but they also lend the community an air of long-settled tranquility. The countryside may have disappeared years ago, but its spirit lingers in the leafy canopy that unfolds over the neighborhood each spring.

The appearances are, to some degree, deceiving. Thurston Woods is actually a mid-twentieth-century community, developed on either side of World War II by Milwaukeeans moving up from older neighborhoods to the south; it's not markedly different from large sections of Menomonee Falls or Germantown. Although its history is relatively brief, the community preserves a unique ambience. What attracted the first urban settlers is the same combination of qualities that keeps today's residents in place: a wide range of affordable housing choices, easy access to jobs and commerce, and an unmistakable edge-of-the-city feeling. Enhanced by the abundance of trees, that sense of living on the urban fringe persists long after the actual fringe migrated miles to the north.

Thurston Woods

1. Agape Community Center
2. Carleton School
3. Christ Memorial Lutheran Church
4. Growing Power hoophouses
5. Havenwoods Environmental Awareness Center
6. Mason Temple Church of God in Christ
7. R.H. Bierman Home (log cabin)
8. Sigma-Aldrich Chemical Plant (American Can Company Site)
9. Silver Mill (Northland) Shopping Center
10. Thurston Woods Campus – Milwaukee Public Schools (St. Albert Catholic School Site)

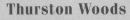

0   1,000 FT

N

Searching for Mr. Thurston

There was no Thurston at the neighborhood's inception. When the first white settlers arrived in the 1830s, the land that became Thurston Woods was an anonymous section of the Town of Granville, which covered thirty-six square miles of unincorporated land in the northwest corner of Milwaukee County. Like the rest of the county, Granville was, in the *Milwaukee Sentinel's* phrase, "a promising wilderness" practically covered with trees. The forest was quickly cleared to create farmland, but not in every case; many farmers preserved woodlots for fuel, maple syrup, or simple sentiment. The scenic grove around the intersection of Thurston Avenue and Thirty-fourth Street—the psychological heart of Thurston Woods—began as one of those woodlots.

Farming in Granville was much the same as farming elsewhere in Wisconsin: first wheat, then mixed crops, and finally dairying. What set the township apart was its proximity to the Milwaukee market. Local farmers had easy access to the city along the Cedarburg Road (today's Teutonia Avenue), and as transportation improved, particularly in the twentieth century, they specialized in table crops that required more intensive cultivation but offered more lucrative returns. The Wilcox family tended row upon row of raspberries in what is now the northwest corner of Thurston Woods—on the site of the appropriately named Berryland housing project. A half-mile east, between Teutonia Avenue and Thirty-fifth Street, local growers built a cluster of greenhouses that supplied carnations, poinsettias, and other flowers to the Milwaukee market. The southern border of that cluster was Florist Avenue—another appropriate name choice.

Although agriculture dominated its past, industry helped to determine the neighborhood's future. In the early 1890s a new settlement began to take shape literally next door: North Milwaukee. Located at the crossing of

■ *The Town of Granville was covered with pioneer farms like this homestead on Green Bay Road.*

Milwaukee County Historical Society

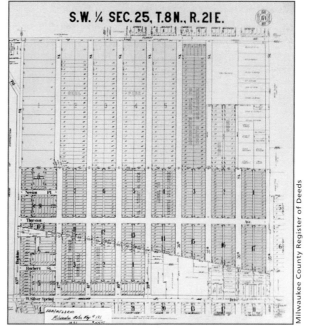

S.W. ¼ SEC. 25, T.8 N., R. 21 E.

two major railroad lines, North Milwaukee blossomed as an industrial suburb filled with trackside industries whose products ranged from bicycles to bridges. When the settlement incorporated as a free-standing village in 1897, its northern border was Silver Spring Road— the southern limit of what would eventually become Thurston Woods.

The same rail lines that created North Milwaukee continued on both sides of Thurston Woods, and developers sensed an opportunity. Here, finally, Mr. Thurston makes his entrance. He was not, as you might imagine, a local farmer who saved part of the original forest from the ravages of the axe. Researcher Carl Baehr identified the man behind the name as William H. Thurston, "an oyster dealer who dabbled in real estate," and further study uncovered his likely connection. In 1893 Milwaukee lawyer George A. West platted one of the first subdivisions in today's neighborhood: G.A. West & Co's. Addition to North Milwaukee, which stretched from Thirty-fifth Street to Sherman Boulevard north of Silver Spring. The subdivision was laid out in thirty-foot lots, suggesting that it was intended for industrial workers like those flocking to North Milwaukee.

West's partners in the venture included William Thurston, whom local papers described as "the Grand Avenue oyster king," and George West decided to name the subdivision's major east-west street for his partner and hunting buddy. (West and Thurston shot 392 geese on one 1895 foray to North Dakota.) William Thurston never lived in the neighborhood—in fact, he was never more than a minor investor in its development—but Thurston Avenue put his name on the map. The original roadway ended at Thirty-fifth Street. When it was extended lakeward to Teutonia Avenue, the

■ (above left) *Greenhouses and fields of flowers dominated the landscape in this aerial view of the rectangle bordered by Green Bay Avenue and Thirty-fifth Street north of Florist. Florist Avenue itself* (above) *was named for the local specialty.*

■ *George West, whose subdivision is shown in pink, named its main street for his friend and hunting partner, William Thurston. The Thurston connection proved to be permanent.*

street practically bisected the old woodlot east of Thirty-fifth. Thurston Avenue went through the woods, in other words, providing a probable, or at least plausible, reason to call the neighborhood Thurston Woods. The fact that the woodlot was later subdivided as Thurston Forest adds weight to the theory.

George West, William Thurston, and their associates had good instincts but poor timing. It took nearly thirty years for North Milwaukee to fill in completely, and traffic on the north side of Silver Spring Road was light indeed. William Thurston had cashed in his various holdings and retired to Los Angeles long before the first urban settlers arrived. By the time the oyster magnate died there in 1902 (he's buried in Hollywood Cemetery), only a handful of lots in G.A. West & Co's. Addition had been sold. The development was, in hindsight, decades premature.

Although Thurston Woods remained a promoter's dream, there were some interesting developments on its margins. A handful of

factories went up along the railroad tracks east of Teutonia, and a more ambitious project took shape on the opposite side of the future neighborhood. In 1917 Milwaukee County moved its House of Correction from an antiquated facility on the South Side to a 420-acre parcel just west of Sherman Boulevard. It was a minimum-security prison for up to 1,000 inmates, most serving short terms for alcohol-related offenses. (The advent of Prohibition in 1919 pushed the population to record levels.) Committed to the "safekeeping, reformation, and employment" of inmates, the House of Correction provided all of them with jobs. Some worked in a well-equipped chair factory, while a greater number labored on the prison farm. Convicts unaccustomed to rural chores tended Holsteins, managed chickens, and tilled fields that produced tons of butter, thousands of eggs, and truckloads of vegetables for themselves and the residents of other county institutions.

■ *The Milwaukee County House of Correction moved from the South Side to the Thurston Woods area in 1917 and steadily expanded its campus.*

Havenwoods State Forest

John Gurda

Milwaukee Public Library

It was in the 1920s that the long-antici-pated neighborhood finally began to take shape. With an industrial suburb to its south, the House of Correction to its west, and a thin belt of industries to its east, Thurston Woods grew up in the space between. There was a rash of subdivision activity north of Silver Spring after 1925 and a corresponding surge in lot sales that lasted into the early 1930s. Most of the new dwellings were rel-atively small workers' homes like those that blanketed North Milwaukee, but by no means all. The old woodlot around Thirty-fourth and Thurston attracted a notably upscale clientele. Platted as the Thurston Forest subdivision in 1931 (with additions in 1936 and 1940), its lots were covered with the brick and stone homes of merchants, business owners, and professionals who could just as easily have settled in Shorewood or Whitefish Bay. The most distinctive home in Thurston For-est—and in all of Thurston Woods, for that matter—was a modified log cabin on Thir-ty-fourth and Thurston. Completed in 1931, it was a genuine hybrid, combining materials from a pioneer log house found nearby with new construction. The reconfigured home's first owner was R.H. Bierman, the architect

who designed it. In keeping with the pioneer theme, there were, by common consent of local homeowners, no sidewalks, no curbs, and no sewer grates in the Thurston Forest subdivisions—a throwback to rural times that survives to the present.

The neighborhood's forward progress came to a halt with the onset of the De-pression. Lots were still sold and homes were still built during the hard times—the Town of Granville put up Carleton School in 1940 to accommodate the growing num-ber of children—but development slowed to a languid pace that didn't quicken until the end of World War II. The most notable activity in the vicinity of Thurston Woods took place on its western border. Soon after Pearl Harbor, the federal government leased part of the House of Correction for the internment of "enemy aliens," whose only offense, in most cases, was their German birth. Later in the conflict, the U.S. Army commandeered the facility, using it first as a camp for German prisoners of war and then as a "disciplinary barracks"—a mili-tary prison—for court-martialed American soldiers. The rest of the neighborhood lay dormant, awaiting the return of peacetime.

■ (above left)
Carleton School, built by the Town of Wauwatosa in 1940, became a Milwaukee public school after the area was annexed by the city.

■ (above)
A modest business district developed along Silver Spring Road near its intersection with Thirty-fifth Street.

293

Becoming an Urban Neighborhood

The postwar period marked Thurston Woods' emergence in its modern form. Returning GIs, many of them about to start families, came home to an unprecedented housing shortage. There had been relatively little construction activity during the Depression and war years, and now developers had to make up for lost time. The result was an explosion—the longest sustained building boom in American history. Because it had been at the leading edge of settlement before the war, Thurston Woods was among the first Milwaukee neighborhoods to feel the blast. The few hundred housing units built north of Silver Spring before 1940 mushroomed to nearly 2,500 as the neighborhood filled out to its limits. There were some larger homes in the mix, but most of the new dwellings were Cape Cods, small ranches, and a variety of "prefabs" nailed together in a matter of days and anchored to concrete slabs.

Even hurry-up housing couldn't satisfy the continuing demand. The City of Milwaukee, after experimenting with barracks and Quonset huts, began to develop permanent housing specifically for veterans and their families. The first two projects, Northlawn and Southlawn, were completed in 1949, and the third, Berryland, filled the northwest corner of Thurston Woods in 1950. Acres of raspberry canes were plowed under to make way for 76 rowhouses with a combined total of 391 units, ranging in size from one to three bedrooms, each with its own basement, laundry, and small yard. Berryland offered a high-density alternative to the single-family homes popping up everywhere else in the neighborhood.

Whether they rented in Berryland or owned their own homes, the people of Thurston Woods had much in common. The greatest number had moved from older neighborhoods on the North Side, and they typically commuted back to industrial jobs in central Milwaukee. Reflecting the ethnic makeup of their old communities, most were descended from German immigrants; as recently as 1980, 51 percent

■ *Berryland was built by the City of Milwaukee to ease a critical shortage of housing for World War II veterans and their families. The complex is shown* (from top) *under construction in 1949, from the air in 1961, and at street level in 1965.*

of Thurston Woods residents claimed at least some German ancestry. The newcomers also brought their religious traditions with them. One of the neighborhood's more dynamic churches was Christ Memorial Lutheran (Missouri Synod) on Teutonia Avenue. The congregation built its first home in 1946 and experienced such rapid growth—drawing up to 1,000 worshipers each Sunday—that it was forced to erect a larger sanctuary next door in 1961.

The last vestiges of rural life faded as Thurston Woods filled in. Milwaukee's city limits had been frozen at Silver Spring Road since 1929, but they thawed steadily northward following World War II. Thurston Woods was annexed in stages between 1945 and 1951, with the biggest parcels joining the city in 1948. Once annexation was complete, Silver Spring was widened, interior streets were paved, and sidewalks were installed—with the notable exception of the Thurston Forest subdivisions. There were also some major non-residential developments. In 1950 the American Can Company built a massive plant at the railroad crossing east of Teutonia Avenue and quickly became a major supplier of containers for Milwaukee's breweries. Practically across the street, where greenhouses had once broadcast the scent of flowers, the Northland (later Silver Mill) shopping center opened to meet the neighborhood's commercial needs.

By 1960 the settlement of Thurston Woods was virtually complete. What had once been the countryside became an urban neighborhood, and so it has remained ever since. Old trees have died and their offspring have grown taller, but Thurston Woods looks much the same in the twenty-first century as it did in the closing decades of the twentieth. Not that there haven't been changes, and plenty of them. Retail businesses have turned over, the Sigma-Aldrich chemical plant has replaced the American Can factory on Teutonia Avenue, and Berryland's population has changed. In the 1970s, with the postwar housing shortage only a memory, the project's townhomes were opened to all moderate-income applicants, with veterans still given priority.

■ *Thurston Woods grew so fast that in 1961 Christ Lutheran had to add a new sanctuary* (right) *to its original 1946 church.*

■ *The American Can Company, a major supplier to Milwaukee breweries, became the neighborhood's largest industry in 1950.*

The biggest change of all has been cultural. Just as the postwar wave of homeseekers, most of them German by ancestry, swept into Thurston Woods from Milwaukee's North Side, the current generation of residents, most of them African-American, migrated northward from the same neighborhoods. The community's African-American population swelled from 2 percent of the total in 1970 to 37 percent in 1990 and 81 percent in 2010. Most of the newer arrivals occupy the same middle-income stratum as the people they replaced, but the cultural shift has caused some dislocations, particularly for historically white religious congregations. St. Albert's Church, the center of Catholicism in the

neighborhood since 1955, closed in 1991, and its combination church-school on Thirty-fifth Street was sold to become Thurston Woods Public School. At Christ Memorial Lutheran, the two-sanctuary church on Teutonia that had once drawn 1,000 faithful to worship, Sunday attendance dropped to seventy. In the meantime, Mason Temple Church of God in Christ, an African-American congregation with deep roots on the North Side, built a spacious church on Thirty-Fifth Street in 2006 that served more than 200.

As the community changed and aged, it began to experience some of the challenges common to many urban neighborhoods, including absentee landlords, public safety concerns, and a spate of foreclosures following the 2008 mortgage crisis. Local residents have also found resources to deal with those problems, beginning with Agape Community Center. Founded in 1986 by a religious order of women whose motherhouse once stood nearby on Teutonia Avenue, Agape built a full-service center in the heart of Berryland in 2000. It offers after-school and summer programs for young people, community meals, health screenings, career fairs, and a variety of initiatives to build a sense of neighborhood, including block clubs, community gardens, home improvement contests, and even low-cost flower seeds. Agape's activities have encouraged a flowering of pride in the neighborhood, visible in everything from stepped-up home maintenance efforts to Thurston Woods' very own neighborhood flag.

That resurgent spirit is perhaps best symbolized by a development on the neighborhood's western border. The former House of Correction, after periods as a POW camp, an Army disciplinary barracks, and a Nike anti-aircraft missile site, was virtually abandoned in the late 1960s, its buildings left to vandals and its land gone to seed. In 1980, fulfilling the dream of a community task force, the property was reborn as Havenwoods State Forest, the first urban unit in Wisconsin's forest system. Year by year, tree by tree, Havenwoods has returned to a state of nature, giving Thurston Woods a living point of contact with its rural beginnings.

■ *Home sweet home is sweet indeed in Thurston Woods.*

all photos on these two pages by John Gurda

The neighborhood is, in fact, an intriguing hybrid. Thurston Woods shares in equal parts the green ambience of Havenwoods, the post-industrial character of North Milwaukee, and the suburban atmosphere of neighboring Glendale. Its homes bridge the gap from prewar to postwar architecture. Some blocks match the best of what Shorewood or Sherman Park have to offer, while others were built in a hurry to meet a desperate demand for housing. Although today's population is largely African-American, diversity remains one of the neighborhood's core strengths, and local residents wouldn't have it any other way. "This neighborhood is the best-kept secret in Milwaukee," said Mavis McCallum, a proud resident since 1973. "It's so peaceful here, with the stately trees and the solid housing. You don't have to pay Shorewood prices for Shorewood-type homes. It's just a great place to live." Mr. Thurston is long gone, but the neighborhood that bears his name is still there, offering a picturesque haven at the edge of the city.

■ *The former House of Correction site experienced an unlikely rebirth in 1980, when it became Havenwoods State Forest. Prairie plants blossomed where inmates had once tended cows on the prison farm.*

■ *The urban forest reaches stately heights in Thurston Woods.*

■ *(center)*
Growing Power, a powerhouse in urban agriculture, maintains a cluster of hoophouses behind Carleton School.

■ *(bottom)*
Deer are permanent residents of Havenwoods State Forest, and its nature center (bottom right) offers a year-round schedule of educational programs.

all photos on these two pages by John Gurda

East Side

In a city with a land area of roughly 100 square miles, the East Side occupies only four. That statistic surprises most Milwaukeeans because it seems to understate the district's influence by a wide margin. What the East Side lacks in size, however, it makes up for in density and diversity. The result is a district best understood as a compact collection of different worlds. The East Side has room for multitudes, in lake-bluff towers, riverfront condos, and detached homes that run the gamut from modest to magnificent. The residential choices are broad, but they fall into two well-defined corridors of settlement—wealthy near the lake and working-class along the river.

That historic contrast is the district's defining characteristic, but the differences transcend income and occupation. Since settlement began in the mid-1800s, the East Side has accommodated successive waves of immigrants and various incarnations of the youth culture, taking on a cosmopolitan personality unique in the city. Add a major university to the mix and the district's cultural quotient climbs even higher. The East Side may occupy only four percent of Milwaukee's real estate, but it plays an oversized role in the life of the larger city.

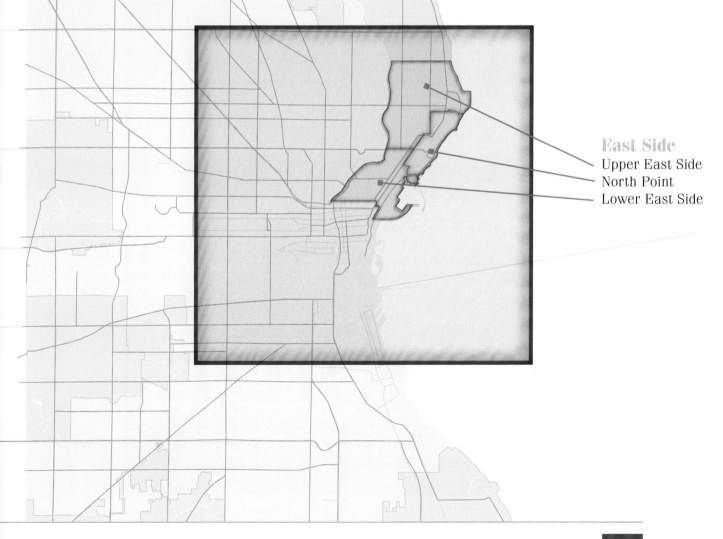

East Side
Upper East Side
North Point
Lower East Side

LOWER

EAST SIDE

M·I·L·W·A·U·K·E·E

Lower East Side

The Lower East Side is a narrow crown of land, less than a mile wide in most places, that separates the final stretch of the Milwaukee River from Lake Michigan. Perched on that crown is a neighborhood of extremes. The area's homes range from upscale condominium towers to cozy backyard cottages, its residents vary from Old World immigrants to New World entrepreneurs, and its businesses run the gamut from yoga studios to pasta parlors. "You name it," said one proud resident, "and we've got it." If diversity is the hallmark of a truly great city, the Lower East Side is a major component of Milwaukee's greatness.

Lower East Side

1. Charles Allis Art Museum
2. East Pointe Commons
3. Holy Rosary Catholic Church – Three Holy Women Parish
4. Jewish Museum Milwaukee
5. Kane Commons
6. Kenilworth Square – UW-Milwaukee
7. McKinley Marina
8. Milwaukee Community Sailing Center
9. Milwaukee River Flushing Station (Colectivo Coffee)
10. Milwaukee Yacht Club
11. North Avenue Dam Site
12. Oriental Theater
13. St. Hedwig's Catholic Church – Three Holy Women Parish
14. St. Rita's Catholic Church – Three Holy Women Parish
15. Wisconsin Conservatory of Music

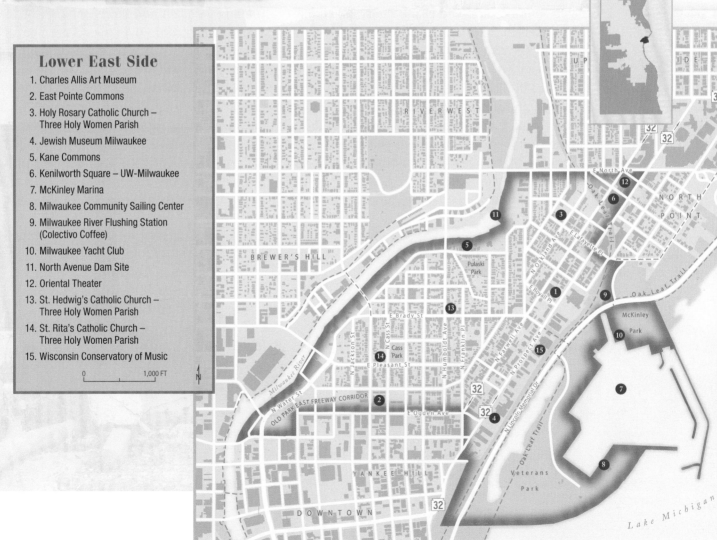

Same Place, Different Worlds

The Lower East Side has been a neighborhood of contrasts from the very beginning. The extremes, in fact, were even more pronounced in the community's formative years, particularly between the wealthy and the working class. The original East Siders included grain traders, lumber barons, lawyers, merchants, bankers, and assorted other plutocrats. Nearly all were Yankees from New England and New York, and many were former residents of Yankee Hill, the affluent neighborhood south of Ogden Avenue. In the 1870s, with Yankee Hill nearly filled to capacity, these members of the civic elite began to build homes on Prospect Avenue. Once an Indian trail and later a muddy turnpike, the avenue soon boasted one of the finest collections of Victorian mansions in the Midwest. "As far as the eye can see," wrote an 1881 observer, "Prospect Avenue is lined with houses, many of which fall little short of palaces." With its fine homes and even finer "prospect" of the lake, this "broad and splendid avenue" became a mandatory stop for visitors to Milwaukee.

A few blocks west, something quite different was happening. In the 1860s a group of Polish immigrants began to settle on the river bluff north of Brady Street. Most were natives of Poland's Kaszuby region on the Baltic seacoast, and the Lower East Side's chief attraction was jobs. A millrace below the North Avenue dam was filling in with sawmills, tanneries, and flour mills, and the train shops of the Milwaukee Road were just across the river at Humboldt and North Avenues until 1880. With an abundance of entry-level jobs close by, the Polish "Kaszubs" covered the blocks north of Brady Street with modest cottages and two-story flats. Their settlement was extremely dense by modern standards; some lots contained two or three houses, not to mention cow sheds and chicken coops.

In 1871 the immigrants organized St. Hedwig's Parish and built a church on Brady Street and Franklin Place. (The men of the parish dug the foundation with their own hands.) They added a school two years later, and in 1887, when membership topped 600 families, the congregation completed the present church on Humboldt Avenue and Brady Street. St. Hedwig's was only the second Polish congregation in Milwaukee (following St. Stanislaus on the South Side), and the church became the cornerstone of the community that grew up in its shadow.

■ *The Lower East Side began as a neighborhood of extremes, from cottages near the river, like these immigrant dwellings on Van Buren Street, to castles on the lake bluff. This Prospect Avenue mansion belonged to banker and grain merchant Charles Ray.*

Milwaukee County Historical Society

Milwaukee Public Library

Archdiocese of Milwaukee

Milwaukee Public Library

■ (left)
The Polish presence was particularly strong in the neighborhood's formative years. Established in 1871, St. Hedwig's was the second Polish church in Milwaukee.

■ (right)
Pulaski Street, a filled-in ravine, ran through the center of one of the most densely settled districts in Milwaukee.

The Lower East Side, then, began as a row of castles on the lake bluff and a cluster of cottages near the river. The pattern became more complex as development continued. Between 1870 and 1900 the neighborhood's central blocks filled in with residents who ranged from tannery workers to corporate attorneys. They were a diverse group, but the newcomers tended to occupy a middle ground in the neighborhood, economically as well as physically. They made the blocks south of Brady Street a stronghold of vintage Victorians, complete with Gothic peaks, scrollwork porches, and the highest concentration of rowhouses in the city. The new residents also reflected the ethnic makeup of communities to the south. The interior blocks attracted Anglo-Saxons from Yankee Hill, Germans from the City Hall area, and Irish families from the Third Ward. In 1885 the Irish organized Holy Rosary Parish and began to build a church on Oakland Avenue. Like St. Hedwig's a few blocks away, it became an anchor of community life.

By 1900 the Lower East Side was a settled neighborhood, but its evolution continued without pause. Milwaukee's population quadrupled between 1870 and 1900 and, as the city grew, so did the demand for housing near its center. The first apartment buildings went up on Prospect Avenue before 1910, and their numbers multiplied in the next two decades. A few

Milwaukee County Historical Society

dowagers stayed behind, but most of Prospect Avenue's wealthier families moved to newly minted suburbs like Shorewood and Whitefish Bay. To the west, St. Hedwig's remained the center of a staunchly Polish community after 1900, but that community, too, was spreading beyond its original borders. Dozens of Polish families moved across the Humboldt Avenue bridge to new homes in the Riverwest neighborhood, where they established two new Catholic parishes: St. Casimir's (1893) and St. Mary Czestochowa (1907).

As the original families moved away, newcomers settled in the neighborhood, including a large number of Italians. In the late 1800s Sicilian families had begun to replace the

■ *Grocers like Frank Wojciechowski supplied their Polish neighbors with goods they couldn't make themselves.*

305

■ *Employment was always close by, and so was entertainment. Pfister & Vogel's riverfront tannery provided hundreds of jobs, and the Oriental Theater, completed in 1927, gave tired workers a chance to escape for an hour or two.*

Irish community in the Third Ward and, like the Irish, many of them moved to the Lower East Side as they made economic headway. In 1919 St. Rita's Mission was opened on Cass Street near Ogden Avenue to serve the new East Siders. The mission became St. Rita's Church twenty years later, and its new building on Cass and Pleasant Streets became a focal point of identity for Milwaukee's Italian community.

The pace of change accelerated in the 1920s; general prosperity brought new cultural groups, new apartment buildings, and new landmarks to the Lower East Side. One

of the boldest additions to the area was the Oriental Theater, which opened in 1927. Built on the site of an old streetcar barn, the Oriental was promoted as "the most beautiful and artistic temple of Oriental art to be found anywhere in America." It was certainly one of the most eclectic; the theater's designers borrowed liberally from Buddhist, Islamic, Egyptian, Indian, and a variety of other traditions. With the advent of "talkies" in the late 1920s, the Oriental became one of the most popular movie palaces in Milwaukee.

Development of all kinds came to a standstill during the Depression and World War

■ *City officials created recreational opportunities on both sides of this populous neighborhood. The Caesar's Park wading pool was constructed next to the North Avenue dam in 1929, and the Juneau Park lagoon was enclosed by landfill during the same decade.*

II, but the neighborhood's transformation resumed with new speed when peacetime returned in 1945. Dozens of Prospect Avenue mansions fell before the wrecking ball, and the neighborhood's eastern skyline fairly bristled with high-rise apartment towers. The Brady Street area remained heavily Polish for a time; in 1950 three-fourths of St. Hedwig's 3,130 members were Polish by birth or background. Eventually, however, the Polish community dispersed to newer neighborhoods. The Italian presence on Brady Street became more pronounced, but the neighborhood's diversity came to reflect

the confluence of many streams rather than a conspicuous few. Year by year and block by block, the Lower East Side moved steadily away from the intensely ethnic, family-centered patterns of its early years.

The establishment of the University of Wisconsin-Milwaukee in 1956 added another layer to the area's cultural life. The Lower East Side had the greatest concentration of student-priced housing in the general vicinity of the campus, and it soon became a haven for young people. The emphasis on youth was even more obvious in the late 1960s, when Brady Street became the offbeat epicenter

307

the East Pointe Commons apartment project was completed. On Prospect Avenue, in the meantime, the high-rises kept getting higher, and they included condominium towers as well as apartment buildings. The ranks of the old mansions on Prospect continued to thin; those that survived typically became professional offices or private schools. Comparable development pressures have transformed the river side of the neighborhood in more recent years, particularly along Water Street. The apartment blocks and condo towers there represent a marked departure from the working-class housing of the formative years. Linking the river and the lake is the Oak Leaf Trail, set in the narrow bed of the old Chicago & North Western Railroad. The trail enables bikers, joggers, skaters, and strollers to traverse one of Milwaukee's most congested neighborhoods without once stopping for a traffic signal.

Ethnically, too, the Lower East Side has evolved away from its nineteenth-century roots. Although there is still an obvious Italian presence on Brady Street, the sharp distinctions of years past have blurred significantly. Change was evident in 2000, when the Lower East Side's three Catholic parishes—St. Hedwig's (Polish), Holy Rosary (Irish), and St. Rita's (Italian)—came together as Three Holy Women. The merger would have been unthinkable in any previous generation. As the old lines have faded, new groups have made their homes in the neighborhood. In 2010 African Americans, Latinos, and Asians made up roughly 20 percent of the Lower East Side's population, and they are dispersed throughout the community.

Not only is the neighborhood internally diverse, but it also attracts a wide range of visitors from throughout the region. There are at any given moment at least forty restaurants and a comparable number of nightspots operating on the Lower East Side. If there's a new fusion dish, a cutting-edge hair style, a fresh take on the martini, or a novel commercial idea, this is where Milwaukeeans are likely to find it first. They can take self-guided gastronomic tours featuring the cuisines of Italy, Korea, Ethiopia, Mexico, Thailand, Greece, the Mideast, and Japan, or browse local stores for vintage clothing, Turkish imports, Italian pastries, juggling

■ *The Brady Street Festival was a summertime highlight during the street's reign as capital of Milwaukee's counterculture.*

of Milwaukee's counterculture. Shops selling candles and sandals, books and beads proliferated, and the scent of incense and other substances wafted out over the streets from second-floor apartment windows. Older residents were mystified, but the young people kept coming. Water Tower Park, near the neighborhood's northeast corner, became their favored gathering spot.

Everyone's Neighborhood

The Lower East Side's evolution has continued since the heyday of hippiedom, and it has proceeded by both addition and subtraction. A block-wide swath of buildings along Ogden Avenue was cleared in the late 1960s for a freeway that was never constructed. The Park East corridor was an open wound on the neighborhood's southern border until 1991, when

John Gurda

■ *St. Rita's Church preserved its Italian heritage through the 1970s and beyond. A pre-Lenten celebration called St. Joseph's Table featured a cake baked in the shape of Sicily, the ancestral home of most parishioners.*

supplies, and Oriental rugs. On weekend evenings, even in winter, the club scene on Brady Street and North Avenue is perhaps the most vibrant in the city. There are also impressive cultural resources, from the studied elegance of the Charles Allis Art Museum to the ersatz splendor of the Oriental Theater. The Lower East Side, in short, is everyone's neighborhood. Home to a variety of cultures and host to many more, this is where a transplanted Easterner might go if he or she felt lonesome for the density and diversity of the Atlantic seaboard.

Although variety is the keynote, some broad demographic patterns unite this complex community. The Lower East Side is, first of all, a neighborhood of adults. Only 3 percent of its residents were under sixteen in 2010, compared with 24 percent for the city as a whole; children are a rarity on most blocks. The two dominant groups are young adults and senior citizens. In 2010 nearly 20 percent of all Lower East Siders were ages twenty to twenty-four—twice the city average—and 14 percent were older than sixty-five—50 percent higher than the city as a whole. Whether old or young, East Siders tend to be single, and they tend to be renters; in 2010 more than 80 percent of the neighborhood's housing units were renter-occupied.

The landscape that these single adults share is, paradoxically, anonymous and intimate at the same time. Precisely because the area is so dense, so diverse, and so heavily traveled, it might seem that the Lower East Side would discourage a sense of belonging. On the ground level, however, the neighborhood is a collection of pockets, each with its own powerful sense of home. The major sub-communities of the past—the Victorian stronghold south of Brady Street, the Polish enclave around St. Hedwig's Church, the middle-income settlement along Oakland Avenue, the Prospect Avenue high-rise corridor—are still physically intact, and each adds a vital ingredient to the character of the whole. In some ways the Lower East Side is more a confederation of communities than a single neighborhood. Then there are the pockets within pockets, like the Kane Commons "urban courtyard" complex above the Milwaukee River or the knot of Victorians on Jackson Street, that make the same point on an even smaller scale.

The intimate/anonymous paradox is reinforced by the area's street network. The Lower East Side marks the intersection of two major street systems—one running parallel to the lake bluff and the other conforming to the

■ (right)
The Oak Leaf Trail fills the old North Western Railroad corridor.

standard rectangular grid. The result is topographic chaos. There are short streets, long streets, busy boulevards, and side streets as narrow as alleys. They join and part at every angle imaginable, heightening the neighborhood's unpredictability and strengthening the contrast between public and private space. The major arterials belong to everyone, but only insiders can navigate the neighborhood's interior with confidence.

The complex interplay of history and geography has given the Lower East Side a character not typically found in a mid-sized city like Milwaukee. There is a sense that, within obvious limits, anything goes. No single group or institution holds moral sway, and the only norm that a resident could possibly conform to is nonconformity. What Lower East Siders share instead is a point of view—one

that values convenience, diversity, and that complex of traits sometimes called urbanism. The community's live-and-let-live mentality is palpable. The Lower East Side has provided a home for so many different people and so many different ideas for such a long time that tolerance has become second nature to its residents. That tolerance, long-practiced, often-tested, and blended with affection, is among the neighborhood's most distinctive and most valuable resources.

From the mid-1800s to the twenty-first century, from the phalanx of high-rises overlooking Lake Michigan to the cluster of cottages along the Milwaukee River, the neighborhood has always been a cosmopolitan collection of different worlds. No true Lower East Sider would have it any other way.

Christopher Winters

Jessica Lothman

Christopher Winters

■ *Street life abounds on the Lower East Side,
which ends in a solid wall of high-rises on Prospect Avenue.*

Christopher Winters

Jessica Lothman

Christopher Winters

Christopher Winters

■ (above)
The former Northwestern Hanna Fuel Company headquarters on Farwell Avenue, an Art Deco gem built in 1934

Jessica Lothman

Jessica Lothman

Christopher Winters

■ (top)
Colectivo Coffee occupies an 1888 pumphouse that pulled fresh lake water under the East Side to flush the putrid Milwaukee River.

■ (above)
The Wisconsin Conservatory of Music is housed in a Prospect Avenue mansion.

■ (left)
Brady Street after dark

NORTHPOINT

M·I·L·W·A·U·K·E·E

North Point

A picturesque water tower, a lighthouse, and a hospital—those are the landmarks you see on North Point's skyline from the far side of Milwaukee Bay. The view from within the neighborhood, below the treeline, is substantially different. North Point is a narrow band of gracious homes inlaid on the lake bluff like architectural gems; the fine homes and the prevailing sense of privacy have made North Point one of Milwaukee's most desirable addresses for well over a century. But the neighborhood is also an integral part of the intensely urban East Side. Apartment-dwellers are actually more numerous than single-family homeowners, and the community lies barely two miles north of Downtown. Its hybrid character and prime location have given North Point a place of distinction in the city's history, geography, and civic life—a place the community continues to occupy with unmistakable pride.

North Point

1. Bradford Beach
2. Columbia St. Mary's Hospital Campus
3. East Branch – Milwaukee Public Library
4. Eastcastle Place (Protestant Home)
5. Downer Theater
6. Maryland Avenue Montessori School – Milwaukee Public Schools
7. McKinley Beach
8. Milwaukee Catholic Home
9. Milwaukee River Flushing Station (Colectivo Coffee)
10. North Point Lighthouse
11. North Point Water Tower
12. Oriental Theatre
13. Sendik's Market
14. Villa Terrace Decorative Arts Museum

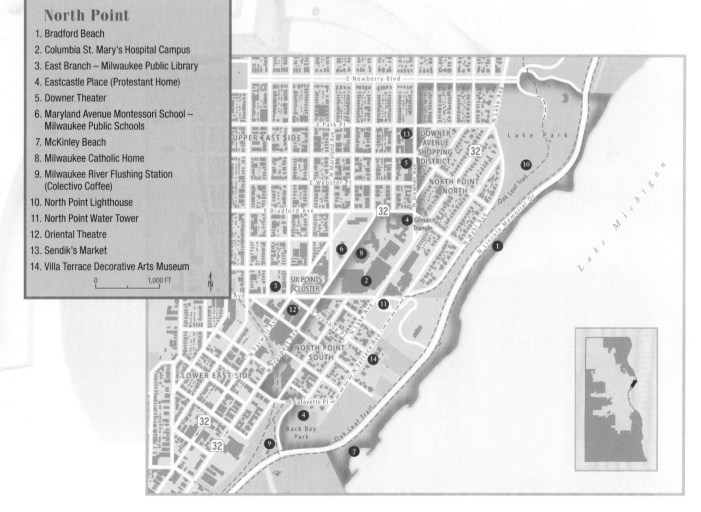

In the Tower's Shadow

North Point's history began Downtown. In the 1840s, when Milwaukee's social order was beginning to crystallize, the city's most prominent families clustered on the high ground between the Milwaukee River and the lake, overlooking the future site of City Hall. There, within a stone's throw of their shops and offices, prosperous businessmen and professionals built the most imposing homes of their time. As other neighborhoods filled in with immigrants, the high ground became a haven for American-born newcomers of British stock, most of them transplanted from New York and New England. Their neighborhood was called, fittingly, Yankee Hill.

■ *Health care came to North Point before housing. The area's earliest buildings included an isolation facility for the indigent ill (top) and St. Mary's, the first private hospital in Wisconsin.*

Milwaukee County Historical Society

Columbia St. Mary's

As Milwaukee grew, so did Yankee Hill. Fortunes were being made in milling, meat-packing, finance, railroads, and the grain trade, and architects worked overtime designing homes for the city's burgeoning elite. A second affluent district developed along Grand Avenue, west of Downtown, but Yankee Hill was the older and larger of the two gold coasts. Year by year the neighborhood expanded to the north and east, reaching the lake bluff in the 1860s and then edging up Prospect Avenue. By 1890 the avenue, with its magnificent "prospect" of the lake, boasted one of the finest collections of Victorian mansions in the Midwest.

Speculators who owned property in the North Point area had long sensed that a wave of affluence was headed their way. The land in North Point South (between North Avenue and Lafayette Place) was subdivided and offered for sale as early as 1854. One prominent speculator, John Lockwood, built a lavish Italianate home on the site of Back Bay Park two years later, presumably trying to start a trend. His instincts were correct, but his timing was unfortunate; it would take another forty years for the vanguard of wealth to reach North Point. Lockwood left town for other pursuits in 1863. His mansion, much abused after his departure, was demolished in the 1880s.

As speculators played their waiting game, development of another kind was well underway in North Point. The first known building in the neighborhood was, ironically, a poorhouse. In 1846, the year Milwaukee was chartered, the city bought a forty-acre parcel to be used "for welfare or charitable" purposes. The tract was bordered by today's Downer and Maryland Avenues between Bradford and North. A primitive hospital for the indigent, the poorhouse was erected in 1846, followed by a "pesthouse" for patients with infectious diseases. The Daughters of Charity moved up from Downtown and opened St. Mary's Hospital in 1858. A public school, Protestant and Catholic homes for the elderly, and an orphanage were added later in the century. The school, the homes, and a much-expanded hospital are still on the original forty-acre site, giving North Point one of the densest clusters of health and human service institutions in the city.

Public works projects also shaped the area's appearance, beginning decades before homeowners arrived. In 1855 the North Point lighthouse was erected between two ravines on the lake bluff. Its beacon was a welcome sight for mariners at a time when lake traffic was absolutely essential to Milwaukee's welfare. By 1888 erosion of the bluff was so far advanced that the lighthouse had to be moved 100 feet west to its present location.

In 1871 construction of the city's first water system began. A powerhouse on the beach below St. Mary's Hospital pumped untreated lake water up the bluff and under North Avenue to a large reservoir just west of the Milwaukee River. From there it flowed by gravity to the city's homes and businesses. The original pumps were as steady as a heartbeat, sending the water uphill in an endless series of surges. The constant fluctuation in pressure created stress on the water main, and so engineers connected it to a vertical pipe, 125 feet high and 4 feet wide, at the top of the bluff. The standpipe absorbed the surges and stabilized the flow of water to the reservoir. In a moment of inspired whimsy, city officials decided to enclose the pipe in an ornate limestone tower. New pumps installed in 1908 made the standpipe obsolete, but the tower retains its fairy-tale quality—and its power as a neighborhood icon.

The last public improvement of the nineteenth century was Lake Park. In 1890 the city's Park Commission, then only a year old, purchased 120 acres on the lake bluff. The commission hired the firm of Frederick Law Olmsted, America's most prominent landscape architect, to design a park on the site. (His firm's other projects included Washington Park in Milwaukee and Central Park in New York.) The Olmsted plan called for an elaborate system of carriageways, pedestrian promenades, and tree plantings that would divide the park into visually

distinct sub-areas. The plan was not executed in its entirety, but Lake Park became, and remains, one of the most artfully crafted links in a world-class park system. The movement's leader, and the Park Commission's first president, was Christian Wahl, a retired glue manufacturer whose name lives on in the avenue that skirts the southern end of the park.

■ *There were also some pioneering public works in the area* (from top)*: the North Point lighthouse, a fixture since 1855; the North Point water tower, designed to equalize pressure on the city's water mains; and Lake Park, one of the first major purchases in a community famous for its parks.*

317

Turn Right at Lafayette

It was in the 1890s, when Lake Park was under development, that the long-awaited residential boom finally reached North Point. As Prospect Avenue filled to capacity, well-to-do Milwaukeeans turned right at Lafayette Place and turned North Point into one of the most prestigious residential districts Milwaukee has ever known. Pabsts, Blatzes, Falks, Vogels, Brumders, and Smiths built homes that epitomized the latest and most luxurious in architectural trends. Some were simple, almost chaste, in their elegance, while others would have satisfied the appetite of any Eastern tycoon.

The neighborhood's development continued over a forty-year period. North Point South was an established community by 1910, although some vacant lots remained into the 1920s. North Point North developed a decade or two later, and its northern blocks, because of their proximity to Lake Park, filled in first. The homes on Newberry Boulevard (conceived as a link between Lake and Riverside Parks) are actually older, on average, than those on Terrace Avenue to the south. By 1930, however, settlement in both sections was virtually complete.

Nearly 400 houses remain from that first, heady stage of development in North Point. The presence of so many homes of such high quality in such a small area makes the neighborhood physically unique. No two dwellings are identical, and all are substantial. Brick and stone are so common that frame houses are a rarity. Libraries, multiple fireplaces, and maid's quarters are practically standard. North Point's homes embody the talent of Milwaukee's finest architects, the skill of the finest local craftsmen, and the material success of the neighborhood's first residents.

The community's architectural character might best be described as eclectic. North Point came to life as the Victorian era was ending and designers were reviving older styles, all with European roots. English Tudor homes are most numerous, but Georgian, Mediterranean, and German and French Renaissance styles are present as well. Architects adapted the traditions freely, producing distinctive homes that are often hard to classify with accuracy. Significantly, some of Milwaukee's most prominent architects lived among their clients in North Point, including the Alexander Eschweilers (Sr. and Jr.), Alfred Clas, Charles Crane, and Armin Frank.

■ *Beer baron Gustav Pabst's Terrace Avenue home was a typical specimen of North Point residential architecture, and his backyard, rolling down to the lakeshore, was even more impressive than the front.*

North Point in its original form was different from Milwaukee's earlier gold coasts in three important respects. It was, first of all, ethnically mixed. When Yankee Hill developed, Milwaukee was a commercial center whose leaders were, by and large, transplanted Easterners of British descent. By 1890 the city was a major industrial center, and scores of immigrants (and their sons) had become captains of industry. German, Irish, Czech, and other European families took their place alongside Yankees in North Point.

A second point of distinction was the neighborhood's status as a second-generation settlement. It was not the immigrants and Easterners themselves who built homes in North Point, but their children, many of whom headed the family businesses. Villa Terrace, for instance, now a museum of the decorative arts, was built for industrialist A.O. Smith's son, Ray. His neighbors to the north included Gustav Pabst, Captain Frederick Pabst's son; and Elsie Cudahy Beck, Patrick Cudahy's daughter.

North Point was, thirdly, a metropolitan gold coast, especially after 1900. In the nineteenth century, practically every neighborhood had its own well-to-do sections. As horse-drawn carriages gave way to automobiles after 1900, affluent families were the first to embrace America's new-found mobility, and they migrated to the lakeshore practically as a body. The city's elite relocated from Grand Avenue on the West Side, from Walker's Point on the South Side, and from First Street on the North Side. A home near the lake bluff—in North Point or farther up the shoreline—became Milwaukee's ultimate status symbol.

The lake bluff itself was a problem as well as an attraction. Homeowners with frontage on the lake found themselves literally losing ground as violent storms tore away at the bluff every year. The problem was solved in the 1920s, when the city began an ambitious landfill project at the base of North Point. One result was a democratization of the lakefront. As the erosion process was reversed and the land grew lakeward, every Milwaukeean had access to a stunning stretch of urban shoreline. Lincoln Memorial Drive, dedicated in 1929, ranked among the most beautiful parkways on the Great Lakes.

In the 1920s, as the lakefront drive neared completion, a wave of change began to move north from Downtown. Milwaukee

■ *One of Pabst's neighbors on Terrace was Lloyd Raymond Smith, head of the A.O. Smith Company, who built a lavish Mediterranean-styled mansion in 1923. It is now the Villa Terrace Decorative Arts Museum.*

Milwaukee County Historical Society

Milwaukee County Parks Department

Milwaukee County Parks Department

■ *The lakeshore itself was enlarged by landfill for both recreation and erosion control. Completed in 1929, Lincoln Memorial Drive (above right) was an overnight success, and brand-new Bradford Beach was just as popular.*

Milwaukee County Parks Department

was growing rapidly, and its central business district was absorbing the neighborhoods around it. Yankee Hill in its heyday was already a memory, and now the wave surged up Prospect Avenue. Dozens of mansions were torn down to make way for apartment buildings. The large homes that remained were converted to schools, offices, or rooming houses, and the original gold coast utterly vanished.

The wave of change bypassed North Point to the west, along Prospect and Downer Avenues. A few apartment buildings went up, and a few mansions were divided into rental units, but the neighborhood retained its genteel residential character. The original homeowners typically stayed at least until their children were grown, and those children often bought homes nearby. Intermarriage was common—a Gallun to a Pritzlaff, a Friedmann to a Schuster— and so the neighborhood's stability was reinforced by family as well as social ties. Change would come, but North Point remained remarkably intact until well after World War II.

Preserving a Legacy

North Point seems to be, at first glance, a haven for the affluent: stately homes on tree-lined streets, abundant parkland, magnificent views of the lake, expensive cars in the driveways. The neighborhood's housing values are among the very highest in the city, as are the income and educational levels of its residents. Perched above the lake, North Point is at a pinnacle, both physically and socially.

But the community's social standing obscures its genuinely urban character. North Point is the east side of the East Side. Its residents overlook what is, in summer, the busiest expanse of parkland in Milwaukee. They look west and south to a high-density district of smaller homes and large apartment buildings. One of the city's most popular nightlife districts—the "six points" cluster at Farwell and North—lies on the neighborhood's western border. The historic St. Mary's Hospital complex, significantly enlarged in 2010 after a merger with Columbia Hospital, occupies the very heart of the neighborhood. North Point residents are among those who buy their groceries at Sendik's, watch films at the Downer or the Oriental, dine at neighborhood restaurants, and borrow books from the East Library. Other East Siders (and other Milwaukeeans) use North Point in turn. Especially during the warm months, the blufftop parks attract an array of strollers, sitters, joggers, parkers, dog-walkers, bikers, and other people who appreciate the finest in urban scenery.

As an integral part of the East Side, North Point's residents mirror the cosmopolitan diversity of the larger district. There are businesspeople, professionals, professors, and artists. Political views span the spectrum. There are retired couples, young singles, and families with pre-school children. Most of Milwaukee's major ethnic and religious groups are represented. Three things unite this diverse assemblage: material success, an interest in historic preservation, and a taste for city life.

That taste was conspicuously absent in the decade or two before 1970. Although it survived long after similar districts had disappeared, North Point was, until the later 1900s, an endangered neighborhood. In the 1950s and '60s, many of the old-line families moved out to newer homes in the North Shore suburbs, just as their ancestors had moved to North Point from Yankee Hill and other affluent districts. Some mansions were donated to religious or charitable groups. Several were bought and razed by Milwaukee County to create more parkland—an approach to green space that most modern preservationists would describe as overzealous. Developers assembled blocks of houses and made plans for high-rise apartment buildings. As the University of Wisconsin-Milwaukee (established in 1956) drew more students every year, there was a growing demand for high-density housing in the vicinity. Local institutions, particularly St. Mary's Hospital, also began to acquire land for

■ (left)
The fountain in Water Tower Park, a 1968 addition, became an instant gathering place for young people, including those protesting the Vietnam War.

■ (right)
St. Mary's Hospital underwent a major expansion in 1976, building a cloverleaf facility described as "tomorrow's hospital today."

Milwaukee Public Library

Columbia St. Mary's

expansion. There was a widespread belief that North Point would become another Prospect Avenue—a high-rise row whose older homes were expendable or, at best, suitable primarily for professional offices. Housing values were depressed, and lenders required abnormally large down payments from the prospective buyers of single-family homes.

A countercurrent was visible by 1970. The preservation movement was gaining traction, and there was a steady growth of interest in historic old homes. New residents arrived, including a sizable number from other states who were amazed at the quality and affordability of North Point's houses.

The new owners joined a stable core of long-time residents to cement a character that had been cracking. The neighborhood mounted a long and continuing campaign to ward off any and all threats to its low-density residential identity.

The effort was informal until 1973, when the Water Tower Landmark Trust was established. Later renamed the Historic Water Tower Neighborhood, Inc. (HWTN), the organization blossomed into one of the most effective neighborhood groups in the city. Its leaders lobbied for a new zoning ordinance and more rigorous building code enforcement. They negotiated with local institutions and developers. HWTN spearheaded efforts to secure landmark status for the neighborhood—both sections of North Point were National Register historic districts by 1985—and there was a social side as well. Neighbors got to know each other through an ongoing round of celebrations and open houses, and North Point became increasingly a community of interest.

Since the Historic Water Tower Neighborhood group was formed in 1973, the trend has been steadily upward. Housing values have soared with the rebound of interest in historic architecture. The Falks and Pabsts,

■ *The original North Point water tower remains the focal point of a substantially changed Columbia St. Mary's Hospital campus.*

the Brumders and Harnischfegers who built North Point's homes have long since departed, but they have been replaced by residents of comparable status, or not far from it. Many of them have moved back into town from the suburbs, and there is a growing concentration of young families—an important sign for the neighborhood's future.

In an area so favored by geography, pressures on the district's integrity are ever-present—from developers, from local institutions, and from simple age—but North Point has shown an impressive ability to meet its challenges. The grand single-family homes are largely intact, and North Point remains a stratum of quiet elegance positioned squarely between the scenic busyness of the lakefront and the commercial buzz of the Prospect-Downer shopping district. Fine homes, even finer views, and a deeply felt connection with Milwaukee's past—those are North Point's enduring assets, and local residents are determined to preserve them for future generations to enjoy.

■ *The North Point lighthouse and keeper's quarters became a museum in 2007.*

John Gurda

Jessica Lothman

Jessica Lothman

■ (right)
The gracious interior of a Wahl Avenue mansion

■ (far right)
"Nite-glow golf" at the Lake Park course

■ (below)
Villa Terrace and its painstakingly planted garden on a cold winter's night

Christopher Winters

Christopher Winters

Christopher Winters

■ Lake Park's "lion bridges" are a cherished North Point landmark.

Jessica Lothman

■ Summertime on Bradford Beach

■ (lower left) *Some North Point houses come with gables galore.*

■ (below) *This Frank Lloyd Wright-designed home on Terrace Avenue was built for Frederick Bogk in 1917.*

Christopher Winters

Jessica Lothman

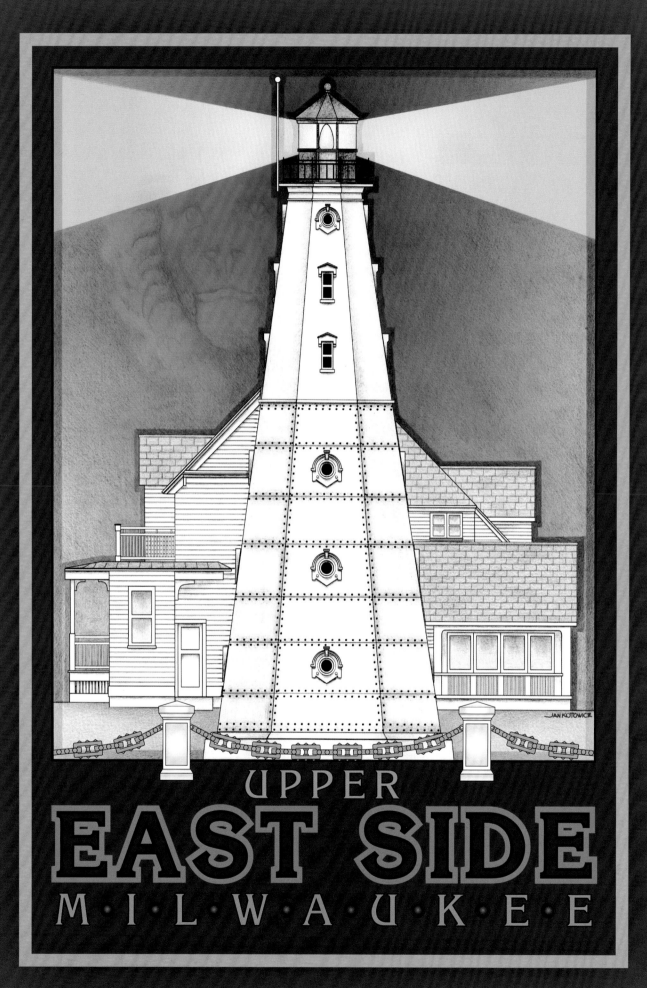

UPPER
EAST SIDE
M·I·L·W·A·U·K·E·E

Upper East Side

The landscape of Milwaukee's Upper East Side is a study in stark but satisfying contrasts. The homes on its eastern margin, overlooking Lake Michigan, are simply the finest in the city. Their counterparts near the Milwaukee River, many built for factory workers, range from moderate to downright modest. In between lies the second-largest university in Wisconsin, with an enrollment of nearly 30,000.

The contrasts reflect a pattern that originated miles south and generations past. The glacial ridge that forms the greater East Side has always been settled by working-class residents near the river and wealthy Milwaukeeans near the lake, and the pattern held as both groups crossed North Avenue to create the Upper East Side. With 20,000 residents, the district is too large and various to be understood as a single homogeneous neighborhood, but it is one world nonetheless. Whatever their differences, local residents have two things in common: a shared sensibility that is by turns urban and urbane, and a shared crown of land, only a mile wide, that slopes off on both sides to some of the most appealing parkland in the city.

Upper East Side

1. Boat house
2. Columbia Hospital Site
3. Downer Woods
4. East Branch – Milwaukee Public Library
5. East Side Baptist Church
6. Engelmann Hall, UW-Milwaukee (Milwaukee University School Site)
7. Epikos (Westminster Presbyterian)
8. Hartford Avenue Public School
9. Helene Zelazo Center for the Performing Arts, UW-Milwaukee (Temple Emanu-El)
10. Milwaukee-Downer College Site
11. Milwaukee-Downer Seminary Site
12. Mitchell Hall, UW-Milwaukee
13. North Avenue Dam Site
14. North Point Lighthouse
15. Riverside University High School
16. Salem Lutheran Church
17. Sts. Peter & Paul Catholic Church
18. Urban Ecology Center - Riverside Park
19. Wisconsin Paperboard Corporation (Hummel & Downing Company)

0   1,000 FT

Between River and Lake

A perceptive observer would have seen it coming. First there were the aristocrats perched on Yankee Hill and the impoverished Irish and German immigrants trying to keep their feet dry on the reclaimed swamp below. Then came the Victorian castles on Prospect Avenue and the humble Polish cottages bordering Brady Street. That odd couple spawned the well-heeled North Point neighborhood and another working-class district west of Oakland Avenue. By 1900, when the Lower East Side was settled to its border at North Avenue, there was little doubt that the contrasts would endure as Milwaukee kept growing outward from its core.

As if to prepare the way, industry had already claimed much of the Upper East Side's river frontage. The Milwaukee Worsted Mills, a yarn factory, opened in 1888 just south of the future Riverside Park. Farther south, near North Avenue, a cluster of icehouses stored rectangles of "hard water" harvested from the river for local brewers, meat-packers, saloonkeepers, and householders. The icehouses gave way during World War I to the block-long plant of the Hummel & Downing Company, a manufacturer of cardboard boxes that evolved into today's Wisconsin Paperboard Corporation—a factory still easy to identify by both sight and smell. The largest industry on the river was National Brake & Electric, whose multi-shop complex at the foot of Belleview Place produced air brakes for the nation's railroads.

True to established form, industrial workers accompanied the march of industry into the Upper East Side. The neighborhood's oldest homes, dating to the 1880s, fill its southwest corner, close by the original factory district. Densely packed, primarily of frame construction, and intermixed with stores and saloons, they formed a cultural landscape that closely resembled those of working-class districts on the North and South Sides.

■ The river side of the neighborhood attracted industries whose workers built relatively modest homes in the surrounding blocks. The largest employer was the National Brake & Electric Company, located just south of today's Riverside Park.

Milwaukee Public Library

Along the lake bluff, the expected evidences of wealth were slower to materialize. For many years the area's only non-agricultural settlers were the families who kept the North Point lighthouse, a fixture on the lake bluff since 1855. (The lighthouse retreated to its present position in 1888, before lake erosion could claim its original perch.) The Lueddemann family operated a bucolic picnic grounds on the bluff near Kenwood Boulevard. Overheated Milwaukeeans came out to "Lueddemann's on the Lake" in droves during the warmest months, and some continued up the Lake Drive turnpike, a toll road, to resorts in Whitefish Bay and Fox Point.

The earliest inkling of urban development came when the City of Milwaukee purchased land for Lake Park in 1890. The park commissioners hired Frederick Law Olmsted's firm to create a plan for their new property, and his nationally renowned team responded with a masterful blend of open meadows, scenic groves, and carriage paths that offered scope for both passive enjoyment and active recreation. Committed to geographic balance, the commissioners purchased land for Riverside

Milwaukee County Parks Department

Milwaukee Public Museum

■ *The lake side was considerably more scenic, with landmarks like the North Point lighthouse and the Lake Park pavilion.*

■ *Residential development on the lake side was at the highest reaches of the income scale, particularly on Lake Drive.*

Milwaukee Public Library

Milwaukee County Parks Department

■ *Riverside Park was a green counterpoint to Lake Park, and skaters flocked to the river with the first good ice.*

Park at the same time, giving the Upper East Side's blue-collar quarter a welcome grove of green. Between Lake and Riverside Parks stretched Newberry Boulevard, a scenic parkway in its own right.

Lake Park was like a green light to developers who were betting that the affluence of North Point would spill over into the open land north of Newberry Boulevard. Clarence Shepard platted his Kenwood Park subdivision in 1891, one year after Lake Park was purchased (and the same year Milwaukee's borders reached their present limit at Edgewood Avenue). Kenwood Park covered seventy-two acres between Kenwood Boulevard and Hartford Avenue east of Downer Avenue. Two years later, Edward Hackett and others recorded the Prospect Hill subdivision, immediately south of Shepard's development and west of Olmsted's Lake Park. Although they were on the map (and Shepard and Hackett would stay on the map as street names), the subdivisions didn't attract much interest until after 1900. North Point was still filling in, and the beer barons

and meat magnates, the blue-chip industrialists and financial executives could afford to take their time. They eventually covered the blocks east of Downer Avenue with elegant homes designed by prominent architects with large budgets at their disposal. Lake Drive, in particular, was synonymous with wealth, but the entire district east of Downer Avenue became an architectural showcase worthy of regional attention.

Filling in the Middle

The middle blocks of the Upper East Side, neatly defined by Oakland Avenue on the west and Downer Avenue on the east, occupied a natural middle ground between the majesty of the lake bluff and the modesty of the riverbank. Turn-of-the-century newcomers built a broad assortment of detached homes there, both duplexes and single-families, that split the difference between the margins both architecturally and economically. The area also became a northerly extension of the apartment corridor that had literally risen on Prospect

330

Milwaukee Public Library

Avenue. Dozens of apartment buildings were interspersed among the detached houses between Oakland and Downer, some with names that suggested aspirations to gentility, like the Chateau, the Malvern, the Belleview, and the Millette. The middle blocks attracted a significant number of churches as well, most with roots farther south. Saints Peter and Paul Catholic (1892) and Salem Lutheran (1911) drew their faithful from the German current that flowed north from the heart of town; Westminster Presbyterian (1895, now Epikos) and East Side Baptist (1912) had a more distinct Yankee flavor that reflected ties to Yankee Hill.

The middle was by no means all homes and churches. Although development was accelerating, there was still open land on the Upper East Side well into the twentieth century. In one of the more unusual developments in the history of Milwaukee neighborhoods, the central blocks became, of all things, a golf course. In November 1894, three upper-income Milwaukeeans who had been bitten by the golf bug during a visit to Chicago laid out the city's first primitive links in a cow pasture bordered

roughly by Downer and Oakland Avenues between Locust Street and Hartford Avenue. (Their sport was known as "pasture pool" in some circles.) Homes were already going up in the area; the golfers rented a room on nearby Frederick Avenue to change into their knickerbockers and knee socks. They used tomato cans in place of cups on the shaggy greens, and their flags were bandannas tied to fishing poles. The group continued to play even after the snow began to fall, using red balls to avoid unfindable lies. Such was the origin of the Milwaukee Country Club. Its tenure on the Upper East Side was brief; the course was relocated to the far side of Edgewood Avenue in 1895 and then to River Hills in 1911, both times in response to development pressure.

Much of that pressure was applied by educational institutions. Wisconsin had long been a pioneer in women's education, led by the Milwaukee Female Seminary (1848) in the state's largest city and Wisconsin Female College (1855) in Fox Lake, sixty miles northwest. Both schools experienced financial distress and political turmoil that

■ *The neighborhood's middle blocks split the architectural difference between lake and river. This stretch of Locust Street looking east toward Oakland was still developing in 1913.*

led to reorganizations; the older of the two became Milwaukee College, and its Fox Lake counterpart was rechristened Downer College in honor of its primary benefactor, Judge Jason Downer. In 1895 the sister schools joined forces as Milwaukee-Downer College. Four years later, the combined institution moved to a new campus on Milwaukee's Upper East Side, at the northwest corner of Hartford and Downer Avenues. Milwaukee-Downer's footprint grew to forty-three acres, including a forested tract still known as Downer Woods, and its graceful red brick buildings blended well with the residential quarter taking shape to the east. In 1910, as enrollment swelled, the college's high school department became Milwaukee-Downer Seminary and moved to a campus of its own on the south side of Hartford Avenue.

A school destined to become many times larger had already opened just south of Downer Seminary. In 1909, after nearly twenty-five years at Eighteenth and Wells, the Wisconsin State Normal School, a teachers college, relocated to the northwest corner of Downer Avenue and Kenwood Boulevard. Its single building would eventually become Mitchell Hall, which, more than a century later, plays the role of Old Main on the University of Wisconsin-Milwaukee campus.

Three more institutions came to life around a single intersection west of Milwaukee-Downer and the Normal School. In 1919 Columbia Hospital moved from Downtown to a sixty-bed facility at the northwest corner of Hartford and Maryland Avenues. Columbia prospered as a non-sectarian teaching hospital for both physicians and nurses, built around the best medical laboratory in town. In the same year that Columbia made its move, Hartford Avenue Public School opened diagonally across the street; its enrollment soared as the surrounding area drew families in their child-bearing years. In 1927, finally, Milwaukee University School left its historic Downtown home for new quarters on Hartford Avenue near Maryland. Founded in 1851 as the German-English Academy, the school was simply following its students up the lakeshore as their families ascended the social ladder.

This rather imposing quintet—Milwaukee-Downer College, the State Normal School,

Milwaukee County Historical Society

■ *A pioneer in women's education, Milwaukee-Downer College moved to Downer Avenue in 1899. Its buildings are now the most venerable section of UW-Milwaukee's campus.*

Milwaukee County Historical Society

Columbia Hospital, Hartford Avenue School, and University School—formed a solid block of institutions in the northern heart of the Upper East Side. The sites they occupied had previously been open farmland in most cases; a handful of pioneer golfers were displaced, but relatively few homeowners. Residential development continued on both sides of the neighborhood as the middle filled in with institutions. Shorewood's incorporation (as East Milwaukee) in 1900 set a northern edge to Milwaukee's expansion. By 1930 both the riverside and lakeside channels had reached the city limits at Edgewood Avenue, and settlement of the Upper East Side was complete.

Although the blocks closest to the lake bluff remained conspicuously affluent—some of the Lake Drive mansions were nothing short of sumptuous—a noticeable difference had emerged along the river. The houses that went up north of Locust Street—bungalows, colonials, and a 1924 standout built in the shape of a boat—were hardly castles, but they were generally larger than those south of Locust; riverside residents had graduated from the working class to the middle class. Still there were disparities. Where the nabobs east of Downer Avenue had a Great Lake at their doorstep, anyone living west of Oakland had industrial smokestacks and the Chicago & North Western Railroad, whose locomotives spewed coal smoke that settled on clotheslines and windowsills with every west wind.

■ *Other institutions developed nearby, including Columbia Hospital, along a very muddy Maryland Avenue. The woods on the left became UW-Milwaukee's Downer Woods.*

■ *Milwaukee University School was eventually transformed into Engelmann Hall, a university building whose name honors the founder of MUS.*

■ *The most important addition to the landscape was the Wisconsin State Normal School, which is now UWM's Mitchell Hall.*

UW-Milwaukee Libraries

Town and Gown

■ *From its humble origins in 1956, UW-Milwaukee became a powerhouse in the city and state, in time absorbing all of its neighboring institutions.*

By 1930, as settlement of the Upper East Side was winding down, so was the American economy. The next fifteen years, from the onset of the Depression to the end of World War II, were a period of anxious lassitude, with few changes of any kind in the neighborhood's population or its landscape. When peacetime returned, a great leveling period began, a lifting up and wearing down that erased at least some of the sharper differences between the lake and river districts. Mansions fell out of favor for a time after World War II, particularly older mansions with antiquated kitchens and post-Victorian heating plants. Americans were embracing the new, and affluent East Siders turned their attention to Fox Point, Bayside, Mequon, and other North Shore suburbs with lots for sale. The market for their old homes sagged alarmingly. Some of the former showcases east of Downer were cut up for multi-family use, while others were donated outright to schools or religious groups.

On the west side of Downer Avenue, a change was under way that would affect, even transform, the entire Upper East Side. In 1956, as part of a larger effort to build a system of comprehensive four-year schools, the Wisconsin State College on Downer merged with the Downtown campus of the University of Wisconsin Extension to form the University of Wisconsin-Milwaukee. UWM opened with 4,481 students, most attending classes in Mitchell Hall, and enrollment climbed quickly to 25,000. The campus became a permanent construction zone, as new buildings were erected and older ones were acquired and refitted. One by one, the Normal School's former neighbors sold their facilities to UWM and closed or moved away: first Milwaukee-Downer Seminary and College, then Milwaukee University School, and finally, in 2010, Columbia Hospital. The spaces between them were filled with classroom buildings, administrative offices, a state-of-the-art library, and a student union whose amenities included a ten-lane bowling alley.

As UWM's physical footprint expanded, so did its impact on the surrounding neighborhood. Former mansions were converted to dormitories, office space, and conference centers. Campus ministries and student-oriented businesses replaced a number of homes. Temple Emanu-El, a Kenwood Boulevard landmark since 1923, was repurposed as a performing arts center. Students and faculty—and their cars—became a dominant influence on neighborhood life, and the local real estate market was completely remade, as both groups sought housing close to campus.

Despite abundant fears to the contrary, the Upper East Side never became a student ghetto. The community's residential character was too deeply entrenched, and the preservation movement of the 1970s brought back into vogue the very kinds of houses that the neighborhood had in such enviable abundance. Milwaukeeans who appreciated vintage architecture came to the Upper East Side by the hundreds, some buying, a greater number renting. There was a home for practically every taste and budget, and the resurgence of interest was accompanied by a new spirit of grassroots activism, much of it oriented to the university. As the block clubs and community groups multiplied, the Upper East Side became a loose-knit confederation of subneighborhoods: Murray Hill south of campus, Cambridge Woods to the west, Kenwood Park and Prospect Hill to the east.

Rather than denature a historic community —the prevailing fear—the university's presence has served instead to intensify the Upper East Side's historic contrasts. Tenured professors and tender freshmen live on the same blocks. Lake Drive doctors and struggling doctoral candidates shop in the same stores. Architectural jewels shine down the street from worn-out student flats. Old businesses have found new customers, and new businesses have opened in old storefronts, including a global assortment of restaurants.

The relationship between town and gown has never been free of friction. Some blocks on the Upper East Side are an unstirred gumbo of families raising kids and of students, on occasion, raising Cain. Conflict, in such close quarters, is probably inevitable, but, as in any

Milwaukee County Historical Society

campus community, the university also brings the currents of the wider world to bear on its surroundings—through its international students, its well-traveled faculty, and its full calendar of cultural events. UWM lends the community a cosmopolitan air that is rare in the larger city. Some Milwaukee neighborhoods are insular, sufficient unto themselves. The Upper East Side is quite the opposite; rather than an island, it more closely resembles a fast-moving stream that is constantly bringing in new people, new ideas, new life.

For all the changes that the university has wrought, some things have hardly changed at all. The neighborhood remains a study in contrasts that date back to its earliest years, particularly the contrast between river and lake. East of Downer Avenue, brick and stone are the standard building materials, practically every home was designed by an architect, and the yards are not just mowed but landscaped. West of Oakland Avenue, a humbler aesthetic prevails. On Kenwood Boulevard, there are fifteen houses per block

■ *The presence of a major university made the Upper East Side a center of youth culture in the 1960s, with regular concerts in Lake Park.*

near the lake and twice that many at the river. The homes of Newberry Boulevard ascend from frame at Oakland Avenue to masonry at Lake Drive. Maryland Avenue is still the approximate line between homeowners and renters above Park Place, as it has been for decades. The neighborhood's average lot width is thirty feet in the southwest corner, sixty feet in the northeast.

The contrasts are indelible, baked into the landscape, but in recent years something resembling parity has emerged. On the river side, living conditions have improved steadily since the late 1900s. Deindustrialization has taken all the factories except Wisconsin Paperboard, and changes in transportation have taken the trains; what had been a smoky urban canyon has become a well-used urban bicycle trail. Bordering the Oak Leaf Trail is an ongoing experiment in community-building: the Urban Ecology Center. Founded in 1991 by Upper East Side neighbors intent on reclaiming Riverside Park from crime and neglect, it has become a nationally acclaimed leader in environmental education. Housed in one of the state's greenest buildings, the Urban Ecology Center introduces young people from within a two-mile radius to the miracles and mysteries of the natural world.

The center was also a powerful catalyst in the development of the Milwaukee River Greenway. The opening of the North Avenue dam in 1991 created first a mess and then an opportunity, one the conservation community moved quickly to seize. The Greenway blossomed as an in-town wilderness, with rustic hiking trails, native plantings, and a stunning increase in wildlife, including game fish that had been absent from the river for generations. One mile east, of course, lies another, grander green way, a line of wooded bluffs with views that stretch over Lake Michigan to the eastern horizon.

Part gold coast, part college campus, part mainstream Milwaukee neighborhood, the Upper East Side is a genuine hybrid. It is a bookish community bookended by parks, an urban landscape both intimate and anonymous, a constellation of contrasts that have been evolving for well over a century. Bordered by the lake and the river from the very beginning, the Upper East Side has borrowed something from both. The neighborhood is a place of broad views, shifting currents, and constant motion, forever flowing into a future as dynamic as its past.

■ *The Oak Leaf Trail carries bikers and hikers down a leafy corridor once filled with the smoke of locomotives.*

Jessica Lothman

Christopher Winters

■ *Running the rapids on the Milwaukee River*

Christopher Winters

■ *In 1924 Edmund Gustorf, a traveling salesman with the gift of whimsy, built his Cambridge Avenue house in the shape of a boat.*

■ *Outdoor dining on Downer Avenue*

Jessica Lothman

Jessica Lothman

■ The Urban Ecology Center's climbing wall

Jessica Lothman

■ Riverside Park frames a sweeping view of Riverside High School and the towers of UWM.

John Gurda

Christopher Winters

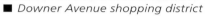
■ *Downer Avenue shopping district*

Christopher Winters

■ *Replanting the past: Ecology Center crews help native tree seedlings take root on the banks of the Milwaukee River.*

Christopher Winters

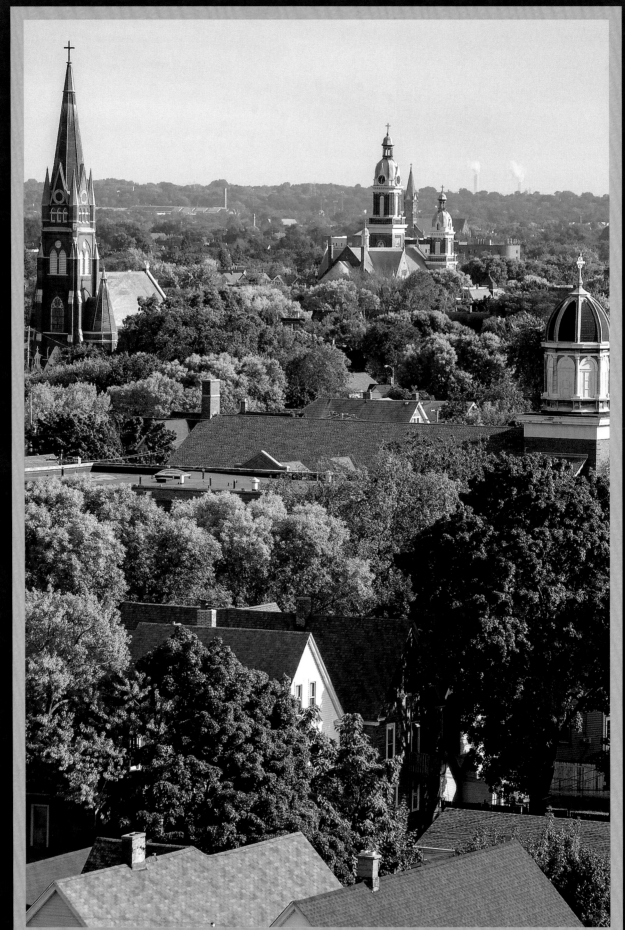

South Side

"In the beginning was the Valley." That would be the first line in any Book of Genesis recounting the history of the South Side. Dividing Milwaukee practically in half, the Menomonee Valley created the district geographically. North of the Valley are the North, East, and West Sides; everything below belongs to the South Side. But the central wetland was more than a defining natural barrier. When landfill transformed the Valley into a center of heavy industry, it provided thousands of jobs that supported the area economically.

Although it's all one district, the South Side is anything but monolithic. North of Greenfield Avenue is a string of polyglot blue-collar neighborhoods that form a well-defined corridor. European in the nineteenth century, they have become specimens of truly global diversity in the twenty-first. South of Greenfield was a *Polonia* (Polish-American community) numbered among the largest in the country—an area that has since become the home of Wisconsin's largest concentration of Latinos. To the southwest are neighborhoods developed both before and after World War II, and to the southeast is Bay View, a former industrial suburb currently enjoying a renaissance. Although their differences are clear, the South Side's neighborhoods tend to share a distinctive cultural landscape: packed with houses, ringed by railroads, and spiked with steeples, all legacies of the district's heritage as a magnet for both industries and immigrants.

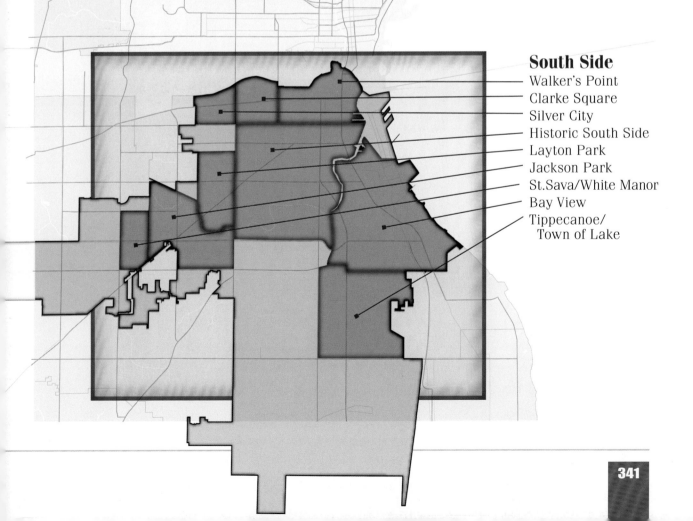

South Side
Walker's Point
Clarke Square
Silver City
Historic South Side
Layton Park
Jackson Park
St.Sava/White Manor
Bay View
Tippecanoe/
  Town of Lake

Walker's Point

Walker's Point is Milwaukee's oldest neighborhood. Of the three settlements that made up pioneer Milwaukee, it is the only one that has retained both its name and key aspects of its original appearance. Some residents, in fact, describe their neighborhood as a "living museum" of housing types and styles dating from the city's earliest years.

That fidelity to the past has made Walker's Point a magnet for preservationists, but it is a vital human community as well, one whose defining quality has always been diversity. From first to last, from the broad European currents of the 1840s to the global blend of the twenty-first century, each generation has left its mark on the neighborhood, and the result is a human richness uncommon by any measure.

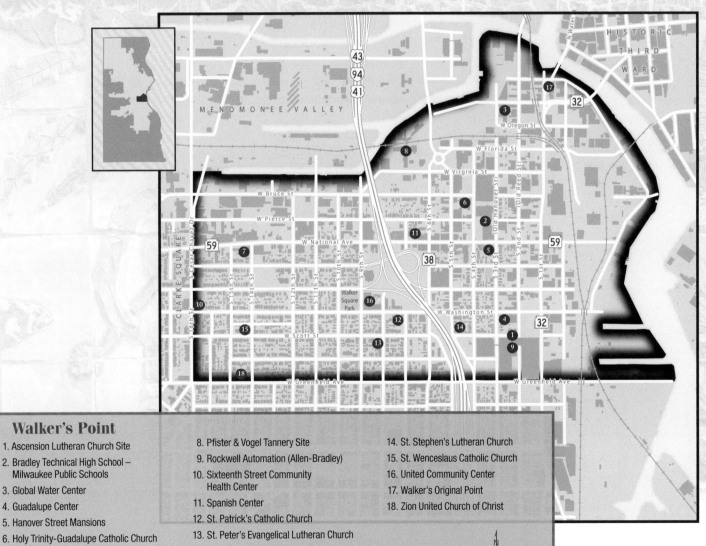

Walker's Point

1. Ascension Lutheran Church Site
2. Bradley Technical High School – Milwaukee Public Schools
3. Global Water Center
4. Guadalupe Center
5. Hanover Street Mansions
6. Holy Trinity-Guadalupe Catholic Church
7. Milwaukee Christian Center

8. Pfister & Vogel Tannery Site
9. Rockwell Automation (Allen-Bradley)
10. Sixteenth Street Community Health Center
11. Spanish Center
12. St. Patrick's Catholic Church
13. St. Peter's Evangelical Lutheran Church

14. St. Stephen's Lutheran Church
15. St. Wenceslaus Catholic Church
16. United Community Center
17. Walker's Original Point
18. Zion United Church of Christ

Making a Point

In 1834 George Walker, a twenty-three-year-old native of Virginia, settled in the Milwaukee wilderness. Solomon Juneau and Byron Kilbourn had already claimed the east and west sides of today's Downtown. Walker built his cabin downstream, on the tip of a narrow peninsula surrounded by marshland. (The peninsula, about twelve feet high and four blocks long, ended near today's Water Street bridge.) "Walker's Point" was soon competing for settlers, and it boasted an important geographic advantage over its upriver rivals: better access to both the river mouth and overland roads from the south.

George Walker had positioned himself at Milwaukee's front door, but he labored under multiple handicaps, including a lack of capital, a bare minimum of political connections, and certain temperamental shortcomings. "He was a free liver," wrote fellow pioneer Enoch Chase, "somewhat careless in his business habits, and while

■ *George Walker, the genial son of Virginia who founded Milwaukee's South Side*

■ *His point extended to what is now the south end of the Water Street bridge.*

he laid the foundations of what might have been a great fortune, he was never in easy circumstances." Walker's most serious problems may have been legal. Green Bay speculators jumped his claim in 1835, and seven years passed before he could secure a clear title. In the meantime, progress on the Point was slow, and Juneautown and Kilbourntown became the dominant settlements. In 1850, four years after Milwaukee incorporated, Walker's Point, the new Fifth Ward, had less than 13 percent of the city's population.

Although it was outpaced by the communities upstream, Walker's Point became a self-contained urban village. Equipped with picks and shovels, a small army of laborers leveled the peninsula and shaved down the nearby bluffs to fill in the surrounding marshland. As development claimed the interior blocks, Second Street (originally Reed) emerged as the neighborhood's commercial district. Third Street (Hanover) was lined with the homes of wealthier residents, particularly merchants, and Walker Square, a gift of the founder, remained an oasis of green as the community developed around it.

Despite its relatively small size, Walker's Point quickly became the most ethnically mixed section of the city. Yankee, German, Irish, and Czech families made up more than three-fourths of its population in 1860. There was a sizable colony of Norwegians as well, attracted by maritime jobs on the developing waterfront at the neighborhood's eastern edge. The groups were mixed on most blocks, giving Walker's Point a polyglot character quite different from the pattern seen elsewhere in Milwaukee.

One legacy of that compact diversity is an amazing abundance of churches. Viewed from the I-94 expressway, the skyline of Walker's Point is practically a thicket of steeples. Germans of different religious traditions built Holy Trinity, St. Stephen's, St. Peter's, and Zion. Norwegian Lutherans erected Ascension and Our Savior's. Irish Catholics established

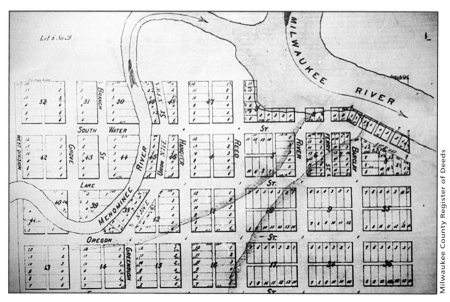

■ *Walker Square, a gift of George himself, has been a green breathing spot for local residents since the mid-1800s.*

St. Patrick's, Czech immigrants founded St. Wenceslaus, and Yankee and English settlers built a variety of Protestant churches. Most of the buildings serve different ethnic groups today, but all are towering testaments to the neighborhood's historic diversity.

Nearly all of Walker's Point's homes and churches were built on the high ground south of Oregon Street and west of Second, the neighborhood's original bluff line. As the adjoining wetlands were filled in, factories sprang up on the fringes of the residential district. Walker's Point offered abundant land, abundant water, and access to both the harbor and (after 1855) railroad lines. As Milwaukee became the "Machine Shop of the World," Walker's Point became the machine shop of Milwaukee. There were factories and foundries as early as the 1840s, and by 1900 Walker's Point had the most densely developed industrial district in the city. Some of Milwaukee's leading manufacturers grew from roots on Walker's old claim, among them Allis-Chalmers, A.O. Smith, Allen-Bradley, Nordberg, Chain Belt, Filer & Stowell, Harnischfeger, Kearney & Trecker, and Ladish. Local factories produced everything from mine hoists to church bells, from steam engines to chocolate bars, and the largest firms sold their products all over the world.

■ *Gravel streets and wooden sidewalks were standard in the later 1800s. The view is east from Fourth and Pierce Streets to St. John's Episcopal Church, a Yankee congregation whose founders included George Walker.*

■ *Built by German immigrants in 1850, Holy Trinity was the first Catholic church on the South Side.*

■ *Walker's Point prospered as Milwaukee's major industrial incubator. One of the largest employers was the Allis Reliance Works, forerunner of the Allis-Chalmers Company.*
(right)
The Allis shops forged parts that dwarfed the men who made them.

Milwaukee Public Library

Milwaukee County Historical Society

■ *The Allen-Bradley industrial controls plant was another giant that grew from humble roots in Walker's Point.*

Milwaukee Journal Sentinel

■ *Just a few blocks up S. First Street, A.O. Smith became a pioneer in the manufacture of automobile frames.*

A.O. Smith Corp.

By the turn of the twentieth century, Walker's Point was not the only neighborhood on the South Side. Sons and daughters of the first residents had relocated west of Sixteenth Street, and Polish immigrants had covered the blocks south of Greenfield Avenue with small houses and large churches. Walker's Point remained a commercial and industrial hub for the entire district. Some of the larger industries left for more spacious quarters, often in the Menomonee Valley, but the neighborhood's manufacturing quarter remained a major source of employment and an incubator for new ideas. When a business group founded Boys' Technical and Trade School in 1906 (the forerunner of today's Bradley Tech), the school was placed, naturally, in Walker's Point.

The community played an even more crucial role in the city: as a point of entry for new Milwaukeeans. Serbs, Slovenes, Croats, Greeks, Poles, Austrians, and even Bulgarians updated the neighborhood's long-standing diversity after 1900, but it was Latinos who were destined to have the most profound influence. Their movement dates from the early 1920s, when the first Mexicans were recruited to work at the Pfister & Vogel tannery on Sixth Street. They established social clubs, started a newspaper, and in 1926 opened the Mission of Our Lady of Guadalupe in a former blacksmith shop on Fifth Street. Emigration from Mexico and migration from the Southwest continued, and there was a parallel migration from Puerto Rico in the 1940s. Walker's Point became the largest Spanish-speaking community in the state, and it has remained so ever since.

Milwaukee Public Library

Milwaukee Public Schools

Milwaukee County Historical Society

courtesy Arnoldo Sevilla

Milwaukee County Historical Society

■ (top left)
National Avenue was Walker's Point's commercial center for most of the nineteenth century.

■ (top right)
Boys' Technical and Trade School, universally known as Boys' Tech, trained young men for jobs in local industries.

■ (center pair)
Industrial prosperity drew a steady stream of immigrants, including the Topitzes family (left), who came from Greece to open a National Avenue grocery store, and hundreds of young Mexicans who began to arrive in the 1920s.

■ (left)
Many Walker's Point Latinos were recruited to work in the sprawling Pfister & Vogel tannery complex.

■ *The Mexican community dedicated the Mission of Our Lady of Guadalupe on Fifth Street in 1926. It moved to other homes in the neighborhood before merging with Holy Trinity Church in 1966.*

courtesy Arnoldo Sevilla

■ *Allen-Bradley, now Rockwell Automation, topped its 1964 addition with a mammoth four-faced clock that told the time for residents of every background.*

Milwaukee Public Library

There was physical as well as cultural change, especially in the later 1900s. Allen-Bradley (now Rockwell Automation) completed its last major expansion in 1964, capping its addition with a gigantic four-faced clock that soon became the South Side's most visible landmark. Interstate 94 cut a block-wide swath through the neighborhood later in the decade, destroying scores of homes and displacing hundreds of residents. The freeway split the neighborhood in two, but the barrier is entirely artificial; the development patterns are continuous from one side of I-94 to the other.

Although Walker's Point changed, it retained a great deal of its physical integrity. In their original forms, Juneautown and Kilbourntown had long since disappeared under successive waves of Downtown development. Walker's Point, by contrast, still had both its name and many of its early buildings. Other Milwaukeeans began to take notice in the late 1960s. Walking tours, architectural studies, and restoration projects added a new dimension to life in the community. Historic Walker's Point, Inc., a predecessor of Historic Milwaukee, Inc., was established in 1973 to focus attention on the area's architectural heritage. In 1978 the blocks east of the freeway became the first section of Milwaukee to be honored with a listing on the National Register of Historic Places.

The resurgence of interest was made possible, ironically, by George Walker's early lack of success. His title problems and other obstacles made Walker's Point a relatively quiet, relatively isolated section of the city, and that character persisted for decades. The result was an unplanned preservation of the landscape. Walker's Point endured long enough to win the attention (and the investment dollars) of a new generation of Milwaukeeans.

Building on the Past

You can look at Walker's Point today from a number of different perspectives. The first focuses on the area's physical heritage and ongoing efforts to preserve and restore it. Walker's Point has been called Milwaukee's "last relatively intact nineteenth-century neighborhood," and with good reason. Although there are communities of comparable age in the city—Brewer's Hill, sections of Bay View and the Lower East Side—none has both the variety and the number of older homes present in Walker's Point. They constitute a builder's book of architectural styles from the 1800s: the simple symmetry of the Greek Revival, the brackets and arches of the Italianate, the layered textures of the Queen Anne, and the points and peaks of the Gothic Revival.

The presence of history is impossible to escape in Walker's Point, and it is by no means confined to the area's housing stock. The neighborhood's major business thoroughfares—particularly Second Street, Fifth Street, and National Avenue—are lined with some of the finest Victorian storefronts in the region. Appropriately, a number of those vintage structures house antique dealerships. Ghost signs on the sides of soiled brick buildings offer mute evidence of the products once made in the community, from shoes to sausage and from cardboard boxes to looseleaf binders. Religious architecture is even more prominent. Walker's Point's crowning glory is its churches, and nowhere else in Wisconsin will you find so many historic houses of worship in such a small area.

The neighborhood's physical attractions are obvious, but Walker's Point is also the living, breathing home of nearly 9,000 people. The community's Spanish accent is unmistakable. Nearly a century after *los primeros*—the pioneers—arrived from south of the border, Walker's Point is the undisputed center of Latino life in Milwaukee—Mexican, most visibly, but also Puerto Rican and a variety of Central and South American cultures. Homes, churches, schools, and businesses all reflect the prevailing influence. The community has

any number of *carnicerias* and *dulceterias*, but Latino commerce is much more than meats and sweets. A stroll down Cesar Chavez Drive—the former S. Sixteenth Street—is like walking down the main street of a border town, with businesses offering a full range of clothes, groceries, music, and even piñatas. Walker's Point boasts nearly twenty Latino restaurants, both Mexican and Puerto Rican, and the culinary choices are especially plentiful in the vicinity of Fifth and National.

Although the neighborhood is predominantly Latino, it is not exclusively so. African Americans and Southeast Asians are present in significant numbers, and several European groups continue to worship in their historic churches. There has also been an explosion of metropolitan nightlife in recent decades.

■ *From well-stocked stores to outdoor markets, shopping in Walker's Point has an international flavor.*

A number of tired old saloons along First and Second Streets have been reborn as first-rate entertainment destinations, typically with their massive oak back bars and pressed-tin ceilings intact. They draw patrons—gay and straight, young and old—from throughout the Milwaukee region. Art galleries are another metropolitan attraction. Most are nonprofit (though not always intentionally so), and each adds something unique to the neighborhood's cultural ferment. Once a quiet, self-contained section of the city, Walker's Point has become a magnet for visitors.

Nonprofit social service agencies work to meet the needs of the resident population. In keeping with the local theme of preservation, some of the oldest and largest are housed in community landmarks. The United Community Center has developed an impressively complete campus in the Walker Square area, with programs in housing, education, employment, elderly services, and athletics, but its core building was once the parish hall of St. John the Evangelist, a Slovenian Catholic church. Sixteenth Street Community Health Center has likewise extended its reach, but the organization's home is a converted jewelry store on Cesar Chavez Drive. Guadalupe Center offers programs for young people in a former telephone exchange, and the Spanish Center, another agency with deep roots in the neighborhood, is based in a venerable commercial building on National Avenue.

It has been nearly fifty years since Milwaukee's preservation movement began in Walker's Point. Hundreds of homes have been restored in that time—and restored again, in many cases—but another trend has surfaced in recent years: the conversion of old industrial buildings to residential and commercial space. Gigantic enterprises like Pfister & Vogel, Harnischfeger, and Nordberg have long since left the neighborhood, but their buildings remain—solid blocks of brick and steel with high ceilings supported by wooden beams. Dozens of these old landmarks have taken on new life as condominiums, apartments, hotels, business offices, and retail space. The conversions include the Global Water Center, an incubator for water technologies that seeks to build on Milwaukee's heritage of innovation. The continuing wave of redevelopment is a welcome spillover from the Third Ward, just across the river from the pioneer peninsula, and some developers have accordingly taken to calling George Walker's old claim "the Fifth Ward."

It is the blend of old and new that makes Walker's Point a special place: the mixture of cultures, the mixture of long-time residents and new condo-dwellers, the mixture of nineteenth-century buildings and twenty-first-century concerns. The community is a museum, a barrio, an architectural showcase, a nightlife district, and a center of new energy rolled into one. Walker's Point has multiple personalities, each completely authentic and all rooted in the community's long history. Milwaukee's oldest neighborhood has also become one of its most fascinating.

■ *The United Community Center (center of page) provides a full range of services for one of Milwaukee's most densely settled neighborhoods.*

Christopher Winters

Jessica Lothman

Christopher Winters

■ *Walker's Point landmarks include* (clockwise from top left) *the western hemisphere's largest clock, a decorative plaster works, a shrine to Our Lady of Guadalupe, Milwaukee's largest mural, and Holy Trinity-Guadalupe Church, a center of Latino worship for nearly fifty years.*

Jessica Lothman

Jessica Lothman

Christopher Winters

Christopher Winters

■ *From modern nightlife to ancient crafts,*
Walker's Point offers a rich panorama of urban living.

Christopher Winters

Christopher Winters

Jessica Lothman

Jessica Lothman

Christopher Winters

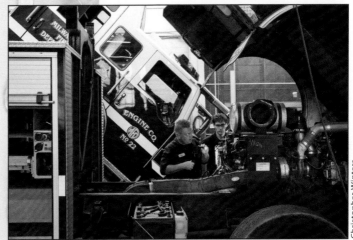

Christopher Winters

Christopher Winters

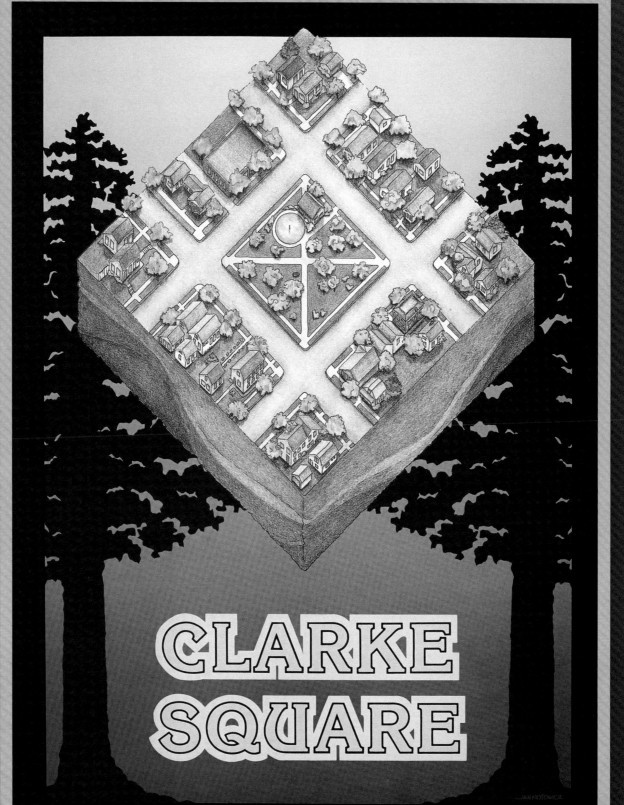

CLARKE SQUARE

M·I·L·W·A·U·K·E·E

Clarke Square

It's an old neighborhood that grew out of an even older one. Clarke Square developed in the late 1800s, when Walker's Point residents began moving west to new homes along the southern edge of the Menomonee Valley. They found a small square of public green space waiting for them, an untended park that would one day give the community its name.

Those early arrivals set the tone for all who followed. There has been a constant procession of groups through Clarke Square since the 1800s, but the neighborhood's most important quality has not changed at all: diversity. In its homes, its institutions, and above all in its people, Clarke Square has always been a rich mixture of different worlds sharing one crisply defined geography.

Clarke Square

1. Ascension Lutheran Church
2. Badger Mutual Insurance Company
3. Bethany Presbyterian Church Site
4. Christ Lutheran Church
5. El Rey Market
6. Faith Lutheran Church
7. International Harvester Company, Milwaukee Works Site
8. Journey House
9. Journey House Packers Football Field
10. Knitting Factory Lofts
11. Lao Buddhist Temple (Knights of Pythias Crystal Palace)
12. Lao Family Center (Scandinavian-American Home)
13. Leidersdorf Estate Site
14. Longfellow School – Milwaukee Public Schools
15. Masonic Excelsior Temple Site
16. Mitchell Park Domes Horticultural Conservatory
17. New Life Hmong Alliance Church (Simpson Methodist Church)
18. Sixteenth Street Community Health Center (Jensen Jewelers Site)
19. St. John's Episcopal Church Site
20. St. Matthew's Catholic Church – Prince of Peace Parish

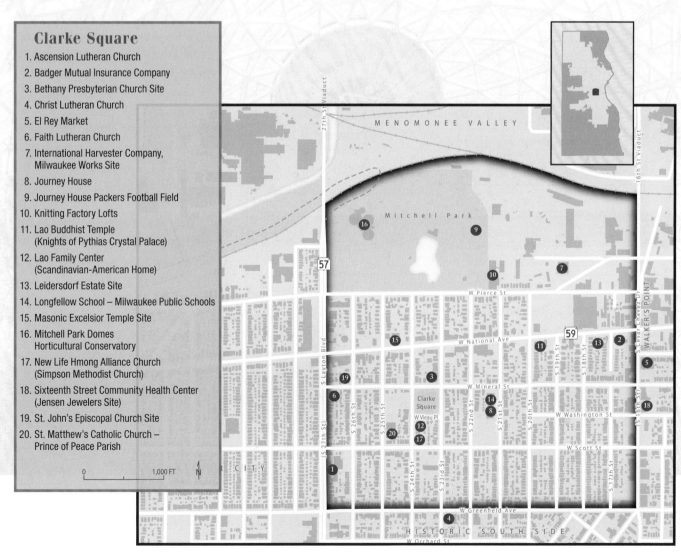

A Second-Generation Settlement

■ *"Clarks Addition" appeared prominently on this 1876 map, but practically no one lived there.*

■ (bottom)
By the early 1900s the neighborhood was settled to its western border at Layton Boulevard.

In 1837, two years after the first public land sale, Milwaukee's leading industry was real estate. Speculators were sure that a great city would arise on the banks of the Milwaukee River, and even non-residents were eager to bet on its future. Two of the gamblers were Norman and Lydia Clarke, a Racine couple who had moved west from Vermont. The Clarkes purchased the 160-acre parcel bordered by Twentieth Street, Layton Boulevard, Pierce Street, and Greenfield Avenue in 1837. They drew plans for a subdivision called

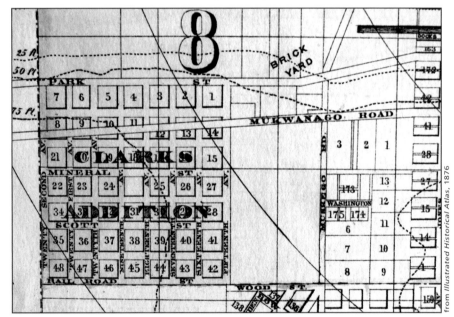

from Illustrated Historical Atlas, 1876

Milwaukee County Parks Department

Clarke's Addition and even reserved two acres at its center for a public park. The land purchase was strictly an investment; the couple remained in Racine for the rest of their lives.

It was not, in hindsight, an inspired use of capital. The parcel was more than two miles from the center of town, and Milwaukee did not become a city until 1846. The South Side, in particular, grew far more slowly than its promoters had hoped. A few lots became homesites in the 1850s, but Clarke's Addition existed largely on paper.

To the east was a real community: Walker's Point. Founded by Virginia-born George Walker, it was one of three rival settlements that made up pioneer Milwaukee, and it was by far the smallest of the three—even after the founder had overcome his early title problems. What it lacked in size, Walker's Point made up for in diversity. Its residents included Yankees from the Eastern states and immigrants from Germany, Norway, Ireland, Bohemia, and other European countries. Each group built its own churches, and their steeples are still the dominant features on the neighborhood's skyline.

It took a few decades, but Walker's Point, covering the blocks north of Greenfield Avenue and east of Sixteenth Street, eventually filled to capacity. In the late 1800s second-generation South Siders began looking farther west for room to expand, and the result was a new community. The long-neglected park at the center of Norman and Lydia Clarke's original purchase was finally named for its donors in 1890. Within a decade or two, the surge of settlement had reached Layton Boulevard (Twenty-seventh Street), and the remaining lots filled in quickly. More than fifty years after it was subdivided, the Clarke Square area became a neighborhood.

Most of the new residents looked back to roots in Walker's Point, and they brought the old neighborhood's ethnic diversity with them. The people of Clarke Square constituted a small-scale United Nations. They included

Germans (the largest group), Anglo-Saxons (children of the original Yankees), Irish families, Norwegians, Swedes, and even a sprinkling of Scots. The emerging neighborhoods south of Greenfield Avenue were heavily Polish, but Clarke Square and its parent—Walker's Point—were studies in diversity.

The community's complex ethnic patterns were best expressed in its striking profusion of churches. As the largest group, Germans established the greatest number: Christ Lutheran (Twenty-third and Greenfield, 1884), Third German Methodist (Twenty-second and Mineral, 1885), and St. Lawrence Catholic (Layton Boulevard and Orchard, 1889). Yankee Protestants built two places of worship: Simpson Methodist (Twenty-fourth and Scott, 1888) and Bethany Presbyterian (Nineteenth and Washington, 1892). Bethany began as a mission effort of Downtown Presbyterian churches, and many of its charter members were natives of Scotland. Swedish Methodists worshiped in a building on Twenty-second and Scott, and Irish Catholics built St. Matthew's Church (Twenty-fifth and Scott) in 1892. St. Matthew's was the South Side counterpart of St. Rose Church, another Irish stronghold on the opposite side of the Menomonee Valley in Merrill Park.

Although the multilingual residents of Clarke Square were moving west naturally, they were also drawn by the promise of jobs close to their new homes. The Menomonee Valley developed the state's largest constellation of industries after 1870, including machine shops, packing houses, tanneries, millwork plants, and foundries. The Chicago, Milwaukee & St. Paul Railroad (known in later years as the Milwaukee Road) opened its complex west of Thirty-fifth Street in 1880 and quickly made it the workshop of a system that reached all the way to the Pacific Ocean. Two years later Milwaukee (later International) Harvester built another huge factory on the south rim of the Valley near Nineteenth Street. Milwaukee Harvester's agricultural machines were soon a common sight on farms from Kansas to Connecticut. Both the Milwaukee Road and Milwaukee Harvester employed hundreds of men who walked to work from the Clarke Square neighborhood.

There were also employment opportunities in the heart of the community. Until the city adopted its first zoning ordinance in 1920, industries could locate wherever they chose. In 1886 John Graf moved his soda water and

Prince of Peace Parish

■ St. Matthew's Church, built for Irish Catholics in 1892, was just one of a generous assortment of Clarke Square churches.

from *Milwaukee's Great Industries*, 1892

■ The Milwaukee Harvester plant produced agricultural equipment on the neighborhood's northern edge.

weiss beer plant from Walker's Point to Twenty-second and Greenfield. "Grandpa Graf," as he was later known, became one of the best-known bottlers in the region. One block north, near Twenty-second and Scott, William Hafner built a packing plant, complete with holding pens and a slaughterhouse. It was in the middle of a growing residential neighborhood, and runaway cattle added an occasional touch of the Wild West to the streets of Clarke Square. The largest local industry was the National Straw Works, a ladies' hat factory that covered most of the block between Twenty-third and Twenty-fourth Streets south of Scott. The company remained in business until the 1930s, and one of its warehouses still stands at 1223 S. Twenty-third Street.

■ *The Leidersdorf estate on National Avenue was a picturesque rural retreat, while just blocks away the Mitchell Park conservatory* (bottom) *attracted thousands of visitors.*

Although most local residents held factory jobs, Clarke Square was not exclusively a working-class neighborhood. National Avenue, in particular, became a gold coast in the late 1800s. It was already one of the South Side's most historic thoroughfares. Originally an Indian trail and then a plank road to Mukwonago, National Avenue was named for the National Soldiers Home, a rest and recuperation center established for Union veterans of the Civil War. (The facility evolved into the much-larger Veterans Administration Center on today's National Avenue.) Wealthy South Siders built lavish homes along the highway before 1900, and one of the wealthiest was Bernhard Leidersdorf, a German Jewish immigrant who owned a large tobacco wholesaling business in the Third Ward. Leidersdorf's homestead was a six-acre estate on National Avenue between Seventeenth and Eighteenth Streets—a showplace that boasted a small lake and a variety of trees and shrubs imported from Europe. The estate was subdivided after Leidersdorf's death in 1912, but the red brick wall that defined his front yard still stands, punched through in several places for the driveways of homes built in the 1920s.

Whether they were rich or poor, Clarke Square residents had an abundance of green space nearby. In 1890 the city's original Park Commission purchased the land that became Mitchell Park. Eight years later, the commission built an elegant glass conservatory that was filled with exotic plants—the forerunner of today's Mitchell Park Domes. Clarke Square itself was developed at the same time. City crews installed a fountain and planted trees that would grow with the neighborhood. While Mitchell Park attracted visitors from around the world, Clarke Square provided an oasis of green for residents of the surrounding blocks.

Other institutions emerged in the neighborhood's formative years. Longfellow School was built in 1886 to serve local youngsters, and it remains in use as one of the oldest buildings in the public school system. Local merchants developed thriving commercial districts, particularly on Sixteenth Street. Establishments like Jahr's Grocery, the Wisconsin State Bank, Patterson's Pharmacy, Dudenhoefer's Hall,

Milwaukee County Historical Society

Milwaukee County Parks Department

and Jensen Jewelers drew customers from throughout the South Side. The jewelry store, on Sixteenth and Washington, advertised its presence with a large street clock that became the last of its kind in Milwaukee. Fully restored, the antique timepiece now stands outside the Milwaukee Public Museum.

Although Clarke Square was a settled neighborhood by 1900, it continued to evolve in the twentieth century. National Avenue gradually changed from an affluent residential corridor to a strip of apartment houses, large businesses, and even larger institutions. Two fraternal groups erected massive homes on the avenue in the 1920s; the Masons built the Excelsior Temple at Twenty-fifth in 1922, and the Knights of Pythias completed the Crystal Palace at Twentieth five years later. Farther east, at Seventeenth Street, Badger Mutual Insurance Company moved into its striking Art Deco home office in 1937. Clarke Square also had no fewer than four movie theaters: the Alamo and the Mozart, both on Sixteenth Street; the Abbey on Greenfield Avenue; and the National on Twenty-sixth and National Avenue. With a seating capacity of 1,400, the National was by far the largest. Its marble pillars, hanging plants, and splashing fountains evoked the atmosphere of a Roman garden.

New churches enhanced the area's already-impressive religious diversity. Ascension Lutheran, founded by Norwegian immigrants, moved from Walker's Point to Layton Boulevard in 1923. Within thirty years, it was among the largest Protestant churches in the state. The Scandinavian presence was reinforced in 1928, when the Scandinavian-American Home, a retirement facility, opened at Twenty-fourth and Vieau Place, directly across the street from Clarke Square. The English-speaking Germans of Faith Lutheran Church moved to a new home on Twenty-sixth and Mineral in 1923, but they soon sold it to St. John's Episcopal, an old Walker's Point congregation that had been forced to leave when its church was razed for an addition to Boys Technical High School. (George Walker himself was an early church officer.) When St. John's took over its building, Faith Lutheran moved down the block to Layton Boulevard. Bethany Presbyterian

Milwaukee County Parks Department

Milwaukee County Historical Society

Milwaukee Public Library

■ (top)
Clarke Square itself, shown in 1914, developed in tandem with the surrounding neighborhood.

■ (above)
The corner of Sixteenth and National was the heart of a bustling commercial district.

■ (left)
The National Theater, completed in 1928, was one of Milwaukee's finest movie palaces.

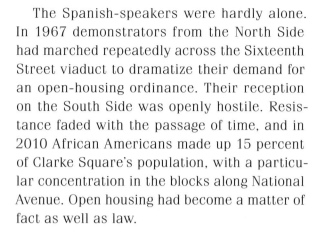

outgrew its original home during the same period. In 1931 the congregation moved from Nineteenth and Washington to a larger church at Twenty-third and Mineral, just across Clarke Square from the Scandinavian-American Home.

By the time the full impact of the Depression hit in the early 1930s, there were ten churches in the neighborhood or on its borders—roughly one for every four square blocks. The area's religious history resembles, in some respects, a complex game of musical chairs, but the remarkable variety of churches embodies, in brick and mortar, the neighborhood's tradition of diversity.

Maintaining the Tradition

That tradition remained vital, but it assumed different forms as the years passed. After a painful slowdown during the Depression and World War II, the pace of change accelerated in the 1950s. As sons and daughters grew up and moved south and west to new homes, Clarke Square became increasingly a community of older residents. Other families eventually arrived, following the well-worn path from Walker's Point. First among them were natives of rural Wisconsin who had come to Milwaukee in search of jobs. Like the European immigrants of the previous century, many had farming roots, and they traded work in the fields for work in the factories. Walker's Point and then Clarke Square provided them with a foothold, and Milwaukee industries provided them with a livelihood.

An even larger group was on the way. In about 1920 Walker's Point tanneries began to recruit workers from Mexico, creating the nucleus of a Latino community that has been growing ever since. Like virtually every other group that has called Clarke Square home, the Latinos started in Walker's Point and then expanded, reaching Sixteenth Street in the 1970s and spreading west. As Mexican families were joined by newcomers from Puerto Rico and Central America, the neighborhood's Latino population rose to 16 percent of the total in 1980 and kept climbing to more than 60 percent in 2010.

The Spanish-speakers were hardly alone. In 1967 demonstrators from the North Side had marched repeatedly across the Sixteenth Street viaduct to dramatize their demand for an open-housing ordinance. Their reception on the South Side was openly hostile. Resistance faded with the passage of time, and in 2010 African Americans made up 15 percent of Clarke Square's population, with a particular concentration in the blocks along National Avenue. Open housing had become a matter of fact as well as law.

Yet another group began to put down roots in the 1980s: newcomers from the war-torn lands of southeast Asia. Vietnamese and Laotian families were prominent in the movement, but the largest single group was Hmong refugees from the highlands of northern Laos. Staunch allies of the United States during the Vietnam War, they were exposed to terrible persecution when American forces left the region. Thousands of Hmong families resettled in Wisconsin, the greatest number in Milwaukee. Clarke Square provided many of them with a place to start over.

In addition to Latinos, African Americans, and Southeast Asians, the community counted Native Americans among its residents, as well as a sizable number of white households—18 percent in 2010—who chose to stay. Clarke Square, in short, became one of the most diverse neighborhoods in Milwaukee. When residents are asked what makes their community unusual, the response is always the same. "Everyone lives here," said one young man. "It's everybody and everything."

Local institutions have clearly reflected the larger patterns. The former Simpson Methodist Church on Scott Street became the New Life Hmong Alliance Church. An old Schlitz saloon on Twenty-fifth and Greenfield, once known for its German ambience, was transformed to a Mexican restaurant. The Knights of Pythias Hall on National Avenue became a Buddhist temple. St. Matthew's and St. Lawrence, the original Irish and German Catholic congregations, merged as Prince of Peace, a largely Latino parish. The Scandinavian-American Home became the Lao Family Center, a Hmong-oriented social

Milwaukee Journal Sentinel

service agency. Ascension Lutheran found new life as a tri-cornered congregation, with an active ministry to Latino and Hmong worshipers as well as its traditional members.

The cultural shift is most apparent on Sixteenth Street. After generations as an Anglo-American commercial district, the corridor has been reborn as the primary "downtown" for Milwaukee's Latino community. Local merchants offer an assortment of goods and services more typically found in a Texas border town. There are one or two taquerias on nearly every block, and shoppers can buy everything from cowboy hats to piñatas. El Rey, at Mineral Street, has become the largest Latino grocery store in the city. In 1996, reflecting the newest chapter in the neighborhood's long history, S. Sixteenth Street was renamed Cesar Chavez Drive in honor of the Mexican-American labor leader.

Clarke Square's current residents represent a global update of the European diversity that had long been the neighborhood's hallmark. There is no doubt that the context

of that diversity has changed. Incomes are lower, relatively speaking, than they were in earlier generations, in part because job opportunities are fewer. International Harvester, the Milwaukee Road shops, and other local giants closed long ago, leaving an employment vacuum that has affected residents of every background. There have been physical losses as well, including every movie theater in the neighborhood and landmarks like the National Liquor Bar, a working-class mainstay for decades.

There are, at the same time, some impressive constants. A chorus of church bells still greets the people of Clarke Square every Sunday morning. The square itself, a gift of the pioneers, is still a central oasis of green space. Scores of residents live in houses their families have owned for generations. A number of those historic homes have been completely restored, and one historic industry, a 1912 knitting factory at Twenty-first and Pierce, has been converted to apartments called, naturally, the Knitting Factory Lofts. Renovation is also on display at the Mitchell Park Domes. Updated

■ *Opened in stages between 1964 and 1967, the Mitchell Park Domes continued a horticultural tradition established in 1898.*

from top to bottom in 2008, the Domes draw visitors from across the globe, but the rest of Mitchell Park—pond, playfields, and paths—serves the citizens of the neighborhood, just as it has since 1890.

In an earlier time churches provided much of the mortar that bound the neighborhood together. Faith communities are still vital anchors for their members, but secular organizations now play the larger role in addressing Clarke Square's challenges. The Sixteenth Street Community Health Center, established in 1969, provides comprehensive health services to low-income South Siders from a facility built around the old Jensen Jewelry store. The Milwaukee Christian Center, a presence in the neighborhood since 1967, serves everyone from senior citizens to juvenile offenders. After nearly fifty years in a building erected on the site of John Graf's old soda water plant, the Christian Center moved to a new facility on Fourteenth and National in 2013.

One organization has focused with particularly intensity on the Clarke Square neighborhood: Journey House. It was founded in 1969 as a youth center in the former Patterson Drug Store on Sixteenth and Washington. The agency "journeyed" to a number of nearby facilities over the years, adding adult education, workforce development, and youth athletics to its mission. In 2012 Journey House consolidated its programs in a $6 million facility attached to Longfellow School, in the very heart of the neighborhood. A few blocks north, in Mitchell Park, Journey House football teams began to compete on a brand-new field overlooking the Menomonee Valley. Its centerpiece is a synthetic playing surface originally used in the Green Bay Packers' practice facility. Donated by the team and installed in 2012, the turf came complete with the iconic "G" at midfield.

Building the center and scoring the play-field were big-league wins for both Journey

■ *Founded in 1969, Journey House offered a variety of activities for the neighborhood's young people, including Easter egg hunts in Clarke Square. The author is at upper right.*

John Gurda

House and the community. They were also among the first "catalytic projects" envisioned by local leaders working with the Zilber Neighborhood Initiative. Launched by real estate mogul Joseph Zilber in 2008, the Initiative seeks to identify and multiply local assets to enhance the community's quality of life. In Clarke Square's case, those assets are many: historic housing stock, ample green space, a thriving commercial district on Chavez Drive, a location on the edge of the reborn Menomonee Valley and, above all, an uncommonly rich tradition of human diversity. That tradition has been the neighborhood's signature for well over a century. It has undergone several translations without losing an ounce of its power, and the landscape of today bears its indelible imprint.

■ (above left) *The Journey House Packers practice in Mitchell Park.*

■ (above right) *Multicultural classrooms are typical of Clarke Square's schools.*

■ *Steeples punctuate the neighborhood's skyline.*

Christopher Winters

■ (right)
*Longfellow
School is one of
the longest-
serving buildings
in the city's
public system.*

■ (center right)
*Clarke Square
is still the green
heart of the
neighborhood.*

James Schnepf for Zilber Neighborhood Initiative

Jessica Lothman

Christopher Winters

Christopher Winters

■ *Eclectic architecture and a place near the center of the city (bottom panorama) are two of Clarke Square's obvious attractions.*

■ *(below) Journey House serves the neighborhood from a $6 million facility connected to Longfellow School.*

Christopher Winters

Christopher Winters

SIEGFRIED
BLOCK

JAN KOTOWICZ

SILVER CITY
MILWAUKEE

Silver City

The name might suggest a mining town or a jewelry center, but Silver City has a less exotic history. It began as a rural resort and became an urban neighborhood filled with industrial workers, many of whom looked back to roots in northern and central Europe. Those first- and second-generation Americans walked to jobs in the Menomonee Valley—the neighborhood's northern border—and spent their hard-earned silver dollars at the commercial crossroads of Thirty-fifth Street and National Avenue.

The Valley, though less industrial today, is still the area's dominant geographic feature, and National Avenue is still lined with businesses, but Silver City has changed over the decades. In a fascinating example of urban evolution, this once-European stronghold has become the home of Latinos, Asians, and African-Americans as well as white residents. For all its changes, however, Silver City retains the small-scale character, the prime location, and the range of residential options that drew the very first urban settlers.

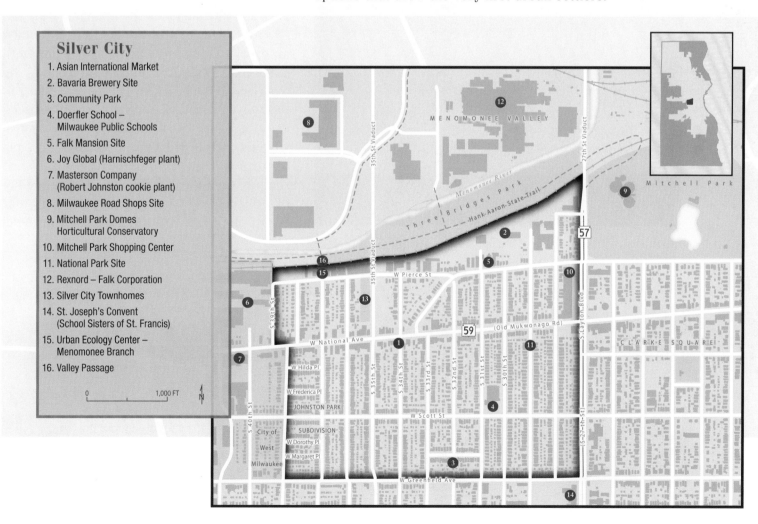

Silver City

1. Asian International Market
2. Bavaria Brewery Site
3. Community Park
4. Doerfler School –
   Milwaukee Public Schools
5. Falk Mansion Site
6. Joy Global (Harnischfeger plant)
7. Masterson Company
   (Robert Johnston cookie plant)
8. Milwaukee Road Shops Site
9. Mitchell Park Domes
   Horticultural Conservatory
10. Mitchell Park Shopping Center
11. National Park Site
12. Rexnord – Falk Corporation
13. Silver City Townhomes
14. St. Joseph's Convent
    (School Sisters of St. Francis)
15. Urban Ecology Center –
    Menomonee Branch
16. Valley Passage

0   1,000 FT

Public Roads and Private Parks

■ *The National Soldiers Home provided a haven for disabled Union soldiers and a name for Silver City's main street.*

■ *(bottom pair) National Park was one of Milwaukee's most popular "pleasure groves" from 1883 to 1899. Its features included a half-mile race track that drew the region's finest trotters.*

Native Americans blazed the earliest trail through Silver City. For centuries before the first Europeans arrived, local residents, including the Potawatomi, walked a well-worn path from their villages in Milwaukee to Mukwonago, an important settlement on the Fox River. Their trail hugged the south rim of the Menomonee Valley before angling southwest toward Waukesha County. Substantially improved, the trail became a territorial road after Wisconsin split off from Michigan in 1836 and was further upgraded to a plank road following statehood in 1848. As the surrounding forest was cleared for agriculture, a growing number of farmers and other travelers depended on the highway, and they paid for the privilege with every trip.

Milwaukee's pioneers knew the thoroughfare as the Mukwonago—or Mequanigo—Road for a decade or two. The name was sufficient until 1867, when the federal government opened the National Soldiers Home for disabled Union veterans on 410 acres of rolling land just west of Milwaukee. The former Indian trail became the southern entrance to the complex, prompting a name change, first to the National Home Road and ultimately to National Avenue. The graceful old buildings continue to anchor what is now a major Veterans Administration facility.

It was not just battle-scarred soldiers and area farmers who used National Avenue. As Milwaukee's population grew, so did the demand for leisure spots within easy reach of the city's center. Public green space was barely an afterthought until 1889, when the Milwaukee Park Commission was established, and the resulting vacuum was at least partially filled by private operators. National Avenue, with its easy access to the interior, was one of the more obvious routes to rural recreation. In 1883 two local promoters opened National Park on what is now the southwest corner of Layton Boulevard (Twenty-seventh Street) and National Avenue. The park's borders stretched south to Greenfield Avenue and west to Thirty-first Street, enclosing an area of forty-four acres. The owners left much of the surviving

Milwaukee County Historical Society

Milwaukee Public Library

from *The Book of Milwaukee*, 1901

native forest intact, but they added a half-mile race track, a small artificial lake, a two-story pavilion (complete with bowling alley), and extensive playing fields. With streetcars running directly to its gates, National Park was an instant success, providing a venue for trotting horse and bicycle races, military encampments, the annual Scottish Highland games, fox hunts (with live foxes), trapshooting tournaments (with live pigeons), cricket and baseball games, labor picnics that drew up to 10,000 people, and Milwaukee's very first roller coaster. The cars traveled a 500-foot circle that took thirteen seconds to complete, and thrill-seekers paid a nickel for two rides.

Although none rivaled National Park in size or amenities, other "pleasure grounds" took shape in the present Silver City area. Conrad's Grove, at Thirty-third and National, hosted everything from Gypsy camps to Methodist tent revivals. Berninger's Park, on the lip of the Menomonee Valley at Thirtieth Street, advertised itself as "The Most Delightful Grove in the Vicinity of the City" and "Just the Place for Public and Private Picnics." All the parks served beer, some of it produced practically next door. In 1856 Franz Falk, a German immigrant, and his partner, Frederick Goes, opened the Bavaria Brewery at the foot of the Menomonee bluff on Thirtieth Street, bordering Berninger's Park. They were soon the fourth-largest producers in a city known for beer. Franz Falk, the managing partner, had a short commute; he and his family lived in a mansion literally overlooking the brewery. Although it has been substantially altered, the residence still stands at 3022R W. Pierce Street. Once the home of a single affluent family, it is now a ten-unit rooming house.

The Falk mansion was not the only notable residence in the vicinity of Silver City. *Milwaukee of Today*, a promotional book perhaps slightly given to exaggeration, described the area in 1892: "The principal thoroughfare is National avenue, along which business extends nearly to the limits, and which continues as a broad residence avenue, bordered with beautiful homes to the Soldiers' Home. Along this splendid avenue, and on drives breaking away from it, are some of the finest summer homes and fancy model farms to be

found anywhere in the country." The homes of National Avenue are still uniformly larger than those on Silver City's side streets, and a handful survive from the neighborhood's days of semi-rural splendor.

Industry Comes to the Valley

Fine homes and festive beer gardens marked a colorful beginning to Silver City's history, but they were not the neighborhood's destiny. As Milwaukee began to flex its industrial muscles in the 1870s, factory space near the heart of town grew scarcer by the year. Manufacturers turned instinctively to the Menomonee Valley, a wetland that covered well over a square mile at the very heart of the city. Beginning in 1869, the marsh was filled in to become an industrial

■ *Franz Falk's Bavaria Brewery was well beyond the city limits, but it became Milwaukee's fourth-largest producer.*

■ *(bottom) Falk's neighbors included banker William Jacobs, one of several gentleman farmers who built lavish homes on National Avenue.*

from *Illustrated Historical Atlas*, 1876

Milwaukee County Historical Society

center of global importance. Honeycombed with canals and crisscrossed with railroad tracks, it drew hundreds of businesses that employed tens of thousands of workers.

Some of the largest enterprises came to life at Silver City's doorstep. In 1880 the Chicago, Milwaukee & St. Paul Railroad, familiarly known as the Milwaukee Road, built a massive shop complex on the valley floor

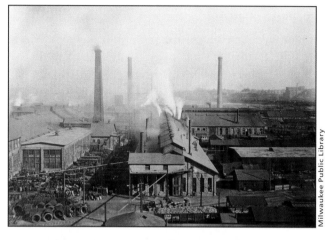

Milwaukee Public Library

Milwaukee Public Library

■ *The Menomonee Valley was filled with world-class industries that provided a living for hundreds of Silver City residents. They included* (from top) *the Milwaukee Road train shops, the Harnischfeger crane plant, and the Falk gear factory and foundry. Shown is the pattern for a "snailshell" turbine case.*

Rexnord Industries

west of Thirty-fifth street. A small army of workers—1,800 in 1885 and 2,500 five years later—turned out two locomotives a week and twenty freight cars a day, in addition to a high volume of repair work. A second giant arrived in 1905, when Henry Harnischfeger moved his overhead crane plant from Walker's Point to the western end of the Menomonee Valley. The suburb of West Milwaukee, Silver City's next-door neighbor, incorporated one year later, in part to capture the Harnischfeger factory's property tax revenue. A home-grown entrepreneur was already at work nearby. In 1892, after his family sold its brewery to Pabst, Herman Falk, one of the younger sons, hung out his shingle as a machinist. Herman eventually became a world-class manufacturer of precision industrial gears, building his factory on a reclaimed marsh just across the river from the Bavaria Brewery. Eventually a unit of Rexnord Industries, it remained in operation until 2015.

Although the Menomonee Valley contained the largest single concentration of industry in the state, there was no shortage of factories along the Valley's tributaries. In 1902 the Chicago & North Western Railroad completed a spur line around the South Side parallel to S. Forty-third Street (now Miller Park Way). It formed the spine of a second industrial corridor that was lined from Lincoln Avenue north to the Valley with malting plants, machine shops, and other large employers. One of the most unusual newcomers was the Robert A. Johnston Company, a maker of cookies and candies that built a stylish seven-story plant on Fortieth and National in 1920. The sweet smell of Johnston chocolate mingled with the odors of roasting malt, hot metal, and coal smoke that wafted over the district for decades.

Such an intense concentration of industry naturally spawned an intense concentration of industrial workers. As the Menomonee Valley developed, so did the neighborhoods on the adjacent bluffs and lowlands. Merrill Park and Pigsville were the most prominent settlements on the north side of the Valley. On the south side, Walker's Point was an early industrial incubator that spawned Clarke Square and then Silver City. Both residential enclaves were closely linked to nearby factories. Silver City, in fact, took shape at the intersection of two industrial corridors: the Menomonee Valley and the North Western spur line. Development of the neighborhood started in the 1880s, not long after the Milwaukee Road shops opened, and references to "Silver City" began to appear in Milwaukee newspapers in the mid-1890s. The name was rooted in the local economy. Most wage workers of the time were paid in silver coin, and the area's saloons were practically awash in silver every payday. There were, by one census count, twenty-four taverns on the south rim of the Valley in 1896. Some catered to the thirsty veterans of the Soldiers Home, while a greater number served the area's factory workers. Together they provided plenty of channels for the tide of silver that flowed through the neighborhood every week.

Although much of that silver went across the bar, most of it was applied to the purchase of homes. As the Menomonee Valley industrialized, local developers worked to satisfy the growing demand for residential lots. John Johnston, a Downtown banker (and no relation to cookie-maker Robert Johnston), platted Johnston Park southwest of Thirty-fifth and National in 1893. The native Scot named several streets in his subdivision for the women in his life: wife Margaret, daughter Hilda, niece Dorothy, and sister-in-law Frederica. That sorority still keeps company on the neighborhood's western margin. Farther east, near Layton Boulevard, horse races and labor picnics were no longer the highest use for land lying so close to the city's industrial heart. After sixteen years of country fun, National Park was sold in 1899 and then subdivided into lots. A few sprawling old homes from the resort era survived, but block after block sprouted new houses that reflected a wide range of income levels. The choices ranged from cottages for laborers to towering duplexes for skilled workers and tradesmen to a sprinkling of spacious single-families for businessmen and professionals. There were no mansions in the mix, but Silver City developed a residential variety that has survived to the present.

Although it was a brand-new neighborhood, Silver City clearly reflected the influence of older communities to the east. Walker's Point, the nucleus of settlement on the South Side, had always been home to a polyglot blend of northern and central Europeans. As the immigrants and their children moved west, the ethnic patterns weakened but didn't disappear. Germans were easily the largest group in Silver City, and they shared the community with Norwegian and Irish families; all three groups looked back to addresses in Walker's Point. By contrast, the blocks south of Greenfield Avenue—the neighborhood's southern

Milwaukee Public Library

■ *A footbridge over the Menomonee River took Silver City factory hands directly to work in the Valley.*

■ *The Johnston cookie plant, built in 1920, sweetened the air over this heavily industrial neighborhood.*

Milwaukee County Historical Society

border—were filled with Poles, a group barely represented in Silver City until decades later.

By 1900 Silver City was an established community of more than 2,000 people, with a variety of churches, schools, and businesses that were supported by a cluster of nationally important industries. The neighborhood occupied the extreme southeast corner of the Town of Wauwatosa, a largely rural polity that provided a bare minimum of services. A series of costly fires underlined Silver City's need for a more adequate form of government. Although there was a flurry of interest in forming an independent village, it made more sense to join Milwaukee. Some of the area's less-reputable saloonkeepers opposed the move because it meant more police oversight (the *Milwaukee Sentinel* blamed them for Silver City's "reputation of

being a tough place"), but the vast majority of residents favored annexation—and so, after some debate, did the Common Council. In 1900 the "suburb" of Silver City became part of the City of Milwaukee.

Bridges Past and Future

Silver City matured at a steady pace in the first decades of the twentieth century, and as it matured, the neighborhood changed. Residential development continued through the 1920s, when the last open lots filled in with Milwaukee bungalows. New ethnic groups arrived, including an unusual (for the South Side) sprinkling of Italian families and a larger number of Serbs and Slovenes moving west from Walker's Point. The intersection of Thirty-fifth and National, Silver City's "downtown" from the beginning, attracted an increasingly diverse range of businesses. In 1921 the establishments on National Avenue between Thirty-fourth and Thirty-ninth Streets included two hardware dealers, four barbers, three butchers, four grocers, two drugstores (both with soda fountains), two doctors, two shoe dealers, a baker, a jeweler, an undertaker, and eight saloons masquerading as "soft drink parlors" during Prohibition.

The greatest number of saloon patrons and their neighbors continued to work in nearby industries, and Silver City's ties to the Milwaukee Road shops were especially close. Those connections were expressed physically. A tunnel at the foot of Thirty-ninth Street passed beneath the railroad tracks to a footbridge across the Menomonee River, which joined a walkway that took workers directly to the shops. A saloon adjacent to the tunnel was called, for a time, The Subway. A much larger bridge had an even greater impact on the neighborhood. In 1933 the Thirty-fifth Street viaduct was completed across the Menomonee Valley. Silver City had been a relatively isolated community since its early years, linked to the rest of the city primarily by National Avenue. The viaduct opened a north-south connection that gave Silver City residents much better access to the commercial, cultural, and employment opportunities on the far side of the Valley.

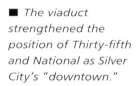

■ *It may have been the bottom of the Depression, but hundreds of Milwaukeeans turned out for the opening of the Thirty-fifth Street viaduct in 1933. The view is northeast.*

■ *The viaduct strengthened the position of Thirty-fifth and National as Silver City's "downtown."*

Milwaukee Journal Sentinel

Milwaukee Public Library

The new bridge was finished in the depths of the Depression, a time of radically reduced activity for Silver City and every other Milwaukee neighborhood. The pace quickened during World War II, when the Menomonee Valley became a pivotally important center of defense production, and remained brisk through the early postwar decades. Silver City experienced a minor surge of new development. A handful of apartment buildings went up, and the old streetcar station on Layton Boulevard and National Avenue—a neighborhood landmark for nearly sixty years—was torn down in 1959 to make way for the Mitchell Park Shopping Center, a suburban-style strip mall. In Mitchell Park itself, three beehive-shaped domes replaced an old horticultural conservatory in the mid-1960s. The Domes blossomed into a major tourist attraction on Silver City's eastern border.

The greater changes were internal. Just as the early German, Norwegian, and Irish residents had moved to Silver City from the east, and just as Croats and Slovenes had followed them in the Teens and Twenties, new ethnic groups arrived from Walker's Point in the late 1900s. Latinos were by far the largest—Mexicans, primarily, but also Puerto Ricans and

Central Americans. Milwaukee's first Latinos had settled in Walker's Point in the 1920s, and they spread steadily westward, reaching Silver City in the 1970s. The proportion of Latino residents in the census tract surrounding Thirty-fifth and National surged from 2 percent in 1970 to 16 percent in 1990 and 62 percent in 2010. African Americans and Asian immigrants together constituted another 18 percent in the 2010 census year. A number of African-American families had moved from the North Side in search of quieter neighborhoods, and most of the Asians were Hmong, Lao, and Thai refugees who had fled their homelands in the wake of the Vietnam War.

The new groups, particularly the Latinos and Southeast Asians, practically transformed Silver City's main shopping district. In 1960 the businesses within a block of Thirty-fifth and National had included Quality Auto Sales, Diliberti Plumbing, National Paint and Wallpaper, the Golden Spike Tavern, Sophie's Coffee Shop, Bomberg Bakery, the Bottoms Up Bar, Ben Franklin 5 & 10, and Charlie's Meat Market. Fifty years later, in 2010, the same blocks were the home of El Jaliscience Auto Sales, the Asian International Market, Thai Barbeque, Nat Singh

John Gurda

■ *Spacious homes rose on the site of National Park. The view is southwest from Layton Boulevard and National Avenue in 1973.*

Food Mart, Asia Apparel and Unique Tailor, Sammy's Silver City Café, the Consulate General of Nicaragua, Vietnam Super Grocery, and the Hispanic Medical Center.

As the neighborhood's demographics changed, so did the manufacturing district on its northern border. The wave of deindustrialization that swept through the American economy after 1980 did not spare the Menomonee Valley, and the largest single casualty was the largest single employer: the Milwaukee Road shops. After the railroad declared bankruptcy in 1977, the shops limped along for a time before closing with a whimper in the mid-1980s. The Thirty-ninth Street footbridge was already gone by that time, and the pedestrian tunnel that fed it was barricaded with metal fencing and barbed wire.

By the end of the twentieth century, there was ample cause for concern about Silver City's future: declining employment, rising poverty, and falling rates of owner-occupancy. There was, at the same time, a clear awareness of how much remained. The Harnischfeger plant and the Johnston cookie factory were still very much in business, even though they had become Joy Global and Masterson. The merchants on National Avenue may have spoken different languages than their predecessors, but they still attracted loyal customers. Silver City's housing stock was still sound and as varied as ever. Its central location, on the edge of the city but within easy reach of two freeways, was still an advantage. Even some of the original landmarks were still standing, including the Falk mansion and the icehouse from the old Falk brewery.

In 1995 a new neighborhood group, Layton Boulevard West Neighbors, was formed to build on the area's traditional strengths and tackle its emerging problems. Founded by the School Sisters of St. Francis, whose motherhouse has stood on Layton Boulevard since 1887, LBWN serves an area extending from Lincoln Avenue to the Menomonee Valley. With key support from the Zilber Neighborhood Initiative launched by real estate developer Joseph Zilber, the group has distinguished itself as one of the most effective grassroots organizations in Milwaukee. In Silver City, Layton Boulevard West's efforts have ranged from housing rehab to neighborhood beautification and from crime prevention to economic development. One of the group's signature projects is Silver City Townhomes, a complex of rent-to-own housing units developed in 2010 in the shadow of the Thirty-fifth Street viaduct. The project's amenities include a green roof where a whimsical flock of artificial sheep grazes contentedly.

The spirit of rebirth has lifted the Menomonee Valley as well. In 1999 Menomonee Valley Partners, Inc., a coalition of public and private interests, was established to bring the

■ *Apartment buildings line the rim of the Menomonee Valley on Pierce Street. The river below them has found new popularity as an urban waterway.*

Jessica Lothman

old industrial stronghold back to life. Plans for the Silver City end of the Valley called for a blend of clean industry and public green space that has been largely realized. Sleek new factories stand literally across the street from the Hank Aaron State Trail and within sight of Three Bridges Park, a creatively reclaimed railyard. Perhaps the most symbolic transformation took place in 2010, when the forlorn and forbidding pedestrian tunnel at Thirty-ninth Street was rebuilt as Valley Passage, an attractive walkway covered with murals and connected to a new footbridge. In 2012 the former Subway tavern adjoining the tunnel was rebuilt as the third branch of the Urban Ecology Center, which uses the Valley as an outdoor classroom for area youngsters.

The symbolism was unmistakable. The tunnel and the tavern served generations of railroad workers when Silver City was inextricably linked to the Menomonee Valley. A new connection has been forged in the twenty-first century, one that promises greater, greener things for the neighborhood, the Valley, and the environment that supports them both.

■ *A Green Bay Packers Sunday at Mamie's Bar and Grill*

Jessica Lothman

Jessica Lothman

■ *Fisherfolk who want to do it themselves flock to Reinke's tackle shop on Greenfield Avenue.*

Christopher Winters

Christopher Winters

Jessica Lothman

■ (top)
The Silver City
Townhomes were
built with a
rent-to-own
model in mind.

■ (above)
The Asian
International Mart
on National
Avenue draws
customers from
throughout the
region, including
many non-Asians.

John Gurda

Urban Ecology Center

■ (above)
The Menomonee Valley branch of the Urban Ecology Center opened to an enthusiastic reception in 2012.

■ (left)
The Thirty-fifth Street viaduct puts a roof over the neighborhood's northern blocks.

Christopher Winters

377

Kościół Św. Stanisława B. iM.

H · I · S · T · O · R · I · C
SOUTH SIDE
M I L W A U K E E

Historic South Side

Of all the neighborhoods that make up Milwaukee, the Historic South Side is the largest, the densest and, in terms of its population, one of the youngest. With a land area of four square miles and roughly 47,000 residents, many of them children, the community plays an oversized role in the life of the larger city.

Its role in Milwaukee's development has been even more profound. The Historic South Side is the heartland, the homeland, the traditional hub of the entire southern half of Milwaukee County. It is here, in this community of modest homes, corner taverns, and church steeples, that two of Milwaukee's major ethnic groups, Poles and Latinos, have grown to maturity, and it is here that uniquely urban patterns of diversity continue to evolve.

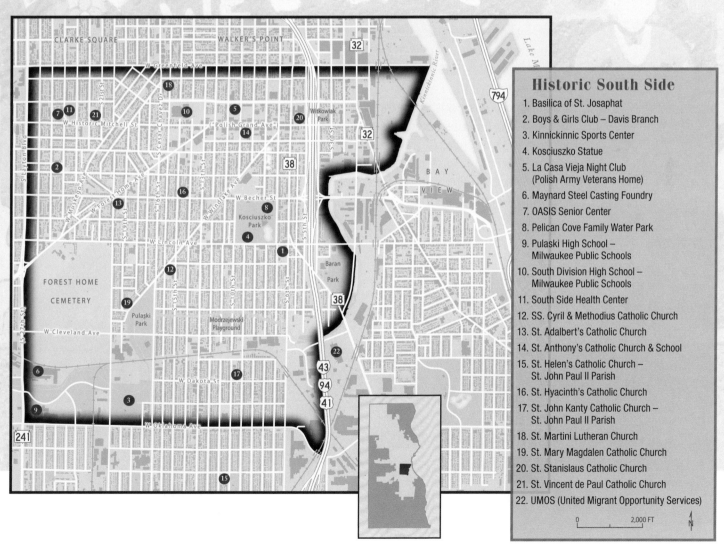

Historic South Side

1. Basilica of St. Josaphat
2. Boys & Girls Club – Davis Branch
3. Kinnickinnic Sports Center
4. Kosciuszko Statue
5. La Casa Vieja Night Club
(Polish Army Veterans Home)
6. Maynard Steel Casting Foundry
7. OASIS Senior Center
8. Pelican Cove Family Water Park
9. Pulaski High School –
Milwaukee Public Schools
10. South Division High School –
Milwaukee Public Schools
11. South Side Health Center
12. SS. Cyril & Methodius Catholic Church
13. St. Adalbert's Catholic Church
14. St. Anthony's Catholic Church & School
15. St. Helen's Catholic Church –
St. John Paul II Parish
16. St. Hyacinth's Catholic Church
17. St. John Kanty Catholic Church –
St. John Paul II Parish
18. St. Martini Lutheran Church
19. St. Mary Magdalen Catholic Church
20. St. Stanislaus Catholic Church
21. St. Vincent de Paul Catholic Church
22. UMOS (United Migrant Opportunity Services)

0   2,000 FT

The South Side *Polonia*

The Poles came first, of course. By the time they arrived, Milwaukee was already an intensely "foreign" city; immigrants and their children made up a majority of the population as early as 1850. Beginning in the 1870s, Poles added a Slavic flavor to the prevailing Germanic tone of the community. They became the second-largest ethnic group in Milwaukee, and the Historic South Side was their particular stronghold.

The South Side *Polonia* (Polish-American community) was different from other immigrant neighborhoods of the time. Most newcomers of the late 1800s settled in the heart of the city, moving into homes handed down from earlier arrivals. The Poles, by contrast, displayed an intense desire to build homes of their own. They bypassed older neighborhoods like Walker's Point and moved directly to the open land south of Greenfield Avenue. The jobs they found in local factories paid modest wages at best, but the immigrants were able to cover nearly four square miles with new houses. Development was both uniform and rapid. Construction peaked near the turn of the twentieth century, and by 1915 the settlement had reached its southern and western borders: Oklahoma Avenue and Twenty-seventh Street.

The homes that emerged in the first generation were variations on a theme that might kindly be described as "cozy." The immigrants built what they could afford, and their homes were monuments to sacrifice and thrift. One- and two-story frame dwellings were most numerous, practically all of them built on thirty-foot lots. Although traditional Milwaukee duplexes accounted for more than a third of its homes, the area's most distinctive house type is still known locally as the Polish flat. The typical homeowner built in stages, beginning with a simple one-story cottage resting on cedar posts. As the years passed and savings accounts grew, the cottage was jacked up from its foundations and a second living unit was added in the half-basement below it. The Polish flat was an affordable duplex, and this form of "additive architecture" helped to bolster a sense of pride and self-respect; the flat's owner was not merely a landowner in America, but a land*lord*.

The South Side *Polonia* quickly developed its own institutions. Mitchell Street became the neighborhood's "downtown" in the late 1800s, and before long it was nearly as busy as N. Third Street, the German community's

■ *The streets of the Historic South Side were among the most densely settled in the city, and the most popular house type was the Polish flat (right), a homegrown testament to immigrant thrift.*

major shopping district. Although its merchants were Jewish and German as well as Polish, Mitchell Street was dubbed "the Polish Grand Avenue." As the neighborhood expanded, other streets filled in with shops—Lincoln Avenue, most notably, but also Thirteenth Street, Muskego Avenue, and Forest Home Avenue. Commercial development was not limited to the major streets. Nearly every block had a bakery, a butcher shop, a grocery store or, at the very least, a neighborhood saloon.

The Historic South Side also developed institutions that met the deeper needs of its residents: mutual aid societies, political organizations, newspapers and, above all, churches. St. Stanislaus Church, founded in 1866, was the first Polish church in urban America. (Its present home, at Fifth and Mitchell, was erected in 1872.) "St. Stan's," whose twin spires are among Milwaukee's most recognizable landmarks, became the mother church of more than twenty Polish Catholic congregations, most of them on the South Side. The growth of the Polish community can be traced, in fact, by following the progress of its steeples. The congregations established south of St. Stanislaus include St. Hyacinth (Fifteenth and Becher, 1883), St. Josaphat's (Sixth and Lincoln, 1888), Saints Cyril and Methodius (Fifteenth and Windlake, 1893), and St. John Kanty (Tenth and Dakota, 1907). Congregations that developed to the west and southwest of the mother church were St. Vincent de Paul (Twenty-first and Mitchell, 1888), St. Adalbert (Nineteenth and Forest Home, 1908), and St. Mary Magdalen (Nineteenth and Windlake, 1925). All eight churches are within the borders of the Historic South Side.

The Polish community's churches were more than places of worship. They were centers of family, social, and political life as well, and some were architectural masterpieces. St. Josaphat's rose to the loftiest heights. Built with materials salvaged from an old federal building in Chicago, it became the largest church in Milwaukee and the first of

(from top)

■ *Mitchell Street was unquestionably the neighborhood's downtown, but there were hundreds of businesses elsewhere in the district, including Bzdawka's butcher shop on Lincoln Avenue and Willmert's saloon on Greenfield Avenue, pictured in the dog days of summer.*

Milwaukee Public Library

Basilica of St. Josaphat

■ *Anchoring the east end of Mitchell Street, St. Stanislaus was the mother church of more than twenty Polish Catholic congregations in Milwaukee, including* (right) *the magnificent St. Josaphat's Basilica, shown under construction in about 1900.*

Wisconsin's two basilicas—a designation of special honor in the Catholic Church. (Holy Hill, near Hartford, is the other.) St. Josaphat's massive copper dome is one of the first sights to greet travelers entering Milwaukee from the south. The influence of the basilica and its sister churches was so strong that the South Side became, for many residents, a cluster of subneighborhoods defined by parish boundaries.

Although Poles were by far the largest group in the community (making up roughly 75 percent of the population in 1905), they were by no means the only one. A scattering of other Slavic immigrants settled in the neighborhood, and there was a sizable German minority, particularly along the area's northern and western borders. The Germans established churches of their own, including St. Martini Lutheran on Sixteenth Street and two congregations on Mitchell Street: St. Anthony Catholic and St. Jacobi Lutheran. Both

Mitchell Street churches were within sight of the spires of St. Stanislaus.

The Historic South Side remained one of Milwaukee's most stable neighborhoods for generations. The community's children frequently attended the same schools, joined the same parishes, and took the same kinds of jobs as their parents. The greater South Side expanded, of course; in the Teens and Twenties, new neighborhoods developed to the south and west of the historic heart. But it was not until the boom following World War II that large-scale out-migration began. The sons and daughters of the neighborhood found new homes in Greenfield, Franklin, Oak Creek, Hales Corners, and on the fringes of the city proper. They took with them the memories and values they had developed on the Historic South Side. Those who stayed behind were joined by a variety of newcomers, and the stage was set for a distinctive new chapter in the community's evolution.

Milwaukee County Parks Department

■ Nearly 20,000 people filled Kosciuszko Park for a Polish Liberty Loan drive in 1920.

■ (below left)
Gen. Kosciuszko watched over the park from his original perch on Becher Street.

■ (below)
The Kosciuszko Reds were a talented semi-pro team whose home field was a cozy ballpark (bottom) on Fifth and Harrison. The dome of St. Josaphat's is visible in the background.

Milwaukee County Parks Department

UW-Milwaukee Libraries

UW-Milwaukee Libraries

Se Habla Español Aquí

"Welcome to El Paso," reads a large banner on S. Third Street. The sign refers to the grocery store it adorns, but the message could apply with equal relevance to the surrounding neighborhood. Although other cultural layers are present, the Historic South Side has come to resemble a border community—like El Paso, for instance—whose context is American but whose primary language is Spanish.

Unlike the *Polonia* that preceded it, the South Side's Latino community is a second-generation settlement. Milwaukee's first Latinos, nearly all of them Mexicans, arrived in the 1920s and settled in the Walker's Point neighborhood, where jobs in local industries, particularly tanneries, gave them the financial resources to plant a community. Social clubs, newspapers, athletic associations, and churches followed in short order. The community's growth was halted by the Depression but resumed with new vigor during and after World War II. Year by year the ranks of the newcomers swelled until they began to spill across Greenfield Avenue—the southern border of Walker's Point—into the Historic South Side.

The transition began in earnest during the 1980s and accelerated at the century's turn. By 2010—almost overnight, in demographic terms—Latinos made up more than 70 percent of the Historic South Side's population, and they were no longer exclusively Mexican. Fully one-fourth of the neighborhood's Hispanic residents trace their origins to non-Mexican cultures. Puerto Ricans, who have been U.S. citizens since 1917, reached Milwaukee in the 1940s and eventually crossed Greenfield Avenue. They were joined by Cubans, Salvadorans, Guatemalans, and a number of other Spanish-language groups with distinct cultural identities. Families with children dominated the movement; as the neighborhood changed ethnically, it also became younger. The Historic South Side's median age dropped to 26.5 years in 2010—nearly five years below the city median.

■ *A rampart of duplexes on Harrison Street*

Just as the neighborhood was never exclusively Polish, it did not become exclusively Latino. African Americans made up more than 11 percent of the population in 2010, and thousands of Polish Americans, most of them older adults, still live in homes they have occupied for decades. When residents are asked to describe their neighborhood's make-up, they typically respond with a single word: "Mixed." Given its powerful Latino presence, the Historic South Side does indeed resemble a border community, but it's also a living mosaic of contrasting cultural traditions.

The physical landscape shared by this rather exotic blend of groups is all one piece. From block to block and border to border, the neighborhood has an absolutely unique sense of place. Although it is flanked by historic belts of industry, the community itself is thoroughly residential: four square miles of homes punctuated by shopping districts and parks. The land surface is gently rolling, and the profile of the area's rooftops is just as even. There are no skyscrapers, no high-rise condominiums. The tallest buildings are churches, and the neighborhood's skyline is studded with steeples. Small businesses dominate the commercial sections, just as small

all photos on these two pages by John Gurda

homes dominate the interior blocks. The Historic South Side is a human-scale community, built for living.

This distinctive physical landscape is the lasting legacy of the first arrivals, naturally. It was Polish immigrants who built the small homes and the big churches, and the Polish presence lingers in other ways. Local parks, again built at the human scale, are still welcome oases of green in this compact community. The three largest—Kosciuszko, Pulaski, and Baran—are named for Polish-American heroes. Generals Thaddeus Kosciuszko and Casimir Pulaski were Polish patriots who fought on the colonial side during the American Revolution. (The statue of Kosciuszko, after a brief stint in architectural rehab, was restored to its rightful perch on Lincoln Avenue in 2013.) Father Felix Baran was pastor of St. Josaphat's from 1914 to 1942, and it was during his tenure that the basilica's magnificent interior was completed.

There is undoubtedly some irony in the transitions of the recent past. An old house on Tenth Street that once served as the Polish Army Veterans Home has been converted to La Casa Vieja night club. A Lincoln Avenue bakery that once turned out *chrusciki* and *paczki*—favorite Polish pastries—makes *empanadas* and *churros* under new ownership. Harlfinger's Meats on Muskego Avenue has become El Indio Carniceria. The contrasts may seem extreme at times, but the neighborhood's older institutions, including its churches, have shown an impressive capacity to adapt and survive. A sign above the entrance to St. Hyacinth's Church bids visitors *Witamy* and *Bienvenidos*—"Welcome" in Polish and Spanish. The traditional Polka Fest at St. Helen's Church has morphed into a Polka Fiesta. St. Josaphat's Basilica, gloriously restored in recent years, displays two matching Madonnas on its side altars: Our Lady of Czestochowa for Polish worshipers and Our Lady of Guadalupe for the Mexican faithful. St. Anthony's Church, once a German stronghold, sponsors the largest K-12 Catholic school in Wisconsin, and nearly all of its students are Latino.

Although the contrasts are striking, the distance between the neighborhood's past and present may not be so great as it appears. The two groups who have played the leading roles in its story—Poles and Latinos—have some important cultural characteristics in

■ The spires of "St. Stan's" are still local landmarks, but Mitchell Street (below) has evolved to serve a new generation of South Siders.

common: a native language other than English, a traditional fidelity to the Catholic Church, a strong work ethic, large and close-knit families, and a starting position at the entry level of the American economy. The living conditions—and the challenges—experienced by nineteenth-century Poles and twenty-first-century Latinos are remarkably similar. Members of the first group eventually rose to economic prosperity from a solid foundation on the Historic South Side. Their experience offers hope—and a possible example—for the second group.

That sense of hope is amplified by developments under way in the neighborhood. Although Historic South Siders face problems common to practically all low-income communities, some countervailing forces

are at work. Nonprofit agencies with long tenures in the community are building on the neighborhood's traditional strengths to improve life for all age groups, among them La Causa, UMOS, the South Side Health Center, the Davis Boys & Girls Club, and the OASIS Senior Center. There is also a sprinkling of upscale restaurants, luxury condos, and artists' lofts that indicate yet another possible scenario for the Historic South Side in years to come.

Whatever its future holds, the community has a unique and distinguished past. The Historic South Side has been a heartland, a homeland, and a hub for two of Milwaukee's major ethnic groups. As its evolution continues, there is no better place to witness the once and future Milwaukee.

■ *St. Josaphat's Basilica provides a picturesque backdrop for the Kosciuszko Park lagoon.*

all photos on these two pages by John Gurda

■ (center left) A robin finds a monumental perch in Forest Home Cemetery, while diners can find dozens of fine restaurants in the neighborhood.

■ Its ornate wooden altar is the pride of St. Anthony's Church, a Mitchell Street mainstay built by German Catholics.

■ (center left) Bridal gowns have long been a Mitchell Street specialty.

■ Front porches and front stoops have always been favorite South Side sitting spots.

■ *A skyline bristling with steeples: the Historic South Side from the Hoan Bridge*

■ (bottom left)
St. Adalbert's Church towers over the neighborhood's rooftops.

■ (bottom right)
The Pabst family plot in historic Forest Home Cemetery

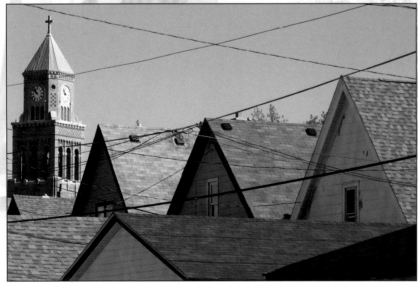

all photos on these two pages by John Gurda

■ (above)
An alley cat prowls behind Saints Cyril and Methodius Church.

■ *From Polish specialties on Lincoln Avenue to hot peppers on Greenfield, the South Side has a wide range of culinary choices.*

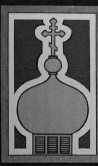

LAYTON
PARK
· SZKOŁA ·
SW · BARBARY ·
M·I·L·W·A·U·K·E·E

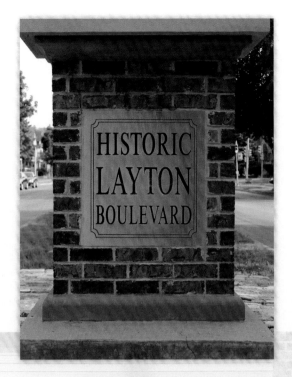

Layton Park

Layton Park is an edge-of-the-city neighborhood. Tucked into a quiet corner of the old South Side, it borders the industrial suburb of West Milwaukee on the west and the sleepy Kinnickinnic River on the south. Where the houses of Layton Park abruptly end, the businesses of West Milwaukee and the green swale of Kinnickinnic Parkway begin, creating an unmistakable line of demarcation.

Within its borders, the neighborhood preserves multiple layers of urban history, including remnants of the earliest, and its population reflects multiple generations of urban change. Once a stronghold of the Polish and German working class, Layton Park is a largely Latino neighborhood today. Whether they are relative newcomers or fifth-generation homesteaders, neighborhood residents share common roots on the South Side, an uncommonly rich heritage, and a comfortably middle-of-the-road lifestyle that has changed little in decades.

Layton Park

1. American System-Built Homes
2. Aurora St. Luke's Medical Center (St. Luke's Hospital)
3. Froedtert Malt
4. Gethsemane Lutheran Church
5. Gurda Hardware Site
6. Heil Company Site
7. Holy Ghost Catholic Church Site
8. Layton House
9. Maynard Steel Casting Foundry
10. St. Rafael the Archangel Catholic Church (St. Barbara's)
11. Sylvester Wabiszewski Home
12. Templo Adventista del Septimo Dia (Layton Park Lutheran Church)
13. Sts. Cyril & Methodius Orthodox Church

Plank Roads and Packing Houses

Native Americans once lived throughout the Milwaukee area, of course, but no neighborhood showed more abundant signs of their presence than Layton Park. Over a period of centuries, local tribes cleared a wide circle of land around the present intersection of Twenty-seventh Street and Forest Home Avenue. Indian Fields, as early white settlers called the site, contained more than fifty effigy mounds, by far the largest grouping in Milwaukee County, and it also featured the region's most extensive plantings of corn. The chief of the local village was named, fittingly, Cornstalk.

Indian Fields was still being cultivated in the mid-1830s, when farmers of a different sort began to arrive. The mounds and the corn hills quickly disappeared under the plows of English-speaking pioneers, and the original settlers soon disappeared as well. In 1838 all the Native Americans remaining in the Milwaukee area were gathered at Indian Fields and herded to reservations west of the Mississippi. Known in Potawatomi lore as the "Trail of Death," the journey was catastrophic for a tribe that had called the region home since the 1600s.

As the rest of southern Wisconsin was cleared and cultivated, the farmers who had displaced the Potawatomi needed highways to bring their crops to market. Lakeshore port cities, particularly Milwaukee, provided the necessary outlet. Plank roads—oversized wooden sidewalks, essentially—were the first solution to the region's transportation problems, and one of the busiest was the Janesville Plank Road. Chartered in 1848, it became the main-traveled highway between Milwaukee and all points southwest. The road practically bisected Indian Fields on its way to Janesville, and it's still in use—as Forest Home Avenue.

There were farmers on the Milwaukee end of the plank road as well. One of them was John Layton, an English immigrant who owned the large triangle of land bordered by Lincoln and Forest Home Avenues east of Thirty-first Street. Layton also owned a Downtown meat market, and he used his rural acreage as pasture land for livestock that were sold, piecemeal, over the counter of his shop. The immigrant had even grander plans. In 1849 he opened a large hotel on the plank road just west of its crossing with Lincoln Avenue. The Layton House was immediately popular among travelers heading into Milwaukee. Each patron received a night's lodging, two meals, bedding and feed for his team, a glass of whiskey, and a cigar—all for

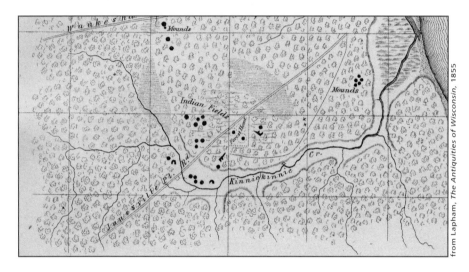

from Lapham, The Antiquities of Wisconsin, 1855

Wisconsin Historical Society

about sixty-five cents. John Layton continued to work Downtown, running his hotel as a sideline. Within a decade of its grand opening, the pioneer butcher had leased the Layton House to another family, and it remained in operation for more than a half-century.

In the early 1850s, Layton built a home for his own family on the north side of the plank road near Thirty-first Street. He thus became Layton Park's first white resident as well as its first commuter. Both the hotel and the Layton residence were large Federal-style buildings— simple cubes with gently pitched roofs and long front porches. The first was of brick, the second of frame construction. The Layton home has long since vanished, but the Layton House, amazingly, is still standing, not quite hidden by buildings of much later vintage.

John's son, Frederick, was a teenager when the family settled in Milwaukee. He joined his father's meat business, but the young man remained open to larger opportunities. Farmers in the region were producing more beef cattle and hogs than the local market could absorb. Frederick Layton was one of the foresighted few who began to pack the surplus meat for sale to a wider market. In partnership with John Plankinton and later on his own, Frederick became one of the industry leaders in a city that was, by 1871, the fourth-largest producer of packed meat in the nation. Layton also became a leading local philanthropist. In 1888 he gave

Milwaukee its first public art gallery, complete with a fine collection of paintings and a $100,000 endowment.

The Janesville Plank Road was not exclusively for farmers and meat-packers. In 1850 St. Paul's Episcopal Church, an affluent Yankee Hill congregation, began to develop seventy-two acres on the highway near Twenty-seventh Street as "a cemetery for the city." Few resting places were truly final in a community growing as fast as Milwaukee, and St. Paul's created an alternative that was both dignified and permanent. Forest Home Cemetery, the result of the church's efforts, was soon hailed as one of

■ *Frederick Layton, the meat-packing magnate whose family gave the neighborhood its name*

Milwaukee County Historical Society

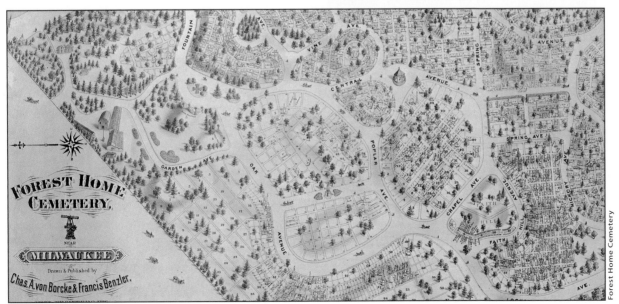

Forest Home Cemetery

■ *Forest Home Cemetery was as carefully landscaped as the finest park, and it attracted hundreds of visitors on summer Sundays.*

the best-planned and most beautiful burial grounds in the American West. It was also one of the most prestigious. Industrialists, politicians, bankers, and other prominent figures from the city and state chose Forest Home as their final address. By the late 1800s the roster of burials amounted to a Who Was Who in Milwaukee.

The cemetery became a haven for living Milwaukeeans as well. There were scandalously few public parks in the city, and hundreds of residents starved for green space came to Forest Home on summer weekends. Although the cemetery was well beyond Milwaukee's limits, horse-drawn omnibuses made three daily trips from Downtown as early as 1857. Visitors enjoyed the beautifully landscaped grounds and the elaborately carved monuments, and it is likely that more than a few raised a glass in the tap room of the Layton House before returning to the city. The cemetery became such a popular destination that the eastern end of the Janesville Plank Road was renamed Forest Home Avenue in 1872, thus becoming the only street in Milwaukee's history to be named for a graveyard. A somewhat more modest cemetery opened just down the avenue in 1880: Pilgrim's Rest. Established by St. Stephen's Lutheran Church, a German congregation in the Walker's Point neighborhood, its entrance was just down the block from John Layton's old residence, and many of its "pilgrims" were natives of Germany who had made Milwaukee their home.

The rest of the future Layton Park neighborhood was farmland but, in keeping with a larger local theme, even some of the farms were unusual. The land northwest of Twenty-seventh and Lincoln was a peat bog in the first years of settlement, covered with a soil that was rich, black, and wet. In about 1880 at least two farmers, Henry Comstock and William Trowbridge, began to use it for the production of celery. Their harvest totaled six million stalks in a typical year and, according to one historian, Layton Park celery had "a bouquet equalled only by that produced in Kalamazoo, Michigan, and in southern California."

A Center of Industry

From Indian Fields to celery fields, Layton Park had a fascinating early history, but it was not yet a neighborhood. Urban development began in the late 1800s, and it was shaped by a newer medium of transportation. Just as a plank road to Janesville had opened the area to agricultural development, a railroad to Madison attracted the first urban residents. In 1885 the Chicago and North Western completed a new mainline around the southern edge of the city, a line that stretched inland from Bay View and crossed Forest Home Avenue at today's Thirty-third Street.

Milwaukee was industrializing rapidly at the time. There was a ready market for factory land served by rail and not too far from an ample supply of workers. Layton Park qualified on both counts. A tack plant established in 1891 was the area's first industry, and it was followed in the next decade or two by firms that made furniture, farm implements, bathtubs and toilets, millwork, wire, and a variety of other durable goods. The two largest industries were the Heil Company (tanks and truck bodies), which moved from the North Side in 1908, and Maynard Steel Casting, which moved from Walker's Point ten years later.

The factories formed a gauntlet along the North Western mainline and created the southern border of an incipient neighborhood. When the railroad built a spur line parallel to Forty-third Street (now Miller Park Way) in 1902, the future Layton Park had industries to its west as well. The Forty-third Street corridor was soon lined with millers, steel fabricators, and so many maltsters that it was known locally as "the malt belt." (Malt, or sprouted barley, is a key ingredient in the beverage that made Milwaukee famous.) The towering concrete elevators of Froedtert Malt, a firm that moved from the North Side in 1922, have dominated the neighborhood's skyline ever since.

Milwaukee was already growing to the southwest when the first trackside factories opened, and the presence of industrial employers accelerated the trend. In 1887, only two years after the North Western mainline

■ *Gears were some of the larger products cast in the Maynard Steel foundry, a heavy industry that helped put Layton Park on the map.*

was finished, real estate promoters subdivided the old Layton farm and began to develop a neighborhood named, of course, Layton Park. Sales were not brisk at first; residential development proceeded, not surprisingly, in tandem with industrial development. In 1900 there were fewer than 200 homes south of Lincoln Avenue.

Settlement north of the avenue began even later. The resident celery farmers were in no hurry to develop their land, and it was not until 1913 that the blocks between Lincoln and Burnham were subdivided. Celery cultivation continued west of Thirty-fifth, but the original fields were covered with homes in the Teens and Twenties. (Some new residents were dismayed to find their foundations shifting as the houses settled into the spongy subsoil.) As the speed of industrial development increased, residential construction kept pace. By 1930 Layton Park was filled almost to capacity.

The homes that blanketed the new neighborhood were medium-sized variations on characteristic Milwaukee themes. The oldest, concentrated in the blocks closest to the North Western tracks, were late Victorian homes from the 1890s, generally two stories in height and often trimmed with architectural "gingerbread." They were followed by somewhat simpler frame houses, including a large number of duplexes built after 1900. Layton Park's development peaked in the 1920s, and the signature home of the decade was the bungalow. Local bungalows ranged

■ *The Froedtert plant anchored the "malt belt" on the neighborhood's western border.*

■ *Forest Home Avenue ran through Layton Park like a pipeline. The view is southwest from Thirty-third Street in 1926.*

from modest tract-built homes to imposing brick houses with leaded-glass windows and built-in oak cabinets.

Some of Layton Park's homes would have been standouts in any neighborhood. Frank Lloyd Wright, a native Wisconsinite, had a lifelong interest in affordable housing, and one of his pet projects utilized precut lumber, prepackaged materials, and standardized designs to minimize building costs. In 1916 a Milwaukee developer completed a row of these "System-Built Homes"—four duplexes and two single-families—just west of Layton Boulevard on Burnham Street. The

System-Built concept failed to transform American architecture, but it gave Layton Park what is probably the greatest concentration of Wright-designed homes on a single block anywhere in the world.

Although they were hardly Frank Lloyd Wright originals, many of the homes on nearby Layton Boulevard were exceptional in their own right. The boulevard (S. Twenty-seventh Street) was Milwaukee's city limits until 1903, and it played the role of the South Side's "suburbs" in the pre-Depression era. The blocks north of Lincoln Avenue were lined with the substantial homes of merchants, professionals, manufacturers, and other South Siders who had done unusually well. Several of the homes wouldn't have been out of place on Lake Drive or Newberry Boulevard. The largest, at 2146 S. Layton, was built for Sylvester Wabiszewski, chief executive of the Maynard Steel foundry one mile south.

Whether they were well-off or merely comfortable, most of Layton Park's newcomers were former residents of the Historic South Side. For virtually all of them, the change of address was a step up. As laborers became skilled machinists and entry-level employees became foremen or even owners, they traded the cramped cottages of their original neighborhoods for the more spacious homes of Layton Park. Blue-collar workers predominated in the movement, many of them drawn

■ Layton Boulevard was lined with fine homes for its entire length, including the mansion built for Sylvester Wabiszewski, Maynard Steel's chief executive.

Anders Gurda

■ Frank Lloyd Wright's American System-Built Homes reached their peak of development on Burnham Street.

Milwaukee Public Library

396

by jobs on the nearby rail corridors, but they tended to be the more-experienced and better-paid hands in the industrial work force.

The neighborhood's ethnic profile was as individual as its employment patterns. The two major ethnic groups in Layton Park were Germans and Poles, including both immigrants and their American-born children. The earliest arrivals were uniformly German, and they were most numerous south of Lincoln Avenue. The blocks north of Lincoln, the site of the old celery fields, were more heavily Polish. Most blocks became ethnically mixed as the years passed, and there was a great deal of intermarriage. The typical Layton Park family was Polish, German, or Polish-German, combining in one neighborhood Milwaukee's two largest ethnic groups at the turn of the twentieth century.

The community's churches reflected the prevailing ethnic patterns. In 1893, two years after the first factory was built, a group of seven German residents organized Gethsemane Lutheran Church. Fifteen years later, Layton Park Lutheran was established by the faithful who preferred to hear services in English. The area's dual ethnic identity created an unusual situation for local Catholics. Holy Ghost Church was built in 1902 to serve German Catholics; St. Barbara's was erected in 1924 to serve Poles. The two churches were only two blocks apart.

Layton Park was not exclusively German or Polish. Norwegian, Czech, Irish, and Italian families were scattered throughout the area. In 1929 a group of Russians purchased an existing house of worship on Thirtieth and Arthur and established Saints Cyril and Methodius Russian Orthodox Church. An onion-shaped dome added to the little building made it an instant Layton Park landmark.

Commerce followed residential and religious development. Lincoln and Forest Home Avenues were lined with neighborhood-serving businesses between 1900 and 1930: bakeries, butcher shops, grocery stores, financial institutions, and hardware stores, including one established by John Gurda (the author's grandfather) on Thirty-second and Lincoln in 1915. Like so many other local businesses, Gurda Hardware served the neighborhood for decades, finally closing in 1965.

With distinct borders, stable employers, a range of housing choices, a distinctive ethnic mix, and thriving commercial districts, Layton Park had all the ingredients of a strong neighborhood, and that's precisely what it became. "Layton Park" was one of Milwaukee's better-known neighborhood names for decades, affixed not only to the community but to some of its major institutions: a bank, the post office, a movie theater, a savings and loan, the railroad depot, a church, and the public library branch. Layton Parkers

■*"Ein prosit":*
The regulars raised their mugs at the Layton Park Exchange saloon on Thirty-first and Forest Home.

Milwaukee Public Library

■ *Gurda Hardware helped keep the neighborhood in paint, nails, and stoves from 1915 to 1965.*

had a sharp sense of geographic identity, and visitors knew they were coming into a cohesive neighborhood. The community even had its own monthly newspaper, the *Clarion*. There was so much going on that in 1922 residents and business-owners formed the Layton Park Civic Association to coordinate it all. The Association sponsored parades, picnics, dances, and even tennis tournaments, all in an effort to "advance the civic welfare of Layton Park."

A Change in Accent

With its "civic welfare" so carefully nurtured, the character that crystallized in Layton Park during the 1920s lasted for generations. There was change, to be sure, highlighted by the intense pressures of the Depression and World War II, but Layton Park did not change in any essential way. Its ethnic, economic, religious, and commercial patterns persisted even as the first urban settlers aged and their children took over their homes and businesses.

It was in the post-World War II years that the face of Layton Park began to change materially, and it has changed by both addition and subtraction. St. Luke's Hospital moved from Walker's Point to the southern edge of the neighborhood in 1952, and it has become the flagship facility of Aurora Health Care, the largest health system in Wisconsin. Three years later the old Rundle bathtub plant at Thirty-third and Forest Home was replaced by a discount mall—an early instance of the deindustrialization that would plague the entire region. The mall has since become an administrative center for Aurora Health Care. The North Western mainline was bridged by a massive viaduct at Thirty-fifth Street in 1959. In a last burst of development, the remaining vacant lots on the neighborhood's western fringe were covered with simple Cape Cod homes after the war. On the other side of the ledger, scores of homes and businesses vanished when Forest Home Avenue and Twenty-seventh Street were widened to become four-lane highways in the early 1970s.

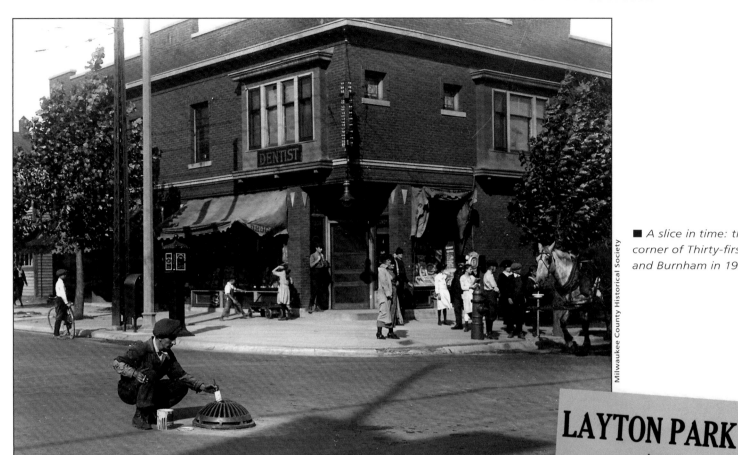

■ *A slice in time: the corner of Thirty-first and Burnham in 1920*

Milwaukee County Historical Society

LAYTON PARK

A

THRIVING COMMUNITY
OF MILWAUKEE

A Book of Our Present Community
Together With a History
of its Growth and
Development

1927

■ *Layton Park was such a strong neighborhood that in 1927 local boosters published a book filled with essays, photographs, and ads for local businesses.*

Layton Park's physical changes have been a predictable, and in some cases inevitable, product of age. The larger transformation has been cultural. The first Layton Parkers—the settlers who came after Indian Fields had been plowed under and the celery fields covered over—were largely Polish or German South Siders who had begun with very little and gradually acquired the means to move to nicer homes on quieter streets. Their descendants showed little inclination to move. In 1980 a majority of Layton Park's residents were Polish or German by ancestry, and hundreds more were both Polish and German. The replacement process finally began, and it followed the same pattern as the very first migration. Another wave of newcomers, most of them Latino this time, looked beyond the old South Side in search of nicer homes on quieter streets, and they found them in Layton Park. The transition took place in a single generation. In 1980 Milwaukeeans of "Spanish origin" (a census category) made up less than 3 percent of the neighborhood's population. By 2010 the proportion of "Hispanic" residents had soared to 64 percent in precisely the same blocks.

Some of the neighborhood's oldest institutions reflected the cultural sea change. Holy Ghost and St. Barbara's Churches, once strongholds of German and Polish Catholicism, merged as St. Rafael the Archangel Parish, and Sunday Mass is now said in Spanish as well as English. Layton Park Lutheran became Templo Adventista del Septimo Dia, a Seventh-day Adventist congregation. El Senorial Restaurant took over what had been La Licata's Little Italy. Saints Cyril and Methodius, once a community of Russian believers, began to advertise itself as "Una Iglesia Ortodoxa Para Todos"—"An Orthodox Church for All People." Taverns where blue-collar Europeans once bent their elbows now play Spanish *corridos* on the jukebox, and the occasional Mexican flag waves from the front porch of a bungalow that might have been built with nails from Gurda Hardware.

399

The transition has taken place with a bare minimum of friction, perhaps because, in some essential ways, Layton Park has remained the kind of community it was at the very beginning. Despite significant losses, there is still a solid cluster of industries along the old North Western rail corridor, and an untold number of Layton Parkers still walk to work there. Local churches still serve as anchors of belonging, just as they did for the original residents. Local taverns are still informal community centers in the best Milwaukee tradition.

On a more fundamental level, traditional values, including pride in property and a strong work ethic, have not been lost in translation. The houses of Layton Park are in generally good repair, and some could easily be on a tour of homes. Those would include the Frank Lloyd Wright dwellings on Burnham, some of them extensively restored and all of them still looking distinctly contemporary a century after they were built. In all sections of the neighborhood, "quiet" is a word you hear repeatedly when residents describe what they like about the area.

The Layton Park Civic Association is long gone, and with its demise the neighborhood's name has lost some currency, but a newer group, Layton Boulevard West Neighbors, was established in 1995 with similar goals. LBWN is a community development organization that strives "to connect neighbors to civic leaders, each other and real solutions" in Layton Park and its adjacent neighborhoods. A growing number of those neighbors are children. In a return to its earliest traditions, Layton Park is increasingly a community of young families. The neighborhood's median age dropped from 30.6 in 1980 to 28.4 in 2010, well below the city average.

Of all the constants that apply on both sides of the cultural transformation, the most important may be what Layton Park signifies. For its current Latino residents no less than for the German and Polish shop hands of the early 1900s, the neighborhood represents a step up and away from the poverty of their first years in Milwaukee. What both groups found in Layton Park is a place on the city's edge but also comfortably in the middle: a community of mid-sized homes, moderate incomes, and typical employment patterns, positioned squarely between the extremes visible elsewhere in the city. Its accent may have changed, but Layton Park still speaks a language that Milwaukeeans of all eras would easily understand.

■ Latinos are the new face of Layton Park.

all photos on these two pages by Anders Gurda

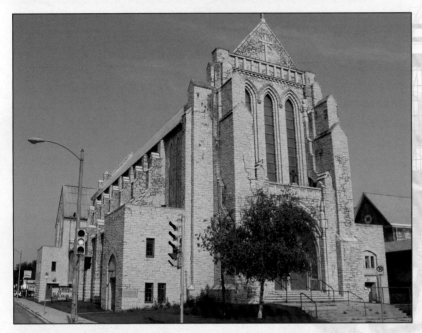

■ (above left) Holy Ghost Church, now St. Rafael, was built to serve German Catholics in 1902.

■ Frank Lloyd Wright's American System-Built homes make Burnham Street a destination for architecture buffs.

■ (opposite page, upper right)
The silos of Froedtert Malt tower over the neighborhood.

■ (opposite page, lower right)
Saints Cyril & Methodius Orthodox Church is Layton Park's most unusual house of worship.

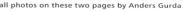
all photos on these two pages by Anders Gurda

JACKSON PARK

M·I·L·W·A·U·K·E·E

Jackson Park

The Jackson Park neighborhood is a community of quiet streets and well-kept homes wrapped around the largest park on the city's South Side. The setting is peaceful, almost pastoral in places, but the Jackson Park area offers more than quiet. Its character is an appealing blend of old and new. Placed squarely between the old South Side and the southwest suburbs, it shares the atmospheres of both, and its homes, bridging the divide between pre- and post-World War II development, make Jackson Park one of the most architecturally diverse districts in Milwaukee.

Jackson Park

1. Aurora St. Luke's Medical Center (St. Luke's Hospital)
2. Blessed Sacrament Catholic Church & School
3. Ebenezer Evangelical Free Church
4. Jackson Park Lutheran Church
5. Leon's Frozen Custard
6. Mitchell Manor (Mitchell Family's Meadowmere Mansion)
7. Southgate Shopping Center Site
8. St. Sava Serbian Orthodox Cathedral
9. Statue of Commerce
10. Wingfoot Homes Development Site
11. Zablocki Branch – Milwaukee Public Library

0   1,000 FT

Between Country and City

The community's lifeline was, and is, Forest Home Avenue. Now a smooth four-lane highway, Forest Home began as an axle-jarring toll road connecting Milwaukee and Janesville. Chartered in 1848, the same year Wisconsin joined the Union, the Janesville Plank Road quickly became the main-traveled highway for the entire region southwest of Milwaukee. When railroad development began to force other toll roads out of business in the 1850s, the Janesville Plank Road's importance actually increased. The Milwaukee & Beloit Railroad—a line that would have paralleled the highway—was stillborn in the late 1850s, and the southwestern townships became the only quadrant of the county without rail service. The Janesville road was virtually the only link between city and countryside in a sprawling agricultural district. Despite regular complaints about maintenance, the owners of the road continued to collect tolls well into the late 1800s.

One of the farmers served by the Janesville Plank Road was Richard Reynolds, a British military veteran who owned 160 acres on the road between today's Thirty-fifth and Forty-third

Streets. Reynolds farmed the land, but he also operated a hotel near the present intersection of Fortieth and Forest Home. Reynolds Grove, as the spot came to be called, served weary travelers on the plank road, but its grounds were also a magnet for Milwaukeeans who wanted to spend a day in the countryside. There is little doubt that beer and more ardent spirits were served on the premises.

Adjoining the Reynolds farm to the northwest was the country estate of John L. Mitchell, a businessman whose career included a term in the U.S. Senate. Mitchell's father, Alexander, was a spectacularly successful capitalist whose ventures in railroads (the Milwaukee Road), banking (the Marine), and insurance (Northwestern National) had made him the richest man in Wisconsin. John Mitchell's son, Billy, was a pioneer aviator who is generally considered the founder of the U.S. Air Force. Fittingly, Milwaukee's airport is named in his honor. The family's Meadowmere estate was one of the premier horse farms in the region, and Mitchell's trotters pranced across 160 acres west of Forty-third Street between Lincoln and Cleveland. Meadowmere's centerpiece was a twenty-eight-room mansion built in 1878.

Both Reynolds Grove and Meadowmere were miles removed from Milwaukee at first, but the city's influence grew more pronounced as the years passed. Forest Home Avenue, the urban end of the Janesville Plank Road, gradually became a major settlement corridor. (The new name was adopted in 1872 to honor the historic cemetery at Twenty-seventh Street.) By the late 1800s Polish and German immigrants were edging out along Forest Home Avenue from the heart of the South Side. They reached the Layton Park neighborhood (between Twenty-seventh and Thirty-fifth) at the turn of the century, and it was clear that the farmland to the southwest would some day become a neighborhood. In 1908 Forest Home Avenue was designated Milwaukee's first county trunk highway.

■ *Long before urban settlers arrived, this one-room Town of Greenfield school stood at the intersection of Forest Home and Oklahoma Avenues.*

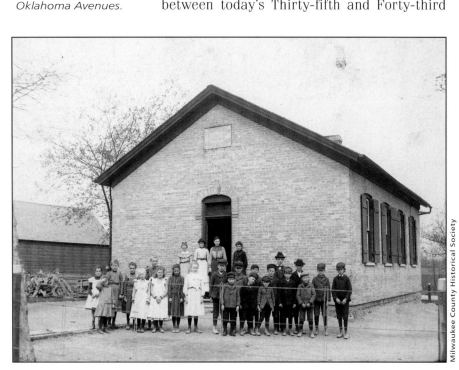

Milwaukee County Historical Society

Meadowmere and Mitchell Manor Communities

Meadowmere and Mitchell Manor Communities

■ (center left) *A twenty-eight-room mansion was the crowning glory of the Mitchell family's Meadowmere estate.*

■ (left) *John L. Mitchell and son Billy wet their lines in the Kinnickinnic River.*

Although urban development was still some years away, the city Park Commission, with characteristic foresight, purchased the northern half of the old Reynolds farm in 1907. Two years later the South Division Civic Association, a group of South Side civic leaders, erected a statue on the former picnic ground, which was soon to become Jackson Park. The statue was a towering zinc goddess representing Commerce, and it had originally graced the entrance of the Chamber of Commerce Building (home of the Grain Exchange) on Broadway and Michigan. (The statue was reportedly removed because it obstructed the view from the windows.) The dedication was attended by 10,000 people.

The statue was virtually the only improvement in Jackson Park for fifteen years. The Park Commission built a watchman's house and put up 3,200 feet of wire fence along Forest Home Avenue, but the park was officially described as "undeveloped." A 1912 Milwaukee guide declared, "This park is a forest in its natural state." A meadow on the southern end of Jackson Park provided seven tons of hay for the park system's horses in 1913, but the rest of the land lay idle, awaiting a neighborhood.

That neighborhood finally began to take shape in the 1920s, a boom period for both the city and the nation. Forest Home Avenue became the spine of a residential district, thinly settled at first, that stretched for miles beyond the city limits. As younger South Side residents built homes around Jackson Park,

Milwaukee Public Library

■ *Forest Home Avenue, the neighborhood's spine, still had a rural appearance in 1925. The view is northeast from Thirty-fifth Street.*

Milwaukee County Parks Department

Milwaukee County Parks Department

■ *Dedicated in 1909, the statue of Commerce was Jackson Park's only amenity for years, but by 1921 the park was developed enough (lower) to host Trinity Lutheran's Sunday School picnic.*

Milwaukee expanded steadily to the southwest. By 1927 the city had annexed most of the present neighborhood.

The newcomers of the 1920s were city residents, but their community was, in a word, suburban. The Jackson Park area became a haven for second- and third-generation South Siders who had achieved some success in business and the professions. The first arrivals built bungalows, those spacious one-and-a-half-story houses so popular in Milwaukee after World War I, but as Jackson Park developed, the bungalow gave way to the Period Revival home. Designers of the 1920s and '30s resurrected the styles of earlier times—Tudor, colonial, English cottage, Mediterranean—and specified brick and Lannon stone as their

building materials. Details like leaded-glass windows, hardwood floors, and working fireplaces were standard. Harder's Oak Park, the subdivision just east of Alverno College, is one of the finest Period Revival developments in Milwaukee, and there are fine specimens of the style both south and west of Jackson Park.

Whether they were merely comfortable or extremely comfortable, most of the Jackson Park area's first residents were either Polish or German by ancestry, reflecting the ethnic composition of their previous neighborhoods. The community's roots were just as obvious in the churches that emerged. In 1927 Polish Catholics formed Blessed Sacrament Parish and built a modest brick church on Fortieth and Oklahoma. Many charter members were sons and daughters of St. Adalbert's Parish, a heavily Polish congregation on Forest Home Avenue at Twentieth. In 1932 a group of German Lutherans built, with their own hands, a small frame chapel at 3056 S. Forty-ninth Street that became the first home of Jackson Park Lutheran Church. An old landmark became a religious institution during the same period. In 1927 John Mitchell's Meadowmere mansion was repurposed as a Catholic orphanage; in 1938 it was converted to St. Joseph's Home for the Aged, serving the opposite end of the age spectrum. St. Joseph's has since evolved into Mitchell Manor, a "senior living community" with a broad continuum of services.

Jackson Park itself developed much faster than the surrounding neighborhood. Between 1922 and 1932, park crews installed electric lights, sidewalks, a new pavilion, athletic fields, and one of the largest swimming pools in the county. In 1928 the Park Commission added 53 acres to its original 80-acre purchase. As development continued, the "forest in its natural state" was reduced to a belt of trees overlooking the Kinnickinnic River, and a section of the river itself was dredged and dammed to form a scenic lagoon. Jackson Park's attendance figures were the lowest in the city, but park planners were confident that the neighborhood would soon fill up with residents eager to use the new facilities.

■ (below)
Period Revival homes began to dot the neighborhood in the 1920s.

■ (bottom)
More than 3,000 South Side Poles gathered in an open field to lay the cornerstone of Blessed Sacrament Church in 1927.

John Gurda

Blessed Sacrament Parish

Time Out,
Then Time to Grow

That confidence vanished in the early 1930s. As a recession became the Depression, the Jackson Park area's developers found themselves unable to pay their taxes, and hundreds of unsold lots reverted to the city. Building activity did not cease completely. Manitoba School was dedicated in 1939, and genteel Harder's Oak Park was developed largely in the Thirties. Jackson Park remained a magnet for South Siders with steady and substantial incomes, but the ranks of those lucky citizens thinned dramatically.

The park fared much better than the neighborhood. Despite the general scarcity of residents in the area, work relief crews, particularly those employed by the Works Progress Administration, finished projects as fast as the Park Commission staff could plan them. Kinnickinnic River Parkway was completed east of Jackson Park in the mid-1930s, the park lagoon was finished in 1940, and there was a flurry of landscaping and remodeling projects. In 1941 park authorities purchased the Kinnickinnic River corridor west of Forty-third Street from the Mitchell estate and lined it with gravel roads. There was also a change of ownership; in 1937 Jackson Park, like every other park in the city, became part of the Milwaukee County system.

Ambitious park improvements and modest residential growth were both brought to a grinding halt by World War II. Severe labor and material shortages made progress on any front practically impossible. A few park projects were completed and a few homes were built, but the area was practically frozen in place for the duration of the conflict. The coolest addition to the landscape, as well as the sweetest, was Leon's Frozen Custard, a drive-in stand that opened on Twenty-seventh Street in 1942.

Although it didn't affect Leon's, fortunately, a dramatic thaw followed the end of the war. The boom of the 1920s paled in comparison with the growth that accompanied the return of peacetime in 1945. Although the Jackson Park neighborhood was an established

■ _Depression-era work relief crews steadily improved Jackson Park. Its attractions included a well-stocked lagoon (lower left) that became the focal point of the South Side's largest park._

community by that time, it was not densely settled by any measure. Barely one-third of the neighborhood's present homes were standing in 1945, and it had taken twenty-five years for them to materialize. In the very first postwar decade, the community was filled to its limits.

What fueled the building boom was a housing shortage of critical proportions. As returning veterans took civilian jobs and started families, many found it impossible to rent a home, much less buy one. Milwaukee County helped matters by erecting temporary housing on land it owned. Fifty Wingfoot homes, painfully small houses with plywood walls, were erected on the present site of Manitoba Park (Forty-ninth and Manitoba) in 1947. The ultimate in starter homes, the Wingfoots remained in place until the early 1950s, when they were sold and moved, many to lake lots in rural Wisconsin. Only the laundry building remained, and it now houses Manitoba Park's rest rooms.

The Wingfoot homes were barely a ripple in the tidal wave of development that engulfed the Jackson Park area after World War II. Conventional homes sold as fast as they could be built, and it took years for

private developers to catch up with the demand. A new style had emerged alongside the Period Revival in the 1930s—the Cape Cod. A basically square house with a simple shed roof, the Cape Cod came into its own just after World War II. Some specimens were prefabricated homes set on concrete slabs; others were conventionally built, with full basements. In the 1950s Jackson Park's Cape Cods were joined by small ranch houses, basic brick apartment buildings, and other housing types that could be erected with a minimum of delay. By 1955 development was practically complete, and the tidal wave continued its sweep to the south and west. As in earlier years, the course of settlement followed Forest Home Avenue.

The most obvious result of the building boom was a fourfold increase in Jackson Park's population between 1945 and 1960. The newcomers who fueled that increase were markedly different from those who had built the neighborhood's first houses. They were generally younger and less affluent, and their homes were, on average, smaller and less elaborate. The vast majority of young families, however, shared the South Side roots and

■ (below)
Hoping to ease a critical postwar housing shortage, Milwaukee County placed fifty temporary Wingfoot homes in what is now Manitoba Park.

■ (bottom right)
More permanent housing tended to be on the modest side, with a strong preference for Cape Cods and small ranch homes.

Milwaukee County Parks Department

Milwaukee County Historical Society

John Gurda

Milwaukee Public Library

Alverno College

Alverno College

the Polish or German ancestry of their older neighbors. The area's two churches, both of which had weathered difficult times during the Depression and war, grew as a result. In 1954 Jackson Park Lutheran moved into a spacious new home on Forty-sixth and Oklahoma. In 1956 Blessed Sacrament dedicated its towering new church on Forty-first and Oklahoma; the old church became an addition to the parish school, whose enrollment soared in the postwar years.

As South Siders moved southwest, South Side institutions followed them. In 1947 Ebenezer Evangelical Free Church, a Walker's Point congregation established by Norwegian immigrants, built a new house of worship on Forty-third and Oklahoma. In 1952 St. Luke's Hospital moved from Walker's Point to Twenty-seventh and Oklahoma; it eventually became the flagship hospital of Aurora Health Care, the largest system in the state. One year later Alverno College began to offer classes at its campus on Thirty-ninth and Morgan. The Catholic women's college was an outgrowth of the teaching, music, and nursing schools operated by the School Sisters of St. Francis at their motherhouse on Layton Boulevard and Greenfield Avenue. In 1958, finally, Milwaukee's Serbs consecrated St. Sava Serbian Orthodox Cathedral, one of the city's most distinctive churches, on Fifty-first Street south of Oklahoma. The Serbian community's roots were in Walker's

Point, and the church had followed its members southwest along the familiar Forest Home Avenue corridor.

One postwar project was without precedent. In 1951 more than 60,000 Milwaukeeans attended the grand opening of Southgate, the metropolitan area's first modern shopping center. Dominating the west side of Twenty-seventh Street north of Morgan, Southgate was an open-air marketplace whose twenty stores shared a single roof and a canopied sidewalk. Customers came in droves, and Southgate's success hastened the transformation of Twenty-seventh Street from a sleepy stretch of Highway 41 to a beehive of automobile-oriented commerce.

■ *Major South Side institutions followed their neighbors to the edge of town. Two of the largest were St. Luke's Hospital (upper left), which moved from Walker's Point in 1952, and Alverno College (both above), a pioneering women's college founded by an order of Franciscan nuns in 1953.*

■ *Completed in 1951, Southgate was Milwaukee's first modern shopping center.*

By the mid-1950s the neighborhood looked much as it does today. There was, however, one more development of note. In the post-war years Forest Home Avenue carried home-seekers deep into the unincorporated territory southwest of Jackson Park. The City of Milwaukee mounted an aggressive annexation campaign on its municipal frontier, sometimes taking in only a few square blocks at a time. The campaign was met with resistance by aspiring suburbs. The City of Greenfield was last to incorporate, in 1957, and the piecemeal annexations came to a halt. The result, in the Jackson Park area, was a municipal border more complicated than the most challenging jigsaw puzzle.

A Place on the Edge

In some important ways, Jackson Park has remained what it was decades ago: a stable, well-kept neighborhood that radiates an appealing blend of old and new, urban and suburban. There are still clear reminders of the area's past. Some oak trees in Jackson Park were shading picnickers when the site was Reynolds Grove. The statue of Commerce still stands watch on a pathway overlooking the park's lagoon. A handful of the oldest residents can still recall the lowing of cattle

from the dairy farms west of Fifty-first Street. Leon's Custard, a throwback to the neon 1950s, continues to serve up contentment, one scoopful at a time.

The neighborhood's past is even more apparent in its homes. World War II was a watershed in American architecture. The contrast between pre- and postwar residential styles is extreme, and no Milwaukee neighborhood typifies that contrast more clearly than Jackson Park. A Period Revival home at 2763 S. Fiftieth, a solitary outlier in the 1920s, is perched high above two simple frame houses built in 1949. A bungalow at 3131 S. Forty-eighth rests between two brick apartment buildings from the 1950s. Some streets, like Forty-third, are dominated by elegant Period Revivals and bungalows; other sections, including Hickory Knoll (north of the Kinnickinnic River), are practically covered with Cape Cods. Many streets feature homes from every period. The result is a range of housing choices and a visual variety usually found in neighborhoods much older and much larger than Jackson Park. The community is both a museum of designs popular over a forty-year period and a mirror of a very significant period in American social history.

Although Jackson Park bears abundant witness to its past, the neighborhood has hardly stood still since the 1950s. There have been some notable additions. St. Luke's Hospital has risen, quite literally, to become the dominant landmark in the neighborhood, and in fact on the entire South Side. Zablocki Library, on Thirty-fifth and Oklahoma, has grown into one of the Milwaukee Public Library system's busiest branches since the landmark opened in 1963; its name honors Clement J. Zablocki, the long-time South Side congressman who lived on nearby Drury Lane until his death in 1983. There have been subtractions as well. Southgate found it increasingly difficult to attract customers in the era of mega-malls and Internet sales. The shopping center was torn down in 1999 to make way for a complex of unrelated businesses anchored by a Walmart. That commercial cluster still dominates the eastern edge of the Jackson Park neighborhood.

■ *Two houses on Fiftieth Street typify Jackson Park's housing stock and hint at its history. The Period Revival dwelling on the left dates from the 1920s, and the ranch house on the right was built in 1949. They were separated in time by the Depression and World War II.*

John Gurda

Other institutions have evolved in place. The churches of Jackson Park have adapted to changes in both American society and their own congregations. Alverno College, with more than 2,600 students, has won national recognition as a model of "ability-based" learning, an approach that stresses lifetime skills like critical thinking and communication as well as academic achievement. Alverno also offers a full schedule of concerts and cultural events that are widely popular in the neighborhood.

The community's population has evolved as well. In the 1950s Jackson Park was largely a neighborhood of young families. By the 1980s, as the newcomers of the postwar era aged with their houses, it had become a neighborhood of grandparents. The replacement process has been under way for years, and it is producing a neighborhood both younger and more diverse than its previous incarnation. Jackson Park's median age has dropped steadily since 1980, and newer residents do not necessarily share the ethnic roots of their predecessors. In 2010 more than 36 percent of Jackson Park's population was either German or Polish by ancestry—substantial, certainly, but a significant drop from 60 percent in 1980. The group that has shown the most dramatic growth is another with

deep roots on the South Side: Latinos, whose population climbed from 2 percent of Jackson Park's total in 1980 to 21 percent in 2010. Local schools, including Catholic institutions that were once filled with Polish-American children, now serve primarily Latino students.

The people and their institutions have changed, but one thing has remained constant from the earliest years: Jackson Park's quality of life. The neighborhood has an abundant variety of sound homes, strong churches, convenient shopping, and a location that allows a suburban lifestyle without sacrificing easy access to the city. Away from the main streets, a general sense of quiet prevails, and the neighborhood is as well-kept as it is tranquil. Fresh paint, weed-free lawns, and colorful flowerbeds—some of them perennial prize-winners—are community standards in Jackson Park. Pride in property is a key Milwaukee trait, and that pride is clearly on display.

At the neighborhood's heart, of course, is Jackson Park itself, and the park adds a vital ingredient to the community's character. Its 117 acres encompass a swimming pool, baseball fields, picnic areas, and a large lagoon that offers skating in winter and fishing in summer. Jackson Park is an important recreational resource, but it plays an even

broader psychological role as the community's centerpiece. The park and its adjoining parkways form a sprawling expanse of well-tended greenery. They lend the neighborhood a feeling of relaxed openness, and together they mirror the neighborhood's concern for quiet, domesticated beauty.

Given the area's assets, it's no wonder that local residents have banded together to preserve them. Jackson Park is the home of one of the strongest grassroots organizations outside the central city—the Jackson Park Community Association. The group was formally organized in 1982, but its activities began in the mid-1970s, when residents came together in opposition to a planned freeway on the western edge of the park. That battle was won in 1983, and the Jackson Park Association has since branched out into activities ranging from business development to Easter egg hunts.

One of the association's most visible projects involved, fittingly, a landmark from the neighborhood's earliest days: the statue of Commerce in Jackson Park. Obscured by underbrush and then damaged by vandals, the zinc goddess was in terrible shape by the 1980s. With funds raised by the Community Association, the statue was carefully restored, relocated to a more prominent place, and rededicated in 1991. At the base of the statue, inscribed in granite, is a wish: "May this statue ever be a silent witness to the progress and growth of Milwaukee." As the community continues to change in the twenty-first century, that wish applies with equal relevance to the growth and progress of the Jackson Park neighborhood.

■ *Leon's in neon, a South Side landmark since 1942*

all photos on these two pages by Jim Hamberg

■ *Blessed Sacrament's "new" church was dedicated in 1956.*

■ (above)
A laundry building from the Wingfoot era now houses Manitoba Park's rest rooms.

■ (left)
The Jackson Park pool is a cool place on a hot day, and the Zablocki Library, named for a congressman who lived nearby, is one of the city's busiest.

John Gurda

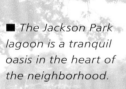 The Jackson Park lagoon is a tranquil oasis in the heart of the neighborhood.

■ (far right) Alverno College is a local institution with a global reputation.

all photos on these two pages by Jim Hamberg except as noted

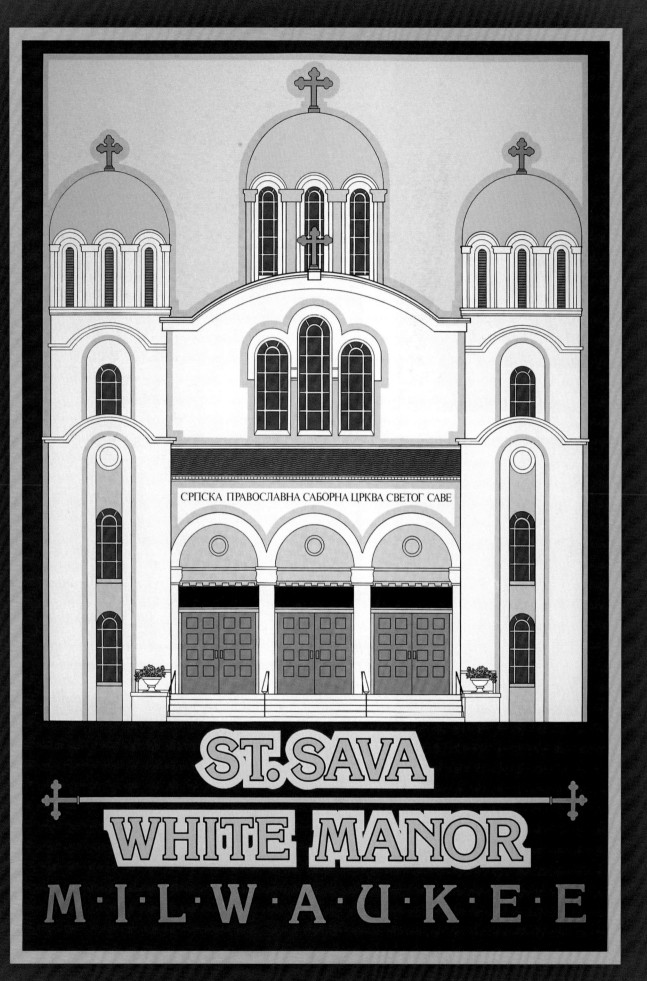

СРПСКА ПРАВОСЛАВНА САБОРНА ЦРКВА СВЕТОГ САВЕ

ST. SAVA

WHITE MANOR

M·I·L·W·A·U·K·E·E

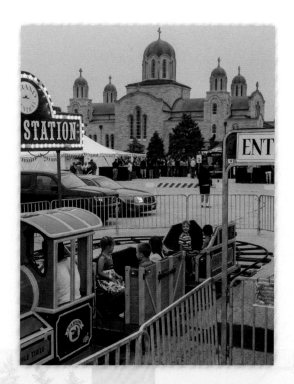

St. Sava/ White Manor

Its major landmark is an ornate Byzantine church, surely an unexpected sight in this semi-suburban neighbor-hood. The picturesque domes of St. Sava Serbian Orthodox Cathedral tower over a community of quiet streets, well-kept homes, and immaculate lawns. The contrast may be vivid, but it's less extreme than appearances might indicate. Both the church and the neighborhood rose from immigrant hopes conceived in Europe and realized in Milwaukee. St. Sava/ White Manor is a place where dreams of a better life on the city's edge came true in the twentieth century. The neigh-borhood continues to play that role for a new generation of residents, not all of them European, in the twenty-first.

St. Sava/White Manor

1. American Serb Memorial Hall
2. El Rey Market (Sentry)
3. Milwaukee Spanish Immersion School (55th Street School)
4. Oklahoma Avenue Lutheran Church
5. St. Gregory the Great Catholic Church & School
6. St. Sava Serbian Orthodox Cathedral
7. St. Sava Serbian Orthodox Cultural Center and School

0   1,000 FT

The South Side Moves West

It was in the 1920s that the Southwest Side began its long transition from farming district to collection of city neighborhoods. Slowly at first, Polish and German South Siders moved out to the countryside, carried by the prosperity of the pre-Depression years and following the Forest Home Avenue corridor. Their first stop was the Jackson Park neighborhood, which is practically bisected by Forest Home, but some of the settlers turned west on Oklahoma Avenue and entered what is now the St. Sava/White Manor area, west of Fifty-first Street. In 1926 the area's first subdivision, Jackson Heights, was platted south of Oklahoma. (The land was part of a farm claimed by Fredcrick Hegelmeyer, a German immigrant, in 1843.) By the early 1930s a thin layer of settlement had begun to cover the old farm. In 1932 some of the area's German Lutherans built a small white chapel on Fifty-fourth and Oklahoma. Established as a mission, it eventually became Oklahoma Avenue Lutheran Church.

The Depression soon stopped development in its tracks. It was not until the late Thirties, when the clouds began to lift, that the real estate market showed even the slightest signs of life. In 1939 the White Manor Park subdivision, north of Oklahoma Avenue, was opened to home-seekers. A few dozen houses were built, but World War II halted development long before the last lot was sold.

With the signing of peace treaties in 1945, the twice-delayed boom began in earnest. A procession of South Siders moved out to the fields west of Fifty-first Street, and at the head of the parade was one of Milwaukee's smallest but most cohesive ethnic groups: the Serbs. Natives of the southern half of the former Yugoslavia, the first Serbs had come to the city at the turn of the twentieth century and settled in Walker's Point, the South Side's oldest neighborhood. In 1912 the community organized St. Sava Serbian Orthodox Church, worshiping in a private home at first, then moving into more dignified quarters on Third Street near National Avenue.

■ **(below)**
In 1912 Milwaukee's first Serbian residents dedicated St. Sava Orthodox Church on S. Third Street.

■ **(center)**
In 1949 the next generation built a hall on Fifty-first and Oklahoma that became one of Milwaukee's most popular gathering places and a major source of funds for a magnificent new house of worship.

St. Sava Serbian Orthodox Cathedral

The Serbian community grew in both size and prosperity over the decades, and the Serbs, like many of their neighbors, began to look to the southwest. In 1945 St. Sava's congregation purchased nearly fifteen acres of land at Fifty-first and Oklahoma. Four years later they built American Serb Memorial Hall on a corner of the property. The hall, owned by the congregation but managed by an independent corporation of parish members, was the cornerstone of the community's long-range plan. Parishioners dreamed that the hall would some day earn enough money to pay for a magnificent new church. Under Mike Potter's astute management, Serb Hall was a resounding success. It gave Milwaukee's Serbs a community center, of course, but it also became a mecca for the city's labor, political, and social gatherings.

Serb Hall was a new landmark in a new neighborhood. Between 1945 and 1960 a tsunami of settlement transformed the area bordered by Fifty-first, Sixtieth, Cleveland, and Morgan. The wave proceeded on three levels at once: annexation, subdivision, and home-building. The entire area was absorbed by the City of Milwaukee between 1946 and 1953, and water and sewer lines were extended soon after annexation. Subdividers added to the original White Manor Park six times between 1942

and 1955, and "White Manor" soon described the entire 160-acre square north of Oklahoma Avenue. The mirror-image square to the south, the old Hegelmeyer farm, was subdivided to its limits between 1947 and 1960. With its usual emphasis on sound planning, the County Park Commission acquired thirteen acres at the heart of the Hegelmeyer tract in 1946. The park that resulted was named for Willard Lyons, a county supervisor from 1924 to 1954. (Lyons was also the uncle of John Doyne, Milwaukee's first county executive.)

■ *Lyons Park preserved a piece of the area's rural past as houses cropped up around it. Mature trees and wooden bridges added to the park's charm.*

American Serb Memorial Hall

Milwaukee County Parks Department

■ Cape Cods were a popular housing choice in the White Manor subdivisions just after World War II.

John Gurda

■ New families in a new neighborhood: scenes from S. Fifty-third Street in the 1940s

all photos this page courtesy Tom Meisenheimer except as noted

As the surrounding land was annexed and subdivided, home-building crews swept through the area like an army of carpenter ants. They built only two types of houses. The first postwar homes were Cape Cods, basically square one-and-a-half-story dwellings with simple shed roofs. In the 1950s Cape Cods gave way to modest early versions of the ranch house. Cape Cods and ranches can be found on the same blocks south of Oklahoma Avenue, but the line between them is crystal-clear in the White Manor subdivisions. To the east of Fifty-fifth Street, Cape Cods predominate, most of them painted (or sided) white, and to the west ranch homes are most numerous. With housing of any kind in short supply after World War II, both types were sold almost as fast as they could be built, and by 1960 the neighborhood's farming heritage was only a memory.

As the neighborhood grew, so did its institutions. In 1952 Fifty-fifth Street School was built in the heart of White Manor to serve the soaring population of youngsters. One year later the members of Oklahoma Avenue Lutheran Church tore down their old wooden chapel and erected the present Lannon-stone structure on Fifty-fourth Street. In 1957 the area's Catholics built St. Gregory the Great Church just west of Sixtieth on Oklahoma; the parish school was expanded several times in the following years.

It was also in 1957 that Milwaukee's Serbs, bolstered by the success of Serb Hall and a massive influx of postwar Serbian refugees, completed the neighborhood's crowning glory: St. Sava Cathedral. The parish's new home was designed in the spirit of fourteenth-century Byzantine Renaissance churches, with a cruciform floor plan, five lantern-shaped domes, and an interior so rich that it seems embroidered. The windows, icons, chandeliers, and mosaics make St. Sava's one of the most striking religious spaces in the region. As an outstanding work of architecture and the home of one of the largest Serbian Orthodox congregations in America, the church was raised to the status of a cathedral by the Orthodox hierarchy.

St. Sava Cathedral is one of a kind, but the church reflects a pattern common to the entire neighborhood: a connection with older neighborhoods on the South Side. St. Luke's

St. Sava Serbian Orthodox Cathedral

St. Sava Serbian Orthodox Cathedral

■ *After years of fund-raising, a new St. Sava's Church began to take shape in the mid-1950s. The Byzantine landmark was completed in 1957 and declared a cathedral six years later.*

Hospital and Alverno College, St. Sava's largest neighbors to the east, both moved from the near South Side in the 1950s, and a number of other churches followed their members to the southwest. The pattern was most obvious in the people themselves. Although the cathedral drew scores of parishioners to homes nearby, Serbs were a minority in the neighborhood. Like the newcomers of the 1920s, the home-builders of the postwar era were largely Polish and German Milwaukeeans whose stories, like the Serbs', had begun on the city end of Forest Home Avenue.

A Tradition Continues

The St. Sava/White Manor neighborhood lies on the edge of town. Only blocks away from West Allis on the north and Greenfield on the south, it has the settled, orderly atmosphere of a postwar suburb. But the neighborhood's institutions have made it a center of metropolitan activity as well. Serb Hall, in particular, is one of the busiest and best-known gathering spots in the region. Its weekly fish fry is the largest in a city famous for fish fries; hungry patrons consume a ton of Icelandic cod on a typical Friday and two tons on Good Friday. There is even a drive-through window for customers who want to enjoy their meals at home. Serb Hall draws from throughout the Milwaukee area, but many of its employees live nearby; hundreds of local young people have earned their first paychecks as waitresses and busboys at the fish fries.

Although Friday is often the most hectic night, Serb Hall is much more than fish. The twelve-lane bowling alley is busy seven days a week during the long bowling season, and Serb Hall has year-round appeal as a gathering place. Wedding receptions, hobby and trade shows, labor assemblies, and political events might bring 5,000 people to the hall during a busy week. The facility becomes a media center during the presidential election season; virtually every major candidate since the building opened has considered Serb Hall a mandatory campaign stop. The landmark's capacity more than doubled in 1987, and its role as a favorite Milwaukee meeting place has grown accordingly.

The cathedral complex to the south is a center for specifically Serbian activities. In 1972 the parish used revenue from Serb Hall to build a full-fledged cultural center on the grounds. The building provides a home for folk dance troupes, singing societies, cultural groups, senior citizen clubs, soccer and basketball teams, and programs that teach young parishioners about Serbian culture and Serbian Orthodoxy. In 1997 the center was expanded to provide room for the first Serbian Orthodox grade school in America. A regulation soccer field adjoins the cultural center and school to the south, and picnics are held in the green space between the cathedral and Serb Hall on every summer weekend. Sponsored by Serbian organizations (and open to the public), the picnics feature lamb and pork roasted slowly over pits of charcoal.

■ *St. Sava's members gathered to bless the cornerstone of a cultural center that opened in 1972.*

St. Sava Serbian Orthodox Cathedral

Of the approximately 6,000 Serbian Americans in the Milwaukee area, the greatest number are affiliated with St. Sava. United by culture and religion, they are nonetheless divided by generation. Some parishioners are descended from immigrants who arrived in the early 1900s, while others came as displaced persons after World War II. Hundreds more fled the violent break-up of Yugoslavia in the early 1990s and started over in Milwaukee. With such regular replenishment, the community's Serbian roots remain strong, supporting a rich cultural life and a robust tradition of bilingualism. The most recent arrivals have long since made the transition from rented apartments to homes of their own, often in the southwest suburbs, but scores of Serbian families still live practically within the shadow of the cathedral's domes.

A different kind of center lies to the north of St. Sava, in the heart of the White Manor section. As part of Milwaukee's desegregation plan in the late 1970s, Fifty-fifth Street School became the Milwaukee Spanish Immersion School. Designed for English-speaking students from kindergarten through fifth grade, the program features regular instruction, in Spanish, from the very earliest ages. Drawing students from throughout the Milwaukee area, the Spanish Immersion School's popularity, and its test scores, have remained high for years.

Serb Hall, the cathedral, the cultural center, and the Spanish Immersion School are metropolitan resources; their influence extends far beyond the borders of the neighborhood. But the St. Sava/White Manor area remains, above all, a community of homes. Away from the bustle of Oklahoma Avenue, a distinct sense of quiet prevails. Trees planted in the postwar years have reached majestic maturity. Homes are meticulously maintained. Some of the yards seem ready for photo layouts in garden magazines. "If you don't get your lawn just right," joked one resident, "you may as well leave the neighborhood."

Pride in property is one tradition transplanted from the older part of the South Side, and the connection persists in other ways. There are Serbian families in abundance, but the greatest number of St. Sava/White Manor residents are still Polish or German by ancestry. Their ranks, however, have thinned, the inevitable result of time and mobility, and most of those who remain have achieved senior status. The neighborhood's median age—more than forty years in 2010—was almost a decade higher than the city median. The inevitable process of replacement is under way, and Latino families, who made up nearly 14 percent of the population in 2010, form the largest single group of newcomers. Most of them look back to the same South Side blocks that sent their younger residents to St. Sava/White Manor in the years following World War II. The location of the Spanish Immersion School seems more appropriate every year, but there's an even more visible sign of change. In 2011 the neighborhood's largest grocery store, a struggling Sentry on Fifty-first and Oklahoma, was purchased by El Rey, Milwaukee's largest Latino-owned grocery chain. After a $1.5 million renovation, El Rey reopened to a brisk business, drawing customers of all backgrounds with a full selection of Hispanic, European, and American foods.

■ *The Spanish Immersion School's location is increasingly appropriate as the neighborhood's accent changes.*

Jessica Lothman

Whether old or young, European or Latino, residents of St. Sava/White Manor typically use the same word to describe their community: "peaceful." The prevailing emphasis on peace and order is nowhere more apparent than in Lyons Park, the neighborhood's largest area of green space. The park is surely one of the undiscovered gems in the county system, a scenic throwback to the early days of fields and forests. A small creek, spanned by three wooden bridges, meanders through a mature oak woods on its way to the Kinnickinnic River. A tot lot, a wading pool, a ballfield, and a community building are tucked among the trees. Wild onions and wildflowers still come up every spring, and a thicket of hawthorns on the park's eastern edge marks the time when a local farmer used the land to pasture his cattle.

Rooted in Milwaukee's South Side, St. Sava/White Manor remains a community of quiet parks, lightly traveled streets, and metropolitan attractions. "Bienvenidos," proclaims a colorful banner at the entrance to the Spanish Immersion School. Welcome, indeed, to a distinctive Milwaukee neighborhood, and to a new generation of residents who inherit a powerful tradition of pride and stability.

■ (right)
Flowers abound in this semi-suburban neighborhood.

■ (center)
The Lyons Park wading pool is a busy place in the sultry days of summer.

■ (below)
Serb Hall's fish fry is a tasty Milwaukee tradition. The hall itself (center) maintains a busy schedule of private and public events.

Christopher Winters

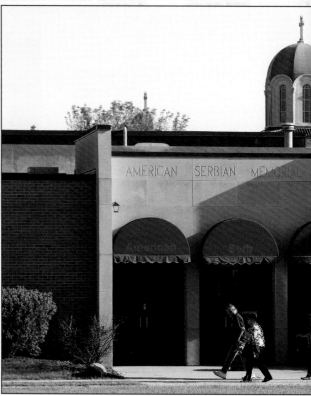

all photos on these two pages by Jessica Lothman except as noted

■ *The interior of St. Sava Cathedral is a wonder of Old World craftsmanship in a New World setting.*

■ *Small homes and large lots are the order of the day in St. Sava/White Manor.*

Christopher Winters

BAY VIEW
M·I·L·W·A·U·K·E·E

Bay View

Of all the neighborhoods that make up Milwaukee, Bay View is one of the most complete. Tucked into a quiet corner of the city, it has a full range of businesses, industries, housing types, parks, places of worship, and even subneighborhoods—all set on the shores of one of the largest freshwater lakes in the world. Once legally autonomous, Bay View has preserved much of its original sense of independence. Once a village, it has kept the leisurely pace and strong sense of community more commonly found miles away from a major city.

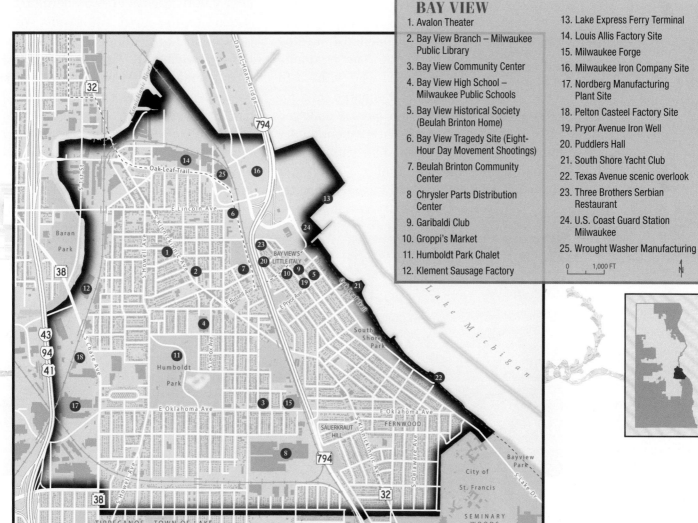

BAY VIEW

1. Avalon Theater
2. Bay View Branch – Milwaukee Public Library
3. Bay View Community Center
4. Bay View High School – Milwaukee Public Schools
5. Bay View Historical Society (Beulah Brinton Home)
6. Bay View Tragedy Site (Eight-Hour Day Movement Shootings)
7. Beulah Brinton Community Center
8. Chrysler Parts Distribution Center
9. Garibaldi Club
10. Groppi's Market
11. Humboldt Park Chalet
12. Klement Sausage Factory
13. Lake Express Ferry Terminal
14. Louis Allis Factory Site
15. Milwaukee Forge
16. Milwaukee Iron Company Site
17. Nordberg Manufacturing Plant Site
18. Pelton Casteel Factory Site
19. Pryor Avenue Iron Well
20. Puddlers Hall
21. South Shore Yacht Club
22. Texas Avenue scenic overlook
23. Three Brothers Serbian Restaurant
24. U.S. Coast Guard Station Milwaukee
25. Wrought Washer Manufacturing

A Milwaukee Mill Town

Bay View was founded by a man who never lived there around a business that no longer exists. The man was Detroit capitalist Eber Brock Ward, and the business he created was the Milwaukee Iron Company. Completed in 1868, Ward's iron mill was the third he built, following earlier ventures in Detroit and Chicago. Within a decade, the mill was the largest employer in the Milwaukee area, providing jobs for more than 1,500 men at peak periods, and it was the second-largest producer of railroad rails in America.

The mill complex covered nearly thirty acres of land at what is now the south end of the Daniel Hoan Bridge, and a compact company town developed in its shadow. The firm built small one-story homes for mill hands with families and opened boarding houses for single workers. The company also sold lots to employees who wanted to build their own homes and donated land for several churches. Bay View quickly emerged as a distinct settlement with a community life so robust that it merited a regular social column in the Milwaukee papers. The roster of homegrown institutions included several churches, a debating society, a temperance band, marching clubs, a newspaper, and a labor union. In 1873 the Sons of Vulcan, a predecessor of the United Steelworkers international union, built Puddlers Hall on St. Clair Street, naming it for one of the skilled trades in the iron mill. Still a popular nightspot in Bay View, Puddlers Hall is among the oldest labor landmarks in the Midwest.

The company town's separate status took legal form in 1879, when the Village of Bay View was incorporated—a move that had the hearty endorsement of the mill's managers. In their view, the rural Town of Lake lacked the resources to support a bustling industrial settlement. The new community took in nearly 900 acres of land bordered by Lincoln Avenue on the north, Oklahoma Avenue on the south, Lake Michigan on the east, and the equivalent of S. First Street on the west.

Bay View was Milwaukee's first suburb as well as its only company town. Those qualities were enough to set it apart, but the community also had an unusual ethnic profile. When the mill opened, few Americans knew anything about the production of iron, and E.B. Ward had to import workers from the industry's center: Great Britain. Emigrants

■ *Eber Brock Ward, the Detroit capitalist who put Bay View on the map*

■ *(right) Ward's Milwaukee Iron Company was the region's first heavy industry and one of the state's largest employers.*

Milwaukee Public Library

Milwaukee Public Library

from *Milwaukee Journal*, Dec. 3, 1933

from England, Scotland, and Wales came to Bay View by the hundreds, adding a distinctly British flavor to an urban area better known for its large German population.

Despite its pioneering suburban status, Bay View's independence was short-lived. As the community's population grew, so did its need for sewers, running water, and streetlights—improvements for which Bay View's chief taxpayer, the mill, was reluctant to pay. In 1887 a majority of Bay Viewites, tired of what they considered substandard services, voted to consolidate with the City of Milwaukee. The neighborhood remains one of only two in the city that were once independent. The second is North Milwaukee, another industrial suburb, which became an incorporated village in 1897 and joined the city in 1929.

In 1886, one year before joining the city, Bay View was the scene of the bloodiest labor disturbance in Wisconsin's history. In early May Milwaukee became a hotbed of agitation for the eight-hour day without a cut in pay. (Industrial workers routinely put

in ten to twelve hours, six days a week, at the time.) On the morning of May 5, 1886, a group of nearly 1,500 strikers, most of them Poles from the South Side, marched on the rolling mill to dramatize their demands. They found the state militia waiting for them. At a distance of 200 yards, the troops opened fire, killing an estimated seven of their fellow Milwaukeeans. The shootings quelled the agitation temporarily, but striking workers rallied to a new People's Party that swept the very next local elections and provided a base for Milwaukee's emergent Socialist movement. Union members have been a potent force on the electoral scene ever since.

Bay View kept growing after the smoke had cleared. Although its legal autonomy lasted only eight years, the neighborhood retained a strong sense of identity after joining the city—much like a woman who keeps her name after getting married. The mill remained a major employer, and it attracted a variety of other ethnic groups in the early 1900s, including a sizable community of northern and central Italians. They made the

■ *Bay View developed as a compact company town that became Milwaukee's first suburb in 1879 and its newest neighborhood in 1887.*

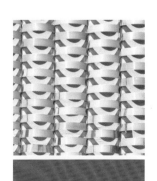

■ *Mill workers like these puddlers endured temperatures of 160 degrees at least ten hours a day and six days a week.*

Milwaukee Public Library

■ *The vast majority were European immigrants. Safety signs were painted in five languages: English, Czech, Hungarian, Serbo-Croatian, and Polish.*

John Steiner

blocks around the mill, particularly north of Russell Avenue, Bay View's "Little Italy" and opened businesses there that became community mainstays, including Groppi's Market, the Garibaldi Club, and DeMarinis Restaurant. An old firehouse on St. Clair Street became Little Italy's official community center. It was named for Beulah Brinton, an early mill executive's wife who had opened her home to the mill workers' families. During the summer months, movies were projected on the huge firehouse doors—a memory that

hundreds of local Italians carried with them into their retirement years.

New ethnic groups were not the only sign of Bay View's growing maturity around the turn of the twentieth century. Gradually at first, the neighborhood began to take on the earmarks of a settled mainstream community. Land was set aside for public parks, beginning with Humboldt in 1890 and continuing with South Shore in 1909. The city limits pushed well beyond the original village border at Oklahoma Avenue. Deer Creek, the source of frequent flooding, was forced to flow underground, beneath Delaware Avenue. After years in a primitive wooden building dubbed "the barracks," Bay View's teenagers moved into a splendid new high school on Lenox Street in 1923. (The budget specified $50,000 for gargoyles.) Kinnickinnic Avenue, an old Indian trail, blossomed as the neighborhood's commercial backbone, with one cluster of businesses at Lincoln Avenue and another at Russell Avenue. The two "downtowns" were connected by a busy streetcar line, the venerable Route 15. Most local businesses catered to a working-class clientele, but one tavern on the Lincoln-Howell-Kinnickinnic triangle featured waiters dressed in tuxedos.

■ *Kinnickinnic Avenue became the commercial center of a bustling twentieth-century neighborhood.*

■ *South Shore Park, acquired in 1909, gave Bay Viewites a welcome and well-used point of contact with Lake Michigan.*

The mill that supported all this activity closed for good in 1929; as an aging and undersized unit of United States Steel, the plant was expendable. Other factories had located along the neighborhood's margins by that time, including giants like Nordberg, Louis Allis, and Pelton Casteel. Bay View was still an industrial community, but its reliance on the mill belonged to the past.

With the rest of Milwaukee, the neighborhood endured the economic collapse of the 1930s. Virtually every family was affected by the endless round of layoffs, and the rusting hulk of the rolling mill provided a handy source of scrap metal for those who were willing to haul it to the junkyard for a few dimes. Memories of the hard times faded quickly after Pearl Harbor, when local industries adopted frantic production schedules to support the Allied effort during World War II. Virtually every able-bodied man who wasn't in a military uniform wore a factory worker's overalls, and thousands of women were enlisted to keep the plants humming.

It was in the postwar years that Bay View returned to its formative traditions. The neighborhood settled into a comfortable rhythm as a family-centered model of residential stability. Children frequently bought homes near their parents, worked in similar jobs, and sent their own children to the same schools they had attended. Change would come eventually, but an independent village had become a strong neighborhood, and so it remained as one generation made way for another.

■ *Families put on their Sunday best for a sail on the lake ...*

■ *(lower) ... but Bay View has always maintained a pleasantly informal pace—a tempo still apparent today.*

■ *(opposite page) Landmarks of the past, at home in the present (from top): the Beulah Brinton House, home of the Bay View Historical Society; a gingerbread cottage on Shore Drive; and Groppi's Market, a neighborhood mainstay since 1913.*

courtesy Meta Lawrie

courtesy Meta Lawrie

Christopher Winters

434

At Home on the Lakeshore

Bay View is an integral part of Milwaukee, and it has been since 1887. Local residents vote in city elections, pay city taxes, and enjoy the full range of city services. They are active participants in the life of the larger community. The neighborhood's major quality, however, is its continuing sense of separateness. Bay Viewites repeatedly use phrases like "a suburb in the city," "an urban small town," and "a place unto itself" when describing their community. It's easy to get the impression that, if an earthquake were to somehow sever Bay View from the rest of Milwaukee, the neighborhood's residents would manage quite nicely.

This paradoxical blend of belonging and independence is, of course, a product of the area's long history. Bay View has been a separate community, in its own view and in the view of outsiders, from the time it was founded, and that feeling has a continuing basis in reality, even in the highly mobile twenty-first century. With the exception of a hospital, Bay View has developed most of the resources necessary to support a community of 25,000 people.

Employment, first of all. Although many of its major industries have gone the way of the iron mill, Bay View is still the home of some traditional mainstays, among them Wrought Washer, Milwaukee Forge, and Klement Sausage. The majority of Bay Viewites work elsewhere in the metropolitan area, but there are plenty of employment opportunities close to home.

The neighborhood's commercial resources are even more impressive. Bay View has grocery stores both major and minor; a bank, a bowling alley, bakeries, and barber shops; doctors, dentists, and druggists; and businesses dealing in fine tea, fine art, and fine fashion. If Bay View had its own version of the Yellow Pages, the list would be impressive indeed. Kinnickinnic Avenue is still the dominant artery of commerce. In keeping with the old-new character of the neighborhood it bisects, the stores on "KK" offer everything from architectural antiques to cutting-edge clothing.

Residents in search of food and entertainment have just as little reason to leave Bay View. The neighborhood has ethnic restaurants in abundance, including hometown favorite Three Brothers (Serbian) and newer

Christopher Winters

Jessica Lothman

Jessica Lothman

435

establishments featuring French, Italian, Vietnamese, and Mexican cuisine. Bay View also occupies a secure place in Milwaukee's thriving theater scene, a tradition started by the Boulevard Theater in 1985. During the summer months, the Humboldt Park Chalet is the venue for a popular weekly concert series that showcases the best in local entertainment. A profusion of coffee shops has made the community a capital of caffeine, and there are dozens of nightspots, from typically well-run, typically friendly corner taverns in the best Milwaukee tradition to well-appointed lounges with their own versions of the latest specialty cocktail.

For those who prefer outdoor recreation, Bay View has an abundance of choices. Humboldt, South Shore, and Bay View Parks attract joggers, bikers, fishermen, tennis enthusiasts, sailors, ice-skaters, swimmers, softball-players, kite-fliers, and Frisbee-throwers. They also offer less strenuous forms of exercise. The oak groves at Humboldt and the beachfront willow trees at Bay View Park are perfect spots for a picnic. Seminary Woods, at the neighborhood's southeastern edge, is a bucolic remnant of the forest that once covered Milwaukee County, and Lake Michigan itself is an overwhelming presence in the neighborhood. A magnificent view of the bay, cooler summers and warmer winters, a welcome feeling of openness—these are some of the lake's gifts to the community. The waterfront parks, linked by a paved trail that runs all the way to Oak Creek, support one of Bay View's favorite pastimes: lake-watching.

The community has a host of other attractions that underscore its distinctiveness. The South Shore Frolic, a summertime staple since 1948, is the city's largest and oldest neighborhood celebration. The Pryor Avenue iron well is Milwaukee's last public well—and the only place within the city limits that you can obtain water that's not from Lake Michigan. Beulah Brinton Community Center is a city-sponsored recreation center that continues the legacy of the compassionate woman for whom it is named. The

■ *Bay View offers lakeside living at its coziest and an increasingly diverse array of local businesses.*

Christopher Winters

Jessica Lothman

Bay View Historical Society, headquartered in Beulah's old home, is Wisconsin's largest neighborhood-based historical society. Bay View Community Center offers programs for every age group from pre-schoolers to senior citizens, and the South Shore Yacht Club, a neighborhood institution since 1912, attracts sailors and power-boaters from throughout the region.

Bay View even has, on the most local level, its own subneighborhoods, defined by parks, rail lines, and major streets. The South Shore Park area—the heart of the original company town—is Bay View's oldest district, and it has an appealing assortment of Victorian homes both large and small. Mill executives and mill hands often built houses on the same streets, producing one of the most democratic landscapes in the city. It is, however, workers' homes that predominate, including a category known locally as "puddler's cottages" for the tradesmen who first occupied them. The Humboldt Park area has a variety of gracious brick and stone

homes from the early decades of the twentieth century, and bungalows and Cape Cods are most numerous in Sauerkraut Hill, a section southwest of Oklahoma and Kinnickinnic Avenues that once housed a large German population. Fernwood, just east of Sauerkraut Hill, is even more diverse, with homes ranging from English cottages to spacious colonials. The overall impression is one of rich visual variety. Few of Bay View's homes are exactly alike, and hundreds have been painstakingly restored, producing a twenty-first-century neighborhood in a nineteenth-century setting.

Bay View has always been a vital community, but there is no doubt that its energy level has increased since the opening of the Dan Hoan Bridge. For generations the neighborhood's major connection with the rest of Milwaukee had been a narrow, congested, and bumpy stretch of Kinnickinnic Avenue. Despite campaigns for better access dating back to the 1920s, nothing was done until the freeway era. The Hoan Bridge was completed without benefit of on- or off-ramps in 1974,

■ The South Shore Frolic parade, a Bay View tradition since 1948

Christopher Winters

creating the temporarily famous "bridge to nowhere." Surface connections were added in 1977, putting Bay View within five minutes of downtown Milwaukee. The results were an end to decades of relative isolation, a spike in real estate values, and an increasingly cosmopolitan population. Hundreds of newcomers—families and individuals, gay and straight, old and young, renters and homeowners—have made their way to Bay View, drawn by its still-affordable prices, lakefront location, and palpable feeling of neighborhood. The newer residents in turn have helped to transform the community into what might be described as the East Side of the South Side—a cultural and commercial hot spot that has become a genuine hybrid. Bay View takes the cultural currents of Brady Street or Downer Avenue, the alternative energy of the Riverwest neighborhood, and swirls them together against the ethnic industrial backdrop of the greater South Side.

For all the new energy that characterizes the neighborhood, Bay View maintains

■ *The Pryor Avenue iron well is Milwaukee's last public well.*

■ *Bay View still makes things, from hats at the Brass Rooster (far right) to aerospace parts at Milwaukee Forge (opposite page left)*

■ *The interchange at the foot of the Hoan Bridge fills the site of the old Bay View rolling mill.*

Jessica Lothman

Christopher Winters

a strong sense of continuity with its own distinctive past. Yesterday is today on Milwaukee's south shore. Bay View's heritage is a living presence, apparent in its eclectic housing stock, its whimsical street system, its home-grown institutions, and its multi-generational families. The iron mill established on the lake shore in 1868 is all but forgotten, but the community it spawned is still a unique presence in Milwaukee—old and yet new, close and yet far, a part of the city apart from the city.

■ (above)
Chill on the Hill is a well-attended summer concert series in Humboldt Park.

■ (left)
Life's a beach, when you live near South Shore Park.

Tippecanoe/
Town of Lake

Tippecanoe is an urban neighborhood with a rural heritage that still lingers in its landscape. Also known as the Town of Lake, the community began as the landlocked dream of a Norwegian ship captain, and it retains an edge-of-town character decades after joining the City of Milwaukee. That character is the product of a distinctive geography as well as an uncommon history. The neighborhood is literally on the edge of town. Tippecanoe's northern border—the line it shares with Bay View—is indeterminate at best, but the remaining boundaries are unmistakable: the City of St. Francis on the east, Sixth Street on the west, and the concrete expanse of Mitchell International Airport on the south.

Within those sharply defined borders lies a complex collection of residential pockets, separated from each other by utility corridors, major arterials, and Interstate 94. Together they showcase the architectural styles that rose to popularity both before and after World War II. Graced by large lots and well-tended gardens—the Garden District is another name for the area—the neighborhood's homes preserve an eminent livability and a vital connection with the natural world that has been Tippecanoe's signature for generations.

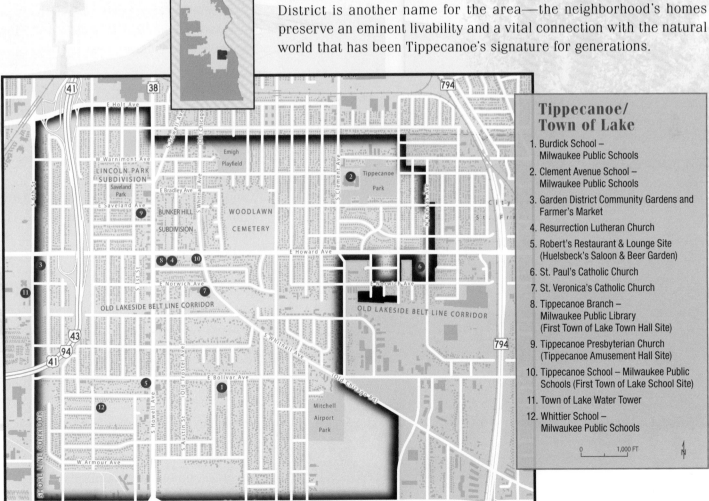

Tippecanoe/
Town of Lake

1. Burdick School –
   Milwaukee Public Schools
2. Clement Avenue School –
   Milwaukee Public Schools
3. Garden District Community Gardens and
   Farmer's Market
4. Resurrection Lutheran Church
5. Robert's Restaurant & Lounge Site
   (Huelsbeck's Saloon & Beer Garden)
6. St. Paul's Catholic Church
7. St. Veronica's Catholic Church
8. Tippecanoe Branch –
   Milwaukee Public Library
   (First Town of Lake Town Hall Site)
9. Tippecanoe Presbyterian Church
   (Tippecanoe Amusement Hall Site)
10. Tippecanoe School – Milwaukee Public
    Schools (First Town of Lake School Site)
11. Town of Lake Water Tower
12. Whittier School –
    Milwaukee Public Schools

0   1,000 FT

Dismantling a Town, Building a Neighborhood

Even before there was a City of Milwaukee, there was a Town of Lake. In the late 1830s, at the beginning of non-native settlement in the region, Milwaukee County was divided into seven townships. The Town of Lake stretched from Greenfield Avenue to College Avenue between Twenty-seventh Street and Lake Michigan—an area of nearly twenty-seven

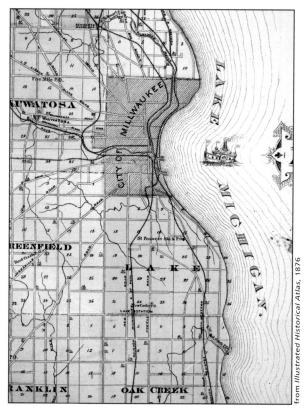

from Illustrated Historical Atlas, 1876

■ *The Town of Lake, highlighted on this 1876 map, once covered twenty-seven square miles at the City of Milwaukee's southern border.*

■ *The town's first school stood at Howard and Whitnall Avenues.*

Milwaukee County Historical Society

square miles. The original town took in places that any Milwaukeean would recognize on today's map, including Bay View, St. Francis, Cudahy, Mitchell Field, and most of the Historic South Side.

Although Wisconsin's towns were, by definition, unincorporated, they provided the rudiments of local government for their residents. Years before Milwaukee became a city in 1846, Town of Lake settlers, nearly all of them farmers, cast their ballots and paid their taxes at the town hall on the corner of Howard and Howell Avenues—still Tippecanoe's principal intersection. Lake's first school was built two blocks east, on the corner of Howard and Whitnall Avenues. Whitnall is one of Milwaukee's oldest highways, laid out by federal crews in 1832 and known for decades as the Old Chicago Road. Some of the early families who farmed along the road—the Howards, Howells, and Austins—are memorialized in today's street names.

The Town of Lake was not destined to remain intact, and the whittling began early. When Milwaukee incorporated in 1846, the city's southern border was Greenfield Avenue—the Town of Lake's northern boundary. Although it provided a ready market for Lake's farmers, Milwaukee's appetite for the town's land grew as fast as its population. The city limits pushed south to Lincoln Avenue in 1857 and reached Oklahoma Avenue in 1887, when Milwaukee annexed Bay View, a former industrial village built around a lakefront iron mill. Rural settlements emerged within the town as well, including St. Francis, named for the Catholic seminary that opened on the south lakeshore in 1856, and New Coeln, a German farming community on Howell Avenue near College Avenue.

Given the Town of Lake's position at Milwaukee's doorstep, it was probably inevitable that real estate promoters would look south for development opportunities. The most ambitious project by far was Tippecanoe, which began as the brainchild of a South Side Norwegian named John Saveland. Like his father and four brothers before him, Saveland had served with distinction as a Great Lakes ship captain. In 1868 he left the lakes to open a new business on South Water Street. Saveland's firm supplied provisions (and sometimes crews) for the steamboats, schooners, and fishing boats that sailed from Milwaukee; his shop stayed open all night during the height of navigation. The proprietor also owned several vessels that were used for hauling everything from railroad ties to tanbark.

Saveland's business interests eventually extended to real estate. In 1887 he led a group of investors who purchased thirty acres in the Town of Lake, bordered by today's Howard, Howell, Bradley, and Whitnall Avenues. His partners included four Great Lakes ship captains and Albert Trostel, one of Milwaukee's leading tanners. (Austin Street was originally named Trostel Avenue in his honor.) The Saveland syndicate soon purchased another thirty acres on the west side of Howell Avenue, centered around today's Saveland Park.

John Saveland apparently hoped to develop an upper-income residential colony on his group's holdings, a South Side equivalent of Shorewood or Whitefish Bay. Milwaukee's streetcar company (in exchange for a sizable subsidy) extended service down Howell Avenue in 1893, and the partners carved their land into lots significantly larger than the city average. Saveland evidently harbored dreams of affluent citizens commuting from their city jobs to estates in the quiet of the countryside. He also demonstrated his patriotism; the promoter's first subdivision (east of Howell Avenue) was called Bunker Hill, and the second was named Lincoln Park.

Saveland himself moved out to Lincoln Park in about 1891, but few Milwaukeeans followed him. When lot sales proved disappointing, the entrepreneur decided to make his project a recreational attraction. In 1894, on the site of Isaac Austin's old barn, Saveland and his partners dedicated a spacious "amusement hall," with a hardwood floor, a huge fireplace, and a wrap-around upper veranda. "It is proposed to make it a sort of club house," reported the

Milwaukee Journal (March 26, 1892), "in which ladies and children may spend the day upon its broad verandas or spacious halls, sheltered from the summer's sun, and in which meetings and amusements may be held." Saveland had already created a small lake nearby, just big enough to float a few canoes and small sailboats. The amusement hall, with a full schedule of recitals, card parties, and dances, gave Milwaukeeans another reason to travel south. The Howell Avenue streetcars were soon bringing a steady stream of city residents out to the Town of Lake for a day of dancing and boating, and the last car didn't return until nearly midnight.

Saveland called his pond Tippecanoe Lake—an overtly political statement. "Tippecanoe and Tyler too!" had been William Henry Harrison's slogan during the 1840 presidential campaign, and later in the century it became a rallying cry for the Republican Party, which succeeded Harrison's Whigs. Tippecanoe Clubs were organized across the country to promote the party's interests. John Saveland was simply expressing his political views, but the name of the lake soon extended to the surrounding area. By 1900 "Tippecanoe" identified the entire community that was slowly emerging around Howard and Howell Avenues.

The dance hall and pond were not the only summertime attractions in Tippecanoe. In 1903 the Huelsbeck family opened a competing business at Howell and Bolivar Avenues, the end of the streetcar line. With a saloon on one corner and a dance hall and beer garden on the other, the Huelsbecks attracted their

■ *Built in 1894, the Tippecanoe Amusement Hall was a destination for residents and visitors alike.*

Milwaukee County Historical Society

share of the pleasure trade. The garden was eventually subdivided for homesites, but the old saloon remained in business; it was known for years as Robert's Restaurant and Lounge, and patrons came from throughout the Milwaukee area.

Tippecanoe was only a warm-weather destination at first, but year by year the city drew closer. By the time John Saveland died in 1909, the area had begun to attract home-seekers. They were not, however, the executives and professionals Saveland had in mind when he launched his project. Most of the newcomers were middle-income South Siders, many in the skilled blue-collar trades, who simply wanted larger homes on larger lots. Ironically, few of them were Republicans. Between 1910 and 1930 they built nearly 500 homes in the Tippecanoe area, most within two or three blocks of Howell Avenue. The streetcar line became the community's lifeline, enabling residents to combine city jobs with a semi-rural lifestyle.

The pre-1930 settlement zone forms the historic core of Tippecanoe. It is an elongated oval bordered roughly by Howell Avenue and the long curve of Whitnall Avenue between Warnimont and Armour Avenues, covering nearly half the neighborhood. Victorian farmhouses are sprinkled throughout the core, but most of the original homes are simple frame dwellings, gracious Period Revivals and, above all, bungalows. Country-sized lots are more the rule than the exception in this oldest section of Tippecanoe. Some lots are literally as large as football fields.

Churches were organized to serve the new residents. The first was Resurrection Lutheran on Howard Avenue and Austin Street, established by German-speakers of the Wisconsin Synod in 1913. Tippecanoe Presbyterian followed four years later. As the surrounding area's focus shifted from recreational to residential, the Tippecanoe dance hall closed its doors, and a Presbyterian minister from Bay View rented the building for Sunday School classes. The hall was eventually purchased and a congregation was formed in 1917. Originally the site of a barn, the amusement hall entered its third incarnation as Tippecanoe Presbyterian Church. The area's Catholics organized two congregations. The first, established in 1919, was St. Paul's on Kansas and Norwich Avenues, but most of its members were (and are) residents of St. Francis. Closer to the heart of

■ *An 1898 ad featured lots for sale in a neighborhood that was slowly coming to life. The drawing shows an equestrienne keeping pace with the Howell Avenue streetcar.*

■ *(center) The former amusement hall was rebuilt as Tippecanoe Presbyterian Church in 1917.*

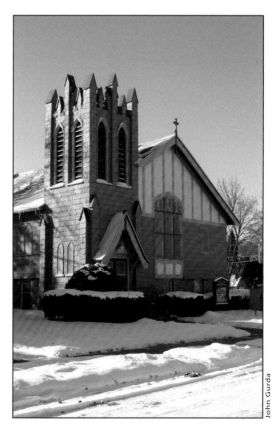

John Gurda

Tippecanoe was St. Veronica's on Whitnall and Norwich Avenues. The parish began with forty families in 1926, and it eventually became one of the largest congregations in the archdiocese.

As the neighborhood took shape around the Howard-Howell intersection, Tippecanoe developed an unexpected secondary identity as a transportation center. The North Shore Line, a high-speed electric railway connecting Milwaukee and Chicago, began to offer service on a dedicated right-of-way adjacent to Sixth Street in 1908. In 1926 Milwaukee County purchased a private airfield south of Layton Avenue for use as a municipal airport. It was a wetland that local farmers had long used as a pasture for sore-footed horses. The airport's first administration building (on Layton Avenue, not Howell) was a remodeled farmhouse. In 1941 the field was named for Billy Mitchell, a Milwaukeean widely considered the father of military aviation.

With the North Shore Line on the west and Milwaukee's airport on the south, two of Tippecanoe's borders were oriented to transportation. In 1930 work began on the Lakeside Belt Line through the very heart of the neighborhood. It was designed as another high-speed electric railway, connecting the Lakeside Power Plant near St. Francis Seminary with the interurban line to East Troy at S. 100th Street. Although the Depression killed the utility's plans for passenger service, the Lakeside right-of-way became an important corridor for high-tension power lines. The block-wide swath of open land remains one of Tippecanoe's major internal borders. The Lakeside Power Plant itself played a different role in the neighborhood's history. From the day it opened in 1921, the plant's assessed valuation was so high that Town of Lake residents, including those in Tippecanoe, paid no property taxes for years.

Joining the City

Although the world was coming to Tippecanoe's door, the neighborhood didn't shed its semi-rural character. In 1926 the only completely paved roads in the district were Howell, Whitnall, and Clement Avenues. Sprawling greenhouses and thriving truck farms still dominated the landscape. Local youngsters hunted pheasants and rabbits in the fields near their homes. But the area's

■ *Years before it became Mitchell Field, Milwaukee's municipal airport was located on Layton Avenue.*

Milwaukee Public Library

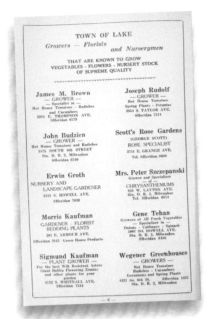

TOWN OF LAKE
Growers — Florists
and Nurserymen

THAT ARE KNOWN TO GROW
VEGETABLES - FLOWERS - NURSERY STOCK
OF SUPREME QUALITY

James M. Brown
— GROWER —
Specialist in —
Hot House Tomatoes - Radishes
and Cucumbers
3203 E. THOMPSON AVE.
SHeridan 6579

Joseph Rudolf
— GROWER —
Hot House Tomatoes
Spring Plants - Petunias
3954 S. TAYLOR AVE.
SHeridan 7574

John Budzien
— GROWER —
Hot House Tomatoes and Radishes
4575 SOUTH 6th STREET
Sta. D. R. 2, Milwaukee
SHeridan 6510

Scott's Rose Gardens
(GEORGE SCOTT)
ROSE SPECIALIST
3751 E. GRANGE AVE.
Tel. SHeridan 5068

Erwin Groth
NURSERY AND
LANDSCAPE GARDENER
4415 S. HOWELL AVE.
SHeridan 7630

Mrs. Peter Szczepanski
— Grower and Specialist —
of —
CHRYSANTHEMUMS
928 W. LAYTON AVE.
Sta. D. R. 2, Milwaukee
Tel. SHeridan 6874

Morris Kaufman
GARDENER - FLORIST
BEDDING PLANTS
201 E. ARMOUR AVE.
SHeridan 7642 Green House Products

Gene Tehan
Growers of All Fresh Vegetables
— Specialize in —
Onions - Cabbages - Spinach
5007 SO. HOWELL AVE.
Sta. D. R. 2, Milwaukee
SHeridan 8466

Sigmund Kaufman
— PLANT GROWER —
For the best Wilt Resistant Asters
Giant Dahlia Flowering Zinnias
and other plants for your
garden
4152 S. WHITNALL AVE.
SHeridan 7544

Wegener Greenhouses
— GROWERS —
Hot House Tomatoes
Radishes - Cucumbers
Geraniums and Spring Plants
4321 So. 6th St.
Sta. D. R. 2, Milwaukee

— 6 —

■ *The 1938-39 Town of Lake directory included ten growers of various kinds. The Budzien boys (below)* pitched horseshoes beside the family greenhouse.

future clearly lay with the City of Milwaukee. New residents wanted urban services, and city officials wanted to grow their tax base—a confluence of interests that led to intense annexation pressures. Between 1927 and 1932 the city limits were extended just beyond Howard Avenue, covering an area that included Tippecanoe Lake. John Saveland's heirs had donated the lake and the land around it to the people of Milwaukee in 1923, and the former resort was named Saveland Park in the founder's honor.

Ironically, the new city limits also took in the town hall on Howell and Howard Avenues; Town of Lake officials technically conducted their business in the City of Milwaukee. They were clearly on the defensive, and one of their chief concerns was water.

Determined to expand, the city was using its water system as a carrot to encourage annexation; Milwaukee refused to extend service to any of its unincorporated neighbors. The Town of Lake relied on a tank truck to supply residents who lacked their own wells, but that proved unworkable as the area's population swelled. Instead of joining the city, however, the town decided to build its own water system. In 1937, with help from a Depression-era federal grant, the Town of Lake dug a well on Sixth Street and Howard Avenue and built a million-gallon water tank above it. The tank was encased in a striking concrete tower that also housed the town's highway, police, and administrative offices. The Art Deco landmark was dedicated with much fanfare in 1940, and it quickly became the focal point of the entire Tippecanoe area.

Although it was legally split between the city and the town, Tippecanoe retained a distinct identity. Between 1949 and 1954 the community even had its own newspaper, a weekly called the *Tippecanoe News*. Before long, however, all of Tippecanoe came into the city. The end of World War II ushered in the greatest building boom in Milwaukee's history. As the movement gathered momentum, South Siders smothered the Town of Lake's farms and greenhouses under thousands of homes, particularly Cape Cods and small ranch houses. Nearly two-thirds of Tippecanoe's present housing stock was built between 1945 and 1960. The neighborhood's historic core was surrounded on all sides by new development, and the line between the pre-Depression and post-World War II eras was razor-sharp in scores of blocks.

Local officials found it hard to keep pace with the demands of growth. To make matters worse, the City of St. Francis incorporated in 1951, taking the Lakeside Power Plant's tax revenue with it, and administration of the town's affairs was marred by corruption serious enough to involve jail terms. By 1953 what remained of the Town of Lake, an area bordered roughly by Howard and College Avenues between Clement Avenue and Twenty-seventh Street, had the highest

courtesy Glenn Budzien

Milwaukee County Parks Department

■ *Saveland Park, donated by founder John Saveland's heirs in 1923, offered a different kind of green.*

property tax rates in Milwaukee County. The only rational choice was consolidation with the City of Milwaukee, and voters decided to make the merger final in 1954. The Lake consolidation was the second-largest in Milwaukee's history (after the Town of Granville acquisition); it added more than nine square miles to the city's land area and nearly 13,000 residents to its population.

Tippecanoe, the largest settlement in the consolidated area, became a full-fledged neighborhood in the 1950s. The signs of growth were everywhere: new churches, new schools, new parks, and a dramatic expansion of Mitchell Field. The last North Shore electric train ran in 1963, but work on Interstate 94 began soon after; one transportation corridor replaced another. By 1960 Tippecanoe's development was nearly complete. It had taken some unexpected turns along the way, but John Saveland's dream of a new community at the city's edge had finally become a reality.

Decades after Tippecanoe's transition from unincorporated settlement to Milwaukee neighborhood, signs of its semi-rural heritage still abound. The stone foundation of the 1894 amusement hall is still plainly visible beneath Tippecanoe Presbyterian Church. The pond in Saveland Park, one of the most attractive vest-pocket parks in Milwaukee County, could float only a toy sailboat today, but it recalls the community's period as a summer resort. Scattered woodlots, like the oak grove bordering Whittier School, are scenic holdovers from the farming period. The vintage homes and oversized lots on many blocks seem more typical of a small town than a large city. The old North Shore right-of-way has been reclaimed for community gardens on both sides of Howard Avenue, adding weight to the area's self-proclaimed identity as the Garden District.

The most obvious legacy of the neighborhood's early years is its name—or names. Although the increased prominence of Bay View in recent years has led some to push that neighborhood's borders to Howard Avenue and even beyond, the community still answers to its original names. "Town of Lake" refers to the township remnant that existed

until 1954, and "Tippecanoe" lives on in Tippecanoe Presbyterian Church, Tippecanoe School (built in 1936 on the site of the Town of Lake's first school), Tippecanoe Park (acquired by the county in 1953), and the Tippecanoe branch library (opened in 1969 on the site of the original town hall).

Although Tippecanoe has a rich rural heritage, it is also an urban community. Interstate 94 and Mitchell International Airport serve as high-volume, high-decibel transportation corridors for the entire region. Howell Avenue has been Tippecanoe's commercial spine since the streetcar era, and it is lined with businesses selling everything from work uniforms to chain saws. Most residents trace their roots to older sections of the city, particularly the Historic South Side and Bay View, and they reflect the cultural patterns of the old neighborhoods, both past and present.

■ *In the wake of World War II, Tippecanoe sprouted hundreds of Cape Cod houses like these on Howard Avenue.*

■ *(bottom) Completed in 1940, a few years before the boom, the Town of Lake water tower represented a last-ditch attempt to preserve the town's independence.*

Milwaukee Public Library

Milwaukee County Historical Society

German and Polish backgrounds predominate, but Latinos made up nearly 14 percent of Tippecanoe's population in 2010, just under the city average.

Whatever their backgrounds, the people of Tippecanoe share one important trait: pride in ownership. Nearly three-fourths of the neighborhood's homes are owner-occupied—one of the highest proportions in the city—and standards of maintenance are uniformly high. With their immaculate lawns, elaborate flower beds, and well-kept houses, Tippecanoe's residents are carrying on one of Milwaukee's most venerable traditions.

It has been well over a century since John Saveland dreamed of a residential enclave in the Town of Lake. The reality that emerged is less grandiose, perhaps, than Saveland's vision, but a rural settlement blossomed into an urban neighborhood, and Tippecanoe's edge-of-the-city character remains proudly intact today.

■ *A light in the urban forest: Many of the neighborhood's trees are older than its houses.*

■ *From community gardens to large, leafy lots and one-of-a-kind businesses, livability is the keynote of the Tippecanoe/ Town of Lake neighborhood.*

Jessica Lothman

all photos this page by Christopher Winters except as noted

■ *Tippecanoe Presbyterian Church has become a center of spirituality with a strong emphasis on social justice.*

■ (opposite page) *A non-working windmill is one of Tippecanoe's more unusual business places.*

■ (below) *Mitchell International Airport is literally at the neighborhood's doorstep.*

■ (opposite page, bottom) *Saveland Park preserves a peaceful connection with the community's rural heritage.*

all photos on these two pages by Christopher Winters except as noted

Jessica Lothman

Index

BAY VIEW
M·I·L·W·A·U·K·E·E

TIPPECANOE
TOWN OF LAKE
M·I·L·W·A·U·K·E·E

DOWNTOWN
M·I·L·W·A·U·K·E·E

THIRD WARD
M·I·L·W·A·U·K·E·E

**MENOMONEE
VALLEY**
M·I·L·W·A·U·K·E·E

AVENUES WEST
M·I·L·W·A·U·K·E·E

CONCORDIA
MILWAUKEE

**MERRILL
PARK**
M·I·L·W·A·U·K·E·E

...S WEST
...UKEE

CONCORDIA
MILWAUKEE

**MERRILL
PARK**
M·I·L·W·A·U·K·E·E

PIGSVILLE
M·I·L·W·A·U·K·E·E

STORY HILL
MILWAUKEE

**JOHNSON'S
WOODS**

MIDTOWN
MILWAUKEE

**WASHINGTON
PARK**

**WAS...
H...**

MIDTOWN
MILWAUKEE

**WASHINGTON
PARK**
M·I·L·W·A·U·K·E·E

**WASHINGTON
HEIGHTS**
M·I·L·W·A·U·K·E·E

SHERMAN PARK
MILWAUKEE

**ENDERIS
PARK**
M·I·L·W·A·U·K·E·E

**BREWER'S
HILL**
M·I·L·W·A·U·K·E·E

HILLSIDE
M·I·L·W·A·U·K·E·E

**HALYARD
PARK**
M·I·L·W·A·U·K·E·E

**...WER'S
...LL**
...UKEE

HILLSIDE
M·I·L·W·A·U·K·E·E

**HALYARD
PARK**
M·I·L·W·A·U·K·E·E

RIVERWEST
M·I·L·W·A·U·K·E·E

HARAMBEE
MILWAUKEE

LINDSAY HEIGHTS
WALNUT WAY

**AMANI
METCALF PARK**

**FRANKLIN
HEIGHTS**
M·I·L·W·A·U·K·E·E

**AMANI
METCALF PARK**

**FRANKLIN
HEIGHTS**
M·I·L·W·A·U·K·E·E

RUFUS KING
MILWAUKEE

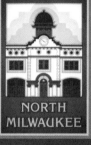

**NORTH
MILWAUKEE**

**THURSTON
WOODS**
M·I·L·W·A·U·K·E·E

EAST SIDE
MILWAUKEE

NORTHPOINT
MILWAUKEE

EAST SIDE

...SIDE
...UKEE

NORTHPOINT
MILWAUKEE

EAST SIDE
M·I·L·W·A·U·K·E·E

WALKER'S POINT
M·I·L·W·A·U·K·E·E

**CLARKE
SQUARE**
M·I·L·W·A·U·K·E·E

SILVER CITY
M·I·L·W·A·U·K·E·E

**HISTORIC
SOUTH SIDE**
MILWAUKEE

**LAYTON
PARK**
M·I·L·W·A·U·K·E·E

**JA...
MIL...**

**HISTORIC
SOUTH SIDE**
MILWAUKEE

**LAYTON
PARK**
M·I·L·W·A·U·K·E·E

**JACKSON
PARK**
MILWAUKEE

**ST·SAVA
WHITE MANOR**
M·I·L·W·A·U·K·E·E

BAY VIEW
M·I·L·W·A·U·K·E·E

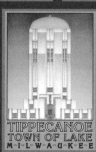

TIPPECANOE
TOWN OF LAKE
M·I·L·W·A·U·K·E·E

DOWNTOWN
M·I·L·W·A·U·K·E·E

THIRD WARD
M·I·L·W·A·U·K·E·E